Bethany in Kansas

the history of
a college

By Emory Lindquist

Emory Lindquist

Bethany College
Lindsborg, Kansas

Bethany College Publications
A. John Pearson, Editor

BETHANY IN KANSAS: THE HISTORY OF A COLLEGE
Copyright © 1975 by
Bethany College, Lindsborg, Kansas 67456.
All rights reserved.
Printed in the United States of America
by Inter-Collegiate Press, Shawnee Mission, Kansas.

First Edition
ISBN: 0-916030-03-2
Library of Congress Catalog Card Number: 75-18910

378.78155
L64b
95284
nov.1975

Illustrations are provided through a gift in memory of
Mrs. Esther Tehlander
from her brother,
Mr. Herbert Johnson, Salina, Kansas.

Library of Congress Cataloging in Publication Data
Lindquist, Emory Kempton, 1908-
  Bethany in Kansas: The History of a College.

  Includes bibliographical references and index.
  1. Bethany College, Lindsborg, Kan.—History. I.
  Title
LD433.L56   378.781'55   75-18910
ISBN 0-916030-03-2

FOREWORD

Time leaves its marks on everything it touches. There are no exceptions to this, and even institutions of higher education have experienced its imprints. These may be imprints of recognized research, vastly expanded facilities, esteemed professors, and graduates who in turn leave their own marks on their period of civilization.

Bethany College also has not escaped the impact of the decades. Time has strengthened it; time has given it distinctive form and function; time has aided it in establishing linkages with the people throughout the world and with those who share in its continuance. Time seemingly has played an unusually significant role in developing the qualities for which Bethany College is known. Stated differently, age has not taken its toll on Bethany College; quite to the contrary, age has made it increasingly alive and vital.

Thus it is now, after almost a century, that we relive its development and study the factors which seem most to have influenced its personality. To rediscover in an orderly and meaningful way requires the talent of a highly skilled historian. Dr. Emory Lindquist, a former Rhodes scholar at Oxford, past student, professor, and president of Bethany College, has provided that quality. His vantage points of living "on the inside" for years and also observing "from the outside" while professor and president at Wichita State University, has led to unusual perceptions and insightful descriptions. Having mastered the discipline of authorship in several historical volumes, Dr. Lindquist has given us the fortunate happening of an unusually skillful analysis of the time that was Bethany's to-date.

To Dr. Lindquist and to the dozens of others who ably assisted in this production, I express my most sincere gratitude.

ARVIN W. HAHN
President, Bethany College

PREFACE AND ACKNOWLEDGEMENTS

A college is an organism with a distinctive life that can be chronicled from the date of origin. The time span of this history of Bethany College is from the founding by Dr. Carl Swensson in 1881 to the end of the academic year 1973-74. It points to the Centennial Year of Jubilee in 1981. This is the first attempt at a comprehensive history of the College.

Two sections identify the contents: Part I describes developments chronologically; Part II is topical.

Many aspects of Bethany's history are recorded in the following pages. The belief in Christian higher education by the Swedish American founders, their associates, and successors; the dedication of faculty; the vision of administrators and board members; the loyalty of the church constituency and the community, locally and also more broadly conceived; the aspirations and activities of students; the special distinction in music and art; the interest and achievement of graduates and former students; the support of friends; and the cooperation of various media sources form the basic content. Faith, sacrifice, devotion, and dedication characterize the annals of Bethany's history. Over and beyond these pages is the unwritten history of Bethany which is known best by those who have shared it.

Two alternatives often confront an historian: the responsibility may be to record the story of an institution or cause that has come to an end; or it may be the happier situation in which the past is a challenging prologue to the present and future. The latter alternative prevails for the historian of Bethany College. A cherished tradition has furnished vital resources for the lively present and the promise of a greater future.

The author had available a mass of primary and secondary sources although limitations of space required difficult choices. It has been an exciting experience to read the documents, to review the printed materials, to share remembrances with alumni, and to observe the dedication of current personnel at the College as they fashion with wisdom and confidence the shape of things to come.

The author's gratitude is great for generous assistance from many people. Inadequacies of the volume are his responsibility. Dr. Arvin W. Hahn, president of Bethany College, has been unfailing in his interest and support. A. John Pearson, director of public relations, has rendered invaluable service as editor of the book. Mrs. Richard Lofgren, secretary to the president of Bethany College, has not only typed the final manuscript with great care, but she also has served as a valuable consultant. William H. Taylor, business manager, Mrs. Delmar Homan, head librarian, Professor Emerita Jen Jenkins, Professor Lambert Dahlsten, Kenneth Sjogren, director of public affairs, L. Stanley Talbott, director of alumni affairs, Ray D. Hahn, athletic director and coach emeritus, E. Keith Rasmussen, former athletic director and coach, and Mrs. Estred Schwantes, a member of the public relations staff, have given substantial support.

In addition to college personnel, several other people have shared their interest and knowledge with the author. Included are Mr. and Mrs. Frank Pedroja, Jr., Wichita, Mr. and Mrs. Edward Almquist, Tib Anderson, curator of the McPherson County Old Mill Museum and Park, Dr. Elmer R. Danielson, Dr. and Mrs. C. P. Greenough 3rd, and Mrs. Elizabeth Jaderborg, Lindsborg. Jacquelyn Black, Wichita, has been an efficient research assistant throughout the preparation of the manuscript. Bianca Ralston, Wichita, assisted in preparing the preliminary version. Nyle H. Miller and his associates at the Kansas Historical Society, Topeka, have been cordial in making available materials. Irma, my wife and a Bethany graduate, has given many constructive suggestions and criticisms. In addition a large number of alumni graciously responded with material for the chapter, "Alumni Remember."

The author hopes that readers who are familiar with the Bethany story will recall happy remembrances of undergraduate years or other relationships with the College and that old and new friends will share together something of the Bethany spirit.

TABLE OF CONTENTS

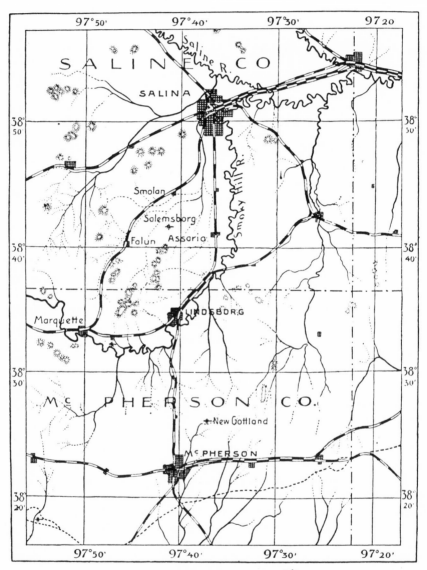

PART ONE
1.

Founding and Early Years
1881-1891

In the pioneer world of 1869 Swedish immigrants from Värmland under the leadership of Pastor Olof Olsson arrived in the Smoky Valley of Central Kansas to begin life in a new land. A variety of circumstances caused them to leave the homeland for the promise of life in America which seemed to them to be *"framtidslandet,"* "the land of the future." An evangelical Swedish Lutheran church was founded in the Lindsborg community two months after their arrival and they named it Bethany in sacred remembrance of that Bethany in Biblical times. Only twelve years later, in 1881, a college was founded in the sacristy of that church and it seemed singularly appropriate to name it Bethany.

The Swedish immigrants did not come to the Smoky Valley as itinerants but as settlers to till the good earth and to share fully in the life of their new homeland. Soon a congregational school and a Swedish lending library were established. In less than a year the immigrant pastor was elected the first superintendent of public instruction of McPherson County which was organized in 1870. One of Olof Olsson's first official acts was to authorize a public school district in Lindsborg.

Pastor Carl Swensson, the founder of Bethany College, citing background factors in the planning of a Christian school in Lindsborg, is the source of the statement: "The plan of locating a school in our Swedish settlements is older than Bethany. Pastor Olsson and his beloved friends from Värmland were, as far as I know, the first to discuss this matter as something they hoped would be realized in the not too distant future." When the Kansas Conference of Swedish Lutheran churches assembled in Osage City in May, 1876, under the presidency of Pastor Olsson, a resolution was passed urging the Augustana Synod to establish a school to train teachers for the Swedish settlements. These new Americans had a genuine understanding of the role of education in developing the talents of their children and in promoting the process of Americanization.[1]

When the beloved Pastor Olof Olsson left the Lindsborg community in 1876, it was upon an urgent call to serve as a professor at Augustana College and Theological Seminary, Rock Island, Illinois. There he met a gifted young Swedish American, Carl Aaron Swensson, son of Pastor and Mrs. Jonas Swensson, who was born on June 25, 1857, at Sugar Grove, Pennsylvania. Olsson described to him confidently the potentialities of the Lindsborg community. Swensson listened attentively and responded enthusiastically. In July, 1879, twenty-two year old Reverend Carl Swensson, who had just graduated from Augustana Theological Seminary, Rock Island, Illinois, was installed as pastor of Bethany Lutheran Church, Lindsborg, by Dr. T. N. Hasselquist, president of Augustana College and Theological Seminary. Bethany College was born in that hour.

Carl Swensson had been pastor of Bethany Church less than six months when the congregation enthusiastically endorsed his proposal at the annual congregational meeting in December, 1879, that a designated area of the church's land should be laid out in city lots and that one-half of the proceeds from the sales should be set aside for founding a Lutheran high school. During the next years several hundred shade trees were planted on one of the blocks, later called the "park," with the site as the prospective location of a school.

Carl Swensson has described the next important development:

> After the meeting of the Augustana Synod at Lindsborg during the summer of 1881, I could not rid myself of the thought that the right time was at hand to make an attempt toward the establishment of a Lutheran high school, or "air castle" as many called it. I saw how God had blessed our settlements in this beautiful, flourishing, and liberty-loving state. But how our children and youth should obtain the necessary Christian education was a question not easily answered.

He expressed the concern that "Without the elevating influence exerted by a good school to mould the character of students and people, we would clearly be in danger of sinking into worship of the almighty dollar and materialism." Moreover, he was concerned that many talents which a school might develop would be hidden and undeveloped.[2]

Carl Swensson was not only a dreamer but a man of dynamic action. He soon disclosed his aspirations to pastors and laymen in the Smoky Valley. The response was heartening. The young pastor decided immediately to found a Christian school at Lindsborg, a village with 700 people. This action was on his private initiative and responsibility since no church, conference, or synod had promised support. Swensson soon engaged J. A. Udden, a recent graduate of Augustana College, as the

OLOF OLSSON   CARL A. SWENSSON   J. A. UDDEN

BETHANY EV. LUTHERAN CHURCH, 1880. Here Pastor Carl A. Swensson and Professor J. A. Udden held the first classes of the academy that was to become Bethany College.

teacher. Udden came to Lindsborg directly from Rock Island after the commencement exercises as a delegate from the West Union congregation in Minnesota to the meeting of the Augustana Synod. Shortly thereafter he enrolled in the county teachers' institute for four weeks at McPherson. After teaching the Bethany Church parochial school west of Lindsborg, he joined Swensson who with Udden were the only teachers of the newly founded Bethany Academy. Udden was twenty-two years old. Swensson was twenty-four.[3]

The chronicle of the first year of the school is brief. Ten students met with Swensson and Udden on October 15, 1881, in the sacristy of the Bethany Lutheran Church to become the first Bethany students. These names are inscribed in the earliest record as having paid $5.00 in tuition that first day: Eric Olsson, Fredrik Carlson, Nora Lind, Otto E. Hawkinson, Andrew Cedarholm, Oscar Hobbart (O. W. Hubbard), John Johnson, Lovisa Olson, Johanna Fälling, and Jenny Carlson. The enrollment reached twenty-seven during the year. The school was coeducational from the outset. Entrance requirements were modest. Mastery of the four elementary operations of arithmetic and ability to read was expected. Students were to be at least twelve years old. The traditional view that no students enrolled the first day may be attributed to a confusion of dates.[4]

All instruction during the first year was provided by Udden except for classes in Bible and religious history which Swensson taught one hour

CARL AND ALMA SWENSSON

The Swedish edition program cover for the first "Messiah" concert on March 28, 1882.

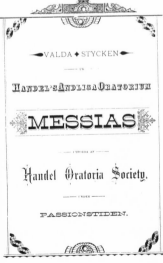

each day. It appears that the students had classes in arithmetic, geography, orthography, English reading, Swedish reading, penmanship, and religion. Udden's salary was $40.00 a month for six months. After paying for his meals at the rate of $20.00 a month and for other expenses, the balance of his funds was $87.75 in April, 1882. There is no evidence indicating when the first year terminated but Swensson and Udden both state that classes did not reassemble after the "Messiah" concerts in March, 1882.[5]

A memorable event occurred on March 28, 1882, when the first rendition of Handel's *Messiah* by the Lindsborg chorus was presented at the Bethany Church. This rendition which initiated a famous tradition was launched by Carl and Alma Swensson and their friends during the first year of Bethany's history.

The treasurer's report for the first year of the new school was encouraging. Income from tuition was $174.50 to which was added $99.75 from the proceeds of the "Messiah" concerts in Lindsborg and churches in the Smoky Valley during the spring, making a total of $274.25. The expenses for the year were $263.50. The building fund for the first year showed as "incomes" a donation from the Handel Oratorio Society and a loan of $500.00 from the Reverend S. P. A. Lindahl, later president of the Augustana Lutheran Synod. The "outlays" were as follows: improvements, $16.00; real estate, $500.00, which was the amount paid for the Lindsborg public school house; other expenses, 25 cents; and a balance of $8.75.[6]

The *Lindsburg Localist* recognized the potential importance of "Swensson's school" in an article in June, 1882: "There is an enterprise underway here that should not be forgotten by our people, namely the Lutheran Bethany Academy. No enterprise could be of greater importance to the city. Talk it up." The editor had reported on March 23 that another city in Kansas, apparently McPherson on the basis of other sources, had offered $10,000.00 as an inducement to move Bethany Academy there. The *Localist* expressed concern on June 15: "Efforts are being made continually by competing towns to have the academy moved there. Lindsborg could not well afford to lose the academy." The *Smoky Valley News* observed solemnly in November, 1882, when commenting about the Lindsborg institution: "We also have the Lindsborg Academy under the supervision of the [local] Lutheran Church, a project that will be of great benefit to our city."[7]

The encouraging response to the new school provided the incentive for the developments that occurred in 1882. The public school house, which had been purchased by Swensson, was moved to the "park" which had been donated by the Bethany congregation. A 16' x 24' addition was built to the school house and the area was then divided into three classrooms, one larger and two smaller. A small steeple to hold a bell was

BETHANY ACADEMY, *the original building.*

EDWARD NELANDER

Above: The Main Street of Lindsborg, 1878.

Left: "Typiskt farmarhem på åttiotalet." Typical farmhome in the 1880s.

added. In July, 1882, the Smoky Hill district of the Kansas Conference of the Augustana Lutheran Synod pledged its congregations and members to support the new school. The following members of a board of directors were elected: The Reverends J. Seleen, A. W. Dahlsten, P. M. Sanquist, and C. A. Swensson and Messrs. Charles Strömquist, J. Thorstenberg, John A. Swenson, and Andrew Lincoln.

The first meeting of the board was held on August 30, 1882. Pastor Sanquist opened the meeting with prayer. Carl Swensson was elected chairman, A. W. Dahlsten, secretary, and John A. Swenson, treasurer. The first action was authorization for Swensson to start a subscription of funds for the school. It was also agreed that income from the noon and evening meals at the festival on October 4 would be used for the purchase of a bell for the tower of the recently acquired public school building. Arrangements were made for the rental of Mrs. S. P. Lindgren's hotel. Mrs. Udden was in charge of the boarding arrangements during the academic year and Udden proudly reported: "There were no complaints about the food that year." Classes were held in the former public school house and at Welin's blacksmith shop on Main Street.[8]

A charter for Bethany Academy was authorized by the State of Kansas in September, 1882. Bethany Academy was dedicated at festive services on October 4, 1882. The *Smoky Valley News* reported: "One of the most interesting events in the history of Lindsborg is undoubtedly the dedication of Bethany Academy. Many people had to stand outside the Academy Building." The Bethany Cornet Band played and the Salemsborg Quartette sang Swedish songs. Addresses were given by the Reverends Carl Swensson, J. Seleen, and S. P. A. Lindahl. The entire dedicatory program and the act of dedication was in Swedish. When the program at the Academy Building was concluded, the band escorted the entire audience to the Tremont House where dinner was served. Exercises in the evening were scheduled for the Academy Building, but the crowd was too large and the wind was too strong for the Chinese lanterns that were to provide illumination, so the festivities were moved to the Bethany Church.[9]

The second year began the next day. Forty-four students signed up the first week, a number that increased to ninety-two by year's end. The divisions were as follows: sub-class, 32; first class, 48; second class, 12. There were 32 males and 16 females in the first class, 11 males and 1 female in the second class, and 27 males and 5 females in the sub-class.[10]

The curriculum had been expanded beyond the basic subjects to include English grammar, Swedish orthography, United States history, and sacred history in the first class. New subjects included Latin, algebra, civil government, physical geography, and natural philosophy in the second class. The charge for tuition and board was $2.00 per week. The catalogue indicated that there might be an increase in the near future. The faculty consisted of J. A. Udden, A.B., instructor in Latin, English language, civil government; E. Nelander, A.B., instructor in mathematics and natural sciences; C. G. Norman, assistant instructor in Swedish language, German, and church history; J. Hasselquist, A.B., instructor in gymnastic; and John T. Anderson, instructor in music. Swensson taught classes in religion.[11]

The enrollment at Bethany in the early years reflected decisively the Swedish background and the Kansas residence of the vast majority of students. In the academic year 1882-83, 65 of the 92 students who matriculated were born in Sweden, 14 in Illinois, 4 in Kansas, 3 in Minnesota and Indiana, and the others in Iowa, Missouri, and Mississippi. In 1885-86, in the enrollment of 179, there were 81 born in Sweden, 36 in Illinois, 37 in Kansas, and the remainder in Minnesota, Iowa, Nebraska, Indiana, Missouri, Mississippi, and Texas.[12]

The place of residence of the vast majority of Bethany students was Kansas in the early years. Students numbering 92 in 1882-83 showed the following distribution: Kansas, 87; Missouri, 2; and 1 each from Illinois, Minnesota, and Sweden. The homes of 79 of these students were within a radius of 50 miles of Lindsborg. The residence distribution in 1885-86 was as follows: Kansas, 151; Illinois, 9; Colorado, 8; and the balance from Nebraska, Missouri, Minnesota, Oregon, Washington, and Sweden. Bethany as a coeducational institution enrolled 112 men and 67 women in 1885-86. A few years later Swensson declared: "Co-education is presently producing good results. The Swedish American woman is worthy of a good and Christian education, and we may blush with shame how often and how long this truth has been disregarded within our denomination."[13]

Udden has described in an interesting manner the first faculty meeting in the autumn of 1882 when Edward Nelander, who had just joined the faculty, was elected to a position that made him president later:

> After two months had elapsed, something happened that required attention. I don't remember what it was but apparently a discipline problem needed consideration. Swensson said that we must meet to discuss the matter. The meeting was held in Nelander's home. Mr. Carl Norman had recently been hired as an assistant teacher . . . . Present were Swensson, Nelander, Norman and I. "Well, who shall we elect to serve as chairman," was Swensson's introductory question. After brief reflection, I proposed Professor Nelander. I have forgotten who seconded the motion but it must have been either Swensson or Norman. I asked for a vote, which when taken immediately was unanimous (for Nelander).[14]

In the summer of 1882 Udden had been asked by Swensson to purchase laboratory equipment and other materials for the new school. In an interesting letter written from Chicago in August he informed Swensson: "It was best to buy a few good things rather than many cheap ones. I therefore bought the best globe and a better electrical machine than they had at Augustana College . . . . An air pump and a set of physiological charts ought perhaps to come next in order. But an air pump for less than $50.00 is worse than nothing." He reported that he had purchased six pupil account books for thirty cents each. "I cannot tell you how important such books are. It trains the teacher as well as the pupil to be particular about small things and to be particular always; and you know nothing is more important for success." Udden also indicated that he recently had received several books for the Bethany library from the Secretary of the State of Minnesota.[15]

The continued growth of the school made it essential to provide additional facilities. In January, 1883, the board of directors decided to add a building which would involve a cash outlay not exceeding $5,000.00. Stone was quarried without cost from the bluffs northwest of Lindsborg. There was a generous response from farmers and others in quarrying the stone, hauling it to the building site east of the park, and in building the structure. The structure, presently the east half of Lane Hart Hall, was ready for occupancy when school began the first week in October, 1883. It was dedicated in a well-attended Luther festival October 16-17. This was a two-story brick and stone building, 35 feet wide and 60 feet long, containing a basement which served as a dining room, classrooms, and two stories of dormitory rooms in which men students were housed. The building was steam-heated.[16]

The school year 1883-84 started not only with improved physical facilities but also with an expanded curriculum that provided a three-year course of study beyond the sub-class. The divisions were the normal, the classical, and the scientific courses. There was also a music department. The design was to prepare the student for entrance into baccalaureate programs. The emphasis in the classical and scientific courses was upon mathematics, English and Swedish languages, history and civil government, while the classical course required Latin each year and the scientific course substituted natural sciences. The normal course stressed pedagogics. Instruction in music was provided through lessons in piano, organ, and vocalization. In August, 1883, when the board of directors was considering college policies, the following resolution was passed: "That in our school the Swedish and English languages shall be considered equally important." The enrollment during the year was eighty-four students. The tuition was placed at $9.00 for the autumn term and $11.00 for the spring term with a matriculation fee of $2.00 payable once. Board-and-room was $2.00 per week.[17]

In May, 1884, commencement exercises for graduates of Bethany Academy were held in the Bethany Church. The graduates were Anton S. Anderson, Lindsborg; Otto Hawkinson, Fremont; George S. Sohlberg, McPherson; Victor Swanson, McPherson; and John Welin, Lindsborg.

The second building on the campus, built in 1883, with what the 1909 Daisy calls "Bethany's first student group."

AUGUSTANA . LIBRARY . PUBLICATIONS
NUMBER 2.

An
Old Indian Village.

BY

JOHAN AUGUST UDDEN.

PUBLISHED BY THE AUTHORITY OF THE BOARD OF DIRECTORS OF
AUGUSTANA COLLEGE AND THEOLOGICAL SEMINARY,
ROCK ISLAND, ILL.

ROCK ISLAND, ILL.
LUTHERAN AUGUSTANA BOOK CONCERN, PRINTERS.
1900.

The first graduates of Bethany while it was an academy, 1884.

J. A. Udden, the first instructor, became a renowned geologist. Some of his work at Paint Creek southwest of Lindsborg is described in this monograph published by his alma mater, where he returned to teach from 1888-1911, before going to Texas.

When the *Smoky Valley News* described the occasion later, the following was recorded: "With tearful partings the students separated, cherishing sacred memories of their school days at Bethany Academy, departing to bring into action the intellectual training and spiritual discipline of their life here."[18]

The motto of Bethany Academy was *"Christo et Ecclessiae"* ("For Christ and the Church"). The catalogue emphasized the religious commitment as follows: "Salvation by a personal living faith in a Divine Saviour is recognized by the authorities of this school as the chief truth in human knowledge. Religious instruction not only forms a part of the daily routine of the school, but every endeavor is also made to surround the student with a healthy religious atmosphere. It is the desire and purpose of both the board of directors and faculty to consecrate the institution to the highest interests of the kingdom of Christ on earth." An appeal to students and their parents from out-of-town was made in these words: "While Lindsborg is free from many of the temptations to vice of large cities, it affords nearly all of their social and educational advantages. This portion of Kansas is noted for its general healthfulness of climate, an important consideration for the student."[19]

The year 1884 witnessed a decisive event when the Kansas Conference of the Augustana Lutheran Synod, meeting at Mariadahl Lutheran Church, near Cleburne, Kansas, passed the following resolution:

> Whereas, Bethany Academy, through its board of directors asks the Conference for its support and protection, be it resolved that the Conference adopt Bethany as its child and that its charter be changed in accordance therewith.
>
> Resolved, that Smoky Hill, Clay Center, and the East districts constitute Bethany Academy's territory, from which its support should be forthcoming.

The Conference further decided that the congregations of the Conference in Nebraska should support Luther College, at Wahoo, and the Colorado District should decide whether it wished to belong to Bethany's or Luther's territory. The action by the Conference at Mariadahl broadened substantially the basis of support for Bethany Academy.[20]

The early years reflect interesting developments. The Linnean Association, organized in 1884, was the first society established on the campus. Named after Carl von Linnaeus, the famous Swedish botanist, the organization was designed to promote interest in scientific knowledge among its members and to collect specimens for the museum. The first leader was President Edward Nelander. The corresponding secretary was J. A. Udden, the first Bethany teacher. The society met at least twice every month. The Lyceum Society, the first of several literary societies in Bethany's history, was also organized during 1884. The purpose of the society was to provide literary and oratorical exercises for its members.

Charles Young was the first president. The group met every Friday evening. The Lyceum Society was active for several decades and became the model for later organizations.

The growth of the school created problems that required early solutions. Swensson described the situation in 1884-85 by pointing out that fifty-six students had been "packed" in the dormitory, thirty-six lived in rented rooms arranged by the College, and the rest had to make arrangements as best they could. The largest classroom was an old blacksmith shop that had been cleaned up and adapted for instructional purposes. The chapel service was conducted in the enlarged former public school house where students sat in four rooms and listened to the speaker who stood in the corridor. Swensson warned the members of the Conference: "We are crowded beyond our capacity, and the school cannot develop without more buildings."[21]

The response of Swensson and the board of directors was to plan expansion of facilities. A farm was purchased in 1885 adjoining the campus and was laid out in lots. In October and November, at a public auction in which J. O. Sundstrom, Lindsborg businessman, served as auctioneer, lots were sold to the amount of $17,000.00 with 122 lots to be sold later. At a meeting of the board in December, 1885, architectural drawings of L. G. Hallberg, well-known Chicago architect, were accepted with only slight changes. At the meeting of the Kansas Conference, March 10-14, 1886, construction of the new building was authorized. It was an important day in Bethany's history when Swensson, A. Lincoln, and J. O. Sundstrom selected the exact place for the construction of the new building. The site was the former Lindsborg cemetery. When the four bids for construction were opened, all were rejected. Arrangements were made to engage the Reverend John Holcomb, Topeka pastor, an experienced builder, as superintendent. Nels Ross, St. Mary's, Kansas, was chosen to be foreman. Swensson later estimated that this arrangement produced a saving of at least $8,000.00.[22]

On November, 1885, the board of directors of the Lindsborg Cemetery Association had voted 28 to 3 to convey by warranty deed to Bethany Academy twenty acres of land, namely, the northeast corner of the northwest quarter of Section 67, Smoky Hill Township. The board of the Academy agreed "to pay the cost of the removal of all bodies now buried in the present burying ground . . . and the removal of all head stones, fences, enclosures, and fixtures of any kind . . . and to move and re-establish them at the new burial ground."[23]

The Smoky Valley people responded enthusiastically to the new building project. Many men offered their services in digging the foundation, hauling stone, doing carpenter work, and related activities. Original plans provided for three full stories, a mansard roof for the top story, and a basement. When Reverend Holcomb assured Swensson that the foun-

The building which became known later as Old Main was built in the 1886-87 year.

Above: Bethany Business College, the room for commercial studies. Below: Second class of Bethany Academy in Old Main.

Above: The chapel was a distinctive feature of the main building. Below: The dining hall.

dation would support another story, the board of directors at a meeting in September, 1886, authorized this addition. The work progressed satisfactorily with the result that a portion of the building was occupied on January 12, 1887.[24]

The new building loomed large on the landscape of the Smoky Valley and in the minds of Bethany faculty, students, and friends. It was advertised as the largest and best in Kansas. It was an imposing structure rising 85 feet in height in its five stories, with a length of 154 feet and a width of 60 feet. The middle part of the roof was designed in the same style as the Grand Central Hotel in Stockholm. The basement contained the museum and natural science department, three large recitation rooms, and a large dining hall. Six recitation rooms, the commercial exchange for the courses in business, the library, and the president's office were provided on the first floor. The chapel extended through the second and third stories with a seating capacity of 850 persons. The four upper stories provided space for 103 student rooms. The response to the new building was a great increase in enrollment from 161 in the academic year 1885-86 to 339 in the following year.[25]

The dedication of the building took place amidst great festivities on June 2, 1887. Ministers read "rare and appropriate texts from the Bible" for about an hour. Several five minute speeches were presented in Swedish and English. The principal speakers were Dr. R. F. Weidner, well-known Lutheran church leader, and Carl Swensson, whose topic was "God is not the God of the dead but of the living." The dedicatory service was concluded by the entire assembly singing the great Reformation hymn, "A Mighty Fortress is Our God." The *Smoky Valley News* reported that 3,000 people attended the dedication. Special trains were run from several communities in Kansas.

Swensson reported to the Kansas Conference in 1887 that the cost of construction of the new building was $45,000.00 plus $6,000.00 for the heating system and $4,000.00 for furniture. The debt was $39,000.00 but there was $13,000.00 in outstanding pledges which could be considered as potential assets.[26]

The developments at Bethany brought some misunderstanding between Swensson and Dr. T. N. Hasselquist, president of Augustana College and Theological Seminary. In October, 1885, Hasselquist wrote to Swensson stating that the latter had misunderstood him and that there was no "discontent on my part with the school at Lindsborg" and that he rejoiced over the progress there. He warned Swensson, however, that "it is easy to begin but intolerably difficult to continue" and that it was essential that Augustana College be strong because then "the synod has at least one center." Swensson was pleased with Hasselquist's attitude. He pointed out, however, that the work in the west involved "striking while the iron is hot, to give one's strength immediately before it is too late."[27]

The relationships of Hasselquist and Swensson became more cordial although the former felt that Bethany had expanded too rapidly. It is clear that Bethany's expansion had exceeded Swensson's original plans. In September, 1882, in the second year of Bethany's history, he had written that the Augustana Synod needed more preparatory schools, pointing out that Bethany and Gustavus Adolphus at St. Peter, Minnesota, should be followed by such schools at Jamestown or Brooklyn, New York, at the Halland settlement in Iowa, and in Saunders County in Nebraska. He concluded his article in *Ungdoms-Vännen* with this observation: "The value of such schools will be great. Out of them will come hidden talents, which after full development in our common institution could be of great use to church and state. Let us therefore support with all our strength our dearly beloved common institution of learning at Rock Island, but let us also in addition establish more preparatory schools within the bounds of our Synod."[28]

The achievement of Bethany Academy had been most encouraging by the end of the fifth year of its history. In contrast with ten students who assembled in the sacristy of the Bethany Church in October, 1881, with one full-time and one part-time teacher, the enrollment in 1886-87 had reached 334 students with a faculty of fifteen. The main building, the largest school structure in Kansas, provided excellent facilities, which were supplemented by a fine dormitory and the original frame building.

Bethany Academy received a new name, Bethany Normal Institute, in March, 1886, identifying the emphasis on teacher education, but this was changed in April, 1887, to Bethany College and Normal Institute. In 1889 Bethany College was designated the official name of the institution.

The academic year 1888-89 brought the first funds for a scholarship and award to students at Bethany. The Emma C. Johnson stipend of $1,-500.00 was established by John A. Johnson, pioneer founder of the Mariadahl community near Cleburne, Kansas, as a tribute to his wife. A scholarship from the income was to be given annually to a needy woman student. The Maria Charlotte Rundström Prize for scholarship was also established during the same year. A "suitable premium for good scholarship was to be awarded to that lady student who in the judgment of the faculty best deserves it." The income from the sale of a horse donated to the College by Dr. John Rundström, pioneer Lindsborg physician, provided the source for this prize in honor of his wife.

Swensson and the board of directors continually sought to improve the facilities of the institution. In 1889 it was reported that a complete system of water works and underground sewers had been completed. Two large tanks had been placed on the roof of the main building to supply water for this structure. Electric bells, operated by batteries, had been installed to give regularity to the class schedule. The College was connected by telephone to the president's residence, the Ladies Dormitory, and a book store on Main Street. Sidewalks had been built between buildings. A special carrier brought mail to the campus twice daily.

Although Carl Swensson, the founder of the College and chairman of the board of directors, provided dynamic leadership for the new institution, the academic policy was fashioned largely by the faculty and by Edward Nelander, who was *rektor,* or principal, or president, titles that were used interchangeably in the period 1882-1889, with the final designation as president in the last three years. Nelander taught a full schedule in a variety of fields including: mathematics and natural science, English language and literature, history, Latin, mental science, pedagogics, and church history. He had received the bachelor of arts degree from Augustana College after attending Knox College for three years. He had studied also at Berlin University. Nelander was a pleasant and cordial person who was highly esteemed by students and associates. The Nelanders shared their home by providing rooms for students. The first Bethany president was enthusiastic about the College and transmitted the vision for a great future which he received from his close identification with Swensson, whom he greatly admired. Nelander's problem was that he overworked with the result that his health was impaired. Swensson persuaded him to stay at Bethany, but during the academic year 1888-89 Nelander maintained his resolve to resign. The resolution at a student mass meeting urging him to continue at Bethany was an indication of the esteem in which he was held by students.[29]

Following Nelander's resignation the board asked Swensson to become president. He accepted the responsibility with the understanding

Old Main at about the turn of the century.

that a search would be made for a permanent appointee. Professor M. Wahlström of Gustavus Adolphus College was called as president in 1889, but he declined the invitation. Swensson contacted Professor Olof Olsson, pioneer founder of Lindsborg, relative to the presidency at Bethany, but he also declined for personal reasons. In 1891 the Reverend G. A. Brandelle, Denver, later president of the Augustana Lutheran Synod, also refused the call to be president. The students had protested the action of the Conference in nominating Brandelle.

In a resolution during a mass meeting the students expressed their opposition to anyone but Carl Swensson. To show the seriousness of their intent, they pledged $1,200.00 for the support of the College if Swensson continued as president. Dr. Erland Carlsson, the famous Augustana Synod pastor then living near Lindsborg, pledged $1,000.00 under the same circumstances. The students' feeling also represented that of the faculty and community with the result that Swensson continued in the position while at the same time serving as pastor of the Bethany Lutheran Church.[30]

Carl Swensson's first address as president of the College was delivered at the opening convocation in September, 1889. He told the students:

> A good education is the greatest of all riches and a condition of liberty. The ignorant man is a slave in proportion to his ignorance. The development of the intellect . . . will furnish knowledge but it must also build character. The latter is the most important of the two. Let us build from the fine marble of the classics, and founded on the granite of ancient wisdom, let the furniture come from the Eddas and the Valas, but allow it to be cemented together by nothing except the unadulterated and divine truth of Christ's religion . . . .

The academy building is in the center of the "park," viewed from atop Old Main. Bethany Lutheran Church is in the distance on the right.

No man is complete, no government is safe, no civilization will be perpetuated
without religion.[31]

Swensson and his colleagues worked hard and planned effectively to
develop the institution. A great landmark was achieved at the end of the
first decade of Bethany's history when the first baccalaureate degrees
were conferred at the commencement exercises in 1891. The academic
organization at that time provided the following departments: 1.
Collegiate, 2. Preparatory, 3. Normal, 4. Conservatory of Music, 5.
Commercial, 6. Model School, 7. Art. The degree curriculum for the
bachelor of arts degree made possible either the classical or scientific
emphasis. The classical course required four years of English, Swedish,
Latin, Greek, and Christianity. Two years of mathematics, history, and
German were included. The following subjects were taken for one year:
chemistry, physics, astronomy, geology, botany, political economy, logic,
and mental science. The scientific emphasis required four years of
English, mathematics, and Christianity, three years of chemistry,
history, and German, and one year of Latin, botany, physics, geology,
astronomy, mental science, political economy, and logic. [32]

The curricula in 1890-91 included the Preparatory Department,
three years; the Model School, six years; the Conservatory of Music,
which offered instruction in piano, organ, harmony, vocal culture, violin,
sight reading; the Commercial Department with courses in bookkeeping,
business practice, commercial arithmetic, rapid calculation, commercial
law, penmanship, English grammar, spelling and defining, test words,
shorthand and typewriting; and the Art Department with offerings in
drawing, crayon work, oil and water color painting. The curriculum in the
Normal Department included English, spelling, reading, Swedish,
Christianity, philosophy, history, civics, geography, physiology, zoology,
botany, chemistry, physics, mathematics, bookkeeping, penmanship,
history of education, physical geography, and methods. Degrees were
offered only in the classical and scientific course on the collegiate level
with certificates available in the Commercial, Normal, Music, and Art
departments.

On the tenth anniversary the president and faculty described briefly
the history and purpose of the College as follows: "Bethany College has a
very encouraging history. It is a child of Providence. It began with
nothing ten years ago. Now it is a large and well-established institution
with seven departments and thorough courses of instruction. Our aim is
to make this college an institution of the people and for the people. The
spirit is that of Christian equality and liberality. Our students have the
privilege and opportunity of choosing a course of study that suits their
special purpose."[33]

The regulations governing student conduct were presented to the
Kansas Conference at the meeting in February, 1891, and included the

following items:

> All secret societies are forbidden.
>
> Indecent or profane language will not be tolerated.
>
> Students are required to attend divine service in some church on Sunday.
>
> No one is allowed to use tobacco in any form in the building or on the premises.
>
> Attending baseball games, horseraces, or any public amusement on Sunday is prohibited.
>
> Study hours begin at 7 p.m. when students are required to be in their rooms. Visiting during study hours is positively forbidden. At 10:30 p.m., lights must be extinguished and students must retire.
>
> Lady students at the Dormitory are not allowed to receive calls from gentlemen except by permission of the Lady Principal, and then only in the parlors of the Lady Principal. Neither are they allowed to accept the company of gentlemen for parties, walks, or rides without the consent of the Lady Principal or to go down town after 6 p.m.
>
> Offenses lead, firstly, to private admonition by the president; secondly, to notification of parents and guardians; and finally suspension or expulsion.

Swensson concluded the report with the observation: "Since there are generally ten or more nationalities represented at our college, one should be very happy over the good discipline and conduct that prevails among us."[34]

The Main Building, the Ladies Hall, and the former public school house (the first building on the campus) provided the physical facilities of the College at the tenth anniversary. The latter building also served as the gymnasium. The library contained 5,000 volumes and several magazines and newspapers. The Museum of Natural History, founded by J. A. Udden, presented general items in the natural sciences and a special collection of fossils from the paleozoic rocks of Illinois. The herbarium included several hundred species of phaenogamous plants. The Conservatory of Music had an adequate number of organs, pianos, and other musical instruments.

The students shared also in improving the facilities. The members of the class of 1891 decided to fresco the Greek classroom in the Main Building. The renovation was executed in the Greek style. The border was Corinthian and from the walls the countenances of Greek philosophers and sages, including Homer, Plato, and Socrates, "looked down in compassion on the eager students of the unsurpassed language of Hellas." Moreover, "From his Olympian throne in the front of the classroom, Zeus will hold guard over all." The same issue of the *Messenger,* student newspaper, reported that the senior class had just completed the study of *Antigone* by Sophocles in the original Greek.[35]

The costs of attending Bethany varied with the course of study. The academic year consisted of a fall term, 11 weeks; a winter term, 15 weeks; and a spring term, 8 weeks. The tuition charges for the three terms of the academic year were as follows: College and Fourth Normal, $34.00;

Commercial, $39.00; Shorthand and Typewriting, $34.00; Piano, Vocal Culture, and Harmony, $66.00; one lesson a week, vocal or instrumental, $17.00. All music students who were enrolled in two music lessons per week were permitted to take two other subjects without cost. Board, including coal oil for a lamp, was $2.00 per week. Room rent was 15 to 30 cents a week according to the size and location of the room. Students living outside Kansas were allowed one-third of their railroad fare for coming to the College, which amount was deducted from regular expenses upon presentation of a receipt.

The financial statement for current operations in the tenth year of Bethany's history, presented by W. A. Granville, treasurer, showed a budget of $24,381.00 for the fiscal year. The largest item was salaries of $7,861.00. The cost of publishing the college catalogue was $173.00. Tuition income was $5,506.00. The Kansas Conference's budgeted item of twenty-five cents per member amounted to $490.77 which was less than the $552.00 value of gifts *in natura* (vegetables, meat, eggs, etc.) which were donated to the college dining hall.[36]

The distribution of enrollment during the academic year 1890-91, the tenth year of Bethany's history, was as follows: College, 33; Normal and College Preparatory, 117; Conservatory of Music, 124; Commercial, 64; Art, 12; and Model School, 72, for a total of 422 with 88 duplicates making a net total of 334. The faculty consisted of nineteen professors and instructors.

The first baccalaureate degree graduates at the commencement in 1891 were Eric Glad, Julius Lincoln, Ernst F. Pihlblad, and J. A. Westerlund. Additional graduates of departments were as follows: *Normal,* Ellida Ellison, Julia Larson, Maria Malmberg, Nellie Rosenstone; *Music,* Hilma Blomgren, Levi Hubbard, Anna Nyquist, Hilder Westerlund; *Commercial,* A. F. Codington, Elmer Johnson, Wm. O. Johnson, C. E. Malmberg, David Pearson, E. W. Peterson, A. J. Thorstenberg, John Vanloon, Charles Vikstrom. The place of birth of the graduates was Illinois, 8; Kansas, 4; Colorado, 3; and 1 each in Missouri, Nebraska, Indiana, Michigan, New Mexico, and Sweden.[37]

The commencement activities began with the baccalaureate service on Sunday, May 17, when Swensson preached in Swedish on the topic, "A True and Sound Philosophy of Life." On the following Wednesday afternoon the baccalaureate graduates defended their theses in oral examinations. In the evening the "disputation" took place with the four graduates as *"disputantes"* and members of the faculty, visiting dignitaries, and selected juniors as *"opponentes."* The topic was "Resolved, That Optimism and not Pessimism embodies the correct view of life." The "disputation" lasted until about 11:00 p.m. May 21 was graduation day, which opened with a prayer service at 9:00 a.m. in the Bethany Lutheran Church.

The commencement program was held in the college chapel later in the morning and included twenty items. The class motto was *"Sic Vos, Non Nobis"* ("Thus do ye, not for yourselves"). Graduates spoke in English and Swedish on a variety of subjects. Ludvig Holmes, the well-known Swedish American poet, read a long Swedish poem which he had written for the occasion. Swensson and E. Nelander, the former president of Bethany, also addressed the assembly. Swensson gave one address in Swedish and another in English.

In the evening a music program was presented by the choir, orchestra, and members of the faculty. A farewell service for the graduates was featured in Bethany Church on the following Sunday when graduates Pihlblad, Lincoln, and Glad spoke briefly. The final event was a meeting later in the day at the Swensson home, when "the group sang in four-part harmony, *Nearer, My God, to Thee,* under the mild summer sky." This became the traditional Bethany hymn for several decades. The first decade of Bethany's history had come to an end.[38]

On May 21, 1891, four men became the first baccalaureate degree graduates of Bethany College. Left to right are: Eric Glad, J. A. Westerlund, Ernst F. Pihlblad, and Julius Lincoln.

"I Skolparken"—A view of the college park at the turn of the century, looking down First Street and what is now the Miller-Stromquist Pedestrian Mall.

THE BETHANY FACULTY OF 1893.

THE BETHANY BOARD OF DIRECTORS, 1893.

2.

Struggle and Victory 1891-1904

The many-sided development of Bethany College continued steadily. Swensson and the members of the faculty worked diligently to strengthen the academic program. The organizational structure in 1901, at the end of two decades, included the College, with a School of Liberal Arts, School of Pedagogy, School of Oratory and Elocution, and Academy; College of Music and Fine Arts with the Musical Conservatory, School of Art, and School of Sloyd, Handiwork, Pyrography, and Embroidery; College of Business with the Commercial Department and School of Shorthand and Typewriting; the Graduate School; and the Summer School.[1]

The College provided a baccalaureate degree through four lines: the classical course, modern languages, natural history, and physics-mathematics areas, each one requiring four academic years of study. The Academy, an administrative unit of the College, presented a four-year college preparatory course. The School of Pedagogy, also a part of the College, enrolled students in a four-year teacher education program, and the Model School offered eight years of elementary education. The School of Oratory and Elocution within the College made available a two-year course which resulted in a Bachelor of Oratory diploma.

The emphasis in the curriculum for the bachelor of arts degree in 1900-01 was upon Latin, Greek, and mathematics. When Swensson reported to the Kansas Conference in 1896, he stated: "We maintain with great emphasis the college course in the old trustworthy classical curriculum. We have not fallen for the elective system." In the November-December 1896 issue of the *Messenger* the editor wrote: "A growing interest for the classics is making itself manifest at our institution this year . . . . This is as it should be. After all the classical course is *the course* which brings forth true culture and refinement." The curriculum provided eighteen semester hours of Greek and eighteen semester hours of Latin beyond the three year prerequisites in high school or academy. Students in the baccalaureate program were required to complete twelve semester hours in religion courses.[2]

The School of Pedagogy, an administrative unit within Liberal Arts and Sciences, provided courses in methods, school law, history of education, philosophy of education, school management, and practice teaching and criticism. The School of Oratory and Physical Culture offered four courses with emphasis upon elocution and gymnastics. The catalogue indicated that in the physical culture course "For health and comfort the clothing shall be light in weight and sufficiently free at neck, shoulders, and hips. The gymnasium dress must be of navy blue cloth with blouse waist and full plain skirt *reaching to the shoe tops.*"[3]

The College of Music and Fine Arts, through the Musical Conservatory, offered instruction in piano with a six-year program and in addition an "artist's course," pipe organ, two years; voice, four years; and violin, varied number of years depending upon previous preparation. Instruction was also provided in harmony, counterpoint, and history of music. Private lessons were available also in wind instruments, guitar, and mandolin. The catalogue for 1900-01 stated "the Conservatory of Music is easily the best in the state, to say nothing of surrounding states. The several departments are well organized and the instruction reliable and superior in kind. Music students here enjoy the advantages of the East at half the price." The instructional program was supplemented by membership in various ensemble groups including the oratorio society, chapel choir, orchestra, and band.[4]

When Birger Sandzén became director of the Art School in 1899, an enriched program of studies was developed in drawing, painting, and art history. The Business School declared its purpose "to actually and really train its students so that they can go right into an office from the school room and take charge of a set of books or do general office work acceptably." The business subjects were taught in fine facilities on the first floor of Old Main where there were simulated offices of a bank and other business enterprises.[5]

In 1894-95 the faculty authorized the awarding of a master of arts degree upon baccalaureate graduates who had spent at least four additional years in professional study or practice; the candidates were required to submit to the faculty a satisfactory literary, philosophical, or scientific paper. Thirty-six of these masters degrees had been conferred by 1901. This arrangement was abandoned in 1901 and a formal course of study in nine areas replaced it. Studies for one year in residence and an acceptable thesis were required.

The facilities for learning were improving steadily so that at the twentieth anniversary in 1901 the college library in Old Main contained upwards of 6,000 volumes and pamphlets in fourteen languages. The Museum of Natural History included an herbarium with representative species of plants, systematically arranged for convenient use. A rich collection of Indian relics from the Paint Creek site southwest of Lindsborg and relics and pottery from various Indian tribes of the Southwest provided good resources. The numismatic collection contained more than 3,000 coins. Laboratories in physics, chemistry, and biology were described as being well-supplied with fine equipment. The music department had adequate resources in organs, pianos, and other musical instruments.

Five scholarships and prizes were available for students. In addition to the Emma C. Johnson Scholarship and the Maria Charlotte Rundström Prize established previously, there were now the Hon. W. W. Thomas, Jr., Prizes for excellence in English and in Swedish oratory, funded by the American minister to Sweden in honor of his father, and the Oscar A. Smith Scholarship, founded by Colonel C. A. Smith, Minneapolis, Minnesota, in memory of his son. Student intellectual life was stimulated by four literary societies—Lyceum, Adelphic, Vim, and Svea, as well as by several debating clubs. The Linnean Society of Science met weekly for lectures, reading of original papers, and discussion. The society also maintained a reading room of scientific periodicals and monographs.

President Carl Swensson was an enthusiastic promoter of the College and its activities. He wrote hundreds of articles for newspapers in English and Swedish. In 1896 he reported to the Conference, "our announcement [advertisement] appeared in 700 newspapers." Other interesting forms of special promotion were used. In 1899 Swensson presented State officials in Topeka with Bethany College ink stands, paper holders, and calendars. Included among other items were aluminum combs in leather cases, men's leather billfolds, and public drinking cups identified with Bethany College.

The philosophy and purpose of Bethany College at this time was stated in the catalogue in 1901 as follows: "In spirit Bethany believes without reservation in the Bible and the Constitution. It is orthodox in its faith; sound in its patriotism; broad in its principles. Bethany believes in hard work on the part of the professor and student alike as conditions of success. Its desire is to give to the young people of Kansas the best and most reliable, liberal, and Christian Education of today."[6]

The College felt its responsibility as serving *in loco parentis:* "The utmost care will be observed in promoting the moral welfare of the students. As to their general conduct, we expect the students to act as ladies and gentlemen under all circumstances. Secret societies, profane language, card playing, late hours, and the use of tobacco in or about the buildings are forbidden." All students were required to attend morning prayer each school day in the college chapel and divine services on Sunday. Student religious organizations included the College Luther League for all students and the Luther League for Young Ladies.[7]

The number of faculty members had increased from 2 in 1881-82 to 7 in 1885-86, then to 21 in 1890-91, to 26 in 1895-96, and finally to 38 in 1900-01. The distribution on the occasion of the twentieth anniversary was as follows: College and School of Pedagogy, 16; Business, Shorthand, and Typewriting, 4; Music, 14, (piano, 7, violin, 2, organ, 2, voice, 2, wind instruments, 1); oratory and elocution, 2; sloyd, 1. The highest salary for a professor was $700.00.[8]

In 1901-02 the tuition for students in the college, normal, art, and professional subjects was $10.00 for each of four terms for the academic year. In commercial subjects it was $12.50 per term. In music the costs varied from $14.00 to $18.00 per term or from $56.00 to $72.00 per year. Meals were available at the college dining hall at two rates, $2.00 or $2.50 per week, the latter providing a better menu than the former. Rooms in the men's dormitory of Old Main rented at 50 to 60 cents per week while the rate at the Ladies Hall was 75 cents per week. Each student paid $1.25 per term for heating costs. The catalogue also recorded the following: "By paying one dollar the student secures the privilege of free baths during his stay at college, be it one or many years."[9]

The budget of Bethany College for current income and expenses in 1900-01, as presented by Carl Johns, treasurer, was $52,852.00. The tuition income was $15,576.00, the largest single item. The churches of the Kansas Conference contributed $1,148.00. The annual Bethany bazaar, which traced its origin to 1889, produced $967.00. Faculty salaries amounted to $14,160.00. There was a net loss of $9,798.00 on operations, including expenditures for repairs. The net worth of the College was $162,555.00. The annual deficits created serious problems with the result that the board of directors agreed at the Conference meeting in 1889 to assume personal responsibility for any deficit in the current operating fund for the next five years. This action was rescinded in the following year.[10]

The net enrollment in 1900-01 was 574 distributed as follows: College, 80; Academy, 74; Normal, 52; Commercial, 101; Conservatory of Music, 275; Elocution, 35; Art, 15; Sloyd and Pyrography, 60; and the Model School, 51. Special students inflated the statistics as judged by contemporary methods of counting enrollment. Fifty graduates received diplomas at the twentieth anniversary commencement exercises. The distribution was as follows: College, 15; Conservatory of Music, 11;

Commercial, 22; Normal and Oratory, 1 each.[11]

The statistics show that at the end of twenty years, 403 students had received degrees or certificates for less than baccalaureate level studies. The number of baccalaureate degrees was 103, involving 90 men and 13 women. The first woman graduate was Jenny Lind, class of 1892, the sister of Mrs. Carl Swensson and secretary to President Swensson for many years. The second woman graduate was Marie Sjöström, class of 1893, the future wife of President Ernst F. Pihlblad. The largest number of graduates was in the Commercial department with 172. The distribution of other graduates was as follows: Academy, 33; Normal, 44; Conservatory of Music, 38; Shorthand and Typing, 10; Oratory, 3.[12]

Although Bethany conferred bachelor of arts degrees for the first time in 1891, academic recognition was soon forthcoming. In 1892 Uppsala and Lund recognized Bethany degrees by permitting the recipients to enroll in the two Swedish universities without taking entrance examinations. In 1893 Bethany graduates could enroll in the graduate schools of Yale and Chicago universities without any further studies or examinations. In April, 1899, the Kansas State Board of Education authorized Bethany to issue life teaching certificates to qualified graduates in accordance with the regulations prescribed by the Kansas legislature.[13]

Moreover, Bethany graduates were stimulated to pursue graduate and professional study. *The Yale Alumni Weekly,* in describing the organization of the Bethany College Club of Yale, reported in 1902: "This club is a very vigorous and active organization . . . . There are now more graduates from Bethany College in the Yale Graduate School than from any other college, Yale excepted." Twenty-one Bethany graduates enrolled at Yale from the classes 1898-1902. Seven of the twelve graduates of the class of 1899 studied in the famous New Haven university.[14]

Although substantial progress was recorded in the academic life of Bethany, a heavy burden of debt hung over the institution. When the main building was completed in 1886 at a cost of approximately $65,-000.00, the debt was $39,000.00. The Reverend Olof Olsson, the pioneer pastor who founded Lindsborg in 1869, a professor at Augustana College and Theological Seminary, moved to Lindsborg in 1888 to assist Swensson in raising funds. At a church meeting on New Year's Day, 1889, Olsson challenged Lindsborg to raise $20,000.00. One-half was subscribed immediately. Although a good response was recorded, the debt was still large. In 1889 a loan for $40,000.00 was negotiated with the Massachusetts Life Insurance Company, Springfield, Massachusetts, through the Hamilton Investment Company, Salina.[15]

In 1891 a campaign for funds was conducted by the Reverend John Telleen, with the result that it was reported at the Conference meeting in 1892 that $35,344.00 had been pledged to pay the debt, with the expectancy that the cash income from the pledges would be considerable. The College, however, was unable to pay either principal or interest on the large loan and on a number of other obligations. The suit by N. Peterson, Galesburg, Illinois, on a $5,000.00 note, which had grown to $7,222.00 when judgment was rendered in December, 1892, included the following notation by Sheriff John Zimmerman when the execution papers were returned: "After diligent search, I fail to find any property to levy on." A different situation prevailed later in Sven B. Johnson's suit on a note dated December 11, 1892, for the recovery of $843.00. The property levied upon included a pipe organ, cabinet organs, pianos, a span of horses, a wagon, stoves, chairs, bedsteads, and 4,000 books. Sheriff Zimmerman attached the property and collected a fee of $1.00 a day as proven by a $40.00 receipt when judgment was released on February 19, 1897.[16]

Many attempts were made to raise funds for the College. In September, 1892, Swensson reported a generous subscription to Bethany by Jernberg and Rylander, Chicago. The development company promised Bethany $25,000.00 in return for assistance from the College in promoting the sale of 1,000 lots in the Belt City area of Chicago. The promotional relationship, authorized by the Kansas Conference, proved disappointing and involved Swensson and the Reverend John Seleen in much unfair criticism and brought much grief to them and others. In 1893 hoped-for income from a gift of 25,000 shares in the Magnolia Mining and Milling Company, Boulder, Colorado, and from 10,000 shares in the Loop Gold Mining Company, Clear Creek County, Colorado, was not forthcoming. In 1889 the board of directors petitioned King Oscar II of Sweden for authorization to receive a collection for Bethany in the churches of Sweden. The monarch's consent was secured. The result was disappointing since only a modest amount was received. In December, 1895, the sum of $814.00 was received from a second collection in Swedish churches which the monarch had authorized.[17]

Pastor John Seleen, Freemount, chairman of the board of directors for several years, was Bethany's contact in Sweden. Seleen reported in his autobiography that his audience with King Oscar II in 1889 was unpleasant and that the King said to him: "You have taken some of our best people, and now you want our money." They "disputed very sharply for over half an hour." However, the relationship became more pleasant, with the result that the monarch not only authorized the offering but donated books from his library for the Bethany library. When Seleen had an audience again with the King in 1894, he was received most cordially and gained the monarch's support for another offering. Seleen rendered great service to Bethany as a solicitor of funds in Kansas and in various sections of the United States.[18]

The indebtedness was reported as $54,936.00 at the meeting of the Kansas Conference in 1895. The College was also seriously in arrears on

The frontispiece for College catalogues in the 1890s.

salaries to members of the faculty. Resolutions were passed at the Conference meeting authorizing the college treasurer to receive student notes for tuition provided that the student could find a faculty member who would take the note as payment toward his salary. In December, 1895, Professor J. E. Welin addressed a letter to the board of directors in which he requested $200.00 on his back salary so that he might attend his own wedding while at the same time inviting the members to be present. The minutes of the board of directors expressed appreciation for the invitation and instructed Swensson to borrow $200.00 in Topeka or other places and to give old notes as collateral security. The shortage of funds was apparent also when the directors "Resolved that Mr. A. Lincoln will get $30.00 today, if that amount is in the treasury, or else as soon as money can be collected for that purpose." Lincoln, a lumber dealer and a great friend of the College, advanced building materials on credit.[19]

Major and Mrs. Lane S. Hart of Hannbury, Pennsylvania, had given the College their interest in the Brunswick Hotel in Lindsborg, amounting to approximately $3,500.00. At the meeting of the Kansas Conference in February, 1897, the following resolution was passed as a protective measure in the difficult situation. "In order to protect this gift from all danger and to keep it tax free, the Bethany College of Music and Fine Arts has been incorporated." This was a separate legal entity from the parent Bethany College.[20]

In the midst of the great strain produced by litigation over the $40,000.00 mortgage of the Massachusetts Mutual Life Insurance Company and following much negotiation by Swensson and other Bethany representatives, a telegram was sent by the creditors in October, 1897, indicating that the mortgage could be liquidated by the payment of $20,-000.00, thus reducing this indebtedness by one-half, if payment occurred by December 20. A chant went up in Lindsborg, "Now or never, Now or never." The *Lindsborg News* observed editorially, "If Bethany lives now, none but God can kill her afterwards."[21]

Swensson and the board of directors launched intensive efforts to reach a goal of $50,000.00 to liquidate the insurance company obligation and other indebtedness. Although some progress was made, the creditors were forced to extend the deadline to prevent legal foreclosure. An intensive drive for funds was made in Lindsborg and in the McPherson District of the Kansas Conference in the spring of 1898 which produced $14,500.00 in cash. Jacob Linn of Halstead made a loan of $5,000.00 at eight per cent. The balance was produced from friends at a special meeting. In a dramatic last minute trip to McPherson, the county seat, Swensson and J. P. Grant of New Gottland brought the payment to the county attorney's office just before the final deadline for foreclosure. The whole Lindsborg community celebrated this great victory from early evening until midnight by the firing of anvils and band music.[22]

The anxiety and burden of debt caused Swensson and his associates, especially the Reverend John Telleen, to explore the possibility of public ownership and support of Bethany. At the session of the Kansas legislature in 1891 Telleen worked closely with Senator H. B. Kelly of McPherson who was willing to introduce a bill seeking a state appropriation. In January, 1891, Telleen reported in a letter to Swensson that Senator Kelly was ready to introduce another bill that would provide for the issue of $60,000.00 in bonds by Smoky Hill Township with the understanding that Bethany would become a township Normal Institute. Telleen was confident that there would be a fine response locally: "I certainly think our township would vote bonds to that amount. Why it would never be felt. And even if it were, the school is worth hundreds of thousands of dollars to our township." Constitutional and other problems made it impossible to bring the matter beyond the discussion stage.[23]

Since the pressing mortgage matter had been settled, Swensson and the board turned to the obligations still creating problems, including salary arrears to the faculty. In September, 1898, the outstanding debt was $32,255.00 including several thousands of dollars of debt to faculty members. In July of that year the board established the Bethany Volunteer Plan. Non-interest bearing script was issued to liquidate the salary indebtedness with one-fifth to be paid annually for five years. In a plea for volunteers Swensson declared: "The war with Spain is over. Other wars are not ended yet. They must go on forever. The war against ignorance and for education cannot, dare not cease." The enlistment was for five years, the length required for paying off the script. The amount for various volunteer ranks ranged from $100.00 for a general to $1.00 for a private during each of the next five years. Yellow and blue buttons which showed the rank of the wearer were issued. The report of the early volunteering showed 1 major general, Carl Swensson, 7 colonels, 1 captain, 3 lieutenants, 4 sergeants, and 11 privates. A substantial relief from the debt to faculty members was achieved by this appeal.[24]

A dramatic example of Carl Swensson's optimism and faith in the midst of critical financial problems is evident in the plans which resulted in the construction of the "Messiah" auditorium later known as Ling Gymnasium. In May, 1895, Swensson had requested permission from the board of directors to construct a large auditorium. Greater attendance at the "Messiah" festival and at other public functions would generate additional funds for current expenses. Fine facilities would be provided for classes in physical education. In a final appeal to the board, written in long-hand on the formal typewritten letter, were these words: "Please let me try it, I pray you."[25]

The minutes of the meeting of the board of directors in July, 1895, recorded receipt of a petition from the Ling Association, a local organization of Bethany boosters, for authorization to construct an auditorium on

LING AUDITORIUM, constructed in 1895 and destroyed by fire in 1946.

the campus. The response of the board was as follows: "The board will not deny a place for the erection of the auditorium, but the board as such will not take upon itself any responsibility, financially or in any other way for this building." A site on the campus was leased to the Ling Association. Swensson proceeded to the work of construction, having received a promise from Colonel C. A. Smith, a Minneapolis lumber baron and philanthropist, to provide essential lumber for the structure. The Ling Association raised a modest amount of funds and provided extensive free labor.[26]

The new building was dedicated in elaborate festivities on October 4-5, 1895. The large auditorium was described by the *Topeka Capital* as "the finest of Kansas auditoriums," allegedly capable of seating 4,000 people. The new building was gaily decorated with flags, bunting, flowers, emblems, and fine crayon portraits of Washington, Lincoln, Cleveland, Oscar II, King of Sweden, John Ericsson, the inventor of the *Monitor,* and Governor Edmund Morrell of Kansas. United States Senator John J. Ingalls surprised the crowd when he declared in an address at the dedication that before people now in middle age had passed away, it would be possible to travel between New York and San Francisco between daylight and darkness by means of airships.[27]

In 1899 a further demonstration of Swensson's faith in the future resulted in the rebuilding and expansion of the Ladies Dormitory. The Brunswick Hotel, a gift of Major and Mrs. Lane Hart, had been sold to George and Sam Shields for $3,500.00. This amount was added to other funds and with much free labor a third story was added to the girls dormitory and a new three-story structure 40 ft. by 50 ft. was built adjoining the original building on the west. The Ladies Dormitory now had a large public reception room, fourteen music practice rooms, and accommodations for almost ninety women students. Bethany's physical facilities were growing to accommodate the increased enrollment and academic program.

Swensson realized the imperative need for establishing permanent financial support for the College when at the meeting of the Kansas Conference in March, 1892, he urged the members to authorize an endowment fund. In his enthusiasm he said: "Think if Bethany College owned a good farm in every one of our Conference parishes how easily the need for security would be achieved." In January, 1895, the *Lindsborg News* announced the likelihood that two farms in Colorado, to be known as the Axel Oxenstierna farm in honor of the great chancellor of Gustavus Adolphus, and another farm, to be called the Uppsala farm, and one, the Stockholm farm in Texas, with a combined value of $10,000.00, would be added to Bethany's assets. The expectations were not realized. In June, 1900, Swensson reported enthusiastically that Dr. R. K. Pearson had offered to contribute $25,000.00 to an endowment fund if friends would raise $75,000.00. C. A. Smith, Minneapolis, gave 25 million feet of timber in Oregon with the understanding that it should never be sold for less than $25,000.00. Although Swensson was optimistic, considerable time elapsed before any substantial sums were added to the fund.[28]

Although there were disappointments, the prospects for Bethany in the early years of the new century seemed encouraging. When Swensson presented his presidential report for the academic year 1901-02, he stated: "The past year has been the happiest in the school's history. The enrollment has been larger than at any other time. Students have been zealous in their studies and exemplary in conduct. The instruction has proceeded with enthusiasm and success. Morale is high." This enthusiasm was apparent in the expanded graduate program that was announced for the following year. The graduate degrees were to include the already established master's plus the doctor of philosophy degree. A detailed curriculum was presented in six areas, namely, philosophy; history; political science and social science; ancient languages and literature; modern languages and literature; natural and physical sciences; and mathematics. There were 118 graduate courses in 19 departments listed in the catalogue for 1902-03. The requirements included three years of graduate study with two years in residence, one major and two minors, and reading knowledge of Latin, French, and German. The doctoral program appeared in the catalogue for three years. No earned Ph.D. degrees were awarded.[29]

The academic year 1902-03 also provided for a school of law with a two-year program at the outset. Dr. Swensson viewed this development as another step in elevating Bethany from the status of a college to a university. There were twenty-three students in the law courses during the first year. This was in the era when graduation from law school was not required for admission to the Kansas bar.   Carl Edwin Anderson and Lewis Johnson were the first graduates in 1904. The program was expanded to a three-year curriculum in 1904-05. In that year the law library consisted of more than 1,200 volumes. There were ten law students. A bachelor of arts degree was required for admission. Several successful Kansas members of the bar received their legal training at Bethany. The law school was discontinued in 1911.[30]

In January, 1903, consternation struck the Lindsborg community when an article in the *Kansas City Star* suggested that consideration was being given to the possibility of moving Bethany to Kansas City, Missouri. The issue was soon discussed in the *Messenger:* "Shall Bethany be moved to Kansas City? In the halls and corridors, in the literary societies and in the stores, on the street corners, through the press, everywhere has this question been a subject of much discussion." Although the editor felt that the matter might be explored, he was convinced that Bethany should not move.[31]

President Swensson acknowledged that contacts had been made with him about moving Bethany. He indicated that $100,000.00 had been promised by one source and that there had been an offer of property on the east side of either Fifteenth or Eighteenth Street in Kansas City, although he had never seen it. In an interview published in the *Topeka Daily Capital,* he was quoted as saying: "In my opinion nothing less than an offer of $500,000 in money and real estate would induce the Conference even to think of moving it to the great city at the mouth of the Kaw. If Kansas City would make such an offer, I suppose the Conference would be sorely tempted to accept it. Personally, I am decidedly of the opinion that Bethany is located in the right place." The rumors persisted. In April Dr. G. A. Brandelle, president of the Kansas Conference, was quoted in the *Kansas City Times:* "If Kansas City will give us $500,-000.00, we will make the change. Indeed a proposition from Kansas City will be considered at any time." Brandelle spoke only for himself. Bethany leaders showed no interest and no proposition was placed before the board or the Conference. Swensson, the faculty, the students, the Conference and the community had great faith in the future of the college at Lindsborg.[32]

The progress of Bethany College at this time reflected the dreams and aspirations of Carl Swensson, founder, and president since 1889. His loyalty to Bethany caused him to decline the call to become president of Augustana College and Theological Seminary which had been extended to him at the Burlington, Iowa, meeting of the Augustana Synod in June, 1900. Swensson's great faith and hard work and that of his capable associates were being rewarded. The future was bright with the promise of greater gains. Even the indebtedness of the College, which had been far greater on several occasions, was only $32,000.00 in 1903. But suddenly Carl Swensson's great career came to an abrupt end. On February 14, 1904, the sad message came from California Lutheran Hospital, Los Angeles, that he had died from pneumonia after a brief illness.

The response of students to the death of Bethany's beloved founder and president was recorded in the *Messenger:* "At chapel services we first heard the indefinite rumor. A telegram had been received saying that our president was quite ill in Los Angeles. Our class had French in room 73 the first period. We assembled in our carefree manner, but there was a delay in the appearance of Professor Sandzén. At length he came, but his face was drawn and pale with grief. 'We have received sad news' was all he could say, and he turned to go again. We walked aimlessly up and down the halls with parched lips, sometimes whispering in subdued groups." On a farm near Lindsborg Mrs. John Holmquist wrote in her diary enclosed in wide black lines, expressing the sentiments of the people of the Smoky Valley: "I can scarcely see to write tonight on account of the tears since we have received the sad announcement that our dear pastor is dead. He died this morning in California. We are all enveloped in deep sorrow. May God strengthen the wife and children. It seems so strange that one who was so needed should have been taken away from his place of service."[33]

February 22, 1904, the day of the funeral, was bright and clear. People called it "a Carl Swensson day." Although nature was kindly disposed, there was deep sorrow in the hearts of the people of Lindsborg and elsewhere. Estimates indicate that 3,000 people were in Lindsborg that day to pay their respects to Carl Swensson. A student guard of honor stood by the casket of Bethany's president in the "Messiah" auditorium while people filed by in a continuous line for several hours. Beautiful floral tributes filled the front of the large auditorium. At the memorial service, sermons and eulogies were presented by Dr. L. G. Abrahamson, Dr. G. A. Brandelle, Dr. M. Wahlstrom, President Gustav Andreen of Augustana College, and others. Messages of sympathy addressed to Mrs. Swensson and daughters, Bertha and Annie Theo., were read. The "Messiah" chorus sang Dr. Swensson's favorite, *Worthy is the Lamb*. A sad people followed the funeral cortege to the last resting place, Elmwood Cemetery, east of Lindsborg. At the conclusion of the committal service the group sang the traditional Bethany hymn, *Nearer My God to Thee*.[34]

In the comparatively brief span of forty-seven years, Carl Swensson had fashioned great achievement. His rugged and sturdy physique could scarcely conceal the surging energy and vitality of this pastor of a large congregation and founder, and later president of Bethany College. In

PRESIDENT SWENSSON WITH THE COLLEGE FACULTY

FACULTY OF THE COLLEGE OF MUSIC AND FINE ARTS

The Swensson family, left to right: Carl, An-
nie Theo., Bertha, and Alma.

CARL A. SWENSSON (right) AND
ERNST F. PIHLBLAD

Below: The Carl A. Swensson funeral cortege outside Ling Auditorium.

describing his schedule in the 1880s, he wrote: "I often preached five times a week, sometimes three times on Sunday, and I rode twenty-two miles in a farm wagon. During the week, I delivered five addresses at the college chapel and twelve lectures to classes; articles were sent to three to six newspapers each week. There was additional work on a large book and worry and anxiety day and night for the school's financial situation, together with carrying on correspondence which on occasion amounted to twenty letters a day. In addition there were continuous trips on the railroad. In 1888 I traveled 25,000 miles, in 1889 it was 22,500 miles."[35]

The unfailing energy of Carl Swensson produced an amazing range and amount of work. Four books were written: *I Sverige* (1890), *Åter i Sverige* (1897), books of travel and commentary, *Vid Hemmets Härd* (1897), a large volume for the home, and *I Morgonstund* (1903), a devotional book which has been translated into English, *In the Morning Hour* (1927). He was a major contributor to two volumes: *Forgät-Mig-Ej* (1902) in Swedish and *Forget-Me-Not* (1902) in English, dealing largely with Bethany College and Christian education. He had an impressive role as an editor and co-editor of *Korsbaneret* in the 1880s, an Augustana Synod church annual, and of *Ungdoms-Vännen,* a bi-monthly journal for young people, 1879-1887. He was the founder of *Fosterlandet,* a Swedish American weekly newspaper, and a contributor for twenty years. He was the founder of *Lindsborgs-Posten* in 1897, serving as editor for many years. He was closely identified with the *Lindsborg Record,* founded in 1896. He was a regular correspondent for *Hemlandet, det Gamla och det Nya* and *Svenska-Tribunen,* Chicago weekly newspapers. His column, *Vid Skrifbordet* ("At the Writing Desk") and his pseudonym, "Leopold," were well-known in Swedish America. He was the founder and a contributor to the Bethany College publications, *Framåt, Budbäraren,* and the *Bethany Messenger.*

Carl Swensson was active in the general work of the Lutheran Church. He served as secretary of the Kansas Conference of the Augustana Lutheran Synod, 1880-82, and represented the Conference on the Synodical Council, serving as secretary 1886-88. Although an ardent champion of Lutheranism within Swedish American circles, he realized that the future belonged to a united Lutheran Church with an American orientation. In 1885 he was elected secretary of the General Council of the Evangelical Lutheran Church of North America. In 1895 Carl Swensson was president of this organization.

The arena of public life also received Swensson's time and talent. Citizenship implied responsibility for participation in the life of the body politic. He was a staunch Republican and an especially bitter critic of the Populists in the 1890s. He campaigned extensively in Swedish communities in the United States, devoting full-time for six weeks to the McKinley campaign in 1896. Carl Swensson campaigned for public office on only one occasion, when in 1889 he was drafted and then elected as a Representative to the Kansas legislature on the Republican ticket from McPherson County. He served as one of seven members of the committee on education in the House of Representatives. Included among the bills that he introduced was House Bill No. 299, January 22, 1889. "An Act relative to trusts, and providing for the punishment of persons organizing, managing, controlling, or conducting the same for the purpose of controlling prices and monopolizing purchases and sales of articles for general consumption" and House Bill No. 574, February 6, 1889: "An Act in relation to foreclosure of mortgages," designed to protect the interests of hard-pressed landowners. Swensson declined to serve longer in the legislature, choosing to devote more time to Bethany College.

A dominant characteristic of the founder of Bethany College was faith and optimism. In dark and difficult days he confidently declared: *"I morgon blir det bättre"*—"tomorrow it will be better," and like all great dreamers and leaders, he believed in the future, in the tomorrow's tomorrows. Moreover, his credo in education was expressed in the phrase which he affirmed again and again with zeal and confidence: *"Kunskap är makt"*—"knowledge is power," and, when joined with the Christian view of life and destiny, he believed that it provided the ultimate meaning for individuals and for society. His many admirers on the faculty and in the Lindsborg community believed in him. They sacrificed their personal standard of living to support Bethany; they mortgaged their property in times of crisis so that the College would live; they signed notes to keep the institution solvent; they worked, they prayed, they dreamed dreams for Bethany.

Carl Swensson was dearly loved, esteemed, and respected. Although he had his critics, arising largely from his exuberant enthusiasm for the Republican party or because some felt he promoted the College too rapidly at times, these dissident voices formed only a minimal number. Swensson possessed a certain kind of charisma that was a great personal resource. He inspired his associates and supporters with his own abiding confidence in the promise of the future.

A contemporary described Dr. Swensson: "The doctor has a magnificent physique, a sonorous voice, animated delivery, and majestic presence." Another observer refers to Dr. Swensson as "An interesting person with an imposing figure, high and broad forehead, and an open countenance. There was something magnetic about his whole personality. He inspired confidence. His great optimism was a source of strength in the great burdens he carried." Dr. Julius Lincoln, a member of the first baccalaureate class at Bethany, has cited the following interesting episode from an appearance of the Bethany president at a meeting in Sweden:

A large Hercules with tanned, weatherbeaten features and with flashing eyes that reminded one of glistening swords. One could almost take him for a seafarer who had sailed the world around and stared death in the face repeatedly with perfect equanimity. His physical appearance bespoke a personality . . . . The social question was considered. The leader's thesis was well developed but something was lacking—what shall I call it, life, radiant life. The room was sultry. We needed air. It came. No, not a draught of air merely, but a thunder shower . . . . It was C. A. Swensson. What a voice! It could silence the roaring storm. And the words. They almost struck terror in the hearts of the Swedish listeners. 36

Many honors came to Carl Swensson in the United States and Sweden. Included were the honorary degree of doctor of philosophy from Uppsala University in 1893 and honorary doctor of divinity degrees from Augustana College and Theological Seminary and Thiel College in 1894. In 1901 he was decorated as a Knight of the Royal Order of the North Star by King Oscar II of Sweden through Bishop von Schéele, Visby, who was visiting in the United States.

Carl Swensson—pastor, educator, college founder and president, churchman, editor, author, member of the Kansas legislature, public speaker of great renown, promoter of art and music, co-founder with his wife of the Lindsborg "Messiah" tradition, friend of man—has been described as "the colossus of the Plains," "the giant from Kansas," "the incomparable Dr. Swensson." Ernst Skarstedt, the Swedish American author and journalist, has written: "Swensson loved everything great, noble, and beautiful: poetry, art, and all that lifts and ennobles." At the time of Carl Swensson's death, the *Kansas City Star* observed in an editorial: "It is scarcely too much to say that Dr. Swensson was at the time of his death the most famous man in Kansas and his fame will grow as his remarkable achievements are revealed in the light of history . . . . He accomplished what few men would have thought of attempting."[37]

When the last page of the final chapter of Dr. Carl Swensson's earthly life had been written, the editor of the *Lindsborg Record* penned lines of appreciation in behalf of the people of Lindsborg and elsewhere: "The grief which spread from home to home in our little town is indescribable. The Doctor was the friend of everybody and everybody was his friend . . . . His life has been a constant endeavor for good towards all. He was unselfish, his whole ambition was for Bethany, for the Swedish people and for his country . . . . Money, distinction, personal favor, and high station in life were nothing to him unless it tended toward the elevation and betterment of Bethany College, the child of his ambitions. His very life teemed with enthusiasm for Bethany, for Lindsborg, and for the Smoky Valley."[38]

The great career of Carl Swensson was shared and supported by his wife, Alma. She came as his young bride to Lindsborg in September, 1880, from Moline, Illinois. She was a talented singer and organist. The Swenssons planned together the presentations of the *Messiah* and Alma served as the conductor in rehearsals the first year, and at the renditions she was a soloist. Alma Swensson had an outstanding record in women's work within the Augustana Lutheran Church. Its national Women's Missionary Society was organized in her home in June, 1892, and she served as the recording secretary. She was the first and long-time editor of the official periodical of the Society. Mrs. Swensson taught music in the early years of the College and served as organist of the Bethany Lutheran Church for forty years. She was a member of the oratorio society chorus until two years before her death.

When Alma Swensson passed away on December 13, 1939, Bethany and Lindsborg said farewell to a dedicated and talented woman who has left an enduring legacy of greatness to the College and church.

"BETHANY PIANOS AND ORGANS, for information or prices address Bethany College, Lindsborg, Kansas . . . . " Shown are two styles from among the many promoted by "Bethany College of Music and Fine Arts, a part of Bethany College."

Below: A group of residences on North Second Street, across from the campus near what is now Swensson Street, is shown in about 1907.

3.

Consolidation and Growth 1904-1921

When sorrowing Bethany and Lindsborg followed beloved Dr. Carl Swensson to his last resting place in Elmwood Cemetery that February day in 1904, the future seemed uncertain. Swensson's dynamic leadership had been so dominant it was difficult for some people to envisage what the alternatives might be. When reality was faced again, there was not only hope but a logical solution. Professor Ernst F. Pihlblad was the most qualified successor to the man with whom he had been associated for nine years, the last two as vice-president of the College.

The Reverend Ernst F. Pihlblad was born in Kansas City, Missouri, March 18, 1873, the first of two sons of Mr. and Mrs. John Pihlblad. Ernst's brother Arvid, a Bethany graduate, became a well-known physician in Lindsborg. After attending the public schools in Kansas City, Ernst enrolled in Bethany Academy at the age of eleven. The family had moved to Lindsborg where John Pihlblad was a merchant. In 1891, Ernst, at the age of eighteen, graduated with honors in the first baccalaureate class. He enrolled at Augustana Theological Seminary the following September, and after returning to teach Latin the next year at Bethany, he continued his studies at the seminary. He received the bachelor of divinity degree in 1894. He was ordained as a pastor of the Augustana Lutheran Synod on a call to the Patterson and Passaic, New Jersey, congregations of the Augustana Synod, the year of his graduation from the seminary. He joined the Bethany faculty in September, 1895, as Latin teacher, thus beginning forty-six years of distinguished and uninterrupted service to the institution.[1]

Professor Pihlblad served as acting president until his election to the presidency by members of the Kansas Conference at the annual meeting at the Salemsborg Lutheran Church in April, 1904. Faculty and students, alumni and citizens of Lindsborg, pastors and members of supporting congregations were unanimous in their endorsement of his election. The *Messenger* declared on that occasion: "Not only has the best man for the place succeeded to it, but this man is the one who was closest to Dr. Swensson during the latter's upbuilding of Bethany, the one most intimately touched with the spirit and the inspiration which the late president sought to weld into its every part . . . . We have little doubt that President Pihlblad would have been the doctor's choice for the succession." In October the *Messenger* again affirmed faith in the new president by declaring: "Now the future of Bethany has been placed in President Pihlblad's keeping and we who know him best cannot but feel that it will rest secure."[2]

Ernst Pihlblad was thirty-one years old when he succeeded to the presidency. He brought excellent resources of intellect as well as great dedication and will. He was a fine classical scholar, and as a professor of Latin he was known as a splendid teacher who demanded high standards of achievement. He was an especially gifted speaker. His rich vocabulary, classical learning, and extensive reading provided excellent materials for public addresses. His philosophy of education was clearly founded upon his understanding of the role of liberal arts and sciences in the Christian context of life and learning. His view was stated clearly in his inaugural address as president in May, 1905: "To develop the individual physically, mentally, morally, and spiritually; to teach him his proper place in the universe, his relations and duties to himself, his fellowmen, and his Maker, and to impart to human life that indescribable charm, ripeness, and maturity that we call culture, this I hold to be the purpose of the college. The college should train the man for the highest of all arts, the art of living, and that irrespective of what his profession or calling may eventually be."[3]

The primary function of teaching and learning engaged the attention of the faculty as a new era in Bethany's history was launched. In his first report to the Kansas Conference at its meeting in Fremont in 1905, Pihlblad identified the trends in higher education: "On the basis of the pressure from the outside to follow the modern tendency to make the courses more or less elective, it is necessary to make some modifications in the curriculum . . . . We have sought, however, to retain the traditional approach while at the same time taking advantage of the valuable aspects of the new view by permitting some freedom of choice among areas and within subjects." In March, 1906, the college faculty adopted new requirements for the bachelor's degree which included the following required subjects and distribution: Christianity, 12 hours; foreign languages, 16-18 hours; English, 8 hours; natural history or

ERNST F. PIHLBLAD, when he became president.

The statue of Carl A. Swensson originally was in front of Old Main.

DR. AND MRS. ERNST PIHLBLAD WITH SONS TERENCE AND HELGE

A campus scene: Carnegie Library and Old Main.

Bethany daisies in the college park.

THE SWEDISH PAVILION

biology, 5 hours; chemistry, 5 hours; psychology, 5 hours; mathematics, 3 hours; and history, 3 hours. The admission requirements with emphasis upon foreign languages, mathematics, and English were continued. The four fields of study for the degree were the classical, modern languages, physics-mathematics, and biological sciences. Requirements included the presentation of 132 semester hours of credit.[4]

Candidates for the liberal arts degree presented a written thesis during the senior year and an oral defense of it. The topic could be either in English or Swedish. Included among the thesis topics in 1906 were the following: "The skepticism of Hume compared with the skepticism of the Sophists," "Virgil's influence on literature during the Middle Ages," "Phidias and Polyclites," "The Romantic Era," "Verner von Hedenstam as a poet," "Factors in the dissemination and germination of seeds," "The value of graphical representation on the study of equations," "The relation of the Protestant reformation to popular government," "Socialism or social reform," and "The separation of Sweden and Norway."

An early emphasis by President Pihlblad was to improve the library facilities and the book collection. The two rooms in the main building and the collection of 8,000 volumes were inadequate for achieving the purposes of the College. Pihlblad presented the needs and plans for the library to the Carnegie Corporation, which through the generous benefactions of Andrew Carnegie made possible extensive resources for colleges and communities. College officials were pleased to announce at the Conference meeting in 1907 that a gift of $20,000.00 had been received from the Carnegie Corporation for a library building. Architectural plans for the building were drawn by Hare and Smith, Iola, Kansas. C. F. Rosine, Lindsborg contractor, was engaged as the builder. The structure was occupied during the summer of 1908 and dedicated with appropriate festivities when the Kansas Conference met in Lindsborg in April, 1909. The beautiful two-story building, with impressive Greek columns facing Swensson Street, south and west of the main building, provided space for 20,000 volumes, two large reading rooms and one small reading room, facilities for the meetings of literary societies, space for art classes, and offices for the president and treasurer. Although extra funds for books were in short supply, a special effort had raised money so that 500 new volumes were added by the time the library was formally dedicated. The Carnegie Library continued to serve the College until 1970 when the library building in the Wallerstedt Learning Center was occupied.

The year 1905 had witnessed the removal to the campus of the Swedish Pavilion at the Louisiana Purchase Exhibition at St. Louis the previous year. The Honorable W. W. Thomas, Jr., the United States Minister to Sweden and Norway, purchased the building and donated it to the College. The cost for moving it from St. Louis was $2,000.00. The building was of Swedish manor house design with a large main room and two wings. The coat of arms of Sweden was centered on one wall of the large room. The structure was known variously as the Sweden House or Swedish Pavilion. It was first used as an art exhibition hall and museum. Later a part of the building was used for gymnastic classes, home economics instruction, and one wing served for a number of years as an infirmary. Instruction in art was later provided in the Swedish Pavilion for many years since the space in the library was too limited to accommodate the needs. The Swedish Pavilion was moved to the Swedish type open-air museum in Mill Park in the south part of Lindsborg in 1969.

In addition to the new buildings in the first decade of the new century, the campus profited from signs of progress in Lindsborg. Wednesday, October 25, 1905, was a big day when the installation of the city electric and water works was observed. The faculty voted that classes be dismissed the whole day to celebrate the big event and to permit students and faculty to participate in a festive program at the Auditorium. Shortly thereafter acetylene lighting was replaced with electricity in the main building and in the Ladies Hall. Electric lighting was provided in the auditorium through financial support from the "Messiah" chorus. City water was also installed on the campus at this time.

When the new administration assumed responsibilities following the death of Swensson in 1904, the college debt was approximately $32,-000.00. This was a large amount at that time, and the board and President Pihlblad were anxious to remove this burden. An added incentive was found in the promise of Colonel C. A. Smith, Minneapolis, Minnesota, that if the debt were paid off by January 1, 1907, $25,000.00 worth of timberland in Oregon would be contributed to the endowment fund. The board engaged Frank Nelson, the highly esteemed former member of the faculty and former Kansas superintendent of public instruction, as the campaign director. Plans were developed with gratifying results. The tension mounted as the goal came within sight. Five-hundred people assembled in the auditorium on the evening of December 31 as final reports came in. When Frank Nelson came to the rostrum at 10:45 p.m. the deficit was $641.00. In a few minutes the goal of $34,000.00 had been exceeded by $2.75. The *Messenger* rejoiced: "Hurrah for Bethany! Professor Frank Nelson says that every cent, honestly and bona fide, of the college debt has been subscribed. The sum of $34,000.00 has been raised in the last months. Nine cheers for Frank Nelson." The board was unsuccessful in the attempt to persuade Frank Nelson to accept the position as permanent director of fund raising.[5]

Annual income for current expenses continued to come from gifts *in natura* and through proceeds from the annual Bethany bazaar. The solicitation of gifts *in natura* was made early in the college's history and continued well into the present century. Committees were organized in

"BETHANY FLATS": A 1907 scene at Main and State Streets shows the Bethany Book Concern and the next-door Lindsborg Mercantile Co.

congregations to solicit these gifts. Long lists were published periodically in *Framåt* and *Lindsborgs-Posten*. In February, 1889, *Framåt* carried a list of one hundred donations which included the following: "N. O. Lundquist, 1 butchered hog; J. Stromquist, 200 lbs. meat; Gust Cedarholm, 1 butchered hog, 1 cheese, 2 gallons of milk, and 2 chickens; C. E. Ericson, 4 lbs. butter, 2½ doz. eggs, 2 gallons milk, and 115 lbs. wheat; J. Ahlstedt, 2 lbs. butter, 3 chickens and ½ bu. apples." More than 100 gifts of this type are listed in *Lindsborgs-Posten*, November, 1907. In March, 1909, the following item appeared in *Lindsborgs-Posten* over the names of President Ernst F. Pihlblad and Martin Anderson, manager of the college dining hall: "We wish again this year to come to our friends with a request for Easter eggs for the dining hall. These gifts *in natura* furnish a substantial addition to the college's treasury. Think of Bethany when the hens lay well."[6]

The annual bazaar in the Auditorium was a great occasion for many years until about 1930. An observer recorded his impression in 1905:

The capacious auditorium is the scene of the bazaar. Booths are erected where the different articles and refreshments are sold. One is a candy booth, another is the juniperade booth. Here is one with books and magazines of all sorts for all. From one part of the room are heard reports and noises of the shooting gallery, from another comes the aroma of coffee and the clatter of dishes. The fish pond, the delight of the youngsters, generally holds the conspicuous place among the attractions. Sometimes there is the fortune teller's tent. Some booths are devoted to needlework and embroidery.

A fee was charged for entrance and for each of the games and attractions. A variety program was also presented. The grand finale was a tableau. Bethany faculty members and their wives joined with students and citizens of the Smoky Valley for decades in a gala event that also produced greatly needed funds. The income varied from year to year.[7]

Although Bethany was free of debt in 1907, the financial problems continued to be critical. The debt for current operations reported to the Conference meeting at Walsburg, Kansas, on April 13, 1913, was $16,-000.00. Annual deficits were approximately $5,000.00 a year in the following years. In 1913 Pihlblad and the board persuaded the Conference to authorize the raising of an endowment fund of $100,000.00. The goal on the basis of the expanding needs was increased to $200,000.00 shortly thereafter. In April, 1915, Jens Stensaas, the treasurer, reported that $83,000.00 had been raised since 1911. The financial problems continued to be serious. Dr. Alfred Bergin, chairman of the board, warned the Conference in 1915: "It will be a dismal day if the daily press announces the news: 'Bethany College is closed and the 'Messiah' festivals have been held for the last time in Kansas.' " He made an urgent plea for

The arrival of a "Messiah" excursion train near Ling or "Messiah" Auditorium.

achieving the endowment goal of $200,000.00. President Pihlblad made an effective plea for attaining the endowment goal and for greater per capita support from the congregations. Good news came from Lindsborg. The Lindsborg community had pledged $50,000.00 and $23,000.00 had already been subscribed. In April, 1917, the total endowment fund was listed as $165,704.00 with $49,381.00 of that amount as subscription notes. Another crisis had been met.[8]

When the guns of August, 1914, sounded loudly in Europe with the outbreak of World War I, a new era in the history of mankind came to birth. The European conflict cast its long and dark shadows across the Atlantic with results that radically changed life for individuals and society. Bethany and Lindsborg were in the midst of the annual "Messiah" festival when news came on April 6, 1917, of the declaration of war between the United States and the Central powers. On the previous Sunday, which was Palm Sunday, Galli-Curci, the celebrated Italian coloratura soprano, had filled the auditorium in the afternoon and a full house had heard the rendition of the *Messiah* in the evening. A seriousminded, capacity audience heard Ysaye, the brilliant violinist, in concert Easter Sunday afternoon and the oratorio society's performance in the evening. Many members of the chorus and the audience were to find in distant places the reality of the question in the bass aria, "Why do the nations so furiously rage together?" During the week following the outbreak of war, several Bethany students and Lindsborg residents signed up with Company D, McPherson, a National Guard unit. Herbert Stone, former Bethany student, was the first volunteer as he was sworn in at the Oscar Berglund drugstore, where he worked, by Lt. Leo Mingenback, who had come from McPherson to recruit members for the unit. Other Bethany and Lindsborg men soon enlisted in the regular army or navy.

President Pihlblad, in his annual report to the Kansas Conference two weeks after the declaration of war, emphasized the following: "Restlessness prevails already among young people and this fact affects their studies. Several students have already entered the military service and many more intend to do so soon . . . . There is discussion in state schools whether or not to hold commencement this year." When the new academic year opened in September, the school week was extended to six days in order to provide longer vacations so that students could work outside the campus for extensive periods. The second semester of the current year was also shortened two weeks by Saturday classes.[9]

The impact of the war was summarized by Pihlblad in his annual report to the Conference meeting in Lindsborg in April, 1918: "We find ourselves in trying times . . . . Not only is there a significant decrease in enrollment, but there is a pervasive restlessness which is the natural consequence of a world at war in which our nation has a leading role. The situation greatly affects students and teachers. Our school has to be organized on a war footing. If the war continues long we will be faced by immense problems . . . . The war proves clearly that man alone with all his boasted progress cannot save either himself or society."[10]

The College was actively engaged in the war effort. Faculty members and students were organized for contributions to Liberty Loan bond drives, Red Cross programs, and other war related activities. Home nursing courses were provided for students. In addition there were health problems caused by the persistent and severe epidemics of influenza. In the autumn of 1918 school was discontinued for three weeks because of the heavy toll of the "flu." The epidemic was particularly severe in October according to an account in the *Messenger*. Although private lessons in music were continued, all class work was abandoned. Students were instructed not to congregate in groups and to spend as much time as possible in the open air. All church activities, classes, concerts, and

The Student Army Training Corps (S.A.T.C.) unit is pictured in the 1919 Daisy *annual.*

public assemblies were cancelled. Students were instructed not to leave Lindsborg. The influenza epidemic gained in intensity in December, resulting in a proclamation by Dr. H. G. Johnson, Lindsborg mayor, prohibiting all public gatherings, quarantining homes where people were ill, and forbidding students to go to town unless under emergency conditions. When the epidemic subsided, the restrictions were withdrawn.

Bethany participated directly in the war effort by forming a unit of the Student Army Training Corps (S.A.T.C.) which was established at 500 colleges and universities. The Bethany unit was mustered in on October 1, 1918, when forty-five male students took the oath. Lt. Speer, a regular army officer, and his associates inducted the new soldiers into the army at a colorful outdoor service on the campus. Following the flag raising, President Pihlblad spoke briefly. The public school children stood in rapt attention carrying American flags. The Lindsborg Home Guard unit of 100 men was also in attendance. Martial music was played by the Bethany Band. The *Messenger* wrote: "The soldier boys are under strict rules, regulations, and discipline, the same as at camp. They salute their superiors, march to and from class and to the dining hall."[11]

The S.A.T.C. had enrolled fifty-four Bethany students and twenty awaited enrollment by the time of the Armistice on November 11, 1918. The members were mustered out of service on December 19. A Soldier's Club, or "hostess club," had been established for the S.A.T.C. members on the Johnson property on North Second Street close to the College. The Y.W.C.A. operated a canteen there. The project was supported financially by the Lutheran Brotherhood of America. In October the *Messenger* pointed out in picturesque language one of the alleged effects of developments: "Since the induction of the S.A.T.C. unit, pernicious evil has launched out in wider latitude and ensnared many more young men. Bethany is also grovelling in its hideous claws. We refer to that low-down sly little white slaver, the cigarette."[12]

But the same *Messenger* contained other more critical news. There was great anxiety at times, for instance in the costly battle of St. Mihiel, where the 353rd company saw action with the following Bethany alumni among others: Herbert Rinkle, Harold Cedarholm, George Lundstrom, Clarence Hegberg, Clayton Almquist (Tunny), and Haggerty II.

The number of Bethany graduates and former students in the armed services was approximately 200. They served in various sections of the military forces at home and abroad.

When the war came to an end, the Armistice was made known to Bethany and Lindsborg with the blast of whistles early Monday morning, November 11, 1918. The *Lindsborg News-Record* described the scene: "Everyone, both young and old became filled with patriotic enthusiasm and presto, things started moving. Flags and bunting in profusion soon adorned the shop windows giving a festive appearance to the business section of the city. It seemed out of the question for anyone to work and very soon a parade made up mostly of grade school and Bethany students headed by the Bethany band was marching up and down the Main Street of our city spreading the glad tidings."[13]

The official celebration started at 3 p.m. with a parade that formed at the high school. Heading the parade were President Pihlblad and Lt. Speer, commandant of the S.A.T.C. unit of the College. Then came the Bethany band, the State Guard, and S.A.T.C. men carrying their guns. They were followed by students of Bethany College and the Lindsborg City Schools. The Lindsborg newspaper reported: "The Kaiser in effigy had indeed met his fate, for he was dragged through the streets of the city with a rope around his neck while two of the State Guards put bullet after bullet into his bulky body." The procession then marched to the college auditorium where President Pihlblad presided at a formal program. The day closed with burning "Kaiser Bill" in effigy.[14]

The war years brought attacks on Bethany and Lindsborg from a few critics who wished to demonstrate their super patriotism by impugning the Swedish background of the college and community. The neutral, and at times the apparent pro-German stance of Sweden as viewed by some critics was occasionally transferred to Swedish Americans and their institutions. There were mixed feelings within the college faculty about the cause and course of the war as was true elsewhere in America prior to the entrance of the United States. Carl O. Lincoln, editor of the *Lindsborg News-Record,* summarized effectively the situation in his editorial column in April, 1917: "Wherever our sympathies in the European war might have dwelt until the United States became involved, matters not now. There is but one course to pursue: 'Get behind the Stars and Stripes.' " President Pihlblad served the college and community well in these years of tension by his addresses and statements as well as by the evidence that came from the institution's policies and actions.[15]

The impact of World War I on the College is difficult to identify specifically but certain aspects are readily ascertainable. The new statement of purpose which appeared for the first time in the catalogue for the academic year 1918-19 reflects the war situation and the institution's response to it: "Bethany College, tho representing the desire for knowledge on the part of the early immigrant, is out and out an American college and stands for American institutions pure and simple. The slogan of its founder was 'The Bible and the Constitution.' Its ideal of manhood and womanhood is the Christian American citizen and toward that ideal it seeks to train its youth." This statement of purpose was continued intact until 1927-28 when the words "pure and simple" were eliminated. The declaration appeared for the last time in 1932-33.[16]

An interesting response to the *Rockar, Stockar* yell in 1919 may or may not have reflected the new Americanism after World War I. In October, 1919, a student wrote in the *Messenger:* "Is Bethany an American institution? If so let us be American . . . . In the early days of this institution a yell composed in the Swedish language (*Rockar, Stockar*) was adopted as the 'college yell.' It is a very good yell, if it were used in the right place, for instance, on the other side of the ocean."[17] *Rockar, Stockar* continues to be the major college yell.

The war era made no appreciable changes in the regulations governing student conduct. The 1918-19 statement in the catalogue read as follows:

> Bethany College seeks the harmonious development of the physical, intellectual and moral nature of students. The fewest restrictions consistent with this aim constitutes, in the opinion of the faculty, the best code. All students are placed upon their honor and are expected to conduct themselves by the principles which obtain in polite society. Enrollment in the College is an implied agreement on the part of the student that he will conform to the rules laid down by the institution. The authorities reserve the right to dismiss, at any time, a student, who in their judgment is undesirable, and whose continuation in the College is detrimental to himself or his fellows.

The regulations then identified specific practices which included the following: "The use of tobacco and card-playing is prohibited on the college campus or in its buildings; students shall not leave the city except by permission of the college authorities; every student is required to attend daily chapel exercises, and at least one church service on Sunday."[18]

The College affirmed positively its role as a church college: "Bethany College maintains that there can be no education without the development of the spiritual with the physical and mental. It further believes that spiritual growth shall be promoted under the influence of the church that stands for positive Christian truth. Bethany College endeavors to cast about the students a wholesome religious atmosphere."[19]

The changes in America were, however, influencing certain aspects of college life. In May, 1919, President Pihlblad emphasized the following: "The melting pot process has developed to the point that the Swedish children have been absorbed completely into the life of the American people, and if it is not yet fully complete, it will be so soon with public opinion opposed to everything foreign whether we think so or not." However, instead of lamenting the situation, Pihlblad concluded: "Our mission instead of being curtailed is expanded."[20]

The Bethany president also identified another aspect of the changing pattern of American life: "Our problem is more complex than that of the other schools of the Augustana Synod since our students are less homogeneous. On account of the preeminent role of our music school many of our students are not from the homes of our church members but are such that come from an entirely different environment. This situation is accompanied with problems. In many cases their environment has been foreign to Christian influences as we understand it and this has made it difficult for many of them to understand the rules that a Christian school establishes for students."[21]

When students returned to the campus after war service or when war veterans enrolled for the first time, provision was made for recognizing military service with academic credit. In September, 1919, the faculty passed the following resolution: "All students who have served in the army for fifteen months or more will be given fifteen credits and those who have served less than fifteen months will be given proportionate credit."[22]

The faculty in liberal arts and sciences had studied trends in curriculum and degree requirements during the war years with the result that a new program was introduced in the academic year 1918-19. The studies were divided into eleven groups: English, classical languages, modern languages, mathematics, physical science, biological science, history, philosophy, Bible and religion, home economics, and fine arts. Provision was also made for more concentrated studies through the requirement that the student must present a major of at least twenty-four hours in one group of the first eight groups and two minors of twelve hours each in two other departments. Students were also permitted to select majors in music or art in the bachelor of arts program. The liberal arts degree was bachelor of arts. The bachelor of science degree was not granted until the academic year 1922-23.[23]

There were no substantial changes in the College of Music and Fine Arts, which in the field of music provided a diploma, certificate of merit, artist's certificate, and bachelor of music degree. The department of expression awarded a diploma and the degree, bachelor of expression. The art department was divided into the professional and normal art courses with a certificate and a degree as the credentials. The commerce department made available certificates in typing and shorthand and a two-year course in commercial subjects known as the degree of bachelor of accounts.

In 1918 the position of academic dean was created for the first time at Bethany. Previously, the members of the faculty of each area of study were responsible for planning and administering the program. Professor E. O. Deere became the first dean of the College of Arts and Sciences and Professor Oscar Lofgren was designated the first dean of the College of Fine Arts. Deere also served as vice-president. Both men initiated administrative careers of great importance that terminated after thirty years with their retirements in 1948. Deere continued a heavy schedule of teaching in biological sciences and Lofgren did likewise as a teacher of piano and classroom courses in music. Mrs. Ernst F. Pihlblad began her long service as dean of women in the academic year 1916-17.

When World War I came to an end, the campaign for funds was

promoted forcefully and effectively. At the meeting of the Conference at Salemsborg in May, 1919, after a long session of prayer, the members pledged to raise $75,000.00 by next January 1 to add to the $50,000.00 already pledged by the Lindsborg community. Dr. A. W. Lindquist, Dr. Victor Spong, President Pihlblad, and Arthur J. Lundgren, financial agent, worked diligently and successfully. There was great rejoicing at the meeting of the Conference at Osage City in May, 1920, when it was announced that the goal had been surpassed by raising $128,000.00. Dr. Alfred Bergin, chairman of the board, stated: "The Conference has written the finest chapter in its fifty year history." President Pihlblad gratefully acknowledged that the debt for current operations of approximately $50,000.00 had now been paid and that the endowment fund had reached $208,477.00, exclusive of the Smith timber lands in Oregon.[24]

Four decades of Bethany history were concluded during the academic year 1920-21. When President Pihlblad discussed the situation in April, 1921, it was with great gratitude and optimism: "The past year has been undeniably the happiest in the school's history." He identified a variety of factors that led to this conclusion: student and faculty achievement was on a high level; the net enrollment of over 600 students showed encouraging recovery from the negative impact of World War I; the current budget was in balance and there was no debt; the assets of the institution had increased from $160,189.00 in 1905, when he became president, to $441,891.00 in 1920, including an endowment fund of $209,-000.00; the Kansas Conference had reached a new high in annual support, contributing almost $13,000.00 during the year. The program in music and art continued to make distinctive contributions and the annual "Messiah" festival had become a magnificent tradition. A $10,-000.00 Möller organ had recently been installed in the college chapel. Moreover, the religious life was stimulating, especially as demonstrated by the vigorous activities of the Luther League, the Student Volunteer Movement and prayer circles.[25]

Bethany's president also reflected on the achievements of the College across the years and what he saw was cause for great gratitude. Almost 2,000 persons had graduated from the various divisions and departments, receiving diplomas, certificates, or degrees. The distribution had been as follows: baccalaureate degrees in liberal arts and sciences, 397; certificates and diplomas, academy, 131; normal, 140 (no longer in existence); business, 801; fine arts, 527.[26]

An analysis of the 397 graduates (297 men and 100 women) in arts and sciences since the awarding of the first degrees in 1891 showed a wide distribution of professions and vocational activity including teachers, 120; ministers of the gospel, 87 (80 in the Augustana Lutheran Church); business men, 47; housewives, 34; lawyers, 15; physicians, 13; and lesser numbers in other vocations and professions. The data showed that almost thirty percent of the male graduates in liberal arts and sciences had become ministers of the gospel. Thirty percent of all graduates in arts and sciences were teachers.[27]

When the Conference met in Assaria in April, 1921, the atmosphere was heavily charged with anxiety over the resignation of Ernst Pihlblad as president of Bethany College. His resignation had been unanimously rejected by the board of directors. The Commercial Club of Lindsborg, Bethany students, most of the faculty, other groups and individuals had petitioned the board not to accept the resignation. In describing the problems which had confronted Bethany during the four decades of its history, Pihlblad stated: "Poverty, lack of adequate financial resources, debts, misunderstanding, and the intrigues of false persons, these would be enough to break the strongest will, but when the needs were greatest, the aid from above has always been present. It is my strong conviction that Bethany is God's work, and as He has stood by it in past years, His help will not be lacking in the days ahead."[28]

Since Pihlblad would not withdraw his resignation, the Conference in its seventh resolution on the Bethany reports accepted it, expressed genuine appreciation for his great contribution, and wished for him and his family God's blessings. Meanwhile, a new development had occurred. Resolution number nine recorded this decisive factor: "On the basis of the Oratorio Society's petition relative to President Pihlblad's resignation the following action was taken: 'Resolved, that since the board of directors of Bethany College has declined to accept Dr. E. F. Pihlblad's resignation, the Conference also refuses to accept it.' " The motion passed by somewhat more than a two-thirds majority. Action was also taken that if Pihlblad would not withdraw the resignation, the board was authorized to nominate candidates for the presidency.[29]

The action of the Conference made it clear that Ernst Pihlblad was wanted as president of Bethany College. There was widespread rejoicing and gratitude when he responded affirmatively to the request of the board of directors on May 3 that he would withdraw his resignation and continue as president.[30]

4.

Academic Enrichment 1921-1941

When Dr. Pihlblad responded to the popular demand that he continue as president of Bethany, he and his associates initiated action immediately to strengthen the academic status of the College. Accreditation by the North Central Association of Colleges and Secondary Schools was imperative. President Pihlblad and the faculty fully realized the importance of membership in this association. The first formal step in that direction was taken in the resolution by the faculty in September, 1921, which read: "For the best interests of the school and the alumni, definite steps should be taken to gain entrance to the North Central Association of Colleges." Professors Deere and Welin were requested to investigate the requirements and report to the board. The action was endorsed shortly thereafter by the board.[1]

The administration and faculty studied carefully the requirements of the North Central Association through an analysis of the purposes of the College, faculty, curriculum, students, library, physical facilities, endowment, and related matters. In April, 1923, President Pihlblad reported: "Bethany College has recently sought recognition twice by the North Central Association of Colleges and Secondary Schools . . . but in both instances recognition has been withheld for lack of sufficient endowment. The present requirement for endowment is $300,000.00." Pihlblad explained that the association's regulations did not permit the capitalization of the annual Conference contribution for purposes of meeting the endowment requirement. It was obvious therefore that the present endowment of slightly more than $200,000.00 would not meet this part of the association's requirements.[2]

The inadequate permanent funds and the minimal general operating financial support created several problems. The highest faculty salary in 1923-24 was $1,800.00, substantially below compensation at most colleges and universities. Moreover, the teaching loads were exceedingly heavy. Six of the nine full-time professors in arts and sciences had the following course load: three, six courses; two, seven courses; one, nine courses. Pihlblad pointed out that someone had said: "The history professor at Bethany had a bench rather than a chair." He reported with deep regret in 1924 that only $395.00 had been spent (during the previous year) on library books and $920.00 on laboratory facilities. However, an additional Steinway grand piano had been installed in one of the studios at a cost of $1,650.00.[3]

After the president had portrayed the critical situation, he challenged the delegates to the Conference and other friends of Bethany in 1924 with the following serious declaration:

> We have come to a state in our development when we must either move forward and meet the requirements of the day or retire from the race, which would ultimately mean that Bethany would pass into history. Our buildings are inadequate, the income of the institution is insufficient to warrant the number of teachers to meet present day requirements and to pay salaries sufficient to attract men and women of the right caliber. The integrity of our diploma is being threatened by the withheld recognition of the standardizing agencies of the country, the menace of which is becoming more serious every year. Because of these things, desirable students who would and should come to us are gravitating to other institutions more fortunate in their financial equipment.[4]

The Conference in April, 1923, had authorized the board of the College to prepare plans for a financial campaign to be presented next year. The administration worked diligently in the interim. Dr. O. H. Pankoke, New York City, who had a good record in fund raising, was consulted. The study revealed that $400,000.00 would be a minimum goal. The findings, when reported to the Conference meeting at Marquette in April, 1924, were heartily endorsed. The distribution of funds sought was to be as follows: $175,000.00 for an auditorium, $150,000.00 for endowment, and $75,000.00 for strengthening the College of Liberal Arts and Sciences. The resolution also provided that the Conference would raise $100,000.00 among churches exclusive of the two Lindsborg congregations. Pledges were to be for a four-year period.[5]

The 1924 campaign was the most extensive and thoroughly organized in Bethany's history. Extensive background materials, workers and speakers manuals, deputation teams of faculty and students, newspaper publicity, and special bureaus and committees were included in the vigorous planning. Every congregation in the Conference as well as alumni groups were organized for action. H. H. Motter, well-known Kansan, was chairman of the Kansas Committee of One Hundred, composed of outstanding citizens from all walks of life. After thorough advance preparation under the direction of Dr. H. O. Pankoke, who established a strict and demanding regimen of action, the campaign was concentrated in the period November 16-24.

Great encouragement had come to the campaign when A. J. Holmquist, Salina businessman, pledged $20,000.00 in September, 1924, to the endowment fund. It was the largest money gift in Bethany's history. At the chapel exercises early in October, Bethany students pledged $12,-000.00 to the campaign.[6]

The response to the well-planned efforts was indeed heartening. The amount subscribed was $315,412.00 with additional promises producing a total of $325,000.00. The Kansas Conference, which pledged $100,000.00, subscribed $125,000.00, the alumni contributed $85,000.00, the Lindsborg community about $75,000.00, and the balance of approximately $40,000.00 was contributed by other friends. The campaign provided specifically that the income from the Conference and the alumni would go to the endowment fund and academic purposes while the contribution from the Lindsborg community would be designated for the auditorium. President Pihlblad observed appropriately: "The campaign of 1924 will ever stand in the annals of Bethany as a monument of the unselfish devotion on the part of its friends and supporters."[7]

The successful campaign of 1924 set the stage for the construction of the auditorium, a central need for sustaining the oratorio tradition. The cornerstone was laid in May, 1928. Substantial contributions had come through concerts by the oratorio society. The first specific support for the building was $1,400.00, the income from two "Messiah" concerts at the Oklahoma Teachers' Association in Oklahoma City in February, 1922. Two concerts by the oratorio society at the American Royal convention in Kansas City, Missouri, in November of that year produced $6,700.00. Schumann-Heink gave a benefit concert in May, 1926, saying, "There is only one Lindsborg and I wish to have a part in this one." Her concert and a performance of the *Messiah* in the evening of that same day produced $5,000.00 for the building fund.[8]

The urgent need for additional music studios, classrooms, and rehearsal halls remained. When the auditorium portion was dedicated with a benefit concert in November, 1928, by Marion Talley, $7,000.00 was raised for the building fund. The board of education of the Augustana Synod made available $5,000.00. President Pihlblad had been in close contact with the Presser Foundation, Philadelphia, which, through a large benefaction by Theodore Presser, had made available extensive grants for music buildings at colleges and universities. When previous commitments of the Presser Foundation had been met, Francis J. Cooke, the distinguished president, announced in June, 1929, that Bethany's request for $75,000.00 to aid in the construction of the studio wing had been granted. This was a tremendous morale booster for college officials and for Lindsborg. It was agreed that additional funds of $40,-000.00 would be provided by the College. The complete structure was appropriately named Presser Hall.

Plans for Presser Hall were drawn by Henry C. Eklund, Kansas City, Missouri, architect. The building was constructed by the Swenson Construction Company, also of Kansas City, Godfrey Swenson, president. The cost of the auditorium was $99,368.00 and with equipment, $129,463.00. Francis J. Plym, Niles, Michigan, provided $6,000.00 for the rebuilding and installation in Presser Hall auditorium of the Möller organ which had been located in the old "Messiah" auditorium. The cost of the studio wing was approximately $115,000.00.

Presser Hall provided the College with excellent facilities. The studio wing, three stories and basement, contained twenty-five studios, thirty-two practice rooms, five classrooms, and administration offices. The auditorium had a total seating capacity of 2,200, including more than 2,000 upholstered chairs, with a large main floor and three-sided balcony. Several hundred chairs were marked with the nameplate of donors who contributed $25.00 or more. Behind the large stage, which can seat an orchestra of ninety musicians, is space for approximately 500 members of the "Messiah" chorus. *Etude* magazine described Presser Hall as "one of the finest music buildings in America."[9]

Although the College was absorbed in this period with fund raising and building construction, other developments were also taking place. In 1925 there were 148 graduates distributed as follows: College, 40; Academy, 23; Fine Arts, 55; Commercial, 30. The senior class was the largest in the history of the College. The enrollment in the College was 281, Academy, 72, and Fine Arts, 460, and when duplicates had been eliminated, the net total was 709. The faculty was composed of forty-two members: fourteen in the college department, four in the academy, three jointly in the college and academy, twenty in fine arts and one jointly in the college and fine arts divisions.[10]

Prince Wilhelm of Sweden is greeted by Dr. Pihlblad at the groundbreaking for Presser Hall.

The auditorium portion of Presser Hall was completed in the fall of 1928, and work was begun the following year on the studio wing.

When Presser Hall was finished, it added much-needed facilities for Messiah *renditions, music studios, classrooms, offices, and rehearsal halls.*

The 1920s witnessed the development also of the Summer School program. The first summer session was held in 1896 with principal emphasis upon courses for teachers in the normal department although classes were available in music, art, and business. The enrollment varied, reaching a peak of 234 in 1925 and approaching 200 in 1930. Music students formed the majority of those in attendance. The interest in summer school never recovered from the depression in the early 1930s. In recent years the enrollment has averaged in the range of 100 students.

Changing circumstances in American life brought an end reluctantly to the commercial department in 1925. This area of studies had provided opportunities for pursuing short and full-length courses in business that recently had been absorbed by the public high schools. The number of graduates since the founding of the department in 1885 was 954. The high point in enrollment was 1903-04 when 212 students were in classes in this department. The courses were uniformly of high quality with emphasis upon practical business. The commercial hall comprised the area on first floor of Old Main under the chapel and provided excellent facilities for banking and other commercial transactions as well as for more traditional studies. This has been a cherished place of remembrance for Bethanyites who in a special way have made distinctive contributions to American business and commercial life. The commercial courses were absorbed in the academy and college. After 1928 these courses and others formed the department of economics and business which has had a continuous history.[11]

Expansion and consolidation of courses occurred in this period. In 1925 the faculty of the College of Fine Arts authorized a four-year course in public school music leading to the bachelor of music degree. The first degree was offered at the 1926 commencement. This enriched program of applied music and music education replaced the public school music certificate. This launched a new era in teacher education at Bethany.

The Academy, the oldest academic unit of the College, closed at the end of the academic year 1927-28. This was done with great regret but low enrollment and financial necessity were the causes. The enrollment was fifty-five when the classes came to an end. The annual deficit in the last few years had been approximately $5,000.00. In the quest for accreditation it was necessary to conserve resources for the degree program.

Bethany could look back with satisfaction on the cumulative achievements of the academy during almost half a century. The total number of graduates was 277. The high point in enrollment was 164 in 1903-04. Of the ninety ministers and missionaries who had gone from Bethany College, at least fifty-two had received their preliminary education in the Academy and three were currently attending Augustana Theological Seminary. Between 1911 and 1923, 102 graduates of the academy had enrolled at Bethany, fifty had graduated from the College and thirty-one were presently enrolled. Twenty-four of the 102 graduates had enrolled in the Bethany Conservatory. This unit of the College had served an unusually important function in the Americanization of the early Swedish immigrants. The growth of the public high school was the principal factor in the closing of the Bethany academy. This was also a main factor in closing academies at other church colleges.

When Pihlblad presented his twenty-fifth annual report as president in April, 1929, he described interesting and important historical facts. In 1904 there were thirty-one persons on the instructional staff; the number was thirty-eight a quarter of a century later. Thirteen college personnel in 1904 were still serving Bethany: J. E. Welin, Birger Sandzén, Hagbard Brase, Oscar Lofgren, Jens Stensaas, Anna Carlson, Oscar Thorsen, Thure Jaderborg, Hjalmar Wetterstrom, Lennard Gunnerson, Emil O. Deere, L. M. Anderson, and Mrs. L. M. Anderson. These are names of great distinction in the annals of Bethany. The salary of professors at the early date was $800.00; currently, it was $2,000.00. The fiscal report in April, 1904, showed an indebtedness of approximately $30,000.00 with no endowment. The endowment now was $379,587.00 and the College was debt free. The cost of operations in 1904 was $72,718.00. The corresponding figure in 1929 was $190,142.00. The net worth of the College a quarter century before was $166,964.00. The amount currently was $761,982.00.[12]

The administration, faculty, and board had worked continuously since 1921 to achieve accreditation by the North Central Association. The liberal arts program was reorganized, course duplication was eliminated, and consolidation was achieved. In 1930 the curriculum was reduced to 224 courses in eighteen departments. The master's degree was eliminated in 1929. Only a few candidates had received the degree across the years, the last one in 1927 in religious education. Faculty teaching loads were reduced and class size was stabilized. Several additions to the faculty of persons with the doctor of philosophy degree were announced.

Some of the permanent staff pursued additional graduate studies in summer months. Miss Edla Wahlin, a professional librarian, was appointed. The budget for library books reached $1,750.00. Almost 15,000 volumes formed the collection. Substantial additions were made to laboratory equipment. As indicated earlier, the endowment fund was approaching $400,000.00. The Kansas Conference budget for Bethany, approximately $14,000.00, if capitalized at the normal rate of interest, added substantially to the basis of financial support. The study of alumni had demonstrated the effectiveness of the Bethany education experience. The budget had been balanced regularly in recent years. Moreover, the facilities for teaching in the arts and sciences had been substantially improved through the space vacated in Old Main when the music program was moved to Presser Hall.

An official inspection of Bethany by personnel of the Commission on Colleges and Universities of the North Central Association took place during the early part of the academic year 1931-32. In March, 1932, the good news arrived: Bethany College had been placed on the accredited list subject to reinspection in keeping with the procedure of the association. A decade of effort was rewarded with success. The *Messenger* reported: "Faculty and students had a joyous celebration in the college cafeteria Thursday, March 17. Speeches were given by President Pihlblad, Dean Lofgren, Dean Deere, and Birger Sandzen. Special recognition was given to Pihlblad and Jens Stensaas, treasurer, for their untiring efforts. The Blue Dozen was at hand to liven spirits with their music." In April 1,200 people from the Lindsborg area came to celebrate the accreditation of Bethany. The Little Symphony provided music. President Pihlblad, Dr. G. A. Dorf, president of the Kansas Conference, and Dr. Victor Spong, chairman of the board, addressed the enthusiastic and grateful audience.[13]

The College was reexamined in 1933 and again in 1935. In the latter year Bethany was placed on the list of accredited colleges, this designation replacing, on the basis of the association's regulations, accreditation subject to reinspection. Bethany has been on the North Central list of accredited colleges uninterruptedly since 1935.

When the Great Depression of the 1930s struck with its fury, the impact became a terrible reality to individuals and institutions. Bethany College fully experienced the storm and stress of those years as did other institutions of higher learning. The wisdom of good planning during the 1920s, when endowment funds were raised and a building program was fully financed, received full confirmation by the events which followed the stock market crash in October, 1929. President Pihlblad and his associates had established a sound financial structure. The years ahead were nevertheless exacting and fraught with danger. What might have happened to Bethany without these judicious prior developments could have been fatal.

The grim situation which faced Bethany was described by Pihlblad in April, 1932: "The financial depression which has rested as an incubus over the world for almost three years is not only a low place in the course of economic development, but it appears we shall emerge from it to find the social life of our country entirely changed. . . . In the twenty-eight years of my experience in the service of Bethany College as president, the past year has been the most trying." He described as critical factors the severe decrease in enrollment, the terrible shrinkage of tuition, smaller endowment income, and the dramatic fall in support from the Conference. In the following year he warned the college constituency: "For three years now, difficulties, mountain high, have been heaping themselves to block the onward course of the Church of Christ. . . . The past school year has been fraught with difficulties. As was to be expected, the prolonged depression has made the question of life and death for Bethany a primary issue, and renders the problems of the establishment of a policy for the immediate future a most perplexing one."[14]

The most dramatic impact of the depression was upon enrollment, with the attendant financial repercussions. The full-time enrollment dropped from 359 in the academic year 1929-30 to 253 in 1933-34. The total enrollment decreased from 451 to 330. In 1938-39 the full-time enrollment was 283, with a total enrollment of 330. The enrollment never attained the 1929-30 level until the post World War II year 1946-47, seventeen years later. The greatest percentage decrease during the depression years was in the college of fine arts, which was especially important at Bethany.[15]

The great drop in enrollment was reflected significantly in the budget. Tuition income in 1929-30 was $70,539.00 in contrast with $42,-266.00 in 1933-34. The severe impact in fine arts is demonstrated in the decrease in tuition from $46,948.00 in the earlier period to $21,334.00 in the latter year. Income in fine arts had been substantially higher for many years than in arts and sciences. As a matter of fact, the instructional program in music had supported the rest of the college programs for many years until the severe reversal that occurred in the depression years.[16]

The income from the Conference showed decreases of over one hundred per cent in the depression era. This source of support dropped from $13,209.00 in 1929-30 to $6,252.00 five years later. The Conference budget did not attain the 1929-30 level until 1947. The endowment income did not decrease as extensively since it dropped from $16,333.00 to $14,499.00 during the comparable years above. Fortunately, thanks to the heroic efforts of Jens Stensaas, treasurer, and the investment committee of the board, the endowment income never fell to a lower figure than $11,434.00 during these difficult years.[17]

The great decrease in income required severe curtailment of expenses. In 1932 four faculty positions were eliminated. When other vacancies occurred, the positions were generally not filled. All personnel were requested to contribute ten per cent of their modest salaries, which with other savings produced $12,000.00. Further cuts in salary during these years amounted to thirty percent of all salaries. The high salary in 1934 was $1,400.00 in contrast with the previous high of $2,000.00 before the depression. The figure remained at $1,400.00 until it was raised to $1,500.00 in 1937. The expenditure for salaries according to the report of the chairman of the board of directors was reduced from $91,442.00 in 1931 to $52,251.00 in 1935.[18]

The effective economy measures restored a balanced budget in 1934-35. The report to the Conference in May, 1935, showed that the deficits during these difficult years amounted to $22,632.00, a remarkable achievement during trying circumstances. Administrative, faculty, and staff personnel had borne the brunt of sacrifice.[19]

The NYA (National Youth Administration) program, which made available grants to colleges and universities for the employment of students, provided considerable assistance in this period. In 1934 twenty-one students were employed at thirty cents per hour with maximum earnings of $15.00 per month. The grants were extended so that in 1937 seventy students received compensation for work on the campus under the NYA program. This program enabled a substantial number of students to continue collegiate studies and thus rendered direct support to the institution. The depression produced great hardships, and faculty and students lived on very close margins. Dr. Victor Spong, chairman of the board, observed in May, 1933: "Financially, the student body has been the poorest that has ever attended Bethany."[20]

Although the economic factors were pressing and, at times, almost calamitous, the College sought to make available a more meaningful educational program. The impetus gained by North Central Association accreditation in 1932 carried over into the next year. A study of institutional purposes was completed in 1934. The general aims of Bethany were described as follows: "The ideal of Bethany College is to serve young men and women who are seeking a liberal education under Christian influence. The college aims to promote cultural development, to stimulate intellectual depth, and to aid the student in forming a sound philosophy of life." Among the ten specific goals for students were the following: "to make intelligent choices and to live in sympathetic understanding with his fellows," "to provide an intelligent appreciation for the beautiful things in life," "to acquire a correct understanding of the physical world," "to develop an integrated personality," and "to emphasize the importance of applying the principles of Christ to all human activities and relations."[21]

The structure of the College of Arts and Sciences and of the College of Fine Arts was based upon academic divisions. In the former, the courses leading to the bachelor of arts and bachelor of science degrees were aligned in the divisions of language, literature, and speech; natural sciences and mathematics; social science and history; Bible and education; and fine arts. In the latter college, the program in the school of music, leading to the degrees of bachelor of music and music education, was arranged in the divisions of applied music, theory and history of music, music education, and ensemble. In the school of art, the divisions were painting and art education, leading to the bachelor of fine arts and bachelor of art education. In the department of expression, the courses for the bachelor of expression degree were in the two divisions, expression and dramatics. The program emphasized general education as well as specialization in a particular field. There was also greater emphasis upon the difference in instruction and expectation of achievement between the lower division (freshman, sophomore) and the upper division (junior, senior). Greater emphasis was also placed upon independent study than heretofore.

The faculty decided in connection with the study of objectives that it was appropriate to recognize scholarship in awarding baccalaureate degrees. At the commencement of 1936 the first degrees *cum laude, magna cum laude,* and *summa cum laude* were awarded. In 1940 Beta Tau Sigma was established for recognition of overall scholastic achievement.

The music program at Bethany had a long and distinguished record of achievement. When the College applied for membership in the National Association of Schools of Music, the accrediting agency in this field, membership was readily granted in 1936. This accreditation has been sustained continuously.

In 1933 Bethany was selected as one of twenty-five colleges and universities in the United States to participate in a study of the relation of music to the collegiate experience under the direction of the eminent composer, Randall Thompson. The College received commendation for the close integration that prevailed between fine arts and liberal arts and sciences on campus. In the following year Bethany was one of twenty-three institutions which received a handsome gift from the Carnegie Corporation for the advancement of instruction in music. Included in the equipment valued at $2,500.00 was a Capehart grafanola, 800 records, 262 scores, and 130 volumes on music.

The administration and faculty sought regularly to stimulate greater achievement on the campus. When President Pihlblad addressed the Conference in 1938 about the role of Bethany as a Christian college he declared: "But a Christian college must also be a college—that is, a school manned by recognized schoolmen. Piety is no substitute for scholarship." One aspect of strengthening the College was improving the library collection. The Bethany president emphasized this need continually. In the above year the collection reached 20,000 volumes and received 165 periodicals and newspapers.[22]

In the quest to keep on the line of discovery, the College engaged in further analysis of its program through the leadership of the committee on self-appraisal appointed in 1938. A series of studies resulted on "Student Organizations and Activities," "Student Achievement," "The Faculty and the System of Grading," and "The Role of Counseling." One of the results was greater emphasis upon counseling and the expansion of personnel services. The testing program was enlarged. Innovations were made in methods of instruction.

Great anxiety and sadness came to the campus on May 23, 1938, with the news of the serious automobile accident involving Dr. and Mrs. Pihlblad and Jens Stensaas, treasurer and business manager, when returning to Lindsborg from a business trip to Salina. All were hospitalized in the Lindsborg Community Hospital. President Pihlblad had serious injuries and was unconscious for a long period in addition to having a broken hip. He was taken to Trinity Lutheran Hospital, Kansas City, Missouri, for additional treatment and rehabilitation. The prayers of large numbers of people were answered with the recovery of all three loyal Bethanyites. Dr. Pihlblad demonstrated unusually great courage and fortitude. He resumed full-time responsibility as president in June, 1939. Professor Emory Lindquist, vice-president, served as acting president during the interim.

The College continued the development of programs designed to enrich the academic experience of students. Extensive faculty studies resulted in the requirement of the comprehensive examination program in the senior year. This regulation was introduced in arts and sciences in 1939-40. The program was based upon "The desire of the faculty and administration to make the college degree more meaningful and to serve as an aid towards more intense study by the student and to stimulate research in the improvement of teaching." The series of procedures included written examinations of four to six hours, the presentation of a thesis or project, and an oral examination by a faculty committee. The purpose of the examinations was "to determine the maturity of the student through his ability to think constructively and to apply his knowledge to the solution of problems that may arise in the chosen field of work and in the daily life of the average educated member of society." Fine arts students participated in this program beginning in 1946.[23]

The thesis requirement could be met by the presentation of an original project or composition. A notable example was the full-length operetta, *If This Is New York,* which was presented in a highly successful first performance to a capacity audience in Presser Hall in May, 1950. It was written, directed, and produced by Bruce Montgomery. He also designed the costumes and stage setting.

The program of comprehensive examinations was continued with some modifications until they were abolished in 1955. A senior seminar was instituted twice a week for which students received one semester hour credit.

The quest for enriching the academic program was further stimulated by the committee on self-appraisal which initiated a study of institutional policies in the academic year 1939-40. Extensive studies were made in several areas. The Student Health Service program was also established that year by an arrangement with Dr. William Holwerda, M.D., Lindsborg physician and surgeon, whereby essential medical services were made available for a modest fee collected by the College.

President Pihlblad and the board of directors developed plans for the "Greater Bethany Fund" in 1940. The six goals were: additional endowment, a new women's dormitory, a science hall, a field house and physical education building, an art building, and the repair and modernization of Old Main. An attractive 30-page brochure was printed which set forth the history of Bethany, its record of achievement, and the great needs presently and for the future. In describing recent developments, the committee pointed out that during the past fifteen years Bethany's plant resources had increased 104% and the endowment had grown 72%. The net worth of the College in 1941 was $936,266.00 including $372,929.00 in the endowment fund. There was no indebtedness.[24]

The well-planned design for raising funds was postponed with the resignation of President Pihlblad, and America's entrance into World War II affected adversely fund raising as well as the entire program of the College. It is well to recall, however, that Bethany's long-time president, even at the end of his career, was dreaming dreams of a greater Bethany.

The hopes of President Pihlblad and his associates for improving the dormitory facilities came nearer realization in 1940 when the Women's Missionary Society of the Augustana Lutheran Church pledged $5,000.00 for the construction of the proposed women's dormitory to be known as Alma Swensson Hall, in loving memory of the wife of the founder of Bethany College. The Conference accepted the gift and authorized the board to make plans for the structure.

When the Conference met at Topeka in April, 1941, the matter of greatest concern was the letter of resignation of President Pihlblad. In it he wrote: "Due to the injuries I suffered in the spring of 1938 in the service of the institution, my locomotion has been somewhat impaired. Furthermore, foreseeing the difficulties and the trying years that confront every Christian college, including Bethany in our disturbed age, I have no desire to remain at my present post under a still increased load."[25]

The resignation of Dr. Pihlblad was accepted under the circumstances which he cited and with the following resolution of gratitude: "The Conference as a whole, with grateful hearts, acknowledges the untiring efforts put forth by Dr. Pihlblad, who for nearly half a century has given his time and talents in the service of the church. He has, during these many years, ever held forth the principles and ideas upon which Bethany College was founded, namely, to permeate the life of the student body with a Christian spirit, as evidenced by the large number of the graduates who have entered the Holy Ministry, and the host of men and women who have left its halls of learning to become co-workers in the church at large. The Conference will ever be grateful to Dr. Ernst F. Pihlblad for the place to which he has raised Bethany College in the realm of higher Christian education." In a special session of the Conference, hearty thanks and commendation were expressed to Dr. Pihlblad by Dr. Victor Spong, president, by Mrs. S. E. Johnson, president of the Women's Missionary Society, and by J. O. Stromquist, well-known layman.[26]

When faculty, students, alumni, and friends of Bethany learned of Dr. Pihlblad's resignation after forty-seven years of distinguished service to the College and to church and state generally, they reflected upon a record of great variety and distinction. He had been a member of the Kansas Text Book Commission, 1912-14, and the Kansas State Board of Education, 1933-36. He served later as the first chairman of the Kansas Merit System for civil service employees. In the tradition of Dr. Carl Swensson, he was active in the Republican party, campaigning extensively in behalf of the party's ticket in Kansas and elsewhere. In 1936 President Pihlblad was drafted by the Republican party to run for State Senator from the Harvey-McPherson county senatorial district. No opposing candidate from the opposition party filed against him, a high tribute to the esteem in which he was held throughout the area.

President Pihlblad established a fine record of achievement in the Kansas Senate. Included in the legislation enacted under his sponsorship was Senate Bill 68 of the 1937 session which made the State Board of Education the licensing agency, with only modest exceptions, for the certification of teachers, supervisors, and administrative personnel. Senate Bill 268 in the same session abolished the Textbook Commission and designated the State Board of Education, with the aid of an advisory committee, as the agency for selecting textbooks. In 1937 and 1939 Pihlblad introduced an amendment to the Kansas constitution which was designed to remove the office of the State Superintendent of Public Instruction from politics. He served as vice-chairman of the committee on education in 1937 and as chairman in 1939. The legislation which he sponsored was heartily supported by the Kansas State Teachers Association and represented substantial educational progress. Pihlblad would have been decisively reelected if he had chosen to serve more than one term.

The great promise of Ernst Pihlblad's career was recognized in 1906 when Augustana College and Theological Seminary conferred the honorary doctor of divinity degree upon him. In 1920 he was made a Knight of the Royal Order of Vasa by King Gustaf V of Sweden for outstanding leadership among Swedish Americans. He was a brilliant orator in English and Swedish. Large numbers of church, community, and civic audiences heard his dynamic addresses annually. Bethany students and faculty had the great privilege of listening to his inspirational chapel talks in the era of daily chapel services. His vocabulary reflected his fine classical education and the content identified him as a man of deep insight who was always on the line of discovery. When Pihlblad accompanied the Swedish Male Chorus of America for a grand tour of Sweden in 1920 as the spokesman on public occasions, people were astounded at the excellence of his Swedish and they were almost unbelieving that he was a native-born American. In the midst of his busy life, his calling as a pastor was a central factor as evidenced by his extensive service as a guest preacher and as the pastor for many years of the Falun Lutheran Church. He was also active in various leadership positions within the Augustana Lutheran Church and Lutheranism in America. President Philblad was a close friend of President Herbert Hoover and several Kansas governors.

The Bethany family, the Lindsborg community, and the Kansas Conference often demonstrated their esteem for the Bethany president. The *Messenger* reported the following in March, 1907: " 'What's the matter with Prexy? He's alright!' These words, issuing from several hundred lusty throats, greeted Dr. Pihlblad on the evening of March 18 as he took his departure from the mass meeting at the auditorium on his thirty-fourth birthday anniversary. Armed with torches they escorted him to the College Dining Hall . . . . He was presented with an office chair and a gold-headed cane. He responded in a voice filled with emotion." In March, 1923, on the occasion of his fiftieth birthday, the College and community showed their love and esteem by a festive celebration in the auditorium. In 1928 the Kansas Conference acknowledged Pihlblad's twenty-five years of service by appreciative resolutions. When he retired in the spring of 1941, leading Kansans, including three former governors, were present to review and laud Ernst Pihlblad's great contribution to Bethany and Kansas.[27]

President Pihlblad was supported effectively by his wife, the former Marie Sjöström, a Bethany graduate with the class of 1893, and the second woman to be awarded a Bethany baccalaureate degree. Mrs.

Pihlblad was an intelligent and energetic person who gave full devotion to her family and to the College. She was the first dean of women, serving from 1916-37, except for a few years. She was active in the Bethany Teachers Wives, the oratorio society, and in church groups. The Pihlblad's two sons, Terence, '16 and '17, and Helge, '18, were actively engaged in the life of the College as students. Terence, who taught at Bethany as a young instructor, served as professor of sociology and head of the department at the University of Missouri, where he became known in wide circles as a fine teacher, scholar, and author. Helge was a successful public school administrator in Kansas for many years. Following service in World War II he held an administrative position with the Veterans Administration in Kansas City, Missouri.

On December 9, 1943, Dr. Pihlblad died suddenly at Topeka while attending a meeting of the Kansas State Civil Service Board. When a large congregation, including distinguished leaders of church and state, came to pay their final respects to Dr. Ernst F. Pihlblad at the memorial service in Presser Hall on December 13, 1943, they held in kindly remembrance an esteemed friend, teacher, pastor, college president, and civic leader. The Bethany College Oratorio Society, which he had done so much to promote, sang his favorite choruses. A far larger number of people also mourned the passing of Bethany's distinguished president and shared the sentiment expressed editorially in the *Topeka Capital:* "The death of Doctor Pihlblad is more than the departing of an outstanding individual personality. He was as much a part of his community and of his state as most men can ever hope to be. And although the impress of his career is deep and lasting, and although his influence will continue to be felt in years ahead, Lindsborg and Kansas are conscious of irreparable loss."[28]

The Dr. and Mrs. Ernst F. Pihlblad Memorial Union, on the site of the old "Messiah" auditorium, stands as a symbol of the devotion and achievement of these two great Bethanyites. The meaning of their lives has also been deeply inscribed in the temple of memory of Bethany alumni and friends across four decades and more.

From 1908 through 1970, the locus of much campus scholarship was Carnegie Library—a building that still stands, although it is no longer used as a library.

For many years a campus drinking fountain between Old Main and Ling Auditorium/Gymnasium was a popular meeting place.

A 200-pound walnut plaque memorializing Dr. and Mrs. Pihlblad, created by Mrs. Rosemary Laughlin (now Mrs. John Bashor), was placed in Pihlblad Memorial Union when it was built two decades after Dr. Pihlblad died.

5.

World War II
Years and Later
1941-1958

When Dr. Ernst F. Pihlblad resigned as president of Bethany College in April, 1941, the board of directors was confronted by the problem of finding a successor. The constitution of Bethany College provided that the president must be "a member of the ministerium of the Evangelical Lutheran Augustana Synod." The attempt to amend the constitution at the meeting of the Conference at Topeka in April, 1941, by striking the clause that required the president to be an ordained clergyman of the church, was unsuccessful. However, the board was authorized by the Conference to fill the vacancy. Professor Emory Lindquist, vice-president, was then designated as acting president. As a layman he was not then eligible for the office of president.[1]

At the meeting of the Conference at Kansas City, Kansas, in April, 1942, the college's constitution was amended to provide that the president be a member of the Lutheran Augustana Synod rather than a member of the ministerium. When this action was ratified by the Conference in the spring of 1943 at Lindsborg, Lindquist was unanimously elected president of Bethany College.

Emory Lindquist, a graduate of Bethany with the class of 1930, was a native of Lindsborg. After three years of study, 1930-33, at Oxford University, where he was a Rhodes Scholar, he joined the Bethany faculty. He was awarded the bachelor of arts and master of arts degrees from Oxford with major studies in history. The doctor of philosophy degree was received by him from the University of Colorado in 1941. He was installed as the fourth president of Bethany at services presided over by Dr.

ERNST F. PIHLBLAD

The old bell tower, which was located southwest of Old Main. The bell is now in a new tower outside R. D. Hahn Gymnasium.

Looking north along First Street, into the campus from Olsson Street.

Victor Spong, president of the Kansas Conference, at the Bethany Lutheran Church on September 21, 1943. Lindquist's address was entitled "Things Truly Believed." In his address Dr. Lindquist declared his belief in Bethany College and Christian education because of "The Christian doctrine of man which it affirms, the unique opportunity for a meaningful education which it provides, and for the gospel of salvation, the story of redemption, and the fellowship of reconciliation with which it is identified." A simple installation service seemed most appropriate at a time when America and most of the nations of the world were in the midst of the tragic conflict of World War II.[2]

When Hitler's Nazi panzer army invaded Poland during the first week of September, 1939, a new era came to birth that was destined to cast its dark shadows into the years ahead. The Nazi onslaught on Western Europe raised grave anxiety in the United States. In September, 1940, Congress passed the Selective Service act which introduced compulsory military training. The chain of world developments brought the devastating Japanese attack on Pearl Harbor December 7, 1941. The United States shortly thereafter declared war on Germany and Japan. Colleges and universities faced a new and ominous situation in a world at war.

There was something prophetic in the serious cartoon that was featured on the front page of the *Messenger* in November, 1939, as Hitler's armies were lurching across the border of neighboring nations in the autumn of that year. A Bethany student was portrayed sitting in his dormitory room in contemplation. Dominating the scene in the background was a rigid Nazi soldier with prominent display of his swastika, gun, and gas mask. This unwelcome and uninvited intruder was destined to produce drastic changes in the life of college students and others throughout most of the world.[3]

The situation at Bethany was described by President Pihlblad in April, 1941, nine months before the American declaration of war when he told the members of the Kansas Conference: "There is reason for some misgivings as to attendance during the next school year because of the military draft now in progress. Several students have left for service and others will be called July 1." This early concern became a reality as the decrease in enrollment became increasingly severe, in spite of the government's attempt to provide a measure of student deferment. The lowest enrollment was in the academic year 1943-44, when the number of full-time students dropped to 128 in contrast with 305 in 1939-40. Only twenty-two males were on campus that year. There were sixty-seven students in arts and sciences and sixty-one in fine arts. The total enrollment, including part-time students, was 206 as compared with 362 four years earlier. The full-time enrollment during the war years was as follows: 301 in 1940-41, 256 in 1941-42, 210 in 1942-43, 128 in 1943-44, 160 in 1944-45, and 217 in 1945-46. Moreover, the actual number of students on campus was less than the statistics indicate because students were called to service during the academic year. There were only twenty graduates in 1944, eleven in arts and sciences and nine in fine arts.[4]

The College exerted great efforts to carry out its responsibilities to students and to the nation. The United States government invited colleges and universities to provide service training programs on campus in a variety of areas. Such programs were established at Bethany whenever the circumstances and facilities made it possible. The V-1 program of the U.S. Naval Reserve and the V-7 program of the U.S. Navy offered students the opportunity to continue their academic studies on the basis of selected curricula that would be helpful in later military service. Students also joined the U.S. Army enlisted reserve. Bethany men were called to regular service periodically as their prescribed courses were completed. Members of the faculty and student body accompanied them to the Missouri Pacific railroad station as they left for their assignments accompanied by the strains of the Bethany alma mater performed by a pick-up Blue Dozen band.

In the autumn of 1941 the first unit of the government sponsored pilot training program arrived on campus. Several units were trained under what were known as the WTS and CAA programs. Later units numbering as many as thirty members each were on active duty with the U.S. Navy in the preliminary course of the naval aviation cadet program. The cadets lived on campus, enrolled in ground school courses at the College, and received flight training with the Peterson Flying Service at the McPherson municipal airport. Dean E. O. Deere was the general coordinator. Professional staff provided the military and aviation courses. Several hundred students participated in the various army, navy, and aviation programs during the war years. Members of the faculty also joined the armed services. Vernon E. Johnson, director of public relations, and Dr. Norbert Mahnken, assistant professor of history, were among the first to enter the army.

The administration and faculty responded to the wartime situation by introducing changes in the curriculum and academic calendar. In 1942 an accelerated program made it possible to complete the normal four-year degree program in three years through attendance at twelve-week summer sessions. Some Saturdays were used for instruction. Greater emphasis was placed upon mathematics and natural sciences. Special courses in nutrition, home nursing, and first aid were added to the curriculum. A committee on civilian defense and aid to students was established with Dean Deere as chairman. Provision was made for early student withdrawal because of military service so that the student received appropriate academic credit for studies that were interrupted. Committees were established to cooperate with Red Cross, USO activities, bond drives, civilian defense, and other war related organizations.

The stars on the Bethany service flag in Presser Hall increased steadily to a total of more than 400 representing Bethany students, alumni, former students, and faculty. They served at home and in distant places in the war areas of the world. Other Bethanyites served the nation in a variety of civilian capacities related to the war effort. Bethanyites known to have given their lives in the service of the nation in World War II were Eric B. Bolling, Harry E. Gray, Marvin Hale, Orville H. Poppe, and Harvey K. Snellbacker.

In the midst of a world at war there was a time of remembrance of Bethany's history when the sixtieth anniversary was observed October 15-16, 1941. Principal addresses were delivered by Governor Payne Ratner of Kansas, Dr. L. W. Boe, president of St. Olaf College, Dr. Pihlblad, and Dr. Julius Lincoln, Chicago. Honorary degrees of doctor of humane letters were appropriately conferred upon Pihlblad and Lincoln, classmates in the first baccalaureate class of 1891, who had made great contributions to church and state. Reflections upon the past disclosed the fact that 11,509 students had matriculated at Bethany since that October day in 1881 when ten students met with Carl Swensson and J. A. Udden to begin the Bethany tradition. The records showed that 3,593 men and women had graduated from the various departments of the College. Approximately 435 Bethanyites were teachers in thirty states and in seventy-six colleges and universities while 159 had entered the gospel ministry.[5]

Bethany faculty members sought to be faithful to the commitment of providing quality education in a difficult time. In 1941 the College was invited by a special commission of the North Central Association to be one of twenty-eight colleges and universities to participate in a study of the education of secondary school teachers. This comprehensive study and self-analysis was directed toward the improvement of curriculum, instruction, and services. A local committee with L. W. Soderstrom, chairman, Bethany graduate, superintendent of the Lindsborg public schools and adjunct member of the Bethany faculty, was established. This cooperative study continued for several years with productive results. Dr. Russell M. Cooper, University of Minnesota coordinator of the project, and other resource persons made frequent visits to the campus. The local committee involved members of the faculty, students, and non-campus personnel in the study of various aspects of college life and learning. Special emphasis was placed on the improvement of instruction. It was in this period that the College participated in the American Council of Education's testing of freshmen and sophomores.

The war situation resulted necessarily in the curtailment of activities. The Bethany Choir suspended its activities in 1942-43 for the duration of the war due to the lack of male voices. Founded in February,

1935, by Dr. Hagbard Brase to commemorate the 250th anniversary of the birth of Johann Sebastian Bach, the choir had established a distinguished reputation. In 1938 in the Columbia choral quest of the Columbia Broadcasting System, the Bethany Choir was runner-up in competition with the best college and university choirs in the nation. Other Bethany ensemble groups maintained greatly modified programs. There was no competition by Kansas Collegiate Athletic Conference members in football during the war years. Basketball was played occasionally but not in conference competition.

The "Messiah" festival was sustained during the war years as great crowds attended the renditions. Older male singers rejoined the chorus to fill the vacant places caused by men in the armed services. Certain chairs in the orchestra were filled by visiting musicians. It was not possible to present a full rendition of Johann Sebastian Bach's *The Passion of Our Lord According to St. Matthew,* but the tradition was kept alive by performances that included selected choruses. The continuity of the message was sustained through the use of a reader for solo parts. In 1944 the Easter rendition of the *Messiah* was transmitted on the world network of the Office of War Information. In 1945 the "Voice of America" transmitted the Palm Sunday rendition to Europe and Africa. The college was grateful for letters from former chorus members who had heard the performance while serving in the armed services in distant places. The message and meaning of the *Messiah* and the Lindsborg performances received extensive publicity.

In the month of May, 1945, amidst the splendor of nature and student graduation recitals on the Bethany campus, the glad news came that the war in Europe was over. An Associated Press dispatch caused the victory whistle at the municipal light plant to be blown prematurely at 8:30 a.m. on Monday, May 7. The official end of the war was announced by President Truman from the White House the next day. An informal prayer session of gratitude to God for the end of the war took place on the Bethany campus at 10:00 a.m. on Monday. The community observance was held in Presser Hall under the auspices of the Lindsborg Council of Religious Education. The Reverend J. Theo. Johnson, pastor of the Mission Covenant Church, presided. Mayor Ernest T. Peterson brought greetings, and the Reverend Philemon Smith, pastor of the Bethany Lutheran Church, delivered the address. The service opened as the congregation sang *My Country 'Tis of Thee* and closed with the hymn, *Lead On, O King Eternal.* The *Lindsborg News-Record* reported: "Rejoicing over the surrender of the Germans was definitely tempered by the knowledge that peace had not yet been won and there may be many months of hard fighting to endure before the Pacific front is taken by the Allies."[6]

Months of great anxiety passed slowly until the announcement came from President Truman that Japan had surrendered to the Allies at 6:00

p.m. central war time, Tuesday, August 14, 1945. The *Lindsborg News-Record* gratefully wrote: "The lights once again go on all over the world, the lights of peace." A capacity audience assembled at the Bethany Lutheran Church that evening "to the call of the church bells which rang out in joy at the glad news." The Lindsborg High School band, led by the colors, furnished music for the parade of members of the Emil Pinkall Post of the American Legion, the auxiliary, and other organizations from the Brunswick Hotel to the church. Dr. Emory Lindquist presided at the meeting. Mayor Peterson welcomed the college and community audience and spoke of the great meaning of the occasion. The Rev. J. Theo. Johnson delivered the major address. The audience sang *The Battle Hymn of the Republic.* The service ended as all joined with grateful hearts and firm voices in singing *Now Thank We All Our God.* The congregation silently left the white-spired church with deep feelings of remembrance of the Lindsborg and Bethany men, relatives and friends, who had made the supreme sacrifice during the war. All business places closed on Wednesday to commemorate the end of the war. Main Street was decorated with Stars and Stripes.[7]

The mood at war's end was far more sombre in 1945 than in 1918. In the latter year the college and community celebrated the armistice not only with religious services but also by dragging an effigy of the Kaiser down Main Street, shooting him periodically, and finally hanging this symbol of German autocracy in the city square.

When World War II ended in the summer of 1945, a new era in the history of American colleges and universities was heralded. Returning veterans and a high birth rate in the 1920s produced a large college-age population. The impact on enrollment at Bethany and elsewhere was dramatic. Full-time enrollment increased from 128, the lowest point in 1943-44, to 409 three years later. The increase in total enrollment was from 206 to 472 in the same period. The greatest bulge occurred in 1946-47 when the full-time enrollment was 409 and the total 472 compared with 217 and 302 in the previous year. The faculty made provision for granting academic credits for war training and experiences in accordance with the recommendation of the American Council on Education. Veterans were served by the faculty committee on veterans affairs.[8]

Bethany became certified for veterans educational programs as soon as the regulations were developed by federal agencies. Public Law 16, the vocational rehabilitation act, and Public Law 346, commonly referred to as the "G.I. Bill of Rights," provided grants to veterans in varying programs. The 160 veterans on the campus in 1946-47 represented the highest point. In that year there were 238 freshmen but only 29 graduates, indicative of the toll in the student population during the war years. Facilities were taxed to the utmost capacity. Additional classroom space was created by remodeling in Old Main. The faculty increased from 23 in 1943-44 to 35 in 1947-48. Recruiting faculty was critical in view

An aerial view of the campus, after World War II.

of the nation's great demand for academic personnel compounded by the situation that graduate schools had a low census of students generally during the war years.[9]

Housing created a pressing situation. Remodeling in Lane Hart Hall and crowding of students made it possible to provide for ninety-one women students in that dormitory. Kalmar Hall, a large residence west of the campus on Second Street, was purchased in 1945. It housed twenty-one students. Old Main furnished accommodations for seventy-five men. Twenty veterans' families lived in apartments constructed by the Federal Bureau of Community Facilities on the campus in 1946. Sororities and fraternities acquired rooms for members by leasing large houses or the second story of downtown store buildings. Fine cooperation from Lindsborg citizens made additional rooms available for students. Faculty housing was also in great demand.

When the majority of the returning veterans completed their studies, enrollment showed a marked decrease. This development was further intensified by the great drop in college-age people as a result of the exceedingly low birth rate during the depression years of the 1930s. Moreover, when the Korean war began in June, 1950, large numbers of college-age men and women were required by the armed services. The gravity of this situation was emphasized by President Lindquist in his annual report to the Kansas Conference in April, 1951, when he quoted the following statement by the American Council on Education: "Insofar as the colleges and universities are concerned the effect of the creation of a three million army, navy, and air force will almost be as serious as the total mobilization in World War II."[10]

The cumulative result of the above factors is clearly seen in the enrollment statistics. The number of full-time students dropped to 305 in 1950-51 with a total of 379 full-time and part-time. A new low point was reached during the next academic year when the full-time enrollment was only 257 and the total 316. This was the lowest number since 1945-46.[11]

In the midst of the factors that so vitally influenced the size of the enrollment, the faculty devoted much time and thought to improving the educational program. In the academic year 1947-48 a comprehensive study was made to enrich the program of general education in response to a changing world. The general design was developed in the expanded series of lectures in the orientation program in 1947. The new pattern was introduced in September, 1949. Studies in three areas—humanities, social sciences, and natural sciences—were required of all students for graduation. The president described the goals: "Such studies will orient the student in the basic aspects and developments of life and learning. It should make for more effective citizenship and provide additional cultural resources. The latest methods and techniques in teaching are extensively employed. Cooperative effort on the part of the faculty in building interdepartmental courses is also having gratifying results." Included among the new courses was an interesting two-semester divisional course in the humanities which provided for an integration of literature, music, sculpture, painting, and architecture. There was also greater emphasis upon personnel and guidance services. Profile sheets and inventories of student interest and background were studied carefully and used as aids in counseling and guidance.[12]

An important action in the development of the college's academic achievement was the establishment of a degree program in elementary education in September, 1949. Bethany's identification with teacher education has been continuous since its founding. Degree programs in secondary education had been available for many years. The courses in elementary education, in keeping with certification requirements, were less complete in the 30-hour and 60-hour curricula. The administration and faculty recognized trends in education which pointed appropriately towards greater emphasis upon degree requirements for elementary school teachers. Studies in consultation with professional teachers in Kansas schools produced a fine curriculum. Bethany was fortunate, through the cooperation of the administration of Luther College, Wahoo, Nebraska, to receive the service of Miss Gladys Peterson, a highly esteemed member of the faculty there, to become director of elementary education. The teaching profession in Kansas gave an enthusiastic response to the new degree program. The William Volker Foundation, Kansas City, Missouri, made a grant of $10,000.00 for initial support.

The quality of the various teacher education programs was recognized by the admission of Bethany as a member of the American Association of Colleges for Teacher Education in 1951 following the visit of an accrediting team. Bethany was the first private college in Kansas to be recognized by this accrediting organization which was the predecessor of the current National Council for the Accreditation of Teacher Education (NCATE).

In 1952 degree programs in the healing arts were introduced. In a cooperative program developed by Dean J. L. Hermanson with Trinity Lutheran Hospital, Kansas City, Missouri, a Kansas Conference institution, Bethany students could earn a bachelor's degree and also become a registered nurse (RN). A cooperative degree program in medical technology was also developed. The courses in the art department were expanded so that a major in commercial art was available in addition to the degree programs in painting and art education.

Resources for learning were enriched during this period although, as President Lindquist emphasized again and again, there was urgent need for more funds to meet reasonable needs. It was not until this period that the library collection reached 25,000 volumes. In 1950 slightly more than 26,000 books were available. The expenditures for library services and materials never exceeded $10,000.00 until the academic year 1949-50 when the amount was $11,236.00. In 1949 a "listening room" was equipped in Presser Hall with turntables, headphones, records, music scores, and other materials, thus enriching the formal studies as well as recreational interests of students. An audio-visual education room was also provided in Presser Hall with projectors, tape recorders, films, and film strips. Valuable laboratory equipment, especially in physics and chemistry, was added through the surplus property program of the federal government after World War II.

Financial problems weighed heavily upon the College during the World War II years. The lowest point in enrollment, as indicated above, was reached in 1943-44. In contrast with tuition income of $61,920.00 in 1940-41, the total was only $34,083.00 three years later. The amount would have been lower annually except for the favorable financial benefits of the aviation cadet program. The Conference budget did not average $9,000.00 per year and in the war years it never reached the former $12,000.00-13,000.00 range prior to the depression era. Fortunately, the endowment income, due to the great diligence of Jens Stensaas, treasurer, sustained a steady average of about $16,000.00. There were deficits in the operating budget for six of the ten years between 1940-50. The deficits would have been greater if some unrestricted gifts had not been used for current expenses.[13]

When the war ended in 1945 current operating surpluses prevailed during the years of high veteran enrollment. The following few years were critical for the operating budget. The Korean War and the low birth rate were factors in the low tuition income. The full-time enrollment dropped to 257 in 1951-52. The deficit for that year was $35,983.00. Fortunately, the endowment income exceeded $20,000.00 per year during this period. The contribution of the church exceeded $35,000.00.[14]

In the early 1940s a beginning was made in developing financial support through a program of annual giving known as the Bethany Loyalty Fund. Alumni and friends of the College were invited to contribute for the support of the current budget. The highlight was an annual Bethany Loyalty dinner on the campus. From modest beginnings of a few thousand dollars per year, the income increased gradually until the high point of $14,204.00 was reached in 1951-52. This general fund-raising effort was replaced a few years later when President Robert Mortvedt and his associates promoted a more specific alumni fund and a patrons and friends campaign which was much more productive.

A critical problem historically for the College was the small church constituency of only about 14,000 members during this period. This loyal group deserved the support of a larger church membership. In 1948 the commission on Christian higher education of the Augustana Lutheran Church placed Bethany on its budget for an annual grant of $5,000.00. This amount was increased to $10,000.00 in 1950 with the commitment that it would be $25,000.00 annually by 1957. The Texas Conference of the church supported the College in the early 1950s with an annual appropriation of $1,000.00. In 1952 church budgets produced in excess of $35,000.00 annually. Ten years earlier it had been approximately $9,000.00.

In December, 1952, President Lindquist and the board participated in organizing the Kansas Foundation for Private Colleges. The purpose of the foundation was "To develop, promote, and direct unified approaches to corporations, foundations, and other organizations and individuals for financial support of member institutions." This foundation developed cooperative approaches for the annual support of private colleges in Kansas.

Attempts to raise capital funds through special campaigns were disappointing and only partially successful during this period. In 1946 when the Reverend Samuel E. Johnson, chairman of the board, reported to the Conference, he emphasized the urgency of raising funds for the construction of Alma Swensson Hall, a proposed women's dormitory, and also for a memorial to Dr. Ernst F. Pihlblad. The records showed that $65,000.00 was available at that time. The Conference authorized a fund drive with an initial goal of $150,000.00 to be known as the Greater Bethany Fund.

In the report to the Conference the next year, the sum of $72,891.00 had been made available in cash in addition to a modest amount of pledges. In 1948 a special effort was again made that produced $32,540.00. The Reverend Carl W. Segerhammar, '29, Longmont, Colorado, devoted much time and talent in supporting Bethany's financial needs in this period.[15]

In 1951 the Conference authorized a Bethany College appeal for $75,000.00 in 1952 to remove capital indebtedness. This modest amount was set in the expectation that a substantial goal would be raised within two years through an Augustana Lutheran Church appeal for higher education. Since the church postponed the general campaign for several years, board and Conference officials authorized a development campaign for $200,000.00 which included $16,000.00 for Augustana Theological Seminary, Rock Island, Illinois. If the full amount could be raised, it was expected that all college debts would be liquidated and that there would be $50,000.00 in the Pihlblad Memorial Fund. A professional fund-raising organization was engaged to direct the campaign. Two well-known alumni, Elmer T. Peterson, Oklahoma City editor, and Judge Karl Miller, Dodge City, contributed their time and talent. State-wide alumni, church, and Lindsborg committees exerted their efforts. When the books were closed in September, 1956, eighteen months later than the original date, the cash income was $166,000.00, plus a modest amount of unpaid pledges. Approximately $100,000.00 was contributed by the congregations of the Kansas Conference.[16]

Several sizeable gifts and bequests were received by Bethany during the 1940s. An inventory of amounts of $10,000.00 or more identifies Bethany benefactors during this period. In 1941 the estate of Frank Grattan, McPherson attorney, added $15,000.00 to the Grattan endowment fund to increase it to $30,000.00. In 1943 Mrs. F. O. Johnson, McPherson, a Bethany graduate and board member, made arrangements to add $15,-000.00 to the permanent endowment fund started by her husband, well-known attorney, long-time board member, and, with Mrs. Johnson, a staunch Bethany supporter. This fund reached approximately $30,-000.00. In 1946 the estate of John P. Ericson, Lindsborg, member of a pioneer immigrant family, made available $25,000.00. Maude Collingwood, Plains, established during the same year a $10,000.00 scholarship fund. Frances Brundage, Russell, a Bethany music graduate, provided through her estate an endowment for music scholarships to the annual amount of $3,000.00. It was also in 1946 that the College received $70,000.00 from the Centennial Thankoffering of the Augustana Lutheran Church through the churches of the Kansas Conference. In 1949 the College was beneficiary to the amount of $45,000.00 from the estate of Christian L. Johnson, Hallville. It was also in this year that the William Volker Foundation of Kansas City, Missouri, made a grant of

$10,000.00 for initiating the degree program in elementary education.

The estate of Ludvig Nelson, Wichita, well-known Kansan, former mayor of Lindsborg, close friend of President Pihlblad, and Mrs. Nelson, loyal Bethany boosters, made available in 1950 the largest gift in Bethany's history to that time in a bequest of $100,000.00 for a science hall. Moreover, Bethany later has shared generously in the income of the Ludvig Nelson and Selma Nelson Religious, Educational, and Charitable Trust through the fine action of Mrs. Nelson and the trustees.

Changes in campus facilities occurred during this period. At noon on Sunday, March 31, 1946, the city fire alarm brought to the campus faculty, students, and townspeople, and they watched with great sadness as flames devoured in a few minutes Ling Gymnasium, known for decades as the "Messiah" auditorium. The octagonal frame structure, which had meant so much to Bethany, was built in 1895. A surplus army physical education building at Camp Phillips, near Smolan, was dismantled and rebuilt on the campus later in the year. The building was given to the College by the Bureau of Community Facilities of the federal government and re-erected at a cost upwards of $30,000.00. As indicated previously, Kalmar Hall, a large residence on Second Street near Presser Hall, was purchased in 1945 for housing women students, and twenty apartments for veterans and their families were constructed for the College by the Federal Housing Agency in 1946.

On May 30, 1949, Alma Swensson Hall, an attractive three-story dormitory housing seventy-seven women students, was dedicated. The architect was Emil O. Bayerl and the Swenson Construction Company,

ALMA SWENSSON HALL, residence for women students, built in 1949.

The public lounge in Alma Swensson Hall.

Kansas City, Missouri, was the general contractor. The building was occupied for the first time in September of that year. The total cost was $267,835.00. The Women's Missionary Society of the Augustana Lutheran Church provided the initiative for the project by a grant of $5,000.00 as a memorial to Mrs. Alma Swensson, wife of Bethany's founder and a distinguished leader of the national women's society. The women of the Kansas Conference also contributed effectively to the construction of the dormitory. The Bethany Development Program provided the bulk of the funds. A loan of $76,000.00 from unrestricted endowment funds, as authorized by the Conference's vote to finance the project as seemed best, was required to complete the financing. In 1950 the college chapel in Old Main was completely renovated with new flooring, heating, lighting, redecorating, and the installation of 300 new seats on the lower floor. Money from the Christian L. Johnson bequest was used to modernize and beautify the chapel. In 1953 Bethany acquired for the first time a residence for the president. Property on North Main Street opposite Swensson Memorial Park was purchased through a gift from Mrs. F. O. Johnson, Bethany graduate and benefactress.

In the decade 1942-43 to 1952-53 the permanent endowment fund increased modestly from $396,710.00 to $528,871.00, the plant fund from $557,135.00 to $961,185.00, and the total college value from $954,078.00 to $1,503,000.00. The indebtedness had increased from $24,112.00 to $122,-720.00, of which $74,114.00 was on Alma Swensson Hall and $48,606.00 on accumulated current fund deficits. Financial resources not included above were $100,000.00 in future plant assets from the estate of Ludvig Nelson and remaining income from pledges to the Greater Bethany Fund.[17]

In November, 1952, Emory Lindquist resigned as president effective with the end of the fiscal year. He thus ended twenty years as a member of the faculty and president. In his final report to the Conference he stated, after pointing to sources of satisfaction with his experience in administration: "I would not be honest if I did not also acknowledge my disappointments. My greatest disappointment is related to the indifferences in some quarters about Bethany . . . . I am disappointed that there has not been a more generous response financially to our program." He went on to say: "My resignation comes with the hope that a new president can stimulate the Kansas Conference, alumni, other groups, and individuals to demonstrate a new and greater loyalty and support for Bethany." In accepting the resignation, the members of the Conference passed the following resolution: "Whereas despite difficult conditions caused by national and international problems, the wise and efficient leadership is seen in the maintenance of high academic standards of the College, the securing of additional professional accreditation, the building added to college property, and the substantial increase in the endowment fund."[18]

EMORY LINDQUIST   ROBERT MORTVEDT

After leaving Bethany, Lindquist became a university professor with an interdepartmental assignment at Wichita State University, and later he served as dean of the faculties and president of that university.

When faculty and students arrived on the campus in September, 1953, they were greeted by a new president, Dr. Robert A. L. Mortvedt, who had been elected at the annual meeting of the Kansas Conference in April. Dr. Mortvedt brought excellent credentials as a teacher, scholar, and administrator. A graduate of St. Olaf College, Northfield, Minnesota, he had been awarded the doctor of philosophy degree in English literature from Harvard. He was a Harvard Phi Beta Kappa. Following several years on the faculty at St. Olaf, he was successively professor of English, dean of the College of Liberal Arts and Sciences, and vice-president of the University of Kansas City. Dr. Mortvedt was also well-known as a Lutheran churchman.

Dr. Mortvedt was installed as the fifth president of Bethany at impressive ceremonies on November 12, 1953. The installation service was conducted by Dr. N. Everett Hedeen, president of the Kansas Conference of the Augustana Lutheran Church, and by the Reverend Ervin C. Malm, chairman of the college board of directors. The principal address was delivered by Chancellor Franklin D. Murphy of the University of Kansas. Among the many distinguished delegates were Dr. Oscar Benson, president of the Augustana Lutheran Church, college and university presidents, and representatives of learned societies. A panel discussion, "Academic Freedom in an Era of Crises," was another feature of the program. A reception for delegates and guests was held in the home of President and Mrs. Mortvedt. This was the first full-scale installation of a president in Bethany's history.

In his inaugural address, "Education in the Shadow of the Church," President Mortvedt identified the challenge that confronted Bethany and his commitment to Christian higher education: "In a time when the destinies of millions of the earth's inhabitants are being forged with atomic-powered tools, when social and moral issues are brought into focus as never before, the Church must speak to the culture of the age. It is for this reason that we are here. It is for this reason that our Church colleges must be strong. Their task and their opportunity are monumental. The only question of importance is whether we have the faith, courage, and determination to carry out the task." Bethany's new president then declared his expectations for the future: "It is my earnest hope that the hearts of many people may be opened so that they may be motivated to help Bethany contribute richly to the mighty task which is to be done. There is no better way to add to one's personal dignity and stature than to become a working part of a noble institution; for institutions have a way of living on, even though human beings are forgotten . . . . Great as Bethany's history has been thus far, it can be greater still. That, I am sure, is what all of us desire."[19]

In describing the inaugural events at the luncheon for representatives of institutions and organizations, Dr. Oscar Benson, president of the Augustana Lutheran Church, expressed the sentiments of the large audience at the inaugural ceremony: "Joy, urgency, and reassurance are the three ingredients . . . . There is joy at the installation of Dr. Mortvedt as the new leader of Bethany; there is a feeling of urgency brought out by the challenge of the outstanding address; and there is reassurance that the future of Bethany is in good hands."[20]

There was encouragement during the first year of President Mortvedt's administration in the increase in enrollment from 284 to 310 full-time students with a total increase from 383 to 430. However, the full-time enrollment dropped to 249 in 1955-56, although the total figure was 414, with 77 part-time students from the Smoky Hill Air Force Base.

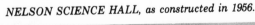

NELSON SCIENCE HALL, as constructed in 1956.

Through concentrated efforts the enrollment reached 353 full-time students in 1957-58, the highest for a decade, with a total of 606, including 155 airmen at Smoky Hill Air Force Base. President Mortvedt, in evaluating the enrollment situation at that time, pointed out that Bethany's pattern in the last several years "has been little different from that of scores of other colleges . . . . The main factor of difficulty was a steady decline in enrollment which resulted from a very low birth rate in the depression-ridden thirties." Moreover, he presented heartening news to Bethany's friends: "The increase in the college-age population, as compared with 1954, for the country as a whole, is estimated as follows: 1960, 16 percent; 1965, 46 percent; 1970, 70 percent.[21]

President Mortvedt soon evaluated effectively the needs of the College. He emphasized for the board and the general constituency of the College the critical situation of the campus facilities as related to "grossly inadequate budget for maintenance, an insufficient staff, and the lack of money for the purchase of essential equipment." Effective steps were taken immediately to deal with this cumulative problem.[22]

The new president also began a study of Bethany's long-range needs. Members of the faculty, board members, alumni, and others were involved in this comprehensive study. In April, 1955, he presented to the Conference, following prior study and approval by the board, a ten-year plan for Bethany College. The full-time enrollment projection was 550-600 in 1964-65. The proposed buildings to be constructed in the order indicated were: science hall; men's dormitory—100 residents; a second men's dormitory—100 residents; Pihlblad Memorial gymnasium; general classroom building; student union; and a Sandzén memorial art building. The endowment fund should be increased by $25,000.00 per year during the ten-year period. The program, according to President Mortvedt, "represents an investment of approximately $1,900,000.00 in buildings, all of which are essential if the youth who come to Bethany are to have substantially the same facilities as they can find in any good college or university." It was expected that $400,000.00 could be borrowed from the federal government through the Housing and Home Finance Agency. It was also proposed that a full-time director of development be engaged.[23]

President Mortvedt launched a building program that greatly

DEERE HALL first unit on the west, residence for men students, dedicated in 1958.

expanded the potential of service to more students with better facilities. The desperate need for a science hall had been recognized as early as 1921, when it was proposed that alumni raise $75,000.00 for this purpose. This hope was not realized. The bequest of Ludvig Nelson in 1949 provided for $100,000.00 for a science hall. Through the generosity of Mrs. Selma Nelson and the trustees of the Ludvig Nelson and Selma Nelson Religious, Educational, and Charitable Trust, and the effectively presented need by President Mortvedt, this amount was matched with another $100,000.00. November 27, 1956, was a joyous day on the Bethany campus when the Nelson Science Hall was dedicated. The attractive two-story brick structure with partial basement included on the first floor a lecture hall, greenhouse, biology laboratory and classroom, physics and optical laboratories, and a science library. The second floor provided for chemistry, mathematics, geology, mechanical engineering, home economics laboratories, and classrooms. The cost of the building was $250,000.00. Fangkiser and Tewkesbury, Kansas City, Missouri, were the architects. The builder was Val Borden Construction Company, Salina.

The second phase of the ten-year plan was heralded on April 5, 1958, with the dedication of Emil O. Deere Hall, a dormitory housing seventy-two men. The two-story brick building on the northwest corner of the campus provided another fine addition to campus resources. The attractive building had built-in beds, desks, and wardrobes with a split level south end, providing a lounge above and recreation room beneath. The cost of approximately $250,000.00 was provided mainly by a $200,-000.00 loan from the federal government through the Housing and Home Finance Agency. This loan is amortized on a regular schedule of payments. A campaign by the Lindsborg Chamber of Commerce raised in excess of $15,000.00. This fine dormitory was named appropriately Deere Hall in recognition of the long service of Dr. Emil O. Deere as professor and dean of the college of liberal arts and sciences. The building was designed by George Tewkesbury, Mission, Kansas, and constructed by the Bradley Construction Company, Salina.

A development of special significance for Bethany and for the enrichment of cultural resources in a wide area was the planning and construc-

At the dedication of Sandzén Memorial Gallery are: Dr. Charles Pelham Greenough 3rd, Mrs. Margaret Sandzén Greenough, and Mrs. Birger Sandzén.

BIRGER SANDZÉN MEMORIAL GALLERY

tion of a fine memorial to Dr. Birger Sandzén, beloved Bethany artist and professor. In March, 1955, the Birger Sandzén Memorial Foundation was established under the leadership of Charles Pelham Greenough 3rd. Dr. Greenough demonstrated great esteem for Birger Sandzén, his father-in-law, as well as a deep devotion to the arts by making available $150,-000.00 towards the construction of the Birger Sandzén Memorial Art Gallery. After initial contributions by the Kansas Federation of Women's Clubs, he led the campaign for funds to complete the project, which resulted in groundbreaking ceremonies on August 29, 1955.

This beautiful gallery was dedicated with appropriate ceremonies on October 20, 1957. The one-story red brick building provides unusually fine facilities for exhibits and displays. Within the dimensions of 65' in width and 149' in length are exhibition rooms, a workshop, a storeroom, and kitchen facilities. An attractive courtyard, featuring a well-known fountain by Carl Milles, the "Little Triton," adds to the charm of the gallery. The gallery's design, lighting, and general arrangements have won approval from knowledgeable people on many occasions. It was singularly appropriate that through the Birger Sandzén Memorial Gallery there is a home not only for the permanent showing of Sandzén's work and that of other artists, but also for invited and travelling exhibitions. The architects for the gallery were Robert Wehrli and Harold Engstrom, Casper, Wyoming. Johnson Bros., Salina, was the contractor.

President Mortvedt and his associates directed their efforts effectively to the perennially critical problem of more funds for current expenses. In the spring of 1954 the alumni association endorsed the alumni and ex-student fund, which separated giving by this group from the Bethany Loyalty Fund. The alumni fund increased in 1954 from $4,070,-00 from 185 donors to $8,456.00 from 358 donors in 1957. There was a substantial decrease in the Loyalty Fund until it was combined with the Patron's Fund, which became an important source of income in the 1960s. A remarkable increase in support from the Church developed in this period. The annual subsidy increased inpressively in the period 1953-58 from $37,000.00 to $78,000.00, representing increased giving from the Conference, and new money from the California Conference, the board of Christian higher education of the Augustana Lutheran Church, and the Texas Conference. Another encouraging development was the support from the Kansas Foundation for Private Colleges which grew from $921.00 in 1953 to $8,932.00 in 1958. The change in current income was from $281,000.00 in 1952-53 to $476,875.00 in 1958. The academic years 1956-57 and 1957-58 showed balanced budgets, a heartening sign for the future, in the background of prior deficits for several years.[24]

Bethany's progress was also apparent in the substantial growth of endowment funds from $528,871.00 in 1952-53 to $680,375.00 in 1957-58. The College received a splendid gift of $115,500.00 from the Ford Foundation in 1955 as part of the magnificent multi-million grant to American colleges and universities. The grant provided that the income for ten years be used for the improvement of teachers' salaries. The Ford Foundation gift increased the endowment fund by about twenty per cent. Another substantial gift came in 1955 when Mr. and Mrs. Emil V. Lillian, Lindsborg, gave $40,000.00 to the College. The increase of total plant fund assets of $943,811.00 in 1952-53 to $1,523,640.00 in 1957-58 was another significant mark of progress. The indebtedness was $88,130.00 in the current fund and $224,546.00 in the plant fund.[25]

The administration and faculty devoted continuous efforts to enrich the curriculum and instruction. In September, 1956, a three-day seminar was held for the study of the general education program and in the following September a similar seminar was devoted to the improvement of instruction. In 1956-57 three new departments were provided, two of them through the process of separating academic disciplines. Sociology, which had been a part of the department of economics and sociology, was divided to create independent departments. A similar goal was achieved when physics was separated from chemistry to provide two independent departments. A major in physical education was provided for the first time. In the same year Dean J. L. Hermanson entered into negotiations with the University of Kansas and Kansas State University, whereby in a five-year program, with the first three years in residence at Bethany, a student could earn a bachelor of science degree from Bethany and a bachelor's degree in engineering from one of the two universities.[26]

President Mortvedt and the board were gravely concerned about faculty salaries, which had been a critical problem for many years. In 1953-54 the top salary was $3,800.00, in 1956-57, $4,400.00, and the budget for 1958-59 brought it to $5,800.00. Income from the Ford Foundation grant in 1955 and the substantial increase in the alumni and ex-student fund was used exclusively for salary improvement. The president pointed out in his annual report in 1958 that in the previous summer three Ph.D.'s had been replaced with three persons with masters' degrees, and although the latter were capable and attractive individuals, the proportion of Ph.D.'s on the faculty was dangerously low.[27]

Action of decisive importance was taken in 1955 when President Mortvedt requested the Conference to amend the constitution of the

College so that a broader basis for membership on the board of directors could be achieved. The current constitution provided that all members of the board, except three alumni representatives, must belong to the Lutheran Church. This limited the personnel of the board while at the same time it failed to represent the facts, namely, that at least one-half of the students and alumni were non-Lutherans. The Conference readily endorsed the proposal in 1955 and with ratification in 1956, Article 1 of the constitution, item 6 provided that "The board of directors may nominate up to four (4) lay candidates who may or may not be members of the Lutheran Church in such a way that a Lutheran majority will always be maintained on the board." This action represented an important gain for strengthening the College in future years. In 1957, by Conference action, the articles of incorporation were brought into conformity with the constitution of the College.[28]

In November, 1957, the campus was shaken by the announcement that President Mortvedt had resigned, effective with the end of the current academic year, to become the first executive director of the board of Christian higher education of the Augustana Lutheran Church. The call to this important post was appropriate recognition of Dr. Mortvedt's talents and his fine achievements as Bethany's president. In concluding his final report to the Conference he stated: "I am grateful for the opportunity which has been mine to try to serve Bethany. My chief desire has been to re-enforce the foundations of the college and to build significantly upon them—as I said five years ago, to try to make a good college better." A splendid record of accomplishment testified to his sought-for goals. The Conference recognized this fact clearly when President Mortvedt was cited "for lifting the college to new heights of education excellence, for projection and implementation of a ten-year development plan, and for inspiration and vision for a greater Bethany."[29]

The years of Dr. Mortvedt as president represent a period of distinctive progress. The changes and developments contributed a broader basis than heretofore for the future development of the College. An effective course for the future had been charted.

Enthusiasm for football runs high as Bethany students get ready for an annual homecoming weekend.

L. DALE LUND

RAY D. HAHN PHYSICAL EDUCATION BUILDING with a versatile gymnasium.

Below: PIHLBLAD MEMORIAL UNION, dedicated 1964.

Below: ANNA MARM HALL, residence for women students, built in 1962.

6.

A Decade of Change 1958-1967

As Bethany approached the end of nine decades of history, Dr. L. Dale Lund was installed as Dr. Mortvedt's successor. He was elected the sixth president of Bethany in April, 1958, at the meeting of the West Central Conference, the successor of the Kansas Conference. Dr. Lund graduated from Gustavus Adolphus College and Augustana Theological Seminary. Following a pastorate in Massachusetts, he joined the faculty of Upsala College, East Orange, New Jersey, in 1947, where he was chaplain and associate professor of Christianity at the time of becoming president of Bethany. He earned the Ph.D. degree from Drew University. A graduate of a Lutheran college and a professor at another, he brought fine understanding of the nature and purposes of Bethany.

The installation of Dr. Lund occurred on "a sun-splashed" campus, October 8, 1958, when a large audience of church officials, fifty college and university representatives, faculty, students, and friends witnessed an impressive service before an altar constructed on the stage of Presser Hall. Russ B. Anderson, chairman of the board of directors, presided. The installing officer was Dr. N. Everett Hedeen, president of the West Central Conference of the Augustana Lutheran Church, assisted by Conference clergy. The installation address was made by Dr. Joseph Sittler, a Lutheran theologian and a member of the Federated Theological Faculty of the University of Chicago. Dr. Lund responded with an inaugural address. In an afternoon session, Dr. Evald B. Lawson, president of Upsala College, was the principal speaker. Musical presentations and a luncheon were a part of the festive occasion.

In his inaugural address, "Wrestling, Humility, and Proclamation,"

Dr. Lund pointed out that the words of the title of his address said much about "the crucial dynamic and essential character of the Christian liberal arts college . . . . We believe that a college where those words become incarnate will become a significant college. We believe it can happen, has happened, and will increasingly happen at Bethany."[1]

The Lund era witnessed substantial growth in enrollment. In the period between 1959-60 and 1964-65, the full-time enrollment increased from 353 to 448, with the high point of 476 in 1962-63. The latter number was the largest in the history of degree candidate enrollment and the highest since the peak of the veteran· enrollment of 409 in 1946-47. Moreover, the total enrollment in 1962-63 was 835, based in part upon nearly 300 airmen at Schilling Air Force Base who took courses offered by the College.[2]

This era witnessed splendid additions to the Bethany campus. Included were a new athletic field, a substantial addition to Deere Hall, and the construction of Ray D. Hahn Physical Education Building, Anna Marm Hall, women's dormitory, the Dr. and Mrs. Ernst F. Pihlblad Memorial Union, and a new president's home.

The need for new facilities in football and track and the replacement of the wood stadium had long been recognized. In the autumn of 1958 Philip Anderson, former student and son of Lindsborg pioneers, gave 12.7 acres to the college adjacent to the same area that he had donated several years earlier. Adequate space was now available for essential expansion. By July, 1959, more than $30,000.00 was raised, largely in Lindsborg, including about $10,000.00 by Bethany students, for a new athletic field and stadium. On October 2 the Philip Anderson Athletic Field and Stadium, constructed at a cost of $62,000.00, was dedicated. This fine facility included football and baseball fields, cinder quarter mile track with a 220-yard straightaway, concrete curbing, new scoreboard, improved lighting, and a chain link fence.

When the Ray D. Hahn Physical Education Building was dedicated in December, 1961, a significant addition was made to campus resources. Since the destruction of Ling Auditorium by fire in 1946, the only college facility was a surplus physical education building from Camp Phillips,

PHILIP ANDERSON ATHLETIC FIELD AND STADIUM, added to the campus in 1959.

near Smolan, which had been reconstructed on the campus. The new and imposing brick building on land given by Philip Anderson east of the former Ling Auditorium provided a fine basketball court with two playing areas for practice, and space for badminton, volleyball, and tennis. There is a classroom for seventy-five students, an exercise room, individual offices for coaches, snack bar, and display area. There is seating for 1500 spectators with opera-type seats in the balcony and roll-out bleachers on the main floor. The $425,000.00 structure was paid for from proceeds of the $825,000.00 share of Bethany in the campaign for the four colleges of the Augustana Lutheran Church known as OCCA (Our Christian College Appeal). The fine building is named in honor of Ray D. Hahn, athletic director and coach since 1938. A plaque inscribed with the following words has great meaning for the many people who hold the honoree in such high esteem: "Ray Dryer Hahn, coach, professor, director of athletics, gentleman." A portrait of Hahn by Professor John Bashor hangs in the building as additional recognition of Ray Hahn's distinguished services to the College. Uel Ramey and Associates were the architects and the general contractor was McBride and Dehmer, Wichita.

The expanding enrollment provided the basis for an addition to Deere Hall, men's dormitory which was occupied for the first time in 1958. In the spring of 1962 an addition running east and west and attached at the north to the first wing was constructed to house 108 men. This extensive addition now made available good housing for more students. The cost of the addition was $296,000.00, financed principally by a loan from the Housing and Home Finance Agency of the federal government. The loan was amortized on a regular schedule.

The need for additional housing for women students became increasingly apparent with the result that plans were made and contracts let for a new dormitory. Construction began in January, 1962, with occupancy occurring in the spring semester of the following year. The "L" shaped two-story building on the south side of Swensson Street in the east part of the campus provided excellent accommodations for eighty-seven women. There were two-room suites for two or three students, one room for study and the other for sleeping, with a bathroom between suites. A federal loan from the Housing and Finance Agency provided $320,000.00 in cost. This dormitory was named Anna Marm Hall in recognition of Miss Marm's thirty-three years of service to the College as professor of mathematics. Uel Raimey and Associates provided architectural services. The builder was McBride and Dehmer, Wichita.

An event of singularly great importance took place on the campus during homecoming, October 17, 1964, when the Dr. and Mrs. Ernst F. Pihlblad Memorial Union was dedicated in festive ceremonies. This occasion witnessed the realization of the long-felt desire to recognize the distinguished contribution of the Pihlblads, both Bethany graduates, who served as a great team in developing Bethany. Dr. Pihlblad made a magnificent contribution during his years as president, 1904-41. Mrs. Pihlblad served effectively as dean of women, 1916 to 1937, except for a few years in the 1920s, in addition to providing staunch support for her husband.

The Pihlblad Memorial Union is a beautiful and functional building on the east edge of the campus facing south on Swensson Street. Its so-called "hip" roof is reminiscent of part of the structure of Ling Gymnasium, the former "Messiah" auditorium which had stood on this site. Serviceable facilities were provided on both floors of the fine structure. The President's Dining Room (a large cafeteria), the Helge Pihlblad Quiet Lounge, and the Blue and Yellow private dining rooms added fine facilities to the campus. This floor also contained a coffee lounge and foyers. On the lower floor were offices for the student council, student publications, offices for the director of the union, student affairs personnel, and the chaplain. A large recreation area, bookstore, and post office were also located on this floor. The cost of Pihlblad Memorial Union was $425,000.00. The project was financed by gifts to the original Pihlblad Memorial Fund, several large gifts from individuals, a challenge gift from the Mabee Foundation of Tulsa, Oklahoma, a substantial gift from the OCCA (Our Christian College Appeal) program of the Augustana Lutheran Church, and a loan from the Housing and Home Finance Agency of the federal government. The architects were Anderson-Johnson, Salina. The builder was Johnson Builders, Inc., Salina. William Hammer, '59, was appointed the first director of the Pihlblad Union. The Union replaced the limited facilities of Swede Inn, which had been located in the basement of Alma Swensson Hall since 1949.

In a reminiscent mood the editor of the *Messenger* described the move to the beautiful and serviceable Pihlblad Memorial Union: "After seventy-eight years the dining hall in Old Main yields to new facilities. Students will leave behind the long tables and red chairs, worn hardwood floors, many memories, and move into a beautiful carpeted dining room with bright colored furnishings and air conditioning."[3]

In addition to the buildings identified above, a new president's home was occupied in January, 1963. This commodious home in the northwest section of Lindsborg provided more adequate resources for entertaining and other public responsibilities of the president's family than the smaller home on Main Street opposite Swensson Memorial Park.

The addition of the buildings to the Bethany campus witnessed the steady attainment of goals set forth in President Mortvedt's ten-year expansion program announced in 1955 and further developed in President Lund's administration. A professionally prepared master campus plan was also adopted by the board of directors in October, 1963.

A fundamental change in the historic administrative pattern of the College was consummated in 1960. Three years earlier, Dr. Gould Wickey, executive secretary of the board of higher education of the United Lutheran Church in America, was requested to evaluate the colleges of the Augustana Lutheran Church. Included in his recommendations for Bethany was the abandonment of the dual structure of a College of Liberal Arts and Sciences and the College of Fine Arts. This structure had its origin in the unique emphasis historically at Bethany upon music and art. President Mortvedt pointed out to the Conference in 1958 that Dr. Wickey considered the present organization "cumbersome, expensive, and divisive."[4]

The board of directors, after studying the Wickey report, recommended on February 3, 1959, that Section 5 of the college constitution which read, "This institution shall consist of a College of Liberal Arts and Sciences and a College of Fine Arts and such other departments as the Conference may authorize," be deleted, and that it be replaced by the following: "The institution shall consist of such departments and administrative structures as the board of directors deems necessary and appropriate to the functioning of an academic program which embraces the liberal arts and sciences, fine arts and music, and leads to baccalaureate degrees in those fields."[5]

The recommendation of this change by the board was adopted by the Conference in April, 1960, after studying this controversial matter for one year. In presenting the recommendation in 1959, President Lund affirmed that "Should such a change occur, it should be made with the clear understanding that the departments of music and art, which now comprise the College of Fine Arts, be maintained with the same care which has made them famous . . . . If this change were adopted, Bethany would be a College of Liberal Arts and Sciences with music and art functioning as departments alongside English, history, and other disciplines."[6]

In April, 1961, President Lund summarized the process of reorganization: "It is now the intention of the president of the college and the board of directors to reorganize the administration and consolidate the academic program into one college with one academic dean. Degree programs will continue as before, with the bachelor of arts, bachelor of fine arts, bachelor of music, and bachelor of science degrees being conferred in course." He pointed out that the following divisions of study would be provided: art, humanities, music, natural science, and social sciences. He also observed: "The chairman of the division of music will serve as director of musical affairs in order that the fine music traditions and festivals may be properly managed and advanced."[7]

The reorganization became effective with the academic year 1962-63.

Dr. Albert A. Zimmer became dean of the College. He held a baccalaureate degree from Pennsylvania State University and the doctor of education degree from Pittsburgh University. He was dean of students and professor of education at Susquehanna University immediately before coming to Bethany. Professor Lambert Dahlsten, a member of the faculty, was appointed director of musical affairs. Dr. J. L. Hermanson, who had been dean of liberal arts and sciences since 1948, continued on the faculty as professor and chairman of the department of chemistry. Lloyd Spear, who had served as dean of the College of Fine Arts since 1948, director of the Bethany College Symphony Orchestra, professor of violin, and for three years director of the Bethany Oratorio Society, left the College in 1959 to continue his splendid career in music teaching, conducting, and administration in the Chicago area.

In September, 1962, an event of far-reaching importance for Bethany College occurred when the organizing convention of the Central States Synod of the Lutheran Church in America met in Topeka. This action followed the merging of the Augustana Lutheran Church and its conferences with the large United Lutheran Church in America and other smaller Lutheran churches earlier that year. The original Kansas Conference, which had been designated the West Central Conference of the Augustana Lutheran Church in 1959, was now absorbed in the larger Lutheran Church in America in the form of the Central States Synod. This synod provided a much larger constituency for Bethany with congregations in Kansas, Arkansas, Oklahoma, and Western Missouri. The new Central States Synod had a baptized membership of 43,000 with 121 congregations and 101 pastors in contrast with 25,000 baptized members, 61 congregations, and 46 pastors in the former Conference. In addition Bethany became the official college of the Rocky Mountain Synod (with Midland Lutheran College) and of the Texas-Louisiana Synod. This new church alignment increased substantially the potential for increased recruiting of students and greater financial support.[8]

The administration and faculty sought to keep on the line of discovery by studying and planning programs and courses of study. In October, 1960, a two-year intensive analysis "resulted in a refined and integrated course of study for all students. A basic 'core curriculum' was provided for all degree candidates including for the first time a minimum number of credits in fine arts for all students." The distribution of courses was as follows: religion, 8 hours; philosophy, 3 hours; English, 12 hours; foreign languages, 6 hours (completion of the second year of college language required for graduation); music or art, 3 hours; history, 6 hours; science, 8 hours; social science, 6 hours (other than history). This required curriculum for all students regardless of majors totaled a minimum of 52 hours. It was effective with the academic year 1961-62.[9]

The major fields of study were identified as follows: 1. The divisional major leading to the bachelor of arts and bachelor of science degrees provided for a concentration of courses taken in one division. 2. The functional major leading to the degree of bachelor of fine arts or bachelor of music. Since the College of Fine Arts had been eliminated, these majors were earned through courses in the department of art and the department of music. This major was described as "preparation for a certain career or for later professional study." 3. The departmental major leading to the degree of bachelor of arts or bachelor of science. Sixteen majors were identified.[10]

Low faculty salaries continued to be the problem of greatest concern to administrators and board members. While gains were made periodically, the increased cost of living and inflation continued to provide a minimal amount for faculty personnel. President Lund emphasized in 1960 a typically historical situation, namely, that salaries were far too low. In the scale of the American Association of University Professors, rating from A to F, Bethany rated F which would have been the rating in prior years also. Although he also pointed out that currently Bethany salaries were at the top among Protestant colleges in Kansas, this only identified the low level in the State. However, in 1965 the president was pleased to indicate that progress in the salary structure was being made since the average salary had increased approximately sixty percent in the last six years.[11]

A very important action involving faculty welfare was taken in the autumn of 1960 when the board of directors authorized and helped to fund participation in the Teachers Insurance and Annuity Association, known among hundreds of American colleges and universities as "TIAA." This joint contributing plan of faculty and college was a proper recognition of faculty welfare and a decisive step in retaining and recruiting faculty. There had been no retirement provisions for lay members of the faculty until the college personnel were included in the social security program of the Department of Health, Education, and Welfare of the federal government on January 1, 1951. The gains represented by the new TIAA plan were heartily applauded by all friends of the College.

When President Lund presented his annual report to the Kansas Conference in April, 1959, he pointed out: "The real problem during the next few years—since the board of directors acted so properly and aggressively in the matter of salaries and 'fringe benefits'—will be obtaining the necessary funds to pay for the concomitant increase in the operating budget." Moreover, he reminded the constituency that the old accumulated operating deficit was about $90,000.00, although the current budget for the past two years had been balanced. The income from all sources increased from $555,369.00 in 1958-59 to $881,586.00 in 1964-65. A most encouraging factor was the steady increase in support from the church which reached $116,974.00 in 1964-65. The total ten years earlier had been $54,160.00. The patrons fund and the alumni efforts produced in excess of $22,000.00 each, a much higher amount than had ever been attained previously. Although tuition income was three times greater at the end of the decade, the expenses increased more rapidly so that the deficits in the current operating fund each year ranged between $17,000.00 to $27,000.00 from 1959-60 to 1964-65. A contributing factor was emergency expenditures for capital needs including the repairs to the heating plant.[12]

These years proved to be very productive in long-range resources. Total endowment funds, which were $680,375.00 in 1957-58 had increased to $889,436.00 in 1964-65. Total assets had almost doubled from $2,225,-335.00 in 1957-58 to $4,332,160.00 in 1964-65, the greatest single development in a similar span of years in Bethany's history. The total indebtedness was $1,194,751.00 which included $979,250.00 in the plant fund and $215,501.00 in the current fund accumulated over many years.[13]

Once again Bethany's president was called to other service in the educational program of the church when President Lund was requested to become dean of the Lutheran School of Theology, Chicago, the newly established seminary of the Lutheran Church in America. The challenge of this important work caused President Lund to resign effective at the end of the academic year 1965. In his last address to the Synod, President Lund described his experiences at Bethany by declaring: "Being president of Bethany has been a privilege and calling of the highest order . . . . I will leave the college I love and believe in because the change seems right for me and for Bethany. My prayer is that Bethany may prosper under the new president and a fine team of colleagues." The Synod expressed appreciation to him for "having effectively and enthusiastically served Bethany College as its president from 1958-65 . . . for securing a strong faculty, developing a meaningful curriculum, and procuring new facilities . . . and expressing genuine appreciation for his outstanding contribution to Christian higher education." The Messenger observed editorially: "Each and every one of us are sad to see Dr. Lund leave Bethany." A symbol of the esteem in which Dr. Lund was held took the form of a plaque which was presented to him by the students for his fine contribution to the College.[14]

President Lund also gained fine recognition outside the campus. He was the first, and to date, the only president of Bethany College who was elected to the commission on higher education of the North Central Association of Colleges and Universities.

When seeking a new president for Bethany following the resignation of Dr. Lund, the selection committee and board of directors turned once again to an experienced academic person at a Lutheran College. Dr. G. Kenneth Andeen, professor of Christianity at Augustana College, Rock

Dr. Andeen discusses blueprints with a group of Bethany students.

G. KENNETH ANDEEN

Island, Illinois, accepted the invitation to become Bethany's seventh president. He was a graduate of Upsala College, East Orange, New Jersey, and Augustana Theological Seminary, and he had been awarded the Master of Arts and Ph.D. degrees from Columbia University. The new Bethany chief executive officer had established a fine record as a teacher and his doctoral research in Christian higher education had further prepared him for the presidency.

On Monday, September 27, 1965, Dr. Andeen was installed as president before a large congregation of visiting academic people, churchmen, Bethany faculty, students, friends, and well-wishers. Dr. Franklin Clark Fry, president of the Lutheran Church in America, delivered the installation address. The installing officer was Dr. N. Everett Hedeen, president of the Central States Synod. A. L. Duckwall, Jr., chairman of the board of directors, presided at the festivities. In his installation address Dr. Andeen declared: "The task and purpose of Bethany College stated simply is 'Bethany is a Christian community at study.' Out of this study the graduate finds his vocation, a calling from God, in which he comes into his own in full Christian maturity, glorifying God in his life and work and unselfishly serving his neighbor in love . . . . We are fortunate [at Bethany College] to be building upon almost a century of sound experience which exhibits itself all about us on campus and in the community." A unique and significant aspect of the installation program was "An Evening with the Students," in which President and Mrs. Andeen shared fellowship with the essential constituency whose interests furnished the reason for the College. This meeting initiated a close relationship with students which characterized President Andeen's tenure at Bethany.[15]

President Andeen and his associates entered heartily into the challenge that confronted Bethany. Since the Bethany College Progress Fund had been delayed by the resignation of President Lund, the new administration reactivated it. In October, 1965, plans were finalized, a campaign organization was established, and a professional fund-raising firm was engaged to provide counsel and direction. The goal for the centennial year, 1981, was set at $7,514,000.00. Included in the design was $3,000,-000.00 for endowment, $2,914,000.00 for future facilities, and $114,000.00 for teaching aids beyond the regular budget. The initial phase provided for raising $1,000,000.00 for the construction of classroom facilities and a library. The first effort involved the Lindsborg community which by April, 1966, had pledged $55,000.00.[16]

Time and attention were also devoted in 1965-66 to the advantages that might accrue from a proposed cooperative venture of six church-related colleges in Central Kansas. Extensive studies and consultation resulted in the formation of the group known as the Associated Colleges of Central Kansas (ACCK) in May, 1966. The purpose of this organization was "to develop areas of cooperation and general policy that would serve to strengthen the respective colleges and supplement their individual programs." Bethany joined with Bethel College, Kansas Wesleyan, McPherson College, Sterling College, and Tabor College to launch a venture in cooperation that was encouraged by the potentiality of public and private funding. The colleges were located within a radius of forty miles.

A new element soon entered into the Bethany situation that was destined to cause great temporary distress but which in the long run proved to be a decisive positive factor. A study of the College was requested by the board of directors in accordance with a policy of the board of education of the Lutheran Church in America whenever a change in administration occurred. The 38-page report of the study committee under the direction of Dr. Francis C. Gamelin, executive director of the LCA board of education, presented in 1966, dealt with college objectives, faculty, student life, facilities, administration, government, costs, and financing significant survival. The study presented data that showed need for curriculum changes, enriching the program, providing new facilities, adding personnel, and increasing substantially the financial support.[17]

Emphasis in the reports was placed upon "the consequences of the prolonged financial starvation" with its dire implications on faculty salaries, program, services, equipment, and facilities. The committee emphasized that the current annual budget must be increased immediately by $300,000.00 in order to achieve valid goals. The implications of the accumulative deficit of $250,000.00 in current operations was stressed. The report also observed, in considering the possible change in the location of Bethany, that "from the social, cultural, and financial points of view, the College is located in a barren area."[18]

Although the basic findings of fact by the study committee were based on appropriately documented evidence, the report may be challenged for not identifying adequately the distinguished reputation, historically and currently, of the College as a unique cultural center based upon a nationally acclaimed music and oratorio tradition, the great achievement in art, the high esteem of alumni in teaching and other professions, and the contribution of the College to American cultural pluralism. The language of the study in its criticism of the vagueness of the statement of the college's objectives made its own contribution to the problem by stating: "A taxonomy of educational objectives will provide them [administrators and faculty] an excellent category of the diverse possibilities open to them." Moreover, it was not possible for the study committee to foresee that the "barren area" could rise to the committee's challenge in a magnificent manner.[19]

The essential thrust of the findings emphasized persistent and inadequate financial support as the central problem of the College. Although the normal course for the presentation of findings of the committee should have been to the board of directors, its authorizing agent, there was prior discussion of certain aspects of the report with persons in Lindsborg under the leadership of a member of the committee. This premature discussion included the possibility of moving Bethany from Lindsborg to Colorado. Dr. Axel Beckman, chairman of the board, identified this action in his report to the Conference in April, 1967, in these words: "An ill-conceived effort to preevaluate the findings of the status study precipitated unfounded rumors of Bethany's removal to another location."[20]

President Andeen found himself in a difficult position. He was fully aware of the dire financial situation and the recommendations of the study committee. His identification with the members of the study committee and his participation in discussions of the future of the College, especially relating to the sensitive point of the possibility of moving the College to Colorado, aroused both concern and anger among certain alumni and townspeople. No one could question President Andeen's sincerity and his concern for what would be best for the College. He knew that something really important must happen in the financial area if Bethany were to be a good college.

In March, 1966, the issue became public as described in the *Messenger:* "Rumors say that Bethany will be moving its campus to Colorado . . . . The first specialist report was submitted in preliminary form Wednesday night." Any plan to move the College was denied by officials of the Conference and board of directors, and in April, 1966, the *Messenger* reported: "The board of directors went on record stating positively and unequivocally that there are no plans for moving Bethany from Lindsborg." The controversy, based upon rumors stemming from the premature release of certain aspects of the study and subsequent discussion, became a very divisive factor in the succeeding months.[21]

These developments resulted in the resignation of President Andeen on February 6, 1967. Dr. Axel Beckman, chairman of the board, in accepting Andeen's resignation, pointed out among other things that the faculty letter sent to the board "was in complete support of Dr. Andeen not only as a man but also as president of the college." In reporting to the Conference, Dr. Beckman said relative to Andeen's resignation: "After comprehensive and earnest consideration of the resignation, the board acted to accept it. While regretting the termination of a relationship which had seemed to hold great promise, the board's decision was made out of a sense of responsibility to Bethany and her several constituencies, the students, the faculty, the staff, the community, and the church."[22]

Regardless of the varied responses to the Andeen presidency the fact remains that his clear and dramatic identification of Bethany's problems, especially financial, created the background elements for a new and decisive response that was crucial for the future of the College. Thus constructive goals were achieved in the midst of problems.

The close relationship between President Andeen and the Bethany students is clearly recorded in the pages of the *Messenger* immediately following his resignation. In "A Note of Farewell" in behalf of the Andeen family, Dr. Andeen wrote: "One of the richest experiences of our lives has been the friendships formed at Bethany College with faculty, students, and the various staff personnel . . . . We express our deepest appreciation for the many kindnesses shown us during our period of service at Bethany." The students' fine feeling toward President Andeen was expressed in a letter from the Student Congress transmitted by the president, Stephen Swanson: "The Student Congress of Bethany College feels a great loss in hearing of your resignation . . . . You have shown interest in students by your policies and leadership. Your integrity and honesty have been a trait of character which has undoubtedly influenced and will in the future continue to influence those students with whom you have come in contact. The series of free discussions which were held, frank criticism and debate, have indeed been a highlight in the eyes of Bethany students. We count it an honor to have known, worked with, and been associated with you."[23]

After leaving Bethany Dr. Andeen served as dean of William Rainey Harper College, Palatine, Illinois. In 1968 he was chosen as president of Wittenberg University, the well-known Lutheran institution at

Springfield, Ohio.

Bethany was now in a crisis situation, a time of agonizing decision that was heavy in implications for the future. In this tense time of February, 1967, the editor of the *Messenger* wrote wisely: "The only true issues now are the positive steps the board is taking both for the future and the immediate needs of the college."[24]

The board of directors acted immediately after President Andeen's resignation to appoint Dr. Albert A. Zimmer, dean and vice-president, as acting president of the College. He was assisted by an administrative committee composed of representatives from the board of directors, the administrative council, and the community. Dr. Conrad Bergendoff, president emeritus of Augustana College, Rock Island, Illinois, a distinguished Lutheran educator and churchman, was appointed consultant to work with the faculty in studying purposes, curriculum, program, and other aspects of college policy. A faculty committee soon went to work on this important assignment. In February, 1967, the board authorized a stepped-up program of student recruitment. Plans were made for adding faculty in speech and drama, modern languages, art, teacher education, and in physical education and athletics. The development committee took steps to revive the Bethany College Progress Fund. There was new excitement and enthusiasm for the future of Bethany. The board's effective leadership deserves the hearty commendation of all friends of Bethany. Their response demonstrated the quality of greatness. The college's extremity had elicited results that transformed crisis into opportunity. There were weeks and months of feverish activity, meetings, conferences, and planning. It was also a time when earnest prayers were made to God that the College might be strengthened to serve His kingdom and the family of man in the years ahead.

Full understanding prevailed as to the intimate relationship between the financial poverty of the College and its present dire circumstance. The response had not been equalled in Bethany's history. As a great example, the Lindsborg community grappled with reality as never before and emerged triumphant. On April 11, 1967, a Town Hall meeting was held in Presser Hall with 700 in attendance under the leadership of Jack Carlin, Lindsborg citizen. The goal was $100,000.00. Walter Ostenberg, '24, a distinguished alumnus, was the principal speaker. When the pledging was over about 10:30 p.m. that night, the handsome sum of $82,-000.00 had been raised. On April 21 the committee announced jubilantly that $100,029.00 had been pledged. This was a great vote of confidence. In explaining this great achievement, several factors were cited: "A new car planned for this year was not bought"; "many vacations were shortened and some cancelled"; "many dug down deeper than ever before." The income from the Lindsborg community campaign was designated for the general operating fund to meet current expenses. The

Messenger reflected that this should be a decisive factor in balancing the budget during the next two fiscal years.

The Central States Synod was informed at its meeting in April of the magnitude of the issues confronting the College. Dr. Axel Beckman, chairman of the board of directors, informed the members: "Boldly imaginative measures are needed, coupling daring with realism. Accordingly, the board and the administration have agreed on a 1967-68 budget which will accentuate student recruitment and a salary-acceleration factor sufficient to attract and hold the kind of faculty Bethany must have. Needless to say, such planning presupposes the discovery of new monies to implement the programmed expenditures."[25]

In the midst of the uncertainties of the year the President's Report for 1966-67 contained much encouragement. Alumni support had reached an all-time high of $99,000.00. This was an increase of $39,000.00 over the previous year. Since the 1962-63 fiscal year, "gifts and grants" for current operations had doubled with $257,821.00 received during 1966-67. The unique "Beth-a-matic" program in 1966-67, with its emphasis upon monthly support, was a great success. Moreover, $200,000.00 had been pledged on the Bethany Progress Fund and $120,000.00 of that amount had been paid to the College.[26]

In the spring of 1967 the finance committee of the board of directors purchased the Carlton Hotel in Lindsborg as an investment from the endowment fund for conversion into a dormitory. The former hotel provided eight double rooms, eight single rooms, an apartment for the resident head, and ample recreation and lobby space. Carlton Hall housed senior women students during the next academic year.

In the midst of the intense activity recounted above, a board-faculty committee was making a thorough search for a candidate to serve as president of Bethany. In April Dr. Albert A. Zimmer, dean and acting president, resigned effective at the end of the fiscal year to become professor of education at Thiel College, Greenville, Pennsylvania. Dr. Zimmer had provided excellent leadership in a crisis situation. The search committee soon had a candidate to present to the board and to the wider constituency. At the commencement exercises in Presser Hall on Sunday, May 29, 1967, Dr. Arvin W. Hahn was introduced as the new president of Bethany College. A new and great era was about to come to birth.

7.

A Miracle in the Making 1967-1974

When Dr. Arvin W. Hahn arrived in Lindsborg in August, 1967, to become president of Bethany College, he brought a splendid record of high level achievement in teaching, scholarship, and administration. A graduate of Concordia Teachers College, River Forest, Illinois, an institution of the Lutheran Church-Missouri Synod, he earned the M.A. degree from the University of Chicago and the Ph.D. degree from Northwestern University. For seventeen years he had been a member of the faculty of Concordia and was serving as dean of graduate studies and director of research at the time of coming to Bethany. He had served as director of placement and director of development. Dr. Hahn had been a visiting professor at other colleges and universities. In 1962 he had made a 27,000-mile study tour of education and geography in Europe and Africa. In addition to several scholarly publications, he was in 1965 collaborator in geography films for the Encyclopedia Britannica. Dr. Hahn had been a member of important public relations and television committees of the Missouri Synod.

President Hahn soon won respect on the campus and in the larger community for his ability, vision, and dedication to Christian higher education. When he visited in Lindsborg at commencement, 1967, he observed: "I have lots of ideas. I plan to make a list of some of them, then

Dr. Arvin W. Hahn arrives in 1967 to assume the Bethany presidency.

THE HAHN FAMILY: DAVID, TIMOTHY, JUDIE, LINDA, AND ARVIN

begin to assign priorities." It soon became apparent that President Hahn had many fine ideas which would be translated into meaningful action within a surprisingly short time.[1]

On Sunday afternoon, October 6, 1968, more than a year later, the largest number of people to witness the inauguration of a Bethany College president assembled in Presser Hall for the ceremony that made Dr. Arvin W. Hahn the eighth president. A large academic procession composed of delegates of colleges, learned societies, professional associations, clergy, Bethany faculty, and members of the board of directors preceded the official party. The inaugural address was delivered by Dr. Louis T. Almen, executive secretary of the board of education of the Lutheran Church in America. A unique but singularly appropriate feature was the conferring of an honorary degree on Professor Herbert H. Gross, Concordia Teachers College, the inspiring friend, teacher, and colleague of Dr. Hahn. Dr. Hahn was installed by the Reverend N. Everett Hedeen, president of the Central States Synod of the LCA.

In an eloquent address President Hahn identified his role and the future of the College. As members of the large audience left the festive occasion they would remember and be grateful for his sincere affirmation: "Today I pledge simply that I will pray fervently and often for the welfare of the college family, that I will engage vigorously and tirelessly in the activities necessary to implement our dreams and aspirations, and I assure you that I will apply all the intelligence at my command toward their fulfillment . . . . It is with these feelings and with total reliance on God's grace and help that I proudly assume the responsibilities of the office of president of this great college, for great it is and great it will be."[2]

Prior to the installation of President Hahn, the Bethany campus had been the scene of intensive activity. A schedule of work had been developed with faculty and staff as a new era in Bethany's history was initiated. The results of thought and planning were soon apparent as the new administration and the faculty worked diligently on several fronts. Dean Albert Zimmer had resigned at the end of the 1966-67 academic year. Dr. Lloyd Foerster came to the College as academic dean in September, 1967. Dean Foerster was a highly esteemed colleague of President Hahn at Concordia Teachers College. A graduate of that college, he had been awarded the master's degree from Rhode Island College and the doctor of education degree from Teachers College, Columbia University. He was a member of the graduate faculty at Concordia and had been a lecturer at Teachers College, Columbia.

The administration and faculty set themselves to a thorough study of the aims and purposes of the College. This involved serious analysis and thought about the historic goals and the current needs. Although the basic principles did not differ fundamentally from the statements that had previously set forth this phase of Bethany's program, the more complete and detailed results of the study presented effective guidelines for the future. The introductory statement of purpose was as follows: "The ultimate aims of Bethany College are to educate students who will contribute significantly toward the development of constructive Christian thought and expression in human life and society, and to provide for the church of Christ on earth dedicated and informed leadership to assist in the determination and implementation of its future goals."[3]

The talent and energy of the faculty and administration were also directed in 1967-68 toward revision and reconstruction of the academic program. As noted previously, the curriculum committee and other faculty groups had initiated a study earlier with Dr. Conrad Bergendoff as consultant. The pace of the study was accelerated through the personal involvement of President Hahn and Dean Foerster. Intensive work was done in the autumn of 1967 through bi-weekly meetings to be climaxed with full-time effort in this important assignment in January, 1968. The curriculum committee was composed of the following faculty members: Roger Thorstenberg, chairman (music), Rosemary Laughlin (art), Jen Jenkins (mathematics), Carl Hansen (religion and philosophy), Gerald Shannon (history), Joe Hermanson (chemistry and former dean of arts and sciences), Willard Nelson, registrar, and Dean Foerster. Dr. Edward Lindell, dean of the College of Arts and Sciences at Denver University, served as a consultant to the committee.

The committee's efforts were framed against the background of the status study, "Towards Significant Survival" (1966), the prospective accreditation visit in 1970 of representatives of the commission on higher education of the North Central Association, the previous studies of the committee, and the new insight and vision provided by President Hahn and Dean Foerster. Moreover, the board of directors had authorized a comprehensive study to be followed by recommendations.

New educational philosophy and recurrent financial necessity were twin forces which operated in the assessment of the historic Bethany program of studies. Enrollment studies and fiscal analysis indicated that the traditional emphasis on music and art, leading to specialized baccalaureate degrees in those fields, was not justified by the current enrollment, staff requirements, and funding resources. The number of graduates in the specialized areas of music and art had decreased from 47 percent of the total number of graduates (35 of 78) in 1950 to 24 percent of the total number of graduates (16 of 68) in 1967. B.F.A. and B.M. degrees required one-fourth of the total staff while their enrollments reflected but one-seventh of the student credit hours. The decision in 1959 to abandon the academic structure which provided for the College of Fine Arts was quite likely a factor in the sharp decrease in the enrollment figures in the music and art courses.[4]

The decision to discontinue the degrees in music and art was made in the context of fiscal reality and educational philosophy. In answer to the query, "What is the central question which is being dealt with in the current review of the College?" the following reply was given: "The central purpose of the review at present is to develop a curriculum which bears quality and at the same time is in line with the funding potential of the school. With the present arrangements in student-faculty ratios and cost-per-student basis, there are few colleges in the nation which could fund the program as outlined in Bethany's current catalogue. Through new curricular developments and greater efficiency on the fiscal side, these two will be brought into greater balance." The recommendations of the committee were carefully discussed, debated, and evaluated by the faculty. In an important meeting of the faculty on January 12, 1968, the new program was adopted. The board of directors had already substituted the one-degree curriculum for the previous three degrees by action on December 18, 1967.[5]

As a result of the action by the board and faculty, the multiple degrees of bachelor of arts, music, and art were merged into the bachelor of arts degree for all graduates. The bachelor of science degree had been combined with the bachelor of arts degree in 1966-67. Provision was made for continuing the degrees in music and art for students already enrolled in those programs. Since the new plan was to become effective in September, 1968, the first class of graduates with the one degree, bachelor of arts, was presented at the commencement in 1972.

Statistics relative to degrees in music and art between 1931 and 1971, the last year of the separate degree pattern, show that 33 percent (816 of 2,472) were in those areas. In the years 1972-74 when only the bachelor of arts degree was conferred, 15.4 percent (70 of 454) were majors in music and art. The largest number of degrees in fine arts was 37 of 80 awarded in 1950; the lowest during a normal period was 11 of 42 in 1955. In the war period of 1944, there were 9 fine arts degrees and 11 in liberal arts. In 1974 there were 25 majors in music and art out of 126, the largest number during the three years of the new degree pattern.[6]

The requirements for graduation in 1968 were revised by substituting thirty-five to thirty-six reorganized and enriched courses for the multiple pattern that had prevailed heretofore. The total number of courses, as a result of consolidation and reconstruction, was reduced by approximately one-third, from 320 to 220. The new schedule provided for two fourteen-week terms separated by a one-month interterm. The 4-1-4 academic program provided a broad spectrum of learning with opportunity for in-depth study. The student normally would enroll in four courses during each fourteen-week term and one course during the four-week term. The courses required for graduation included general education studies in the humanities, social sciences, and natural sciences. Majors were available in eleven academic disciplines and teaching majors in twelve areas. Dr.

Joseph Iverson, St. Olaf College, served as consultant in planning the 4-1-4 arrangement.

The program initiated in September, 1968, has been sustained subsequently with some modifications to provide greater flexibility. The new plan has been well-supported by administrators, faculty, and students. Criticism from some music students was based upon the shorter term and almost daily class meetings of each course which restricted time for practice. Although the new program resulted in a shift from the historic professional emphasis in music and art, the assessment of Bethany's current situation was made on the basis of new conditions. Losses in certain aspects of Bethany's tradition were offset by gains, including emphases which were within the realities of attainable financial support. An exceedingly critical phase of Bethany's history had been resolved in a spirit of judicious reflection and effective compromise.

President Hahn and his associates soon launched efforts to eliminate "a burden heavy to be borne" in the $215,000.00 debt on current operations accumulated over many years. The major source for loans to cover the debt had been the endowment fund. This was the most crucial immediate Bethany problem because the future of the College depended upon financial solvency. A thrilling landmark date in the emergence of the new Bethany was March 11, 1968, when at a large Town Hall meeting in Presser Hall, Dr. Hahn announced that the debt had been eliminated through cash donations and pledges and that provision was being made for a contingency fund for possible fiscal emergencies. The grand total came from the following sources: The Ludvig Nelson and Selma Nelson Religious, Educational, and Charitable Trust, $50,000.00; assignment by the board of directors of $82,500.00 from the Ford Foundation grant a decade earlier in keeping with the foundation's policy that these funds were now unrestricted; and $82,500.00 from the Lindsborg community.[7]

Friends of Bethany had great reason for gratitude and rejoicing. The Nelson Trust had produced, as was to be its pattern across the years, substantial support for the College. Once again the Lindsborg community responded heroically to Bethany's needs by matching the Ford Foundation allocation. Less than a year earlier Lindsborg had raised in excess of $100,000.00 to assist substantially in meeting operational costs for the current and next fiscal year. Jack Carlin, chairman of the Lindsborg committee, his associates, and the citizens responded with support by example that not only met a crisis situation but had wider implications as prospective donors saw clearly the tenacity and will of the community in which the College was located.

The people attending the Town Hall meeting on March 11, 1968, received another unforgettable thrill when President Hahn announced that Mr. and Mrs. Alvar G. Wallerstedt, Pittsburgh, Pennsylvania, had given Bethany a challenge gift of $500,000.00. This was the largest benefaction in Bethany's history. The Wallerstedts' leadership at this point was decisive not only in the large gift but as a significant demonstration of faith in Bethany's future. Wallerstedt, a native of Lindsborg and an alumnus of the commercial department, has a distinguished record of achievement in business and finance. He served as an accountant with private industry and the United States government and for many years he headed the accountants' tax department of the well-known legal firm of Reed, Smith, Shaw and McClay of Pittsburgh. He became associated with Rockwell Standard Corporation in 1936, serving as a director and later as director emeritus. Mr. and Mrs. Wallerstedt showed convincingly high-level citizenship and understanding of Christian higher education by this initial gift which was made at a crucial time in the college's history.

In the background of the great developments of March, 1968, had been serious and effective planning for the future. The campus master plan was revised and enriched. Three distinctive academic features, involving old and proposed new buildings, were provided: a center for the social sciences, a center for the natural sciences, and a center for the humanities. Two additional points of focus were a learning center involving library and audio-visual resources, and an administrative center, later abandoned in the planning. Another feature was outside courts at each center to facilitate discussion among students and teachers. Plans were designed to incorporate the old and new facilities through campus malls thus replacing the two principal streets running through the campus.

The challenge of the Wallerstedt gift and the impressive plans for the future produced a magnificent response by delegates to the annual meeting of the Central States Synod in May, 1968, under the leadership of N. Everett Hedeen, President, when a Bethany fund-raising campaign of $500,000.00 was endorsed. The Synod exceeded the goal in four months. Another great chapter in the annals of Bethany had been written.[8]

When a large assembly of Bethanyites and friends met for another Town Hall meeting at Presser Hall on Sunday afternoon, December 15, 1968, good and great news was compounded as President Hahn recounted recent developments. A total of $1,150,000.00 was now available for proceeding with the initial phases of the new master plan. The Wallerstedt gift of $500,000.00, the Central States Synod successful fund-raising effort of approximately $550,000.00, and the $100,000.00 raised by friends and alumni now provided adequate funds for the construction of "the million dollar circle," consisting of social science facilities and a library. Moreover, Mr. and Mrs. Walter Warner, Salina, had provided $40,000.00 for furnishing of the proposed dormitory which was to be constructed by a loan of $613,000.00 from the federal government. The dormitory was to be known appropriately as Warner Hall. Mr. and Mrs. Warner and Mrs. Warner's parents, Mr. and Mrs. S. I. Nelson, were long-time friends of the College. In addition, the president announced a federal government grant of $250,000.00 for the construction of academic facilities.

The new developments at Bethany involved the need for assessment not only of former patterns of education but also for decisions relative to the future of Old Main. As early as April, 1955, President Mortvedt reported that the study by specialists had indicated that it was doubtful that Old Main could be reconstructed. Further studies verified the early assessment, and late in June, 1968, Old Main was no longer a landmark in the Smoky Valley. It is reported that the grand old structure, for more than eight decades a symbol and fact of Bethany, resisted far more than other buildings the attack of the wrecking crew. In 1958 a sensitive student wrote in the *Messenger:* "The floors of Old Main are worn by the soles of hundreds of shoes, the plaster is cracked and checked, and the upper floors are becoming unsafe as well as uncomfortable for use as a dormitory. But the halls seem to hold the dreams and laughter of long-gone students and the name of 'Old Main' has found its way into the hearts of all Bethanyites."[9]

When the end of an era leads to a new beginning as the past is joined with the future in reverential respect, the sadness of farewell to the old is diminished. Old Main was not abandoned because what it represented had failed nor was the memory of it destroyed. It had played a vital role in the tradition that was now entering a new phase. When the first spade of soil was turned that July day in 1968 for the construction of the Wallerstedt complex, the old and new joined hands, figuratively speaking. Another landmark literally left the campus in the summer of the next year when the Swedish Pavilion found a permanent home in the historic Old Mill park in south Lindsborg. The first college building, the former one-story frame Lindsborg schoolhouse, was also moved there in 1969.

In the development of the master plan, College and Swensson Streets, which for many years had created a serious traffic hazard, were closed so that a new feeling of campus unity could be developed through a pedestrian mall in those areas. The mall, which was planned by the art department, contains rocks and boulders from the Smoky Valley, combined with shrubs and trees to give the patios and planters natural accents. These attractive areas were designated the Miller-Stromquist Mall in 1971 in memory of Mr. and Mrs. Charles A. Miller and the Reverend and Mrs. Luther Stromquist (Rev. Stromquist, '03), former residents of Longmont, Colorado. A gift from Mr. and Mrs. Carl A. Miller (Lorraine Stromquist, '31) in memory of their parents was used to develop the mall.

In the process of change the marble statue of Dr. Carl Swensson, which had been raised in front of Old Main in 1907 with love and esteem, was moved to the west end of the mall on former Swensson Street, facing west. It stands there still as a symbol of love and esteem for today and tomorrow. This generation of Bethany students refers affectionately to Bethany's great founder as "Dr. Carl."[10]

When the Reverend Axel Beckman, chairman of the board of directors, presented his report to the Central States Synod in April, 1970, he stated: "Bethany's song is a hymn of praise these days, and it seems to have only crescendos, no diminuendos." The meaning of that declaration was fully understood on Sunday, October 18, 1970, a "Day of Dedication," when four new buildings were formally dedicated. No event in the history of the College had been similar in relative magnitude since the dedication of Old Main in 1887. The great day started with a service of thanksgiving in Presser Hall at which Dr. Robert J. Marshall, president of the Lutheran Church in America, was the principal speaker. The large congregation then shared in the dedication of the Wallerstedt Social Science Center, the Wallerstedt Library, the Mingenback Art Center, and the Warner Residence Hall.

Two buildings, the social science center and the library, form the Wallerstedt Learning Center, named in honor of Mr. and Mrs. Alvar G. Wallerstedt, Bethany benefactors. Two areas were memorialized for B.G. Grondal, long-time Lindsborg photographer, and Samuel F. Johnson, Bethany friend, through respective gifts by Mr. and Mrs. Paul Nels Carlson, Seattle, and Herbert Johnson, Salina. A third area was named in honor of Mr. and Mrs. Paul Nels Carlson (Edith Grondal), '06. Architectural plans were drawn by Shaver and Company, Salina. The builder was J. S. Frank Construction Company, Salina.

The library and audio-visual building provides on three levels the following facilities: on the lower level, the media center with a foreign language laboratory, listening rooms, a dial access retrieval system, seminar rooms, and the Swedish library; the second level contains reading rooms, open stacks, periodical areas, offices and cataloging room; the top level makes available research and reference rooms. Individual carrels and study tables are available on all levels. The building is designed to furnish space for 90,000 volumes. Shaver and Company, Salina, were the architects. The general contractor was Abbott Construction, Inc., Salina.

Both buildings of the Wallerstedt Learning Center are carpeted and air-conditioned. The space is attractively arranged and beautifully decorated. The cost of construction and furnishings of the two buildings was in excess of one million dollars. Reverend Harvey Prinz, president of the Central States Synod, conducted the dedication rites.

The Mingenback Art Center was the third building dedicated that

WALLERSTEDT LEARNING CENTER is now at the heart of the campus.

Dr. Robert Marshall, President Hahn, Dr. Axel Beckman, Chaplain Stanley Swanson, Dr. Harvey Prinz, Dr. Philip Wahlberg, and Dr. Franklin Heglund process for a service of thanksgiving on Day of Dedication, October 18, 1970.

Part of the crowd at Wallerstedt Learning Center dedication.

Above: WARNER RESIDENCE HALL. Below: MINGENBACK ART CENTER.

An announcement of Day of Dedication.

day. The Reverend Philip L. Wahlberg, Jr., president of the Texas-Louisiana Synod, was in charge of the dedication. This excellent facility was named in memory of Julia J. Mingenback, mother of Mr. E. C. Mingenback, chairman of the board of the Alliance Insurance companies, McPherson. A gift of $100,000.00 from the Mingenback Foundation was supplemented by $100,000.00 from the J. M. McDonald Foundation, Hastings, Nebraska, and by gifts from the Kresge Foundation, Birmingham, Michigan, and by funds from the Texas-Louisiana Synod churches. The facilities include well-equipped studios for drawing, painting, printmaking, sculpture, ceramics, faculty studio-offices, an exhibition room for student works, a small library and conference room, an all-purpose classroom-studio, a wood-working room, and a photographic dark room. The architect was Shaver and Company and the general contractor was Commercial Construction, Inc., McPherson. The Mingenback Art Center is located near the Birger Sandzén Memorial Gallery in the south section of Presser Hall block.

The events of the great day were concluded with the dedication of Warner Residence Hall by the Reverend Franklin C. Heglund, president of the Rocky Mountain Synod. This coeducational hall, which is designed to house 116 students in suites on three of the four floors, includes twenty-nine double-room suites, private floor lounges, a public lounge, a conference room, and an apartment for the residence director. The building is carpeted and air-conditioned. Named in recognition of a $40,-000.00 gift by Mr. and Mrs. Walter Warner, Salina, Kansas, it was financed principally by a $613,000.00 government loan. The hall was built by the J.S. Frank Construction Company, Salina. The architect was Shaver and Company, Salina. Warner Hall serves as a coeducational dormitory during the academic year and provides excellent facilities for conferences and continuing education in the summer months.

A crowd of 2,500 people had witnessed a great achievement in the events of that day. Those in attendance included Governor Robert Docking of Kansas and other dignitaries and many friends. *The Hutchinson*

News in a full report of the activities wrote: "It was called a 'Day of Dedication' but it seemed more of a day of miracles."[11]

In a statement remarkable for its clarity and content, President Hahn early had affirmed his faith in the future of Bethany College. In 1967, writing in the context of the status study of the board of college education of the Lutheran Church in America in 1966, which stated, "Bethany will need miracles to survive significantly as an independent college in Lindsborg," President Hahn declared: "Only God can make a miracle, yet men can pray for one and engage in efforts which will effect great positive change. This is our simple contention, for we firmly believe not only that it can be done, but the process has already begun at Bethany College." He then identified forcefully the "four essentials" required "to make a miracle": "First, the effort must have purpose," pointing to the recently adopted "Aims of the College," involving the training of youth "for a life of selfless service to God and Country." "Second, there must be detailed and effective planning." The third essential is "participation." Finally, "persistence. Success at Bethany College requires long range and untiring dedication to the task at hand." The great events of the "Day of Dedication" witnessed magnificently the achievement of Dr. Hahn's declaration of faith."[12]

When President Hahn reflected during the "Day of Dedication" about recent achievements at Bethany, he observed: "If tomorrow finds you with a sigh of satisfaction that Bethany has indeed arrived, you've missed the point of October 18, 1970. But if you leave these premises with the renewed commitment to move on with the mission that now has an increasingly firm rooting, then, we have reached a more clear understanding."[13]

The seriousness of President Hahn's dedication received magnificent confirmation on October 2, 1972, when the $11,055,000.00 Centennial Decade Development Program was launched. Intensive preparation formed the prelude to the announcement of the magnificent design for Bethany's future at a combined college convocation and special Town Hall meeting at Presser Hall. Bethany's president outlined the nine-year program which had been prepared "following a detailed study of our long-range needs in the areas of academic and student support, new and renovated facilities, and general college advancement through endowment growth." Funds would be sought for three areas: endowment, $5,000,000.00; academic programs, $4,630,000.00; and facility development, $1,425,000.00.

The program also presented a detailed analysis of the proposed use of funds: 1. *Endowment:* professorships, $1,500,000.00; student scholarships, $1,000,000.00; library fund, $500,000.00; departmental programs, $500,000.00; excellence fund, $1,500,000.00. 2. *Academic development:* faculty development and support, $1,600,000.00; student aid, $1,330,000.00; academic support (including library), $900,000.00; current needs and contingencies, $800,000.00. 3. *Facility development:* center for religion and performing arts, $300,000.00; Presser Hall (renovation), $80,000.00; student health center, $25,000.00; indoor swimming pool, $250,000.00; building and grounds center, $200,000.00; Pihlblad Memorial Union (renovation), $150,000.00; Presser Hall pipe organ, $100,000.00; other renovation, $320,000.00.[14]

Planning for the Centennial Decade Development Program also included a carefully-drafted design for leadership to implement the goals. The President's Advisory Council presented thirty representative and distinguished men and women. They declared in a leadership statement: "It is our pleasurable task to share in the revolutionary new developments taking place at Bethany. We are proud of its academic development and equally proud of its physical growth and fiscal progress that have accompanied it. As we share in the progress of Bethany, we share also in the responsibility for achieving these goals." Dr. and Mrs. Alvar Wallerstedt, Pittsburgh, Pennsylvania, were designated as honorary co-chairpersons; Edward Bittner, Kansas City, Missouri, banker, serves as chairman of the Council; Lester Woodward, Denver attorney, is chairman of annual funding; Robert Sunderland, Kansas City, Missouri, business and finance executive, is responsible for capital funding; and Russ Anderson, Emporia attorney and businessman, is chairman of endowment funding.[15]

The Centennial program for the enrichment of the life of the College was auspiciously launched with the immediate announcement that gifts totaling $570,000.00 already had been received toward the goal. The four gifts were as follows: $45,000.00 from the Kresge Foundation; $75,000.00 from Mr. and Mrs. Gene Burnett of Lawrence, Kansas, for renovation of the music department facilities; $200,000.00 from the Burnett family for the construction of a new building to be named the Burnett Center for Religion and the Performing Arts; and $250,000.00 for the establishment of the Mary Mingenback Distinguished Professor of Art. Mrs. Mingenback's generous personal gift established the first endowed professorship at Bethany. In commenting on this gift Mrs. Mingenback said: "After my husband and I helped make it possible to build the new art center at Bethany College, through the Julia J. Mingenback Foundation, it was my decision then to establish a distinguished professorship in art to assist in underwriting the program."[16]

Progress was soon made in implementing the Centennial program. Ray Kahmeyer, head of the art department, was appointed the first Mary Mingenback Distinguished Professor of Art, effective September, 1973. Professor Kahmeyer, who received undergraduate and graduate degrees from Kansas State University, had a splendid record as a teacher and as a creative artist, especially in ceramics.

The Swenson Chapel in Burnett Center for Religion and the Performing Arts.

The dedication of the Burnett Center for Religion and the Performing arts, April 28, 1974.

In April, 1973, the DeWitt Center for Music in Presser Hall was dedicated in memory of Dr. Thomas D. DeWitt, D.O., '53. The complete renovation and enrichment of facilities on the second and third floors of the music building was made possible by the $75,000.00 gift from Dr. DeWitt's sister and her husband, Mr. and Mrs. Gene Burnett, Lawrence, Kansas. Mrs. DeWitt was Evelyn Morton, former Bethany student. The newly refurbished area provided attractive and functional classrooms and studios. Carpeting and appropriate decor produced a transformation of old areas. A special feature was the Wurlitzer Music Laboratory on second floor, which was made possible by a $45,000.00 gift from the Kresge Foundation, Birmingham, Michigan. Twelve student electronic pianos with earphone-microphone headsets and one instructor piano with a built-in communication center and keyboard visualizer enrich the instruction in piano.

In June, 1973, groundbreaking for the Burnett Center for Religion and the Performing Arts took place. This excellent facility was dedicated on Sunday, April 28, 1974, by the Reverend Paul D. Olson, pastor, Trinity Lutheran Church, Lawrence, Kansas. Dean Lloyd Foerster delivered the principal address. The building features a large multi-purpose stage in an auditorium with 243 permanent seats and a capacity of 300 by using temporary seats. A section of the auditorium, including 85 permanent seats, can be mechanically rotated to form a separate soundproof chapel with a permanent worship center and a new Reuter organ. The chapel has been designated as a memorial to Roy Bruce Swenson, son of Mr. and Mrs. Roy Swenson, Washington, D.C. The Burnett Center will serve the college effectively for drama presentations, recitals and concerts, chapel services, and a classroom and meeting area. Several of the beautiful stained glass windows from the former chapel in Old Main are incorporated in the structure. The $300,000.00 facility was designed by the Shaver Partnership, Salina. The builder was Busboom and Rauh, Salina.

Although new facilities graced the campus with attractiveness and utility, improvements were also made in other buildings. In 1972 Deere Hall was completely remodeled and divided into two units with the resident head's office and apartments in the central area. In the same year the first floor and the lower level of Presser Hall were redesigned and renovated with the result that an observer declared: "This can't be the same place." Administrative offices were rearranged, paneling and new lighting were installed, floors were carpeted, a greatly needed conference room was created on first floor, and the two areas were attractively redecorated. The first floor is known as the Rouback Administrative Unit as a memorial to Miss Hannah Rouback, Gorham, Kansas, and her parents. The latter were Swedish immigrants. Bethany was designated as one of the primary recipients of the Rouback Foundation earnings, which have periodically enriched the college's program and facilities.

Substantial improvements were made in the Pihlblad Memorial Union during 1973. The renovation and enlargement provided fine additions to the facilities and made possible the increase of services. The project was financed by a loan of $135,000.00 from the Federal Housing and Urban Development Administration and by a gift of $40,000.00 from Robert Sunderland through the Lester T. Sunderland Foundation, Kansas City, Missouri.

In September, 1973, President Hahn announced that Dr. and Mrs. Alvar G. Wallerstedt, Pittsburgh, Pennsylvania, great Bethany friends and benefactors, had made a $100,000.00 challenge gift for the endowment fund if this gift were matched by the end of the year. This generous action elicited a heartening and prompt response. Toward the end of December President Hahn announced that $118,800.00 had been raised to match the Wallerstedt gift. The president pointed out that $111,000.00 had been raised from twenty-three benefactors in amounts ranging from $1,000.00 to $20,000.00 and that the balance was contributed by nearly 100 persons. The permanent endowment fund was thus enriched by more than $200,000.00.

Bethany's history since the presidency of Dr. Arvin W. Hahn beginning in September, 1967, chronicled magnificent progress in identifying college goals, in reconstructing the curriculum to achieve the declared purposes, in enlarging the financial resources, and in providing the physical facilities for making possible effective campus living and learning. In the midst of this great progress, other outstanding gains were also recorded. Enrollment statistics mounted with unfailing regularity, operational budgets soared but so did the financing with the result that large budgets were unfailingly balanced, the curriculum was enriched, accreditation was reaffirmed and new accreditation achieved, faculty capability and welfare were enhanced, and the esteem for Bethany reached into ever greater constituencies. These developments will furnish the content of the next phase of the history of the new Bethany.

Endowment funding under the Centennial Decade Development Program, 1972-81, is highlighted in this display case in Presser Hall lobby.

8.

New Horizons
1967-1974

A college achieves its purpose only if students come to the campus in sufficient numbers to share in the program of studies and in the many other aspects of college life. The chronicle of Bethany's history in this period presents another impressive chapter. The enrollment increased by 43 percent from 517 in September, 1967, to 737 in September, 1973. There were 20 part-time students in the former and 87 in the latter year. This is a remarkable achievement in a period when either leveling-off or a substantial decline occurred in many colleges and universities. This was the eighth consecutive year that the size of the student body had increased.[1]

Enrollment statistics indicate the broad geographic distribution of Bethany students in 1973. Twenty-four states were represented. Kansas students numbered 497 with 101 coming from adjoining states. New Jersey, 30, Illinois, 28, and New York, 20, provided the next highest numbers of students. A modest number was from abroad. Thirteen religious denominations and organizations were represented. Lutherans numbered 345 of the 688 identified, followed by Methodist, 96, Roman Catholic, 48, and Presbyterian and Baptist, 31 each.[2]

Bethany has maintained an aggressive and well-planned program of student recruitment and admission in recent years. The organizational pattern provides for student, alumni, and church participation in advising and counseling high school students about the College program. The dean of admissions and several admissions counselors and others develop many direct contacts with students in various areas of the nation. Edwin A. Gorsky was director of admissions from 1967-73. In 1973 Leon Burch, '64, succeeded him with the title, dean of admissions.

Substantial gains were recorded during this period in faculty academic achievement and graduate degrees. In 1973 President Hahn reported that members of the faculty with terminal degrees (persons with doctorate or recognized professional degrees or certificates in certain fields) had increased since 1967 from six to thirteen and that the number of staff members working toward terminal degrees had increased from three to nine. The various programs and grants for enriching the faculty were becoming increasingly productive.

In the annual report of President Hahn to the delegates of the Central States Synod in April, 1973, a significant analysis of faculty services was presented: "When comparing 1967 with 1972 faculty-student ratios, it must be noted that about 60 percent more students are being taught with virtually the same number of instructional staff, thus bringing us to highly desirable levels of efficiency in that category."[3]

A memorable gain affecting the entire life and achievement of the college was the substantial improvement in the historically inadequate faculty salaries. In the period from 1966-67 to 1973-74 the average salary increased from $7,575.00 to $10,389.00 and the average for a full professor from $8,720.00 to $13,508.00 during the same period.[4]

The curriculum provides the framework in which teaching and learning is achieved. The program established in 1968 was revised three years later. The general education requirements were drastically reduced from fifteen and one-half to six courses. The following studies meet the general education requirements in the new program: religion, one course; basic communications, one course; and four courses determined in the following manner: two courses selected from each of two divisions outside the student's major with each of the courses being in a different subject area. No study or proficiency test in foreign languages is required for a degree. The six courses constitute a minimum but additional general education courses may be elected. Teacher education candidates must include more courses in general education in order to meet certification requirements.[5]

The three divisions of the curriculum are: 1. *Humanities:* with departments in art, English, speech and drama, foreign languages, music, religion and philosophy. 2. *Natural Science:* with departments in life and earth science and physical science and mathematics. 3. *Social Science:* with departments in behaviorial science, education, and history. The curriculum also provides a variety of courses leading to certification in elementary and secondary education. Majors are available in the following departments: art, English, French, German, music, biology, chemistry, mathematics, economics-business, social work, sociology, elementary education, health and physical education, history-political science, contract major, and divisional majors. A revision in 1971 enriched the area of independent study. Five courses in levels II and III are available for qualified students with approved projects, readings, and

President and Mrs. Hahn visit with freshmen students.

ARVIN W. HAHN

research. The academic year 1971 also inaugurated a new social work major based upon ten courses.

In 1973 the three-year bachelor of arts program was introduced. The purpose of this new arrangement was to enable intellectually superior students who were certain of their educational and vocational objectives to complete the undergraduate course of study in three years. Specific guidelines were established to insure the capability of the student and the integrity of the degree.

Another new development became a formal academic policy with the establishment of an experience-based education program in 1973 following extensive study and experience with pilot programs. Dean Lloyd C. Foerster described this addition to the curriculum: "The intent of this program is to enable students to engage in work experiences which provide a meaningful interaction between the world of ideas and the world of work and which provide career direction." The program is designed to give the student "an added dimension to his total educational experience which would not normally be available on the college campus, providing the student with opportunities for expanding both general and specialized knowledge and for personal development, self-management, career orientation, and preparation."[6]

In the academic year 1973-74 there were experience-based programs involving students in the areas of social work, accounting, retailing, banking, probation, law enforcement, church music, and museum work. A $20,000.00 grant from the federal government was received for the payment of administrative costs in the program, which is also known as cooperative education. Dr. Richard Moore was appointed director of the program beginning with the academic year 1973-74.

The academic year 1973-74 introduced freshmen students to what is known as the "Neighborhood Concept" in their residence halls. The program, which emerged from a Danforth Foundation Institute, was designed to enrich the life of first-year students. The participants are organized into neighborhoods of fifteen students each in men's and women's residence halls on the basis of geographical, cultural, and high school rank heterogeneity. All members have one identical course as a basic unit of common interest. Each group is staffed with a resident hall assistant who works under the direction of the resident head and dean of student affairs.

The responsibility of the College to individuals and society beyond the undergraduate years was recognized in 1971 with the establishment of a formal program of continuing education. The Reverend Carl L. Hansen, '60, assistant professor of religion and philosophy, was appointed director. The program provides for seminars and workshops on campus and for off-campus institutes. In the first year seven seminars were held on campus during the summer for two or three days on the theme, "God's People Facing Today and Tomorrow." There were 570 participants in 1971 with the number increasing to 1000 the following year. Interesting and varied programs bring adults to the campus where they are housed in the attractive and comfortable Warner Residence Hall. Grants from the Aid Association for Lutherans Insurance Company, Appleton, Wisconsin, from the Lutheran Brotherhood Insurance Company, Minneapolis, Minnesota, and from the Lutheran Church in America have been used in supporting the continuing education program.

In January, 1974, a project was shared by 200 Lindsborg residents in the program designated the January "Other Term." Fifteen non-credit courses including such areas as auto mechanics, bread making, conversational Swedish, beginning bridge, and the President of the United States and executive privilege, were presented.

The 4-1-4 curriculum adopted in 1968 provides great flexibility and unique opportunity for learning through the four weeks interterm. A three-week pilot program with twelve courses involved twenty percent of the students and thirty-five percent of the faculty in 1968. The enthusiastic response to the program resulted in a steady enrichment and expansion. In January, 1973, thirty-five interterm courses were available on campus and others in Mexico and in Europe. The campus courses included traditional and highly innovative opportunities.

The curriculum and courses of study form a central part of the college experience which also is greatly enriched by the non-academic resources. Student services are organized with the dean of student affairs as the chief administrative officer. Other persons with important responsibility for student life are the assistant dean of student affairs, the college chaplain, the director of student aid, the college nurses, and the heads of residence halls. The program is carried out through faculty and student committees. Organizational patterns provide for student government, a Pan-Hellenic Council, dormitory council, and a wide variety of other groups. Personal and group counseling are readily available through professional personnel and an open-door policy. The health service provides for the welfare of students in that area. Fred Ray has served as dean of students since 1970. His predecessor was Edward Brake.

A vital educational experience is closely identified with adequate library and related resources. The Wallerstedt Learning Center provides fine facilities and space. The value of such facilities depends upon materials and service. Again, the record is impressive. Library expenditures increased from $37,901.00 in 1966-67 to $84,120.00 in 1973-74. The book collection grew from 45,332 to 64,542 volumes. Current newspapers and periodicals number 503. The learning resources have been enriched from time to time by federal government grants. In 1969 a $12,000.00 grant was received to update and improve the instructional program through the acquisition of maps, transparencies, records, 8 mm. loops, films, and multi-media materials. Mrs. Dorothe Homan has been head librarian since 1966.[7]

Academic resources and programs of learning have been enriched through membership in the Associated Colleges of Central Kansas organized in 1966. This consortium is composed of Bethany College, Bethel College, Kansas Wesleyan, McPherson College, Sterling College, and Tabor College. The colleges started with a budget of $27,600.00 in 1966-67, which expanded to $374,072.00 in 1972-73. The member colleges contributed $72,000.00 that year. Programs under the Title II and Title III of the Higher Education Act of 1965 made available $300,000.00.

The resources of the ACCK involve several areas. The combined catalogue of books owned by the six colleges lists 300,000 entries. The regular courier service makes books and periodicals readily accessible for each institution. Visiting professors employed by the ACCK enrich the curriculum in various fields. Regular academic credit courses are provided by the ACCK for students of all colleges. In 1972-73 seventeen courses were presented as coordinated by the dean of instruction of the ACCK. The consortium makes available computer resources for teaching and administrative purposes. The College is linked to a computer system located in the headquarters at McPherson. The Bethany teletype terminal is installed in Wallerstedt Library.

An important evaluation of a college occurs through the accreditation process. The regional organization for accrediting colleges and universities is the North Central Association of Colleges and Secondary

Schools through its commission on colleges and universities. Representatives of the commission visited the campus in April and July of 1970 in the normal 10-year cycle of review. Prior to that time administrators and faculty had engaged in a self-evaluation and analysis which produced comprehensive materials in the "Institutional Profile" and "Basic Institutional Data." Dean Edward Lindell of the College of Arts and Sciences of the University of Denver rendered valuable service as the North Central consultant beginning in September, 1967, in preparation for the review. Accreditation, first gained in 1932, was reaffirmed by the association for the normal period.

Comprehensive studies and self-appraisal preceded the visit of the accrediting team of the National Council for the Accreditation of Teacher Education to the campus in 1971. Bethany had been the first private college in Kansas to be a member of the American Colleges for the Accreditation of Teacher Education (ACATE), and when this organization was merged to form the NCATE, the college's accreditation was continued. However, the College lost this professional accreditation in the 1960s. There was, therefore, great satisfaction when the programs in elementary and secondary education were once again accredited in May, 1972, retroactive to September, 1971. This status is exceedingly important to Bethany with its historical and current major emphasis upon teacher education. Not only is this accreditation important to graduates seeking positions for the first time, but they and alumni profit from the certification by a number of states of the graduates of institutions accredited by the NCATE.

The expansion of programs of instruction, student services, learning resources, and auxiliary activities required a vast increase in the budget for operating expenses. The extent is dramatically demonstrated by comparing the operating budget for 1967-68 of approximately $1,313,686.00 with that of 1973-74 of $2,199,273.00. The decisive factor is that the current budget has been balanced every year since fiscal year 1967. President Hahn, Kenneth Sjogren, director of public affairs, and their associates and the board of directors have produced a record of distinction in an era when large deficits in operating budgets were common for private colleges.[8]

The splendid achievement financially during these years is shown convincingly by the facts which follow. The annual alumni fund increased in the period from $29,255.00 in 1966-67 to $95,888.00 in 1973-74. The sustaining fund, supported by Lindsborg citizens and other friends, increased from $80,919.00 to $86,136.00 during these years. The allocation from the Lutheran Church maintained a steady range of more than $100,000.00 annually, reaching a high of $130,600.00 in 1967-68. The Kansas Foundation for Private Colleges provided approximately $24,000.00 for current operations in 1973-74 in contrast with about $14,000.00

in 1966-67. The endowment fund increased in this period by $602,802.00 providing a total endowment fund of $1,613,973.00. Gifts and grants from all sources—church, alumni, special funds, capital funds, and governmental grants—reached the handsome sum of $1,017,077.00 in 1973-74. Only $44,046.00 of this amount was from government grants. The total assets of the College were $9,081,220.00 at the end of the academic year 1973-74 in contrast with $4,831,528.00 in 1966-67. The liabilities, principally in the form of amortized loans on dormitories, were $1,518,600.00.[9]

In the period of extensive capital gains and the balancing of ever increasing budgets for current operations, substantial gifts to the endowment were recorded including $85,000.00 from Dora Durham, '01, '18, Beloit; $32,000.00 from Dr. Anna Rimol, '05, Norway; and $40,000.00 from Mrs. E. K. (Anna) Nordin, Salina. These bequests were designated primarily for the scholarship fund.

Student aid of various forms is a vital aspect in building and sustaining enrollment. State and federal scholarships and grants have introduced a vital element in recent years. The total scholarship and student aid in 1973-74 was $638,218.00. College scholarship programs provided $137,000.00. The largest single item was the tuition grant program of the State of Kansas which made available $216,625.00 for 228 students. The next largest item was $195,000.00 in the federal government's national direct student loan program for 219 students. Lesser amounts of federal student aid came from grant programs, college work study, and other loan funds. The total need of 190 Bethany students was met in the academic year 1973-74. Fifty-six percent of the total need of applicants for financial aid was met.[10]

In a unique presentation to the synod in May, 1974, President Hahn summarized composite and substantial gains by citing what he called "Vitality Factors," in contrasting the situation in 1972-73 with that of 1966-67. In the area of non-fiscal "Vitality Factors," the following increases were recorded: overall enrollment, 51 percent; enrollment of low income students, 75 percent; minority students, 600 percent; entering freshmen in upper one-half of high school class, 27 percent; student-faculty ratio, 31 percent; overall student retention, 11 percent; faculty with doctorates, 120 percent and volumes in library, 59 percent.[11]

The same report by Bethany's president showed for the same years an increase of 91 percent in educational expenditures; 118 percent in library investment; 308 percent in student aid expenditures; 139 percent in income from tuition; 205 percent in alumni giving; and overall operating gift income, 54 percent. This magnificent achievement constitutes a record that is distinctive among institutions of higher learning in the United States during this period.[12]

The achievements in finance represent fine leadership by President

Hahn and the creation of a table of organization that includes well-placed personnel and comprehensive as well as detailed guidelines of operation. The administrative organization of the College includes five divisions: admissions, academic affairs, business affairs, student affairs, and public affairs. The latter division is composed of public relations, alumni affairs and parents' program, deferred giving, church relations, and development.

Kenneth Sjogren, '57, is director of public affairs and director of development. He is responsible for the overall program and management of the public affairs division. He joined the Bethany staff in 1961 as director of publicity and alumni affairs. He has been director of development since 1967. Sjogren's energetic and imaginative leadership and his close identification with President Hahn has enabled him to render excellent service to his alma mater. He was recognized by fellow Bethanyites in 1970 as a recipient of the alumni award of merit. As alumni secretary he was responsible for establishing the Phone-a-rama and Beth-a-matic programs for fund raising. He has had a leading role in developing later fund raising projects.

The division of public affairs relies upon well-established as well as more recent organizations and groups to support the College. The alumni association constitutes a basic element. Alumni giving, as indicated, has exceeded $80,000.00 annually in recent years. L. Stanley Talbott, '46, is director of alumni affairs. Since his appointment in 1967 Talbott has strengthened alumni relations through organizational and publication activities. The quarterly *Bethany Magazine* and special bulletins keep alumni well-informed. An expanded number of Bethany clubs and the appointment of class secretaries strengthen the bonds with the College. Talbott organized the Bethany parents' association in September, 1969, "to give parents a sense of direct participation in the affairs of the College and to be a source of great encouragement and assistance to Bethany College." The organization has officers and a regular schedule of meetings.

In 1970 a new organization, the Ambassadors Club, was inaugurated for supporting the current operating budget. Membership is based upon gifts in various categories annually from $100.00 as an associate to $1,000.00 as a challenger. In October, 1970, an anonymous donor challenged alumni and friends of the College to respond by promising $12,500.00 providing $87,500.00 was raised by June 1, 1971, when another gift of $12,500.00 would be added. There were 579 members of the Ambassadors Club in 1974. This unit provided gifts of $147,186.00 in 1973-74. Kenneth Sjogren is responsible for developing this program.

James Attleson, director of deferred giving since July, 1970, has responsibility for promoting various programs which identify opportunities for long-range support. In October, 1972, the "Scroll of Immortals" program was launched. Persons contributing through an estate or other type of planned giving will have their names, or the names of persons they wish to memorialize, inscribed on a Bethany "Scroll of Immortals." On Founder's Day, October, 1973, only one year after the new program was inaugurated, ninety-eight gifts were acknowledged on this very special scroll.

The various aspects of the college's program are described and interpreted through a variety of effective publications and press releases. Substantial expansion of this phase of Bethany's program has occurred during the tenure of A. John Pearson, former Bethany student, director of public relations since August, 1970. Pearson is also responsible for the establishment of very unique and successful newspaper and yearbook summer workshops for high school students.

Milo Miller is assistant to the president and director of church relations. He assists the president in assembling reports, in coordinating activities among functional offices of the College, and he serves as director of church relations.

William Taylor, '40, has been business manager and treasurer since 1952, thus serving with five of Bethany's eight presidents. He is in charge of all financial matters. He serves as an advisory member of the board of directors on fiscal matters. Campus building and grounds, new construction and auxiliary activities come under the jurisdiction of this office. The business manager-treasurer is supported by assistant business manager, office manager, superintendent of buildings and grounds, manager of the bookstore, director of food service, and other personnel. Mrs. Harriett Westman has served in the treasurer's office since 1948. She is currently chief accountant and office manager.

The manifold activities and programs of the college—curriculum, teaching, student services, learning resources, religious programs, campus facilities, public relations, and business affairs—are developed for the high purpose of providing meaningful Christian higher education. This central responsibility was given a new and distinct emphasis in April, 1972, when a covenant was drawn up between the College and the Central States Synod of the Lutheran Church in America, and later with the Rocky Mountain and Texas-Louisiana synods.

In this four-part document the College reaffirmed its purpose as described in Article I of its constitution revised May, 1968, as follows: "The object of this institution shall be to serve Christ and His Church by training young men and women who seek a liberal education under Christian auspices and to acquaint them with the cultural, intellectual, and religious forces in the field of higher education." The Synod, in keeping with Article VIII, section 2 of its constitution, "accepts and sustains a supporting relationship to Bethany College . . . with a three-fold concern for its character as a Christian institution of learning, its academic excellence, and its material welfare." The document concludes, over the signature of the president of the Synod and the president of Bethany College, that the Synod and the College "hereby acknowledge their mutual desire and intention to continue a relationship, and, to preserve and enhance the vitality of the relationship, and, to review this covenant at least every eight years."[13]

In 1968 the College adopted as its slogan, "Bethany College, A Retreat For Learning." The emphasis was upon the unique cultural resources of Lindsborg and the role of learning for abundant living. The symbol, a white bird in flight on a blue background, was adopted to express the intent of the slogan. Harold "Cotton" Smith, Jr., former student 1958-60, was its creator. This striking symbol, a progressive form of Scandinavian design, had two parts: a boxed trademark and a logotype. "The new mark represents freedom and is a symbol of soaring and learning," according to Smith. "Symbolizing light as Christian light, through the open tip of the wing, the mark is modern, yet the symbol of flight is very old." The new symbol does not replace the official college seal adopted in 1907, with the lamb and the cross, and the legend, *Domini Domino* (Of the Lord and for the Lord).[14]

There was something dramatically prophetic in the banner headline of the first issue of a new year for the *Messenger,* September 7, 1967, during the early presidency of Dr. Arvin W. Hahn. In bold letters these words stood out: "A New Administration—A New Bethany." Although this declaration described the shape of things to come, the new Bethany found its resources in the old Bethany, rediscovered, revitalized, enriched, and thrust into the future with faith, wisdom, and energy. Moreover, the sacrifices and struggles of the past decades took on new and happy dimensions in the magnificent achievement of the present and in the great promise of the future. In his first address at the inaugural service, Dr. Hahn had declared: "I proudly assume the responsibilities of the office of president of this great college, for great it is and great it shall be." This statement, like the *Messenger's* comment, had about it a prophetic quality.[15]

Symbol and fact of the esteem in which the Bethany president is held was shown convincingly in April, 1970, when the students observed "Dr. Arvin W. Hahn Appreciation Day." This was a festive day of joy and gratitude. Dr. Hahn was presented a shield-shaped plaque with this inscription: "Outstanding Leadership Award, presented to Dr. Arvin Hahn, with sincere appreciation for 'making a miracle,' by the Associated Students of Bethany College." At the banquet the Bethany president received a standing ovation that will linger long in the memory of the large crowd in attendance. In reporting the event the *Messenger* referred to the President's Ball in which "the band played the rich swing music of Hahn's youth." This was an occasion also for paying tribute to

Mrs. Judie Hahn, the president's wife, who has established her own areas of great esteem for fine service to the College and the community.

Recognition for the splendid achievement of Bethany under the leadership of President Hahn continues to be extensive and complimentary. The remarkable gains in enrollment and financial support have been heralded by the press on a nationwide basis. A splendid feature article by Bryce Nelson in the *Los Angeles Times,* August 29, 1970, was syndicated for national distribution. When President Hahn declined an attractive position as a college president in the spring of 1974, one of several available to him in recent years, a grateful college and constituency again expressed their high esteem and appreciation. A meaningful response occurred in a highly commendatory editorial in the *Wichita Eagle* in March, 1974: "It's good news for Kansas that Dr. Arvin Hahn has rejected the offer of the presidency of a larger college and will remain at Bethany. The state needs people like him . . . . Dr. Hahn has great plans for Bethany, and it will not be surprising to see them fulfilled, for he has vision and energy, and his community supports him. That's a winning combination and serves as an example for the rest of Kansas."[16]

President Hahn has always emphasized that team effort is the decisive element in great achievement. The capacity to accomplish that objective is abundantly demonstrated in the recent history of the College and contains abiding resources for the future as Bethany College moves toward the centennial observance of its founding in 1981.

It's someplace special at Bethany, as students and president get together to talk and to discuss concerns.

THE MILL ON THE SMOKY   *Birger Sandzén*

CORONADO HEIGHTS   *Birger Sandzén*

PART TWO
9.

Colleagues and Co-Workers

In slightly more than nine decades of Bethany history, approximately 440 persons have served on the faculty and in related academic positions on a full-time basis. This includes all departments and divisions. Loyalty to the College has been a distinctive mark of identification.

A very special group of individuals taught at Bethany for fifty years or more. They include names that are written large in the history of the College: Hagbard Brase, Emil O. Deere, Thure Jaderborg, Birger Sandzén, and Oscar Thorsen. Serving forty years or more were Lennard Gunnerson, Oscar Lofgren, Annie Theo. Swensson, Ernst F. Pihlblad, Jens Stensaas, Ellen Strom, John E. Welin, and Hjalmar Wetterstrom. The honor roll of thirty or more years of service includes C. F. Carlbert, Anna Carlson, Ray D. Hahn, J. L. Hermanson, Anna Marm, P. H. Pearson, and Arvid Wallin. In addition, those on the honor roll for membership of twenty-five years or more are Walter Brown, George W. Kleihege, and Amanda Magnusson. Seven persons identified with Bethany for twenty years or more are A. A. Abercrombie, Ina Bell Auld, Emory Lindquist, Ethel Palmquist, Gladys Peterson, Arthur Uhe, and Edla Wahlin. Four members of the faculty in 1974 belonged to this category: Lambert Dahlsten, Roger Thorstenberg, Leon Lungstrom, and Clara Tow.[1]

Bethany alumni have made fine contributions to the College as members of the faculty. Ten of the thirteen teachers who served forty years or more were Bethany graduates. In the total of 440 faculty members from 1881 to the academic year 1973-74, Bethany certificates or diplomas were held by 156 or 35.4 percent. In the years since 1930, the 227 new appointments have included 44 alumni or 19.3 percent. The large numbers of Bethanyites prior to 1930 is related in part to the faculty of the academy and business school. In addition to some highly esteemed

THE BETHANY COLLEGE FACULTY, 1888-89.

OSCAR THORSEN,
EMIL O. DEERE,
THURE JADERBORG

HAGBARD BRASE

BIRGER SANDZÉN

1925 Faculty Members

A current-day faculty meeting in the Blue and Yellow Room of Pihlblad Memorial Union.

non-alumni who gave their entire careers to Bethany, the loyalty of alumni to their alma mater has been a vital factor in providing good instructional personnel.

Instruction during the first year was provided by J. A. Udden as the only full-time teacher. Carl Swensson taught Christianity one hour each day. Edward Nelander became another full-time teacher in the second year, with C. G. Norman as an assistant. Nelander was elected *rektor,* or president in 1882, a position which he held until his resignation in 1889. In 1883 P. T. Lindholm and Miss Hulda Peterson joined the faculty. In 1884 Miss Ella Lawson was added to the teaching staff. Lindholm left his position in 1885. The faculty in 1885-86 consisted of Nelander, Christianity and pedagogy; Udden, natural science; Ella Lawson, English and civics; Miss Jo C. Harper, mathematics; Philip Thelander, Swedish and Latin; G. A. Andreen, English and German; and M. Österholm, natural science and geography.

Udden left the Bethany faculty at the end of the year 1887-88 to join the faculty at Augustana College. He had a distinguished career later as state geologist of Texas and was nationally known as a geologist. In 1886 W. A. Granville came to Bethany to teach business subjects and mathematics. He left at the end of the academic year 1890-91 to complete studies for the Ph.D. at Yale, where he became a member of the faculty. He was for many years president of Gettysburg College, Pennsylvania. J. E. Welin began in 1891 his academic career as a teacher in mathematics and natural history. He served Bethany with distinction for almost half a century. G. A. Andreen began his career at Bethany as a teacher of languages in 1885, and shared his fine talent until 1894. He then continued his studies at Yale where he received the Ph.D. degree and became a member of the faculty. He later served as president of Augustana College and Theological Seminary. J. E. Floren became a teacher of Swedish language and literature in 1891, serving for several years.

Although several outstanding teachers like Udden, Granville, and Andreen moved on to other academic assignments, the College was successful in attracting able replacements. In 1889 C. F. Peterson began a long career as a teacher of history that ended with his death in 1924. He changed his name to Carlbert and was known affectionately as "Doctor Put." He was vice-president for several years. P. H. Pearson joined the faculty at Bethany in 1891 as professor of English language and literature and served until 1920. Pearson was the author of several volumes on English and American literature. A popular lecturer, his career included an assignment with the U.S. Office of Education and as a professor at Upsala College, East Orange, New Jersey. A. W. Kjellstrand, an able instructor of Latin, came to Bethany in 1887; he served until 1895. He was succeeded by Ernst F. Pihlblad. An important addition to the instructional staff occurred when Frank Nelson became instructor in philosophy, methods, and education in the Normal Department in 1892. He was elected Kansas superintendent of public instruction for two terms, 1898-1902. He later was an effective fund raiser for the College. His career included the presidency of Minnesota College, Minneapolis, Minnesota.

Instruction in music began in 1882 with J. F. Anderson as the teacher. Mrs. Carl (Alma) Swensson, a fine organist and musician, taught the following year, and was joined in 1884 by Charles Purdy and Miss Ella Bengtson. In 1885, when the conservatory of music was established, N. A. Krantz, a graduate of the Royal Academy of Music, Stockholm, came to Bethany. He served until 1896. He conducted the "Messiah" chorus for several years. Krantz was the first of a distinguished succession of musicians on the Bethany faculty. In 1887 Victor Lund, a former student at the Royal Conservatory of Music, began his teaching. He was conductor of the "Messiah" chorus 1888-93. K. Döme Geza served from 1889-92 as instructor in violin. Franz Zedler, Stockholm, succeeded Döme Geza in 1893, and continued on the faculty until 1897. Sigfrid Laurin, a colorful personality from Sweden, was a piano teacher 1894-1904. Other music teachers in this early period were Edla Lund, G. Hapgood, and Hilma Blomgren.

When the business department was established in 1884, J. E. Gustus was engaged as the first teacher, a position he held until 1889. In 1889 A. A. Abercrombie, who had been an assistant in the department, became director of the department, a position which he held until 1896. He later rejoined the faculty. Other early teachers were Amelia Jaeger, Margaret E. King, and Hannah Anderson. The establishment of the model school in 1886 brought J. Lewis as the first teacher. Several persons served briefly in the succeeding years. Marie Malmberg taught in the model school for more than a decade beginning in 1895.

Instruction in art began with courses in drawing, water color, and oil painting in 1890. The first teacher was Lucy Osgood, 1890-92. Hannah Swensson, Marie Swensson, and Addie Covell taught during the next few years. Olof Grafstrom taught art from 1893 to 1897, when he joined the faculty of Augustana College. Carl Gustafson Lotave succeeded Grafstrom and continued in that position until 1899. Grafstrom and Lotave became well-known artists. A decisive year in Bethany's history occurred in 1894 when Birger Sandzén began his great career at the College which was continued for almost six decades. He became the principal teacher of art in 1899. Sandzén's great Bethany career is described elsewhere.[2]

When the twentieth anniversary was celebrated in May, 1901, Bethany's faculty consisted of distinguished academic and professional people. Such names as Carl Swensson, C. F. Carlbert, J. Emil Floren, P.

H. Pearson, J. E. Welin, John Ekholm, Birger Sandzén, Sigfrid Laurin, Samuel Thorstenberg, Ernst F. Pihlblad, and Theodore Lindberg were on the role from earlier years. New names included equally gifted persons. Carl Johns, instructor in natural science, had a distinguished career later as professor of chemistry at Yale. Vivian Henmon, professor of pedagogy, had an equally great career at the University of Wisconsin and became nationally known as joint creator of the famous Henmon-Nelson mental ability test. Hagbard Brase, graduate of the Royal Conservatory of Music, Stockholm, had recently joined the Bethany faculty as instructor in organ and harmony, and became the famous conductor of the Bethany College Oratorio Society. Oscar Lofgren, instructor in piano, later became dean of the College of Fine Arts. The names of Thure Jaderborg, instructor in voice, and Oscar Thorsen, instructor in piano, graced the faculty role the next year. This superior group of persons represents undoubtedly the most outstanding faculty in the history of the College. A similar period of greatness prevailed in the early period when a smaller faculty included Carl Swensson, J. A. Udden, Edward Nelander, W. A. Granville, and Gustav Andreen.

The roster of the faculty during the early decades of the twentieth century also included loyal and capable teachers. In the commercial department A. A. Abercrombie rejoined the faculty, teaching from 1906-18. He was a fine teacher and friend of students. His untimely death in the influenza epidemic of 1918 brought great sorrow. George E. Eberhardt taught commercial law, rapid calculation, and penmanship for more than a decade, 1893-1906. Students recall his effectiveness as a teacher and his patience as a counselor. When he resigned from the faculty he entered the banking business in Lindsborg.

Two outstanding musicians, Theodore Lindberg, '95, and Samuel Thorstenberg, '95, were faculty members in this era. Lindberg, who taught violin and conducted the symphony orchestra 1897-1906, was a splendid and popular musician. He was not only a fine violin virtuoso but he brought the symphony orchestra to a high level of achievement. The name of Samuel Thorstenberg plays a prominent role in the Bethany musical tradition. He was an excellent bass singer and teacher. His musicianship served him well as conductor of the oratorio society 1898-1909. Earl Rosenberg taught voice 1908-13 and conducted the oratorio society 1910-13. H. E. Malloy was a voice teacher 1912-14. He served as conductor of the oratorio society in 1914. Rosenberg and Malloy were fine musicians and teachers. Charles D. Wagstaff, who taught piano and theory 1893-1907, was one of the talented musicians on the faculty during this period.

Two teachers of language, G. A. Peterson ("Swede Pete") and Walter Petersen ("Greek Pete") joined the faculty in the latter part of the first decade of the new century. G. A. Peterson, Swedish born, a knowledgeable teacher of Swedish language and literature, impressed his students with his thorough methods and by his friendliness during his tenure, 1907-24. When he left Bethany, he joined the ministerium of the Augustana Lutheran Church. Dr. Walter Petersen was one of the outstanding scholars in the history of Bethany's faculty. In the period 1909-21 he was professor of Greek and philosophy. A Yale Ph.D. with extensive studies in Leipzig, he achieved high levels of excellence in the classroom. In 1919 he published a volume of translations, *Lyric Songs of the Greeks* and contributed articles to learned journals. Henry N. Olson, '01, professor of mathematics 1903-21, was a patient and dedicated teacher. He was quiet in manner but he was always helpful in working with students.

A unique pattern of loyalty and dedication is recorded in the careers of several fine musicians and teachers who devoted their lives to Bethany. Hagbard Brase and Oscar Thorsen were Swedish born and the others were children of Swedish immigrants. Brase, a faculty member 1900-53, studied at the College of Skara, at the Royal Conservatory of Music, Stockholm, and in Germany. Choral director, organist, composer, teacher—his achievement was distinguished in all his fields of professional activity. Famous conductor of the oratorio society, he founded and developed the a capella choir as an ensemble group that attained national recognition. Organ students recall his ability to interpret the score, to develop techniques, and to stimulate musicianship. Oscar Thorsen's, '02, career as a member of the faculty covered the years 1901-55. He early showed fine talent which was further developed by studies with well-known piano teachers in the United States and Germany. Sound musicianship and ceaseless interest in the arts marked him as a person of broad and deep culture. He was an effective and inspirational teacher. Oscar Thorsen was a generous person whose second story studio-apartment on the northwest corner of Main and Saline Streets became the center for hundreds of recitals and social functions. Oscar, as he was affectionately known, and "Sandy," his dog companion, were familiar sights on the streets of Lindsborg.

Oscar Lofgren, '02, served his alma mater with distinction from 1900-48 as teacher of piano and dean of fine arts. He continued postgraduate studies with American and German teachers. He had many loyal private pupils. He responded to the call of the College to become dean of fine arts in 1918. In that assignment he provided effective leadership in curriculum development and accreditation. He was an outstanding Kansas leader in the arts, serving in important offices of trust on a state-wide basis. Thure Jaderborg, '02, teacher of voice 1902-54, studied voice with New York teachers and coaches. His fine bass voice gained favorable reviews from the press and a large following from the public. His emphasis upon repertoire and the careful cultivation of the human voice provided important sources for the development of his students. A large number of his graduates became professional musicians.

Ellen Strom, '04, devoted her professional career to Bethany from 1906-1952. Miss Strom was a talented organist, serving the oratorio society in that capacity for several years, a fine conductor of children's choruses, and an effective teacher of keyboard harmony. Ellen Strom and her sister, Tillie, were generous in their hospitality as large numbers of students and colleagues visited in the Strom home. Hjalmar Wetterstrom, a native of Lindsborg and a Bethany graduate, devoted more than forty years of his life to the College, 1903-50. He was an excellent performer on the trumpet and an accomplished cellist. His natural gifts as a musician and his temperament made him a fine conductor of instrumental ensembles. A large number of band directors across several decades hold "Wet," as he was affectionately known, in kindly remembrance.

Currently with the above group of capable and long-tenured music teachers were other able and devoted colleagues. Arvid Wallin, '03, '05, was on the faculty for more than thirty years in two periods of service, 1909-20 and 1925-48. He was a highly esteemed teacher and a fine pianist. He served professionally as an accompanist. Wallin was also a talented organist who served as accompanist for the oratorio society for many years. He had also sung the tenor solos with the oratorio society in *Messiah* renditions. When Dr. Hagbard Brase retired as conductor of the society in 1946, Arvid Wallin was his logical and capable successor. Until death called him in 1948 in a critical illness, he was serving as conductor of the oratorio society and as professor of piano.

Walter Brown, instructor in woodwind instruments, was a member of the music faculty for more than twenty-five years, 1922-50. He was a fine performer on the clarinet and saxophone and a good teacher. He came to Bethany following extensive professional experience, including membership in well-known professional bands. When Wetterstrom retired as band director, Brown continued the fine tradition of that musical group.

Arthur E. Uhe, violinist, composer, and teacher, joined the Bethany faculty in 1914 and served the College for almost twenty-five years. American born, he studied violin in America and Europe, including among his teachers Ysaye and Cesar Thomson. Early in his career he had successful tours in the Scandinavian countries and on the continent, and later in the United States and Canada. Breitkopf and Hartel, New York, published his many compositions. He was a Victor recording artist. He also served as conductor of the symphony orchestra for several years.

Lennard Gunnerson's commitment to his alma mater covered more than four decades, 1901-44. He was a fine performer on the string bass and taught this instrument to several generations of students. His principal assignment was curator of musical instruments and piano tuner. Many generations of Bethany music students will always remember his helpfulness and counsel.

A key figure in the development of music education at Bethany was Geneva Smith (Mrs. Myron Ross), '16, '23. She began in 1922 a career as instructor and later she was professor of public school music until 1937. The bachelor's degree in public school music was established during her tenure. The rich tradition of Bethany in the education and placement of music teachers received a substantial legacy from the dedication and talent of Geneva Smith.

The late 1920s included other loyal and able teachers. There was Lewis I. Loveland, an Amherst graduate with advanced studies at Yale and Pennsylvania, professor of Greek and Latin 1927-40, who impressed his students not primarily because he had been a student of Latin with the famous Bennet or because he knew President Calvin Coolidge and Dwight Morrow at Amherst, but because he was an example of the belief that the study of Latin and Greek disciplined the mind. Dr. Hans J. Hoff, 1929-43, professor of German and Swedish, had a kindly manner, unfailing trust in students, uniqueness of personality, and comprehensive knowledge of languages identified by his certification with the United States government as an interpreter in ten languages.

In the social sciences for twenty-five years, 1928-52, 1953-54, the central figure was Dr. George W. Kleihege. Caricatured at Stunt Nite by the reams of newspaper clippings which mock surgery uncovered, he introduced students to *The Nation* and *The New Republic,* thus offering alternatives to the status quo in the search for truth. A former candidate for governor of Kansas on the Socialist ticket, Dr. Kleihege's presence on the faculty represented the principle of academic freedom in a church college.

The students of that era, and earlier too and later, hold in kindly remembrance two great women teachers, Anna Carlson, 1901-35, and Amanda Magnusson, 1908-35. Anna Carlson moved from the principalship of the academy to the college where she taught courses in education and religion. Her patience and sensitivity to the welfare of her students and her simple but meaningful commitment to Jesus Christ and His teachings gave her courses a rich dimension. Amanda Magnusson, also a dedicated Christian, was a woman of great intellect and wisdom. Her explanation of psychological terms and principles was clear and comprehensive. An appropriate tribute to Anna Carlson and Amanda Magnusson is found in the words of President Pihlblad: "Both of these handmaidens of the Lord, representing the noblest qualities of Christian womanhood, have exercised an influence on Bethany's student body and on the youth of the church which the years will not be able to efface."[3]

The fifth floor of Old Main was the academic domain of Dr. J. E. Welin, 1891-1936, and Dean Emil O. Deere, 1903-55, who, though differing in temperament, were deeply committed to their calling and profession. A constant flow of future physicians, chemists, and other scientists went on from Bethany to continue their studies in graduate and professional schools. President Pihlblad described the quality of Welin's career: "He met the exacting requirements of a Christian professor of science, evidencing in his personality and in his teaching that a naturalist may at the same time be a disciple of Christ in confession as well as in his daily walk." Dean Deere's broad learning and his knowledge of the interrelationship of the sciences greatly enriched his courses. Whether the course involved a specific consideration of Holmes, *The Biology of the Frog,* or the flora and fauna of nature's great outdoor laboratory, there was always the shared insight in natural phenomena and explanation of the distinctiveness of nature and nature's law. The light burned late in his office-laboratory on fifth floor of Old Main as this intelligent man and Bethany graduate, '04, devoted vast energy to academic, administrative, and extracurricular activities of his alma mater.[4]

For more than a decade, 1920-32, Martin J. Holcomb, '16, '18, was the key faculty figure for many students in their Bethany years. A fine teacher of English and one of the most successful debate coaches in the United States, "Prof," as he was affectionately called, was held in high esteem and affection. His great contribution to forensics at Bethany is described elsewhere.[5]

A dearly loved and highly esteemed member of the faculty for several generations of students was Annie Theo. Swensson, daughter of Dr. and Mrs. Carl Swensson. She taught at Bethany 1907-49. In early years her classes were in English and physical culture until she later concentrated on expression, dramatics, and speech. She distinguished herself for many years through performances of famous plays and literary works in solo reading recitals. Frequent press reports cite such notices as "a large and appreciative crowd heard Annie Theo. Swensson read *Ben Hur"* and "1500 persons listened attentively as Annie Theo. Swensson read Charles Rand Kennedy's *The Servant in the House."* Her fine personal qualities received a new area of influence when she served as dean of women 1937-45. Annie Theo. Swensson will long be remembered for her sterling character, quiet dignity, gracious manner, and professional excellence.

Anna Marm, '09, who shared her talent with students for more than three decades, 1921-55, as professor of mathematics, established a fine record of achievement. Thorough and exacting, she expected and generally received a gratifying response from students. She founded the mathematics club at Bethany. A loyal member of the American Association of University Women, she was a leader in establishing the Lindsborg

ANNIE THEO. SWENSSON   ANNA MARM   INA BELL AULD

branch of that organization. Anna Marm Hall is named in appreciation of her career.

The Reverend Aaron Wahlin family contributed two daughters to the faculty among the five children who were Bethany graduates. Edla Wahlin served for more than two decades during two periods as a teacher in the model school and as head librarian, 1929-44. She rendered fine service as a professional librarian in reorganizing the collection and in establishing sound policies of operation. Vendla Wahlin was an able teacher of English and foreign languages from 1935-49 and as librarian in the later years.

Dr. Ina Bell Auld, professor of English, joined the faculty in 1938 and continued her dedicated career at Bethany until her death in 1960. An editorial in the *Messenger* at the time of her death identified this dedicated teacher: "Dr. Auld exemplified some of the finest traditional values of the scholar and person. We have been taught by her courage and fortitude . . . . Following a wise discipline she learned and taught out of love of intellect for its own sake. Underlying all these was a spiritual quality expressed in parable form by a remark she made about herself: 'You have no idea how often I climbed to the top of Old Main to see how far I could see.' She was one who, in all areas of life, saw far."[6]

When Anna Marm retired in 1955 it was the good fortune of Bethany to have Jen Jenkins as her successor. The latter continued as professor of mathematics until retirement in 1973. Miss Jenkins had been especially active in teacher education. In the period 1965-68 she directed on the

Bethany campus institutes for mathematics teachers sponsored by the National Science Foundation. In addition to excellent achievement in the classroom, she published several articles in professional journals.

Gladys Peterson, '31, concluded twenty years of service at Bethany when she retired in 1969. She made a splendid contribution by establishing and developing the elementary education degree program. Miss Peterson was named a Kansas Master Teacher in 1968. Her dedication and Christian character place her in the great tradition associated with Amanda Magnusson and Anna Carlson.

Included among the Bethany teachers with more than twenty years of service is Ethel D. Palmquist, '18. Her assignment included classes in the academy, and later she taught English and languages in the College of Liberal Arts and Sciences, 1953-63. She is remembered especially for the excellence of her classes in freshman English courses. Inez Esping, '23, became head librarian in 1952 and held that position until 1965. Her professional training and understanding of the Bethany situation brought positive results in strengthening and developing library services. She also devoted much time to the local historical and Swedish collections.

When Dr. Walter Fahrer, professor of German, died in 1960 following a critical illness, Bethany said farewell with great sorrow to a capable and dedicated teacher. After several years of successful teaching at Luther College, Wahoo, Nebraska, he came to Bethany in 1948. President Lund expressed the feelings of Dr. Fahrer's many friends: "He was too young to die and the world still needed him. Yet he was ready, as he always had been for life's next step . . . . His rare scholarship, his master teaching, his friendly counsel, and his humble devotion to duty will inspire us for many years."[7]

Dr. Joe L. Hermanson was a professor and dean for more than three decades. He taught chemistry 1936-42, and in 1948 he returned as dean of liberal arts and sciences, resuming full-time teaching in 1962. He had an outstanding record in sending chemistry majors to graduate and professional schools. His service as dean was excellent in developing programs and in providing leadership in interpreting new trends in higher education. He also published several articles in learned journals. His spirit is demonstrated in a typical statement of his view of life upon retirement in 1973: "Teaching has been my most satisfying work. To see students come alive, take hold, and move ahead is what gives real joy."[8]

The chronicle of selected members of the faculty presents only a partial portrait because many other capable and dedicated persons are not identified. Except in the context of the early years of Bethany, when the foundations were laid, the criterion for selection generally has been that of substantial length of tenure. Similarly, the account does not include fine and able members of the faculty in recent years. As the decades accumulate, their contribution will also become a part of a

The Bethany College Board of Directors in a recent pose.

treasured legacy for Bethany alumni. Fortunately, there have been and there still are dedicated teachers at Bethany of short or long tenure who are reminiscent of the description of Chaucer's scholar in the famous words, "And gladly would he learn and gladly teach."

A vital aspect of the history of Bethany College is related to the decisions and activities of the board of directors. The first members were the Reverends Carl Swensson, Lindsborg; A. W. Dahlsten, Salemsborg; P. M. Sannquist, New Gottland; and laymen John A. Swenson and A. Lincoln, Lindsborg; John Thorstenberg, Assaria; and C. J. Stromquist, Fremont. These persons were all identified with congregations and communities in the Smoky Valley. In more than nine decades ending with the academic year 1973-74, the membership has included 183 regular members, a few of whom were ex officio at some time. Four additional persons have served only in an ex officio capacity.[9]

When Bethany became an institution of the Kansas Conference in 1884, board members were elected at the annual meeting. The number varied from seven to sixteen during the first decade. For more than three decades between 1892-1925, eight regularly elected members formed the board, four clergy and four laymen. An equal ratio of clergy and laymen was maintained until about 1940. The laymen were generally somewhat greater in number than clergy from 1940-1960, but after 1960 there have been at least twice as many laymen as clergy. The president of the Conference and the president of the College were made ex officio members in 1900. The three presidents of the supporting synods became ex officio members in 1962. In 1926 two liberal arts alumni, one clergy and one layman, were added upon nomination by the alumni association and election by the Conference. In 1941 the fine arts alumni received the right to nominate two candidates for one position. Amos Glad, '16, and the Reverend Paul Engstrand, '12, were the first liberal arts representatives. Julius Hultquist, '35, was the first fine arts representative. Dr. G.

A. Dorf, '93, was the first of fifty-four alumni who have served as board members. Beginning in 1943 the Women's Missionary Society of the Kansas Conference designated one member, and in 1951 a member from the Texas Conference joined the board.

Important action was taken by the Conference in 1956 when authorization was given to the board "to nominate up to four (4) lay candidates who may or may not be members of the Lutheran church." Prior to this action, members, except alumni representatives, were required to be Lutheran. The college constitution adopted in 1968 provided for a board of not less than twenty-five nor more than thirty-one members. Except for members at large and representatives of the alumni association, all others must be "a communicant member of a Lutheran congregation." In 1974 the board included the presidents of the Central States, Texas-Louisiana, and Rocky Mountain synods as ex officio members.[10]

An unusual record of dedicated service was rendered by seven individuals who held membership on the board for twenty-five years or more. The Reverend J. E. Liljedahl, pastor of Immanuel Lutheran Church, Salina, was a regularly elected member for thirty-six years between 1916-52. Dr. Alf Bergin, Dr. Victor Spong, Dr. G. A. Dorf, Dr. A. W. Lindquist, C. J. Stromquist, and G. E. Bengtson served for twenty-five years or more. Since 1968 no member of the board may serve continuously for more than two four-year terms.

The preponderant Swedish and Swedish American composition of the board is proven by the fact that it was only in 1943, well into the sixth decade, that the first non-Swedish person was elected to membership. Mrs. Dolores Gaston Runbeck, '27, Lindsborg, a representative of the fine arts alumni association, was that member. Only four of the first one hundred members were non-Swedish. This pattern has changed decisively in recent years with the broadened basis of the church constituency and changes in qualification for membership. Mrs. F. O. Johnson, McPherson, and Mrs. Dolores Gaston Runbeck, Lindsborg, who joined the board in 1943, were the first women members. Thirteen women have served on the board. Membership has been dominantly from Kansas with 116 out of 165 accounted for, or 70 percent. There have been 21 from Colorado, 18 from Missouri, 12 from Texas, and the balance from other states. The occupational profile identifies the clergy as the largest group historically with 80 out of 175 or 45.7 percent on the basis of available data. Businessmen have provided the second largest group historically with 48 or 27 percent. Included among other vocations and professions have been farmers and ranchers, 13, lawyers, 11, educators, 8, housewives, 8, and physicians, 4. The preponderant role of the clergy is based upon the pattern for several decades when the constitution provided that at least one-half of the members must be clergy.

Great responsibility and dedication has characterized the service of eighteen persons who have served as chairmen of the board of directors. Dr. Victor Spong, Kansas City, Missouri, had the longest tenure with twelve years, from 1924-36, followed by that of the Reverend S. E. Johnson, 1939-50. Only five of the chairmen have not been clergy. Prior to 1952-53, C. J. Stromquist was the only lay chairman. Since 1952-53 four of the six chairmen have been laymen. Six of the eighteen chairmen have been Bethany alumni. The following have been chairmen: Rev. C. A. Swensson, Rev. J. Seleen, Mr. C. J. Stromquist, Rev. J. E. Floren, Rev. G. A. Dorf, '93, Rev. Alfred Bergin, Rev. E. P. Olsson, Rev. Victor Spong, '10, Rev. A. W. Lindquist, '95, Rev. S. E. Johnson, '11, Rev. Robert Hurty, '39, Rev. Ervin C. Malm, Mr. Russ B. Anderson, Mr. Carl Engstrom, Dr. Einar Jaderborg, '46, Mr. A. L. Duckwall, Rev. Axel Beckman, and Rev. Verner E. Strand.

Closely identified with the board of directors have been the men who have served as business managers and/or treasurers. Jens Stensaas served faithfully in that position for more than four decades, 1906-48. A Bethany commercial graduate in 1901, he was successively instructor in commerce, professor of commerce, and business manager and treasurer. A quiet man who shunned the public spotlight, he worked hard and effectively for Bethany. Jens Stensaas was one of a small group of dedicated men and women who gave their lives to Bethany and Christian higher education. Closely identified with Jens Stensaas in the heavy work load of the treasurer's office was Delia Berglund, assistant treasurer, who resigned in 1945 after thirty-five years of dedicated service.

Mrs. Carl (Irene) Thorstenberg gives food service keys to her successor, Ray Brax.

JENS STENSAAS   *WILLIAM TAYLOR*

The office of treasurer and/or business manager has been held by the following: John A. Swenson, 1882-83; P. T. Lindholm, 1883-86; G. E. Gustus, 1886-88; W. A. Granville, 1888-91; A. A. Abercrombie, 1891-92; John S. Swensson, 1892-97; G. E. Eberhardt, 1897-99; Carl Johns, 1899-1903; G. E. Anderson, 1903-06; Jens Stensaas, 1906-48; Vernon E. Johnson, 1948-52; and William Taylor, 1952-.

Capable service has been given by several people for shorter or longer periods in various areas. In the 1890s the Reverend John Telleen served the College well as a special financial representative in reducing the heavy debt. Professor Frank Nelson, who had been a member of the faculty for several years in the 1890s, rendered heroic service in removing the debt in the 1907 campaign. Arthur J.Lundgren, '10, a member of the department of business and principal of the school of commerce, was heavily involved in financial campaigns and student recruitment in the years before and after 1920. William Stensaas, '22, who was a member of the English faculty, served also as the financial secretary in the late 1920s. T. E. Dorf, '24, was alumni secretary with broader institutional responsibilities in promotion for a few years in the 1930s.

Vernon E. Johnson, '35, was the first director of public relations, serving in the period 1938-43, prior to military service. He was treasurer 1948-52 and returned as executive assistant to the president 1960-66. Lorin E. Sibley, '32, served for two brief periods as director of public relations in the 1940s. Frank Pedroja, Jr., '46, was director of public relations 1949-55. The tenure of current administrative staff in public affairs and financial matters has been described previously.

Jenny Lind, '92, sister of Mrs. Alma Swensson and the first woman Bethany baccalaureate graduate, served the College faithfully as secretary to President Swensson, and later, to President Pihlblad, and as registrar from shortly after graduation until 1920. Aileen Henmon, former student 1914-15, was secretary to President Pihlblad for more than twenty years beginning in 1920. She was also assistant registrar and director of the placement bureau until her death in 1950. Miss Henmon was the keeper of alumni records for many years and she continued a constant stream of correspondence with alumni and former students. As director of the placement bureau, she was untiring in assisting hundreds of Bethanyites to find a first teaching position and later to assist them in finding further professional opportunities.

Faithful and efficient service has been given by the managers of the food service. In 1930 Mr. and Mrs. Martin Anderson concluded thirty-three years of service as steward and matron of the dining hall and for a few years, as managers of the cafeteria. These three decades brought them into contact with thousands of students who recalled their affability and quaint ways. Mrs. John Altenborg, Sr, served efficiently until 1941 when Mrs. Carl Thorstenberg began two decades as director of food service. Mr. Thorstenberg was supervisor of mechanical and service departments of the College. The Thorstenbergs endeared themselves to succeeding generations of college students through their fine service and genial spirit of cooperation. Mr. and Mrs. Ray Brax have been the capable directors of the food service in Pihlblad Memorial Union since 1962.

Mrs. Olga Anderson rendered fine service to the College in various capacities for more than twenty years, 1949-71. She was the well-liked resident head of Deere Hall for many years prior to retirement.

Bethany has been served well and faithfully by people who have had various assignments in buildings and grounds. In the earlier period John Renander, John C. Peterson, Ed Gibson, and Sven Björn were associated with the College for many years. In October, 1904, Sven Björn died from an explosion while working on a generator in the acetylene gas plant. The *Messenger* reported that "Sven Björn's example of faithful application to duty ought to inspire the students." More recent service over a period of many years have been given by Carl A. Teed, Carl Thorstenberg, Emery Ahlstedt, Hans Carlson, and "Cy" Leland Westman.[11]

Academic Deans

EMIL O.   JOE L. HERMANSON   ALBERT A. ZIMMER   LLOYD C.
DEERE   FOERSTER

OSCAR LOFGREN   LLOYD SPEAR   LAMBERT DAHLSTEN

10.

The Lindsborg "Messiah" Tradition

The achievement in music and art has identified Bethany College as a unique and distinctive collegiate institution with great cultural resources. National attention has come to the College and to the Lindsborg community through the annual "Messiah" festival and the Mid-West Art Exhibition during Holy Week. Thousands of people have made annual pilgrimages to the Smoky Valley of Central Kansas for decades in order to share in these religious and cultural events. Such designations for the college community as "America's Bayreuth" and the "Oberammergau of the Plains" suggest symbols that are distinctive historically and currently. Twin-born with the founding of the College in 1881 was the Handel Oratorio Society which became known as the Bethany College Oratorio Society. The popular reference to this distinguished organization identifies it as the Lindsborg "Messiah" chorus. Endowing the music of the oratorio with deep meaning is the great spiritual message based upon the abiding promises of the Holy Scriptures.

The threads of that story are associated like so many in the history of Lindsborg with Pastor Olof Olsson. The day was Friday, April 4, 1879, when the Lindsborg pioneer pastor, then on a trip to Europe, arrived in London. When reading a newspaper, he learned that Handel's *Messiah* under the direction of Sir Michael Costa was to be presented in Exeter Hall that evening. Immediately he decided to attend the concert and engaged a room near Exeter Hall. Olsson had only modest financial resources and purchased the cheapest ticket available, which, however, gave him a good seat on the balcony directly across from the chorus.

At 7:30 p.m. Sir Michael Costa picked up his baton and for almost three hours Olsson sat spellbound as the chorus and orchestra of six hundred presented Handel's inspiring oratorio. An Englishman seated by Olsson shared his score of the *Messiah* so the visitor from America could closely follow the rendition. It was a thrilling experience from the "Overture" to the last "Amen" as recorded by Olsson:

> I will not even attempt to describe it all for that is beyond my power. At times I was so carried away that I scarcely knew myself. Well, my friends may smile at my childishness. Let them smile. But I don't know what sort of man he would be who had no feeling for beautiful spiritual music. Among other things sung were the names of our Saviour given in the ninth chapter of Isaiah: Wonderful, Counsellor, Mighty God. When the great chorus and the full orchestra intoned those words, I was so enchanted that I feared the shock would be too much for me. That evening in Exeter Hall will stand out, I can well say, as the most beautiful memory of the journey.[1]

Olsson left Exeter Hall that evening with a great song in his heart. It was more than an episode, because his thoughts came back to it again and again. When he returned to Augustana College, he communicated his great enthusiasm for the *Messiah* to friends there. The response was encouraging. A small chorus was assembled for rehearsals. On April 11, 1881, the first rendition was presented at Moline, Illinois. A splendid oratorio tradition at Augustana College had been launched.[2]

Present in the audience at the rendition of Handel's great oratorio by the Augustana chorus at the First Congregational Church, Moline, Illinois, during the commencement activities in 1881 was Carl Swensson. When he returned to Lindsborg following this "Messiah" rendition, he was full of enthusiasm for Handel's great composition. Mrs. Swensson, a talented musician, was also eager to bring the *Messiah* to Lindsborg. Plans were discussed in the first instance with the choir of the Bethany Lutheran Church, where the Swenssons were dearly beloved by the membership. The possibility of organizing a chorus was suggested to the pastors and choir members of neighboring congregations. The response was encouraging although this seemed to be a big venture. Carl Swensson was accustomed to attempting great things, and plans moved forward with certainty.[3]

Announcements of the first rehearsal were made in the Bethany Church and in other churches in the Smoky Valley. On December 8, 1881, the *Smoky Valley News* carried the following statement, the first in a long series in the local, regional, and national press: "We understand that Rev. Swensson and lady and Mr. Hasselquist of this city, are busily engaged in working up a 'Messiah' choir to comprise about one hundred voices. Fifty dollars have already been raised for song books. A leader for the choir and a string orchestra will be engaged from Rock Island. This choir is to give concerts during Easter at the different churches in this vicinity for the benefit of the Swedish Academy of Lindsborg."[4]

The response to the announcement of the first rehearsal of the *Messiah* is also recorded in the *Smoky Valley News* a week later: "The 'Messiah' choir was organized last Sunday with a membership of thirty-eight from Lindsborg. The choir is to contain one hundred voices, and the rest of the choir will be made up from Freemount, Assaria, and Salemsborg churches."[5]

The men and women who assembled in the Bethany Lutheran Church for the first "Messiah" rehearsal that Sunday afternoon in December, 1881, were taking the first step in a tradition that was destined to be unique and distinctive. It was with keen anticipation and some anxiety that Pastor and Mrs. Swensson awaited the arrival of the singers. Then they came, almost forty of them, challenged by the leadership of their pastor and his wife. Carefully they opened the pages of their *Messiah* books. This was new, strange music for them. They had never heard a rendition of the *Messiah*. It seemed difficult. Truly this, too, was an act of faith for Mrs. Swensson, the conductor, and for the singers.

The people who came for that first rehearsal still lived in the pioneer world. Almost all of them were Swedish immigrants who came to sing a new song in a new land. English was still a strange and difficult language for the majority of them, and it was only natural that the explanations were made in Swedish. They understood the great message taken from the prophets, the gospels, the epistles of Paul, and the Revelation of St. John as Swensson eloquently but simply gave the context of each great theme. Rehearsals, like renditions, constituted serious religious services.

Pastor and Mrs. Swensson were motivated to introduce the *Messiah* in Lindsborg by other factors than those based on their appreciation for good music. Life on the Kansas prairies in the seventies and eighties of the last century was barren in many respects. They realized that the life of the people would be greatly enriched as they sang or heard a great oratorio. The *Messiah* was to be identified with the daily life of the people. It was to become a part of them, an expression of their love for the beautiful. They came from simply furnished sod-houses, stone houses, and frame houses to sing the *Messiah*. For some of them it involved a rough ride over roads filled with ruts as the lumber-wagon bounced them here and there. Still others walked miles across the prairies to the stone church which meant so much to them. Neighbor joined neighbor, and as they rode under the clear, starlit, Kansas sky, they intoned a chorus from the *Messiah*. It made life meaningful as they shared in this great venture in cooperation.

Mrs. Swensson sought musical excellence, and she realized that it could not be achieved if they relied only on the general rehearsals. Part-practices were organized, and sopranos, altos, tenors, and basses met separately at the parsonage home of Mrs. Swensson or in the residence of a member. The group worked hard on the specific parts of each chorus.

Individual responsibility was developed as the group grew in understanding of the score. Then followed coffee and Swedish delicacies and excited talk about the first rendition.

It was the plan of Pastor and Mrs. Swensson from the outset that a conductor and the orchestra should be imported for the first rendition. Professor Joseph Osborn, who had conducted the *Messiah* at Augustana College the previous year, was invited to take up the baton at Lindsborg so that Mrs. Swensson could be released to sing the soprano solos. Thirteen members of the orchestra also came from Rock Island, Illinois. Seated at the organ during the first rendition was Dr. Olof Olsson, Lindsborg's founder and first pastor of Bethany Lutheran Church, who also had come from Rock Island to share with his Lindsborg friends in this thrilling venture.

The first rendition of the *Messiah* at Lindsborg took place in the Bethany Lutheran Church at 7:30 p.m., Tuesday, March 28, 1882. Two rehearsals were held with Professor Osborn conducting, Dr. Olsson at the organ, and the orchestra furnishing the accompaniment. The first program provided the following information on the front page: "Selections from Handel's Sacred Oratorio, MESSIAH, performed by the Handel Oratorio Society, during Lent, 1882." The soloists were Mrs. Alma Swensson, soprano, Miss Lydia Andreen, soprano; Miss Anna Swensson, alto; Mr. C. A. Beckman, tenor; and F. Linder, bass.[6]

The program at the first performance consisted of eighteen of the fifty-three numbers in the *Messiah:*

1. "Overture" 2. Recit. (Tenor)—"Comfort ye my people" 4. Chorus—"And the Glory of the Lord" 8. Recit. (Alto)—"Behold! A Virgin shall conceive" 9. Air (Alto) and Chorus—"O thou that tellest good tidings to Zion" 13. "Pastoral Symphony" 20. Air (Alto)—"He shall feed His flock like a shepherd" and Air (Soprano)—"Come unto Him" 22. Chorus—"Behold the Lamb of God" 23. Air (Alto)—"He was despised" 26. Chorus—"All we like sheep have gone astray" 30. Air (Tenor)—"Behold, and see if there be any sorrow" 33. Chorus—"Lift up your heads, O ye gates" 38. Air (Soprano)—"How beautiful are the feet of those who preach the gospel of peace" 44. Chorus—"Hallelujah" 45. Air (Soprano)—"I know that my Redeemer liveth" 46. Single and Double quartette—"Since by man came death" 47. Recit. (Bass)—"Behold, I tell you a mystery" 53. Chorus—"Worthy is the Lamb," "Amen." Separate programs were printed in Swedish and English.

No record is available of the comments which came from members of the audience as they filed out of the stone church that March evening. From the first strains of the "Overture" until the last chorus, they had listened to inspiring messages and thrilling climaxes. Attentively they heard the tenor declare: "Comfort ye, comfort ye my people, saith your God . . . . Prepare ye the way of the Lord, make straight in the desert a highway for our God." There was absolute silence as the chorus arose and sang: "And the glory of the Lord shall be revealed, and all flesh shall see it together; for the mouth of the Lord hath spoken it." And so the great oratorio moved on, and with it, interest and attention mounted. They heard, following the "Pastoral Symphony," the solo, "He shall feed His flock like a shepherd." When the program entered the second part, a new feeling came as the audience heard the chorus sing, "Behold the Lamb of God, that taketh away the sin of the world," to be followed by the aria, "He was despised and rejected of men; a man of sorrows and acquainted with grief." But the spirit and the tempo changed, and soon the audience arose in adoration of Him Who is "King of Kings, Lord of Lords," as the great "Hallelujah" Chorus echoed for the first time in the Smoky Valley.

Although the individual responses that night as people rode home across the Kansas prairies were unrecorded, the editor of the *Lindsburg Localist* recounted his impressions:

> After thorough preparation, the Bethania Chorus, numbering some seventy-five performers, made their first public appearance at the Lutheran Church on the evening of the 28th. The church was filled with a fine audience who enjoyed a rare musical treat. It has always been held that to render the *Messiah* is a most difficult and delicate undertaking, which to accomplish is glory enough for any company of singers. Therefore, anything like success by amateurs is no small praise.
>
> The performance on the whole, was good, while some of it was excellent, especially the 'Hallelujah' Chorus, and the solos by Mrs. Alma Swensson, Soprano, and Miss Anna Swensson, Alto.[7]

The editor, sensing the importance of what he had heard, concluded with this prophetic observation: "The concert is an event in the history of our town. This, together with the object of it all, makes success gratifying to all lovers of the true, the beautiful, and the good." The enthusiastic response to the first "Messiah" rendition was also reflected by a correspondent writing in the *McPherson Republican:* "It is impossible to give an adequate word picture of the performance. Anyone who would undertake to describe, say the 'Hallelujah Chorus,' might as well attempt to imprison the rainbow and spread its colors on canvas. In short, to appreciate or have any sort of conception of it, it must be heard and felt (for in some instances last night many were overcome and in tears)."[8]

The Lindsborg "Messiah" tradition had been launched. The response had been heartening. A series of five concerts had been planned in order that neighboring communities might share in the enterprise. On March 29, the day following the Lindsborg rendition, the society presented the *Messiah* at the Salemsborg Lutheran Church at 3:00 p.m. On March 30 the *Messiah* was sung at the Salina Opera House at 8:00 p.m., on March 31 at the McPherson Opera House at 8:00 p.m., and on April 3 at the Freemount Lutheran Church at 3:00 p.m. The journeys to Salemsborg and Freemount were made in lumberwagons as the jovial groups joined in the happy fellowship of these occasions. The Union Pacific Railroad took the singers and orchestra players to Salina and McPherson. The Bethany Band accompanied the group to Salina and McPherson, playing street concerts to attract attention to the "Messiah" performances in the evening. Admission was 50 cents for adults and 25 cents for children.[9]

The "Messiah" renditions had been planned to provide support for Bethany Academy, which had been established the previous October. This early identification of Bethany College with the great "Messiah" tradition has been a characteristic feature across the decades. The net proceeds of the renditions in 1882 amounted to $224.25, which was turned over to the treasury of the academy. A most significant aspect of the unique resources of Bethany College is the "Messiah" tradition, which established the background for the splendid program of musical studies at the Lindsborg college.[10]

The auspicious beginning of 1882 was followed by annual presentations of the *Messiah*. In 1883 the oratorio was performed at Freemount and Assaria. In November the "Messiah" chorus and Bethany Band joined with friends and supporters to form an excursion party to Rock Island, Illinois, where the Lindsborg organizations performed at a great festive program at Augustana College. One hundred and seventy-five people traveled by special train to the city and college which had been the direct inspiration for the Lindsborg "Messiah." Local interest increased, and the quality of the performances improved appreciably. When Old Main was completed in 1887, renditions were held in the college chapel. By 1897 the *Messiah* had been performed twenty times.[11]

While the response to the *Messiah* was general, there was one individual who felt especially grateful for the fine progress in sacred music that was being made in Lindsborg. That individual was Olof Olsson, the pioneer pastor of Lindsborg, later president of Augustana College and Theological Seminary. As noted above, Olsson was at the organ when the first rendition took place in 1882. He was present for the last time in 1898. After the rendition of number 22, "Behold the Lamb of God," he arose from his seat in the audience and waving his hands to the singers, called out, "Thanks, my young friends; this is the heart of the oratorio," and overcome with emotion, sank back into his place. There was a song in his heart too. He recalled those first days in Lindsborg out on the bare prairies. He remembered also that first Christmas service in the stone and sod church in Section 7 northwest of Lindsborg when a choir had participated in that service of worship. There were other remembrances of sacred song inspired by the beloved Olof Olsson. A new generation had taken up the great message of song, and now his people were singing the *Messiah*. Exeter Hall in London, where Olsson first heard the *Messiah* and dreamed of it for the people in Kansas, seemed very close to the Smoky Valley.[12]

The achievement in the "Messiah" renditions was the result of genuine devotion and patient rehearsal. While there were some fine singers in the early years, many voices had to be developed. Members of the choir rehearsed at home. Housewives would sing parts of choruses while doing the daily duties of the household. At times the men while plowing the soil or planting corn would recall the rehearsal scheduled for the morrow and take upon their lips the words of the *Messiah*. Children, too, caught the spirit of the cause which meant so much to their parents.

The Bethany College Oratorio Society performs in its second "home"—the chapel in Old Main.

At a morning service at the Bethany Lutheran Church in 1887, it was necessary to take out a small girl because she insisted on humming the figurations in "He Shall Purify." She had heard them so frequently in her home that she would hum them on many occasions.[13]

Interest in the "Messiah" chorus increased steadily as reflected in membership statistics. From the initial figure of about 75 in 1882, the number had grown to 102 a decade later. The construction of Ling Auditorium in 1895 increased facilities for the chorus as well as the audience in contrast with the limited space in the college chapel. In 1898 there were 343 singers and at the end of the century almost 400 sang Handel's *Messiah* at Lindsborg. The chorus was composed of more than 500 members each year in thirteen years between 1900-35. The largest recorded membership was 609 in 1923. The *Lindsborg News-Record* reported that 758 people had applied for membership that year. When the auditorium in Presser Hall was completed in 1928, the size of the chorus was limited to somewhat less than 450 members.[14]

LING AUDITORIUM, constructed in 1895, was used for the "Messiah" concerts. It later was a gymnasium for the campus.

The "Messiah" at Lindsborg became nationally known after the turn of the century.

The personnel of the Bethany College Oratorio Society reflects the intimate relationship between college and community. Faculty members and students have joined with residents of Lindsborg and surrounding communities in building the "Messiah" tradition. Every type of employment has been represented in the membership. Farmers, housewives, merchants, physicians, ministers, mechanics, blacksmiths, cattlemen, students, and teachers have met twice a week annually for months to rehearse the *Messiah* and other great oratorios, and to participate in what is actually a great laboratory of community living. In the period 1900-1918 there were more Bethany students every year than non-students except for two years. In 1905, when the membership was 570, there were 355 students and 215 general citizens. In later years a balance between students and non-students has been typical. In 1961, 191 of the 391 members of the chorus were college students. Only 95 of the 200 non-students were Lindsborg residents. The rest were singers from eighteen other communities with Salina and McPherson providing the largest number. The distribution of the 375 members in 1974 was as follows: 44 percent Bethany College students, 30 percent Lindsborg residents, and the balance from seventeen communities around Lindsborg. New members comprised 25 percent of the total. Almost 7 percent of the singers had been in the chorus twenty years or more. Two former members, Fritz Tarnstrom and Hjalmar Winblad, sang the *Messiah* for sixty years. Mrs. Albertha Sundstrom, a member in 1974, has sung for more than fifty years.[15]

The performances of the *Messiah* were held during Lent in the early years. This pattern was interrupted for several years by concerts during commencement week in May. In the late 1890s the oratorio was sung during Holy Week. At the turn of the century performances on Palm Sunday, Good Friday, and Easter Sunday were customary. Exceptions included May renditions in 1902 and 1918. In the latter year the influenza epidemic had delayed the opening date for rehearsals. Occasional performances or partial renditions in Lindsborg were presented at the meetings of church conventions or on anniversary occasions. Five renditions a year were normal for about a decade prior to 1908. In that year three performances became the pattern—Palm Sunday, Good Friday, and Easter Sunday evenings. The Good Friday concert was looked upon as the concert which Lindsborg people should attend. Visiting celebrity artists performed in afternoon concerts on those three days. In 1931 the celebrity concerts on Palm Sunday and Good Friday afternoons were abandoned in the context of the bad economic situation. Beginning that year the *Messiah* was performed on Palm Sunday afternoon. In 1967 the decision was made to present the *Messiah* on Easter Sunday afternoon, thus eliminating the celebrity concert from the "Messiah" week program. *The Passion of Our Lord According to St. Matthew* replaced the *Messiah* on

Good Friday evening in 1929.

Since the first rendition by the "Messiah" chorus in Lindsborg in 1882, and in nearby communities at the time and in the immediate years following, the Bethany College Oratorio Society has presented the oratorio out of town on seven occasions. As noted above, the oratorio society presented selections from the *Messiah* at Rock Island in November, 1883. During World War I the idea was conceived of bringing the chorus to Camp Funston, where thousands of soldiers were stationed prior to assignment in Europe. On May 13, 1918, a glorious spring day, the special train of eleven coaches on the Union Pacific transported the singers and orchestra members on this important journey out of the Smoky Valley. The renditions at Camp Funston were presented at 4:00 p.m. and at 8:00 p.m. in the All Kansas Building, which seated 4000 people. The conductor and performers were inspired by the great mass of men in khaki, many belonging to the 89th division which soon went overseas to participate in critical battles. The response of the men in uniform was enthusiastic. A long-established Lindsborg tradition provides no applause during the concert. It was quite otherwise at Camp Funston that May day. The chorus had to rise again and again to acknowledge the response of the audience. In the evening large groups of soldiers stood outside the building during the performance since no seats were available inside. Across the moonlit landscape of the military reservation resounded the majestic music describing Him Who is "King of Kings, and Lord of Lords . . . Wonderful, Counsellor, the Mighty God, the Everlasting Father, the Prince of Peace." As a grand finale, Dr. Hagbard Brase led the chorus and audience in singing the *Battle Hymn of the Republic*. It had been a day of high inspiration, and as the weary chorus entrained for the little community in the Smoky Valley, where the effect of war was

World War I was a grim reality, but "Messiah" concerts on May 13, 1918, provided an emotional uplift for soldiers of the 89th Division and others who both heard and performed that day at Camp Funston.

The Messiah *was presented by the Bethany Oratorio Society in Kansas City, Missouri, as shown here for December 13 and 14, 1930.*

also a part of a grim reality, it was with a prayer that God would add His blessings to the events of the day.[16]

On February 8-9, 1922, the Bethany College Oratorio Society presented the 114th, 115th, and 116th renditions of the *Messiah* at the Coliseum in Oklahoma City, Oklahoma. The appearances were sponsored by the Oklahoma State Teachers Association. Thousands of people crowded the auditorium and applauded the Lindsborg singers. A special train again brought the chorus and orchestra on this expedition of sacred song. On November 18-19, 1922, the society appeared for the first time in Kansas City, Missouri, when two renditions were presented in connection with the events of the American Royal Stock Show. In two consecutive years, 1929 and 1930, the society presented the *Messiah* in Convention Hall in Kansas City during the Christmas season under the sponsorship of the Kansas City Chamber of Commerce. An enthusiastic response again greeted the Lindsborg chorus with large audiences. In 1934 two "Messiah" renditions were presented in the Forum at Wichita, Kansas, under the sponsorship of the American Legion, and again capacity audiences listened attentively and appreciatively to the message and meaning of the *Messiah*. In November, 1945, the Bethany College Oratorio Society presented selections from the *Messiah* in Kansas City, Missouri, to an audience of 12,000 people at the program in observance of the Eightieth Anniversary of the founding of the Salvation Army.

In 1945 the Oratorio Society returned to Kansas City to perform at a Salvation Army anniversary program.

A national radio network broadcast of a "Messiah" performance originates from Presser Hall on Wednesday, March 20, 1940.

When the magic of radio became available, the *Messiah* reached even greater audiences than could be accommodated in Lindsborg. In April, 1939, selections from the majestic music of Handel's *Messiah,* as presented by the Bethany College Oratorio Society, were heard throughout the nation over the network facilities of the National Broadcasting Company. It was with a feeling of keen anticipation that Conductor Hagbard Brase and members of the orchestra and chorus envisaged a vast unseen audience in all parts of the nation sharing the great message and meaning of the *Messiah.* NBC continued these Easter time broadcasts from Lindsborg periodically.

When America was engaged in the decisive phase of World War II, the Office of War Information in 1945 transcribed the *Messiah* at Lindsborg for transmission to troops overseas and to the population of European countries. In 1949 the Voice of America under the auspices of the State Department beamed a Lindsborg performance of the *Messiah* to Europe to demonstrate the fine quality of life among free people in a small rural community in America. These international broadcasts have been made periodically. WDAF, the broadcasting station of the *Kansas City Star,* Kansas City, Missouri, broadcast the Palm Sunday rendition of the *Messiah* for several years beginning in 1945. In recent years the Palm Sunday performance has been transmitted by the interstate Messiah Festival Radio Network of about a dozen stations, originating with WIBW, Topeka. The Good Friday rendition of Bach's *The Passion of Our Lord According to St. Matthew* has been broadcast since the mid-1940s.

The Bethany College Oratorio Society has sung the *Messiah* so long and so well that some people do not realize that the society has had an extensive repertoire across the years. *The Creation* by Haydn, *Stabat Mater, Elijah,* and *Hymn of Praise* by Mendelssohn, *Messe Solenelle* by Gounod, *Requiem Mass in C minor* by Cherubini, *Christmas Oratorio* and *Sleepers, Wake* by Bach, and *Pilgrims of the Prairie,* a cantata by

Dr. Brase leads the chorus and orchestra for the "Messiah" in Presser auditorium.

Carl Busch, have been presented on various occasions. The latter was commissioned by the College for the dedication of Presser Hall on March 29, 1929. The words were by E. W. Olson, Rock Island, Illinois. Hagbard Brase prepared the chorus for the performance that was directed by Carl Busch, the composer. Stanley Deacon, baritone, was the only soloist. The premiere performance of the cantata, *Genesis to a Beat,* by Walter L. Pelz, a member of the Bethany faculty, was presented in November, 1970, along with a performance of *Gloria* by Vivaldi.

Since 1929, the 200th anniversary of the first performance of Johann Sebastian Bach's *The Passion of Our Lord According to St. Matthew,* this oratorio has been a regular part of the annual Holy Week festival. This great Passion oratorio was introduced by Dr. Hagbard Brase in 1925. The society rehearsed this work in the autumn for several years before formal rendition. The quality of the performance has improved with greater knowledge and understanding of the score. The *St. Matthew Passion* is appropriately presented on Good Friday evening.

The "Messiah" chorus at Lindsborg has been fortunate in its leadership across the years. All conductors except Mrs. Alma Swensson, who organized the chorus and served as the first conductor, and the visiting conductor, Professor J. Osborn in 1882, have been members of the faculty of Bethany College. The following individuals have wielded the baton before the oratorio society: Mrs. Alma Swensson, 1882-83; P. T. Lindholm, 1884-85; N. A. Krantz, 1886-87; Victor Lund, 1888-93; Vilhelm Lindberg, 1894; N. A. Krantz, 1895-96; Sigfrid Laurin, 1897; Samuel Thorstenberg, 1898-1909; Earl Rosenberg, 1910-13; H. E. Malloy, 1914; Hagbard Brase, 1915-46; Arvid Wallin, 1947-48; Ralph Harrel, 1949-51; Rolf Espeseth, 1952-55; Eugene Pearson, 1956; Lloyd Spear,

SAMUEL
THORSTENBERG   HAGBARD BRASE   ARVID WALLIN   ELMER
                                                          COPLEY

1957-59; Elmer Copley, 1960 to the present time, except 1968, when the conductor was Dr. Henry Veld, the famous Augustana College conductor emeritus, who was a visiting professor at Bethany during Copley's sabbatical leave.

The quality of the performances improved with the passing of the years. An historical appraisal of the developments will credit substantial gains under the leadership of Samuel Thorstenberg, 1898-1909, the great growth into a fine musical organization under the brilliant direction of Dr. Hagbard Brase, who served as conductor for three decades from 1915-46, and the continued development under the leadership of Elmer Copley beginning in 1960.

Samuel Thorstenberg was the son of pioneer parents in the Smoky Valley and a graduate of Bethany College. He continued his musical studies in New York and Europe. Thorstenberg was a fine singer and would perform as bass soloist, yielding the baton to the concertmaster for those selections. The chorus increased in membership from 183 in 1892 to 487 during his tenure as conductor. His fine general musicianship and his understanding of the oratorio tradition at Bethany were of great importance in his record of achievement.

The longest tenure as conductor has been that of Dr. Hagbard Brase, and it was a decisive period in developing musical excellence in the "Messiah" renditions. Following studies at Skara College, Brase completed the rigid requirements at the Royal Conservatory of Music in Stockholm. He then studied in Germany. Coming to Bethany College in 1900, he soon established himself as an outstanding musician. He became organ accompanist in 1901 and conductor in 1915.

The years of Brase's leadership were decisive. His splendid qualities of personality and musicianship, his complete understanding of the tradition and chorus, and his ability to inspire confidence were more valuable to the organization than can be adequately described. Brase's period of service witnessed great changes in society produced by two World Wars and consequent post-war adjustments. The interest in the *Messiah* at Lindsborg, however, increased under the leadership of capable Dr. Brase. Voice tests were introduced to insure good quality voices. Rehearsals by individual sections were emphasized. The great Lindsborg tradition might have been of only average quality under a less capable conductor. Brase was deeply loved by members of the society who appreciated his fine character, his keen sense of humor, his deep musicianship, and his contagious enthusiasm. Distinguished in appearance, he walked directly to the podium, gave a kindly glance to chorus and orchestra, and another great rendition was underway. Upon Brase's retirement in 1946 as conductor of the society, a well-known music critic observed that one of the last of the finest type of European music master in America had raised his baton for the last time.

Elmer Copley conducts a recent "Messiah" rendition.

Augustana College conferred upon him the honorary degree of doctor of music in 1930. He was made a Knight of the Royal Order of Vasa by the King of Sweden in 1947 in recognition of his distinguished contribution to music. Brase left the chorus with the greatest esteem and love of everyone surrounding him as he continued as professor of organ and theory.

It was the good fortune of the oratorio society to have Arvid Wallin, a fine musician and intimate friend of Brase's, available for the position following the latter's retirement. As a former conductor of the Bethany Symphony Orchestra and of various choral groups, he had the experience required for the assignment. Moreover, as organ accompanist he had worked for many years with Brase. The "Messiah" chorus under Arvid Wallin continued the fine tradition of his predecessor. The chorus, college, and community mourned his untimely death in September, 1948, following an illness which he bore courageously.

Elmer Copley, who has been conductor of the oratorio society since 1960, is a graduate and former faculty member at Augustana College. He has pursued extensive graduate studies. Copley, a tenor, is widely recognized as a fine singer and teacher. He came to his present position on short notice to succeed the newly appointed conductor, Professor Alvin Reimer, whose untimely death prevented him from taking up the post. Copley is also chairman of the music department.

There was prophetic insight in the comment of a music critic in 1960, Copley's first year at Bethany, when the writer observed: "A feeling is beginning to take hold in Lindsborg that perhaps those who see Copley in action are seeing the beginning of a new legend."[17]

The Lindsborg "Messiah" tradition has attained its great meaning because of the enthusiastic response of so many people to the music and message of Handel's great oratorio. Successive sites of the performances—Bethany Church, the College Chapel, the "Messiah" Auditorium, and Presser Hall Auditorium—have not been able to accommodate all the willing listeners on many occasions and capacity audiences have been a common pattern. In the early 1890s special trains with excursion rates brought many festival visitors. In 1903 there were twenty-five special trains during the week. The *Messenger* described the festive spirit of "Messiah" week in 1907 when even nature cooperated:

> The excursion trains arrived and in due season such immense masses of humanity poured out from the cars that the town literally swarmed with people . . . . Everything appeared in its gala attire. Nature had donned gorgeous spring hues—the lawns in the softest green and the peach and apricot trees in the sweetest and daintiest pink and white velvet. In the tree tops the red birds chirped their welcome and the frisky squirrels hopped and circled about expressing their intense delight with the day. The spirit of festivity pervaded everything and hovered especially over the gray old auditorium, where the first concert of the season was rendered at two-o'clock—surely a glorious beginning of the week's musical fete.[18]

The change produced by the automobile was described in the *Messenger* when in 1922 only a few trains were provided by the Union Pacific: "The long line of cars in front of the auditorium when the roads are good tell a silent tale of how Ford [Henry Ford] beat Gould [Jay Gould, the railroad tycoon] out of the 'Messiah' visitor business." The automobile continued to bring thousands of visitors. President Pihlblad reported in 1930 that 329 standing-room-only tickets were sold for the Easter Sunday evening concert. The attendance at the "Messiah" concerts has also been excellent in recent years. The Palm Sunday concert is generally sold out weeks in advance and a capacity audience fills Presser Hall Auditorium for the Easter Sunday afternoon performance. The attendance at the *St. Matthew Passion* performances on Good Friday evening in recent years has been far greater than ever before in the history of the renditions in Lindsborg.[19]

The response to the "Messiah" festival in the press and through the media generally has been extensive. Dr. Carl Swensson was a promoter, and he soon realized the immense publicity value of the "Messiah" concerts. There is an abundance of material from newspapers describing the Lindsborg "Messiah" festivals during the Swensson era. A turning point, however, in the national scope of "Messiah" publicity was a well-written and interesting article by Charles Harger, well-known editor of the *Abilene, Kansas, Reflector-Chronicle,* in the *Ladies Home Journal,* April, 1900. This magazine, with its large national circulation, called attention to the unique features of a distinctive American cultural achievement on the Kansas prairies.

The Abilene editor described "the octagonal building ablaze with lights most alluring" and "the chorus tier on tier of men and women, nearly 400 of them. The men in black; the maids in pink and white . . . .

Singing "The Messiah" on the Plains

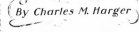

By Charles M. Harger

BECAUSE of its surroundings, and uplifting by its earnest methods and teaching, the Easter performance of "The Messiah" by the Swedish colony at Lindsborg, in Central Kansas, is each spring one of the interesting events of the West. A musical festival that out on the comparatively sparsely settled prairies can bring together ten thousand people during Holy Week, many of them coming two hundred miles, must be excellent indeed. The growth of the audiences in this instance, year after year, indicates a thorough appreciation of a worthy rendering of Handel's great oratorio. The Swedes are a singing people, and the religious sentiment is strong in their hearts. The one cherished day for this colony of perhaps three thousand families is Easter, and the chief glory thereof is "The Messiah." The Lindsborg settlement dates back to 1869, when the Rev. Olof Olson led from Sweden the first comers and founded the colony on the unbroken prairies. The settlers toiled, and prospered, and saved. They were homesick for the scenes of childhood, but learned to love their new home. Amid the struggle against drought and storm they sang their folksongs of cheer.

interpretation. This concert engages the very best of the talent of the college, but it is not the event for which the auditors long.

That comes in the evening. The crisp, frosty air outside and the early darkness make the octagonal auditorium, ablaze with light, most alluring, and its four thousand seats are quickly filled. Over the gathering broods a tenderness appropriate to the memories of the occasion, its influence being manifest in hushed tones, as if this were indeed a service of the heart. Easter is not here, but its forerunner has shed abroad a spirit of consecration.

Before the audience is the chorus—tier on tier of men and maidens, nearly four hundred of them. Bunting and banners transform the stern outlines of the great stage. The men are in black; the maids in pink and white, the costumes making vivid contrast. Whole sections are in a flutter of light; others are sombre and still. The central figure of all, occupying the place of honor, is the powerful organ, and supporting it the orchestra of forty pieces. When the time arrives for the opening Doctor Swensson steps forward and in a few words tells the story of the first Easter—the prelude of the music that is to come.

A tremor passes over the ranks of the singers; they are rising to their feet. The orchestra breaks the stillness.

CARL A. SWENSSON   SAMUEL THORSTENBERG

The Messiah Festival first received national news media attention in the April 1900 issue of The Ladies' Home Journal.

A tremor passes over the singers. The orchestra breaks the stillness." Then this keen observer wrote:

> When the last note has died away, when the final "Amen" has been breathed, the listeners, their hearts warmed with religious fervor and exaltation, go out into the clear starry night as in a dream. The far horizon seems nearer, the wide arch of heaven, bending over the dusky reaches of prairie sod and field, closer at hand . . . . With such concentration of effort, such delight in musical expression, so worthy a theme, and so devout a people, little wonder is it that the singing of the Easter "Messiah" on the plains is an occasion to be anticipated eagerly, enjoyed with zest and remembered long.[20]

In 1913 the music critic of the *Chicago Tribune* described the Lindsborg "Messiah" tradition in an article that was often quoted:

> It is not surprising, therefore, that this chorus attains a tone of surprising unity, and that in all matters of rhythmical and intervallic precision it is unsurpassed. The quality of the tone is beautiful. In all massive efforts it is of overwhelming sonority. Sopranos are remarkable for the purity, the flexibility, and smoothness of the tone produced and the confident ease with which they approach trying altitudes of pitch. The contraltos share the delicious sympathy of tone quality common to most American choruses. Tenors achieve brightness and aggressiveness, and the basses are splendidly sonorous . . . .
>
> The Messiah has been sung by many persons the world over, but it is doubtful if the choruses were ever better sung than when these trained voices, rehearsed for a year, burst forth in divine harmony. They sing it with the scriptural words in their hearts. It is a praise anthem to the God who had prospered them and kept them together.

The music critic of the *Kansas City Star,* in an article in 1970, quoted the first paragraph above and then observed: "So it sounded to Dr. Gunn in 1913 . . . . And so, or nearly so, it sounded in 1969 on Easter Sunday."[21]

Many interesting descriptions of the cultural and religious life of Lindsborg have been made in the context of the "Messiah" tradition.

At the 1950 "Messiah" rendition, Ambassador Eric Bohman of Sweden speaks. Looking on are, left to right, the WDAF announcer, Kansas Governor Frank Carlson, President Emory Lindquist, and conductor Ralph Harrel (standing at right.)

Howard W. Turtle wrote in the *New York Times* in 1939: "When Brase begins his stern beat for one of the great choruses of the *Messiah*, he draws from the chorus a body of tone that is truly magnificent in its splendor. It is an expression in song from voices schooled to near perfection through years of training. But it is more than that. In Lindsborg, the *Messiah* is religion—as much a part of the Swedish people's worship as the church services which they attend every Sunday. It is an outpouring of the story they believe—the voice of John the Baptist crying in the wilderness, the birth of Jesus, His ministry, His crucifixion, and the triumphant resurrection with its resounding 'Hallelujah.' So when they sing their oratorio, it is more than a performance of musical quality. It has behind it a conviction of truth; of high purpose; of religious zeal that lifts its ecstasy to the sky and resounds in countless 'Hallelujahs.' " The *Reader's Digest* in a feature article, "Oberammergau of the Plains," in April, 1944, pointed out that the "Messiah" festival is called by critics "the finest of its kind in the world."[22]

In 1953 the *Washington Star* presented an article that provided this appraisal:

> A musical saga that has no equal in this or any other country reaches its annual climax Easter Sunday in the performance of Handel's *Messiah*. In the small midwestern town of Lindsborg, Kansas, Handel's great oratorio will be given today for the 197th time. For nearly three-quarters of a century it has been the inspiration of the daily life of the inhabitants. The story is one of the most thrilling in American history and in the annals of music. For the performance of the *Messiah* not only testifies to the cultural ideals of this community, but records the preservation until the present, of qualities of mind and spirit that inflamed the pioneers whose contribution to the greatness of this country was directed by God.[23]

The fine achievement of the oratorio society has also been described in recent years. In 1960 the *Kansas City Star* wrote as follows about the 210th rendition:

> The 500-voice chorus was in good form, responsive and sensitive to the direction of the new conductor, Elmer Copley. . . . The chorus rang with magnificent massive tone, clarity of diction, well-balanced, rich sound and finesse. The exaltation and vibrant joy of the singers found receptive response in an audience that filled Presser Hall. An occasional lifting here and there was

used to bring out expression and deep feeling to meet the new conductor's interpretation without lessening the spiritual appeal as interpreted by the program's founder and preserved through the years under the calm Nordic tradition.[24]

The Palm Sunday rendition in 1972, the 234th by the oratorio society, was summarized in the *Topeka Capital-Journal* in these words: "For members of Bethany College's Oratorio Society, and especially for Copley, the *Messiah* is more than great music. It expresses the wonderful joy that grows out of Easter, and through Copley and the singers, it is communicated to all who crowd Presser Hall for the performances on the Bethany campus."[25]

A vital aspect of a fine oratorio performance is the organ accompaniment. Several talented organists have shared this responsibility including Olof Olsson, Alma Swensson, Luther Swensson, A. D. Bodfors, Anton Oeslund, N. A. Krantz, Charles Purdy, Sigfrid Laurin, Samuel Thorstenberg, Hugo Bedinger, Hagbard Brase, Ellen Strom, Arvid Wallin, Mabel Gertrude King Hanson, and Lambert Dahlsten. The longest tenure is that of Lambert Dahlsten, '32 and '33, professor of piano and organ since 1952. After graduating from Bethany he studied piano with Beveridge Webster in New York. He also taught piano for several years in New York. He has studied organ extensively with Gotthard Arner of the Royal Academy of Music in Stockholm, Sweden. Dahlsten has devoted his talent with fine results as organist and pianist for more than two decades as well as accompanying guest soloists during Festival Week. He served as acting dean of the College of Fine Arts, 1959-62.

A sizeable number of alumni have returned to the campus as soloists in performances of the *Messiah* and *St. Matthew Passion.* Included among them are the following: Marvel Biddle, Ethyl Coover, Ethel Cullison, Ernest Davis, Olive Frisk, Thure Jaderborg, Edla Lund, Carl Melander, Daniel Nelson, Minnie Nelson, Allen Stewart, Myrtle Sundstrom, Bertha Swensson, Samuel Thorstenberg, Floyd Townsley, Arvid Wallin, and Raquel Jerrue-Winkler.

G. N. Malm, Lindsborg artist, author, and business man, was a key person in promoting the oratorio tradition. He was a fine painter and a famous author in Swedish American circles. His volumes, *Charlie Johnson* and *Härute,* are classics in Swedish American literature. He came to Lindsborg in 1894 at the request of Dr. Swensson and he soon identified himself fully with the college and the community. He was secretary of the oratorio society as well as historian. He wrote extensively for newspapers and periodicals about music and art activities. Dedicated service came to an end with his death in 1928.

Worthy service to the oratorio society has been given by the secretaries of the various sections of the chorus across the decades.

The management and promotion of the "Messiah" festival required

The 1918 "Messiah" program depicts famous artists from previous Festivals: Ysaye, Schumann-Heink, Sembrich, Gadski, Nordica, Nielsen, Galli-Curci, Claussen.

Oratorio Society officers in the 1926 program are: Pihlblad, president; Mrs. Swensson, vice-president; Brase conductor; Malm, secretary; Stensaas, treasurer.

much planning and extra effort in several college offices. The attendance generally produced surplus income which was used to support the current budget. These funds were especially important in certain years.

A vital aspect of the "Messiah" festival has been the many famous musicians who have appeared in concert. In 1902, prior to the later tradition of great artists during Festival Week, Bethany College presented to the music lovers of Kansas the celebrated singer, Mme. Nordica. Special trains brought great crowds on March 3 to swell an audience that filled the "Messiah" auditorium. When Nordica appeared on the stage resplendent in brilliant attire and flashing jewels, she was received by an audience that rose to its feet and gave her thunderous applause. While the accompanist was arranging the music for the first selection, "Elsa's Dream" from *Lohengrin,* her glance embraced the strange octagonal building, and seeing the large organ, she smiled congratulations. This response was again greeted with great applause. The concert was a thrilling performance for the enthusiastic audience.

When Nordica was ready to leave the auditorium for her private car, "Brunnhilde," on the railroad siding, the members of the Bethany Male Chorus pulled her carriage. As an expression of appreciation for this fine gesture of interest, the renowned singer tossed some roses from her beautiful bouquet. One stem was carefully nurtured by G. N. Malm, and in the next few years, visitors to the Malm residence saw the "Nordica rose." The plant died, but the remembrance of Nordica's memorable recital lived on.

The list of great performers who have appeared during "Messiah" week is a long and impressive one. Schumann-Heink appeared in recitals in 1913, 1916, and 1926, the last a benefit concert for the construction of the new music auditorium. Lindsborg residents recall her wonderful singing and her warm, friendly personality. When appearing in the benefit recital in Lindsborg on May 16, 1926, Schuman-Heink declared: "America has no other Lindsborg. I want to have a part in this one." Friends of the College were thrilled at this identification of a famous figure in the music world with the program and emphasis in the small

The 1889 Bethany Orchestra. *The Bethany Band, under C. D. Wagstaff.*

college town in Central Kansas. Other great artists who have performed in Lindsborg are Eugene Ysaye, Mme. Gadski, Galli-Curci, Mischa Elman, Mme. Olive Fremstad, Frieda Hempel, Pablo Casals, Lucy Gates (twice), Jennie Norelli, Alice Nielsen, Julia Claussen, Gustaf Holmquist, Arthur Middleton (twice), Florence Macbeth, Margaret Matzenauer, Erna Rubinstein, Sophie Breslau (twice), Paul Althouse, Marian Talley (twice), Marie Sundelius (twice), Reinold Werrenrath, Albert Spaulding (two times), Clair Dux, Dusolina Giannini (twice), Kathryn Meisle, Francis Macmillan, Mary Lewis, Richard Crooks, Gina Binnera, Arthur Hacket, Mario Chamlee, Florence Austral, Luella Melius, Elsa Alsen, Efrem Zimbalist, Hilde Reggiani, Gregor Piatigorsky, Joseph Szigeti, Ellabelle Davis, Marjorie Lawrence, Jennie Tourell, Seymour Lipkin, Mack Harrell, Isaac Stern, Blanche Thebom (twice), William Primrose, Irene Jordan, Set Svanholm, Grant Johansson, Michael Rabin, and Gary Graffman. Included among great ensemble groups presented at the festival are the Innes Band, which appeared in 1905, 1906, 1907 for several concerts during the week; the New York Philharmonic, Joseph Strnsky conducting, in 1916; the Flonzaley Quartet in 1926; and other important groups earlier and later.

Closely identified with the oratorio society are other Bethany musical organizations and their personnel. The Bethany Symphony Orchestra traces its origin to 1882 when Lindsborg orchestral musicians joined in the second year of the "Messiah" renditions. As indicated previously, an orchestra was imported from Rock Island, Illinois, for the first year's performance. The orchestra has always shared in the repertoire of the oratorio society. The instrumentation and personnel have made possible concerts which include the great symphony compositions during most of the orchestra's history. A concert is always featured during the "Messiah" festival and other concerts are scheduled during the year. The conductors, except in the early years, have been members of the Bethany faculty and include the following: A. E. Agrelius, Sam E. Carlson, Charles Purdy, N. A. Krantz, K. Döme Geza, Franz Zedler, Theodore Lindberg, H. E. Malloy, Arvid Wallin, Hjalmar Wetterstrom, Arthur E. Uhe, Joseph Kirschbaum, Lloyd Spear, Lowell Boroughs,

The Bethany Male chorus, 1907.

The 1937-38 Bethany A Capella Choir.

Marshall Haddock, David Higbee, and others for shorter periods.

Various choral groups have furnished talented singers for the oratorio society and each organization has developed fine traditions of choral performance. A chapel choir was organized in the early history of the College. This ensemble group has performed intermittently and is active at the present time. In 1895, *Norden,* a male chorus with emphasis upon Swedish repertoire, was organized with N. A. Krantz as conductor. The Bethany Male Chorus made its first public appearance in 1902 and had a continuous history for more than two decades. Samuel Thorstenberg was the first conductor and G. N. Malm, Lindsborg citizen, was a leader in its activities.

The Bethany College A Capella Choir was organized by Dr. Hagbard Brase in 1935. The choir soon established a reputation for excellence in a demanding repertoire. The chorus received splendid press notices in its appearances at home and on tour. In the national Columbia choral quest sponsored by the Columbia Broadcasting System in 1938, the panel of judges ranked the Bethany choir as runner-up in the competition.

Excellence has also characterized the performances of this choir under the leadership of Elmer Copley beginning in 1960. The choir has made several tours to both coasts. Harriett Johnson in the *New York Post* in May, 1973, described the concert in Tully Hall, Lincoln Center, by writing that the performance " . . . was more than professional; it is a remarkable group . . . . There were unforgettable moments . . . . Copley has instilled a strong sense of the lifeblood of music into his chorus, that is—the importance of rhythm. Tone quality was consistently

The Bethany College-Community Symphony Orchestra, directed by David Higbee.

The Bethany Symphonic Band.

Pianist Malcolm Frager and the Kansas City Philharmonic Orchestra in Presser Hall, May 3, 1974.

The Bethany College Choir, directed by Elmer Copley.

The Bethany College Choir performing at the nation's capitol, May 29, 1973.

buoyant, one reason for the impeccable pitch." The *New York Times* observed: " . . . the sound . . . was consistently beguiling. Elmer Copley cultivates unusually mellow tone. This velvety quality prevailed no matter what the dynamic extreme." [26]

The Bethany Choir always sings to a large audience during the "Messiah" festival and on other occasions. Copley introduced a beautiful annual program on the campus, "An Hour of Christmas," which regularly fills Presser Hall to capacity. The Bethany Choir with Copley as conductor, the Bethany Chapel Choir, Dr. Walter L. Pelz, conductor, and the Bethany Choraliers participate. The program often includes compositions by Professor Pelz, who is receiving increasingly great recognition for his compositions, especially in choral music.

The following persons have served as directors of the Bethany Choir: Hagbard Brase, Charles Stief, Ralph Harrel, Rolf Espeseth, Eugene Pearson, Alvin Reimer, Roy Henry Johnson, and Elmer Copley.

The oldest musical organization on the Bethany campus is the Bethany Band. The first instrumental band in Lindsborg was organized in 1877. The group was reorganized at the suggestion of President Swensson in 1881 as the Bethany Silver Cornet Band. The band always performs during the "Messiah" festival and on other occasions. A. E. Agrelius was the first conductor. Succeeding conductors have been N. A. Krantz, Victor Lund, George Hapgood, Charles D. Wagstaff, Hjalmar Wetterstrom, Walter Brown, Lowell Boroughs, Marshall Haddock, David Higbee, and others with briefer tenure.

The Bethany College Choir, the Chapel Choir, and the Choraliers present "An Hour of Christmas" each December to a packed house in Presser Hall.

11.

Art and Artists

A college enriches the life of students in proportion to the opportunities provided for living in a stimulating environment that is friendly to great values. A continuing source of enrichment at Bethany has been the testimonial to beauty through artists and their creativity, the courses in classroom and studio, the variety of exhibitions, the influences of art students upon their associates, and the general commitment to the worth of art for individuals and society. Moreover, Birger Sandzén, master artist-teacher for more than half a century, added a special dimension personally and professionally. Sandzén paintings and prints in countless homes of Bethany alumni and former students witness to an appreciation of art from Bethany years.

Art in the Bethany curriculum traces its origin to the academic year 1890-91. A statement in the catalogue introduced it as follows: "In this department scholars may obtain instruction in drawing, crayon work, oil and watercolor painting . . . . It will be the aim of the teacher to give a critical knowledge of the principles of light and shade, accuracy in outline, and the use of color. A class in sketching can be organized, if any demand is made for it, also composition from original subjects for advanced pupils." Miss Lucy J. Osgood was the first art teacher. Twelve students were enrolled. The classes in art attracted forty-four students in three classes during the next year. Mrs. Hannah Swensson, teacher in painting, and Mrs. Marie Swensson, teacher in crayon work, joined Miss Osgood. In 1892-93 Addie Covell is listed as the only art teacher for forty-seven students.[1]

An art exhibition was held at commencement in 1892. The enthusiasm of Carl Swensson for this new department is reflected in an article in *Hemlandet,* June, 1892, the weekly Swedish newspaper

Views in the Art Hall, circa 1889.

published in Chicago: "We must say some words about the art depart-ment at Bethany College. The exhibition is indeed excellent. Miss Lucy Osgood's exhibits consist of no less than twenty-five splendid oil paint-ings. Mrs. Hannah Swensson and Mrs. Marie Swensson show in the other departments forty-two beautiful proofs of crayon work and oil and we may add that the results seem surprising."[2]

The art program had been so well established that Olof Grafstrom, a well-known artist, joined the faculty in September, 1893. Grafstrom had achieved a good reputation as a painter on the west coast. Swedish born, he had studied painting at the Royal Academy of Art in Stockholm. He emigrated to the United States in 1886, living in Oregon, Washington, and California. He became known for his landscape and altar paintings, creating about 200 of the latter. He was a fine teacher and painter at Bethany until he resigned in 1897 to join the faculty of Augustana College, Rock Island, Illinois. Birger Sandzén, after describing Grafstrom's excellent work as a painter, observed: "Anyone who knows Grafstrom personally cannot but like him for he is a true friend, a generous colleague and a fine gentleman."[3]

The scope of the art instruction in the Grafstrom era and for several years later, was described as follows: "Thorough instruction will be given in the study of drawing, light and shade, still life, the cast, antique, human figure, portrait, interior and landscape composition, animals, fruits, flowers, decorative work, etc. through the usual medium—oil, watercolor, charcoal, crayon, pencil, pen, India ink, and sepia. Special attention will be given to sacred art."[4]

Grafstrom was succeeded in 1897 by another fine artist, Carl G:son (Gustafson) Lotave. Lotave had studied at Stockholm with Anders Zorn and Richard Berg. He was a fellow student of Birger Sandzén at Stockholm. Lotave then studied in Paris for two years. Carl Swensson contacted him, upon the recommendation of Birger Sandzén, while traveling in Sweden in 1897. Lotave joined Swensson on the long trip to Lindsborg. He was an excellent portrait painter. Famous people whose portraits were painted by Lotave include King Albert of Belgium, Generals Joffre, Foch, Hindenburg, and Pershing. When Lotave left Bethany in 1899 for Colorado Springs, he had made a significant con-tribution to the College.

Birger Sandzén, in a reminiscent mood, wrote about his close relationship with Lotave in Stockholm where they visited historical land-marks and painted continuously, and later in Lindsborg, where they not only sought to capture the mood of nature on canvas but also spent time walking in pastures and in valleys hunting rabbits and quail. In assessing Lotave's career Sandzén wrote: "It was early apparent that Lotave was a young man with great talent. Now we see the noble and fine achievement that has been developed. The recognition and admiration which is now lavished upon him is truly deserved because he is an honest artist who paints for the sake of art."[5]

The appointment of Birger Sandzén as professor and head of the art department to succeed Lotave in 1899 was a singularly important development in Bethany's history. Sven Birger was born in the parish of Blidsberg in Västergötland on February 5, 1871, the son of the Reverend and Mrs. John Peter Sandzén. The Sandzén home provided excellent cultural opportunities for Birger and his brothers Gustaf and Carl. Birger has stated that as a child he constantly listened to classical music, "one day Beethoven and Bach and the next day, Bach and Beethoven." His father was a capable violinist. When the family moved to Järpås, also in Västergötland, Gustaf Lundblad, an assistant to Birger's father, observed the boy's talent in drawing and encouraged him to draw with informal lessons. Birger also received lessons in watercolor painting at this time. At the age of ten, he enrolled in the preparatory department of the College of Skara in the cathedral city of Västergötland. In addition to academic studies, he took drawing lessons from Olof Erlandson, a teacher who emphasized fundamentals. He also studied famous prints with Erlandson, thus enriching his knowledge of art.

After completing studies at Skara, Birger enrolled at Lund University. There he concentrated on aesthetics, French language and literature. He also took lessons in watercolor painting with Regina Kilberg, an able teacher. Traditional university studies did not fully satisfy the young man at this time because his greatest interest was in painting and drawing. This desire brought him to Stockholm. He was enrolled in *Tekniska högskolan,* when through fate and good fortune he met a nephew of Anders Zorn, who was perhaps the greatest Swedish painter and printmaker of all time. Zorn's nephew told Birger that Zorn had rented some rooms in Stockholm, and in addition to his own painting, he planned to take a few pupils. Birger hurried to meet Zorn and became his pupil for two years. He was one of eight young men who studied with Zorn in the little studio on Norra Smedjegatan, beginning in the autumn of 1891. When the number of pupils increased, a larger studio on Mäster-Samuelsgatan was used.[6]

The years with Zorn were decisive in the life and career of Birger Sandzén. The student had great admiration for the master. Zorn worked all day long with his students, painting and teaching, as Sandzén did later. The legacy from Zorn included strict discipline of the palette and a direct vigorous use of the brush.

Sandzén had multiple resources for development during the Stockholm years. He studied portrait painting with Richard Berg, who told Birger that he had the potentiality for becoming a portrait painter and could make a living in that field. He received lessons in drawing from Per Hasselberg, a well-known sculptor. Berg and Hasselberg taught in

Zorn's studio. There were also many opportunities to view great works of art and to listen to thought-provoking lectures in Sweden's capital city. Besides working intensively in painting and drawing, he also studied voice in Stockholm.

After two years with Zorn, Sandzén studied for about six months in Paris at the studio of Aman-Jean on the Avenue de Saxe, beginning in February, 1894. The fine instruction, the stimulation from like-minded students of several nationalities, and the helpful artistic milieu deepened Sandzén's devotion to his calling. He also continued his interest in music by taking singing lessons. Americans were among his friends in Paris. He was attracted by the promise of American life as they described it. His feelings were expressed in these words: "A free, new country! It should be heaven for a young painter. Out there in your West an artist could develop a style of his own to fit the country."[7]

Sandzén's interest in America was further stimulated by reading a book by Carl Swensson, president of Bethany College. Swensson's volume, *I Sverige* (1890), included material on America and especially about Kansas and Lindsborg. Young Sandzén sensed something contagious in the enthusiasm of Swensson. In March and April of 1894 when Birger was in Paris, there was correspondence between Dr. Swensson and him. The Bethany president was greatly impressed with the young Swedish student and enthusiastically invited him to join the Bethany faculty. On Tuesday, September 4, 1894, youthful Birger Sandzén saw for the first time the Smoky Valley of Central Kansas. He was twenty-three years old.

The talent of Birger Sandzén was used in the early years at Bethany in teaching languages, especially French, in giving voice lessons, and in painting and drawing. He continued to teach some language classes until the 1930s. His fine voice was heard in the tenor arias for several years in renditions of Handel's *Messiah* and on other occasions. In 1899, as indicated above, he succeeded Carl Lotave as head of the art department.

Birger Sandzén was a magnificent example of the vital concept of artist-teacher. His keen insight as a teacher was supported by his distinction as an artist. In the tradition of his former teacher, Anders Zorn, he taught and painted with his students. Sandzén's emphasis upon drawing, his mastery of design, his understanding of composition and color, joined with his enthusiasm for teaching, fashioned a master teacher. Birger Sandzén's sensitivity and patience made his suggestions the basis for appreciative response from the students. The studio was a partnership in creativity and cultural growth. The very presence of Birger Sandzén added a new dimension as youth were stimulated by example to respect honest and sustained effort.

Birger Sandzén's classes in art history were memorable experiences for many generations of students. His knowledge of music and literature enriched his approach to art of the past, which was not a paralyzing analysis but rather a humanistic response coupled with the historian's respect for names, dates, and places. His great love for Chinese art added new resources to the traditional western tradition. Moreover, his lectures provided the insight that came from a creative and sensitive person.

Although Birger Sandzén was fully occupied with a heavy teaching load and his own creative activities, he developed, with the help of his assistants, an effective curriculum in art. In 1916 the courses were enriched and the staff expanded so that a four-year program leading to the bachelor of painting degree was introduced. A formal two-year normal course, leading to certification by the state board of education, was also provided. In 1929 the curriculum was revised to provide for the bachelor of fine arts in painting, the bachelor of fine arts in art education, and a two-year certificate in commercial art.

The broad expanse of prairie and the wide horizon in Kansas were quite different from Sandzén's native Sweden, which, in contrast, was a land of miniatures with an abundance of birch and pine trees amidst quiet lakes and sparkling streams. The impact of this new milieu was described by the artist in 1915:

> When I came to this part of the country twenty years ago, I had much to learn over again. The atmosphere here is different from the atmosphere in Sweden. There everything is enveloped in a soft clinging atmosphere with colors in greens and blues. But here the air is so thin that the colors become more vivid and the shadows lighter. The colors here are purples and greens and yellows, with everything bright in this clear, ringing atmosphere of the West. When I started to paint here, I had to pitch everything in a higher key.[8]

Sandzén's paintings reflect his artistic response to the American West. He looked at his new world and what he saw excited him as he drew or painted willows and cottonwoods, ponds and river banks, pastures and pioneer houses, rocks and mountains. Oils, watercolors, lithographs, and woodcuts interpret the Smoky Valley with the Spanish Steppes to the north and west and the winding river running through it. Graham County with its Wild Horse Creek was another favorite area. Colorado, Utah, New Mexico, and coastal areas provided numerous subjects for his creativity. His portraits reflect sensitivity to the human situation whether it be a sturdy pioneer or a scout from the western lands. His numerous canvases of sunflowers, peonies, chrysanthemums, coxcombs, and lilacs testify to his love of color, his distinctive style, and his appreciation for the simple beauty of nature.

Birger Sandzén's prints and watercolors were an important part of his career. He was a member of the Society of American Etchers, Gravers, Lithographers, and Woodcutters, the American Water Color Society, the Prairie Water Color Society, which he organized, the California Society of Water Color Painters, the Philadelphia Water Color Club, and he exhibited with the New York Water Color Society. In the volume,

The Graphic Work of Birger Sandzén (1952), Dr. Charles Pelham Greenough 3rd, the editor, has listed, with many illustrations, 204 lithographs, 95 block prints, and 27 dry points from the works of the Bethany artist. This comprehensive catalogue also presents valuable introductory material about the artist and his prints. Sandzén's works are found in the Metropolitan Museum of Art, Chicago Art Institute, British Museum, Library of Congress, New York Public Library, National Museum of Sweden, William Rockhill Nelson Gallery of Art, and in countless churches, schools, and homes.

Critics have praised Dr. Sandzén's understanding of art and the technical mastery of his media and subjects. Although space does not permit citation of many comments of art critics, reference to the New York exhibition in February, 1922, seems appropriate. In reviewing the critics' evaluation, a writer in the *Kansas City Star* observed: "Art critics in New York have been searching their vocabularies for words vigorous enough to describe their impressions on seeing paintings and lithographs of Birger Sandzén." Among those New York critics was Peyton Boswell of the *New York American* who wrote about "the vigor of his [Sandzén's] techniques, the 'rightness' of composition, and the gorgeousness of his color." He continued: "That he has delicacy of touch as well as strength is shown in his watercolors . . . . This group of watercolors establish Sandzén's distinction as an artist and yet he adds effect to effect, power to power by his lithographs and woodcuts." The critic in *America Art News* wrote: "All the reports of the brilliant quality of the art of Birger Sandzén that have come to us from the West are more than justified" and the exhibition makes him "stand out as a bigger and more rounded personality than even report had made him."[9]

The legacy of Birger Sandzén to Kansas and a wider area is rich in his contribution to art appreciation. He was at times a lonely pioneer in his ceaseless efforts to develop greater understanding of beauty. In many schools, churches, and communities he was the first contact thousands of people had with art through hundreds of lectures and exhibitions. Weekends found him boarding a train with as many art portfolios as he could carry. The attendance varied in size and responsiveness, but it is true as Leila Mechlin once wrote: "Birger Sandzén has lit little candles of art knowledge and appreciation all through the Middle West."

In a delightful article in *Prärieblomman 1903*, Birger Sandzén describes the origin of the first formal Bethany art exhibition in the spring of 1899. This established the tradition that has had a continuous history during "Messiah" week ever since that time. Several friends were visiting in Sandzén's room in Old Main when someone suggested that an art exhibition should be held in connection with the "Messiah" festival which would begin the next day. The words led to immediate action as Carl Lotave, head of the art department, G. N. Malm, Lindsborg author, artist, and professional designer, and Sandzén launched into the project. Room 114 Old Main was selected as the location. A frantic search was made for rugs, drapes, potted plants, and other items to make the room as attractive as possible. A sizeable number of paintings were hung. Included were Lotave's *1861, Dödsdans,* the *Nordiska sommarnatt;* a portrait of Lotave and *Paris Street Scene,* by Sandzén; and other works by these two artists and by Malm.[10]

The response during the first day was terribly discouraging—only one person came to the exhibition. Lotave, Sandzén, and Malm reflected on the situation. Arrangements were made to publish circulars to be distributed on the "Messiah" excursion trains and on the campus. Students were engaged to serve as "barkers" to publicize the event. The result was astounding—during the afternoon and evening the room was literally packed with people who paid the ten cents admission fee.[11]

In 1913 Birger Sandzén and his friends organized the Smoky Hill Art Club "to help create by talks and exhibitions a more active interest in art in all its forms and also to establish a permanent fund for the Art School, the income of which is to be given to needy art students." Previously, in 1897, a *Pro Artibus Society* had been formed to stimulate interest in art. The Smoky Hill Art Club greatly enriched the cultural life of the college and community. The society was very active in promoting exhibitions, in purchasing paintings and prints for the permanent collection, in acquiring art books, and in encouraging young artists through the award of scholarships. Sandzén was generous in making available prints as an important aspect of membership promotion. In March, 1920, a chapter of Delta Phi Delta, national collegiate art fraternity, was established on the campus. This organization recognized outstanding student achievement and fostered the growth of professional understanding.[12]

Art instruction was apparently held in a room in Old Main until 1893 when the first college building, the old Lindsborg public school, became the art hall. The numerous windows created a faulty light situation, but in the summer of 1898 this problem was remedied. One half of the building, the studio area, was renovated so that windows were located only on the north side. The other half, which served as an exhibition hall, was improved by the addition of skylights and interior renovation. The annual art exhibitions were held in the art building for several years beginning in 1900. Classes in art were taught and exhibitions presented subsequently during the Sandzén era on the second floor of the Carnegie Library building and in the Swedish Pavilion.

Closely identified with Birger Sandzén in instructional responsibilities have been several talented artists and teachers. Anna Keener Wilton, Jessie Bob Severtson, Dolores Gaston Runbeck, Myra Biggerstaff Holliday, Alice Whittaker, Margaret Sandzén Greenough, Ramona Weddle Raymer, Marie Miller, Katherine Watts Johnson, Gladys Hendricks,

Annie Lee Ross, and Ray Stapp were able colleagues who shared with Dr. Sandzén in the fine achievement of the art department.

Birger Sandzén's personal world provided resources of great meaning. In 1900 Alfrida Leksell, McPherson, a Bethany graduate and teacher of piano, and Birger Sandzén were married. The love and companionship of these kindred spirits enriched immeasurably the life of each of them. Mrs. Sandzén was a talented pianist and teacher who continued her interest in piano until the last days of her life. The Sandzén's daughter Margaret (Mrs. Charles Pelham Greenough 3rd), a former Bethany art teacher, completed the happy family circle. The Sandzén home and studio, on the edge of the campus west of Presser Hall, was the center of unfailing hospitality and great inspiration. Individuals and groups shared pleasant, relaxed conversation in the indescribably meaningful and beautiful milieu of paintings, prints, sculpture, and books.

Birger Sandzén retired from teaching in 1946 to become Artist-in-Residence and Professor Emeritus of Art. He then concluded more than a half century of dedicated and distinguished service to Bethany College. His was a life of unfailing loyalty to the College and Lindsborg, manifested by his decisions to decline calls to assume positions of leadership at several universities and art institutes in America, as well as one notable invitation to return to Sweden to assume a promising post. His life style did not encompass aggressive reach for recognition and prestige. His was a life of dedication to painting and teaching. He had heavy teaching loads, he gave many off-campus lectures, he wrote hundreds of articles, largely in Swedish, for newspapers and periodicals dealing with art and artists, reviews of musical events and of books, and descriptions of the life of the college and community. A book, *Med Pensel och Penna* (c. 1907), 215 pages, provided twenty-two narratives and stories, several with a setting in Spain and Mexico. A dozen reproductions in black and white of Sandzén's oil paintings, water colors and prints are included. Two volumes with reproductions of Sandzén's lithographs and woodcuts have been published: *The Smoky Valley* (1922) and *In the Mountains* (1925). The bibliography of articles in art periodicals and newspapers on his life and career is extensive. Several universities conferred honorary degrees upon Birger Sandzén. In 1940 he was honored by being made a Knight of the Royal Order of the North Star by King Gustaf V of Sweden for his outstanding contribution to Swedish American cultural life. The careers of art graduates during the Sandzén era are described in the chapter, "Alumni Achievement."[13]

The well-established tradition in art was continued and developed by several talented members of the faculty following the retirement of Birger Sandzén in 1946. The classes of Lester Raymer, a graduate of the Chicago Art Institute, profited from his instruction as students worked with an artist of rare ability who has been widely recognized for his creative excellence in several media. Charles B. Rogers is well-known as a painter and teacher. Annie Lee Ross and Ray Stapp were artists who were also versatile and able teachers. They strengthened the program in art education and enriched the curriculum in crafts and design. In 1953 John Bashor began a tenure of more than a decade. He was soon recognized as a fine painter and teacher whose work has received recognition in a wide area. When Rosemary Laughlin was a member of the staff during the 1960s, her ability in sculpture made a valuable addition to campus educational and artistic resources.

Splendid recognition of the role of art historically and currently at Bethany came in 1973 when Mrs. E. C. (Mary) Mingenback, McPherson, established an endowment for the first distinguished professorship at Bethany, to be known as the Mary Mingenback Distinguished Professorship in Art. Professor Ray Kahmeyer, who served as head of the department, is the deserving and talented person to be recognized in this manner. He has received wide recognition for his creativity, especially in ceramics.

The current curriculum in art provides a wide selection of courses in drawing, painting, printmaking, ceramics, sculpture, photography, and art history leading to a major in the bachelor of arts degree. A four-year curriculum is also available which leads to teacher certification. The faculty and enrollment showed a substantial increase in the 1970s. The Mingenback Art Center (1970), described previously, has greatly enriched the physical resources for instruction and student exhibitions.[14]

The Birger Sandzén Memorial Gallery, completed in 1957, provides splendid facilities for the permanent collection and for traveling exhibitions. While the former is comprised principally of oils, watercolors, and prints by Sandzén, paintings in various media by other artists form a respectable share of the collection. The Brase Room is usually hung with a fine group of early Henry Varnum Poors, Lester Raymers, and canvases by John Steuart Curry, Doel Reed, Marsden Hartley, B. J. O. Nordfeldt, Raymond Johnson, John Bashor, and others. Among the prints gathered over a period of years with funds from the Smoky Hill Art Club, there are examples by Rembrandt, Dürer, Zorn, Pennell, and an impressive list of other printmakers. Sculpture ranges from "The Little Triton" by Carl Milles and "Greyhounds Playing" by Anna Hyatt Huntington to a pair of sixteenth century Chinese "Guardian Lions" and three early seventeenth century Japanese bronzes. Because of Sandzén's admiration for oriental art, he acquired, along with his friend Oscar Thorsen, a number of Chinese paintings and Japanese color-prints, a varied assortment of eighteenth and nineteenth century textiles, many bronzes, porcelains, and pottery. Since 1957 a collection of contemporary ceramics has been formed which includes an outstanding group of ceramic sculpture by Rosemary Laughlin Bashor.[15]

Since the opening of the gallery in 1957, over four-hundred exhibitions have been shown. The largest was probably an assemblage of "Swedish Arts and Crafts" sent out by the Swedish Government. Highlights among other exhibitions included a group of large oils by the late Rico Lebrun, IBM traveling shows, Goya's complete "The Disasters of War," a group of Edward Munch's graphics lent by the Museum of Modern Art, a room of 17th century Dutch paintings, special Christmas exhibitions, and shows of African, Mexican, South Pacific, Central American, Australian, and American Indian arts and crafts.

Many group or one-man shows by contemporary artists of Kansas, the Midwest, Colorado, the Southwest, and Lindsborg have been featured. The tradition of continuing the annual Messiah Festival Spring Exhibition has been an important trust which the gallery has carried out every year since its opening in 1957. The work and responsibilities connected with this gallery are effectively carried out by the co-directors, Dr. Charles Pelham Greenough 3rd and Carl William Peterson.

Birger Sandzén at a painting easel.

Ray Kahmeyer and Dan Mason converse in the Mingenback Art Center ceramics classroom.

The great "Terrible Swedes" football team of 1904.

Even in early days football was a popular spectator sport.

Left: Football and track spectators today have a good view from the Philip Anderson Stadium.

Left: The 1971 football "Terrible Swedes" block a field goal attempt to set up their Mineral Water Bowl victory.

12.

Intercollegiate Athletics

Bethany College has followed the pattern of American colleges and universities generally in sponsoring intercollegiate athletics. As early as 1892 the following question was raised in the *Lindsborg News:* "Where are the football clubs? There are many who would take part in such a sport. We already have baseball, lawn tennis, and gymnastics." The question was soon answered. Football was played at Bethany with the beginning of the next fall semester. In October, 1893, the *Messenger* recorded the following: "The Bethany football team has played and lost its first game. The contest was with Kansas Wesleyan University. The Bethany boys played a plucky game but they were no match for the Wesleyans. The game was characterized throughout by gentleness and good feeling. A large crowd of lookers on were present." KWU defeated Bethany by the score of 38-0. Interest was high among the students who produced the first Bethany yell which was led by an elected "Yellmaster":

Rah, rah, rah; Rah, rah, rah;
B-E-T-H-A-N-Y, Bethany College.
Rah, rah, rah.[1]

Football was played in the following year with a schedule of two games against Kansas Wesleyan. The record was one win and one loss. In contrast to the favorable comment about the Wesleyan game the previous year, the *Messenger* reported the following about the second game: "The Swedes did not consider the numerous fainting spells of the Wesleyan captain as being professional. Valuable time was consumed when Brown repeatedly resorted to his unsportsmanlike tactics."[2]

The second season had just been completed when at a meeting of the board of directors on December 3, 1894, President Swensson was requested to present resolutions on the subject of football at the next

meeting. When the members met on February 4 they adopted unanimously the following resolution: "Whereas, the sport of Foot Ball has
caused much unfavorable comment among our friends and patrons, and,
Whereas, the board is assured that Foot Ball is not a suitable game for
our students, giving occasion for brutality and other base passions, and
often accompanied with painful and dangerous accidents, therefore be it
Resolved, that Foot Ball is hereafter prohibited at this institution." In a
letter to the *Topeka Capital*, President Swensson identified the following
reasons for the college's opposition to football: "It is brutal; it is
dangerous; it is a poor substitute for gymnastics; it causes students to
become negligent in studies; it includes noisy boisterousness, savage all-
penetrating yelling, free and unpleasant exhibition of unrestricted lung
power."[3]

No football games were authorized following the action of the board
until 1901. In May of that year a faculty committee consisting of
Professors J. E. Welin, Vivian Henman, and P. J. Wedel presented a
petition urging that competition in football be allowed. The following
reasons were cited: "The game promotes courage and manliness; it exercises the mental faculties; it arouses college spirit and enthusiasm; it
develops keenness and accuracy of thought; it attracts to our school the
healthiest and most robust students; the sentiment of our community
seems to be entirely favorable to the game." On the basis of this faculty
petition, football was authorized for the academic year 1901-02.[4]

When football was resumed in 1901, the sponsorship was furnished
by the Bethany College Athletic Association which had just been organized. Eight games were played with a record of five wins, two losses, and
one tie. Enthusiasm mounted with the result that Benjamin J. "Bennie"
Owen was hired as the coach in 1902. Owen had been a fine athlete at the
University of Kansas, he had served as coach at Washburn College, and
he came to Bethany upon the invitation of President Swensson after serving as an assistant to "Hurry Up" Yost at the University of Michigan.
"Bennie" Owen, who was hired to teach chemistry and coach all sports,
had a great career as football coach 1902-04.

"Bennie" Owen's three years at Bethany produced the greatest
record of victories in the college's history and attracted national attention. The record provided twenty-two victories, two losses, and two ties.
The "Terrible Swedes," as they were known, compiled 796 points to 34
for their opponents. In 1904 Bethany won all seven games, including victories over Kansas State Agricultural College, Manhattan, and the
University of Oklahoma.

The big games in 1903 and 1904 were with Oklahoma University.
The 1903 game was played in Colcord Park in Oklahoma City on
Thanksgiving afternoon. Two hundred Bethany fans went to the Sooner
Capital via special train. The game was only eight minutes in progress

when the Swedes started a ninety-six yard touchdown drive. "Win" Banbury, half-back, made a thirty-yard run for the first touchdown drive. The final score was Bethany 12, Oklahoma University 10.

Owen's Swedes were all victorious when they faced a strong Oklahoma University team at Sportsman's Park in Oklahoma City on Thanksgiving Day, 1904. The Bethany team unleashed a fast, deceptive type of play that confused their opponents. The "spinner," "cross buck," "the unbalanced line," and other plays were used perhaps for the first time in the Plains area by Bethany. The final score was Bethany 36, Oklahoma University 9.[5]

The great success of "Bennie" Owen was followed by his resignation at the end of the 1904 season to become head football coach at the University of Oklahoma. He continued his career as a successful coach and director of athletics for many years at that institution.

The "Terrible Swedes" made history for Bethany in the years of "Bennie" Owen's leadership. Included among the players were: the Banbury brothers from Pratt—Win and Quince—the four Petterson brothers from Mitchell County—Dave, Leslie, Alfred, and Andrew—Fred Troutman, Leonard Runbeck, Frank Henderson, Elmer T. Peterson, "Wink" Busch, E. Wiley, Luther and Martin Swanstrom, George White, "Kacie" Swenson, Edwin Anderson, J. R. Skidmore, Anton Peterson, Eric J. Heurlin, Carl Slatt, Leonard Petterson, Paul N. Carlson, Charlie Clancy, Arthur "Doc" Berquist, Frank Gibbs, Oscar Ostrum, Otto Oleen, Clarence Rapp, Luther Stromquist, John Turner, Evan Pugh, "Bill" Bailey, "Gabe" Carlson, G. Edwin Johnson, Arthur Gibson, Leonard Haggman, Roscoe Peterson, Leonard Swedberg, and Sam Holmberg. The training was intensive. Following long scrimmage, the players would jog to the bridge two miles east of Lindsborg and back. When returning from a football trip, Owen would ask the conductor to stop the train two miles out of Lindsborg, and the coach and team trotted into town. Physical condition and mental alertness were basic factors in Owen's great teams. Morale was high.[6]

The famous *Rockar, Stockar* yell had its origin in the "Bennie" Owen era. It appeared for the first time in the *Messenger*, December, 1902, as the first item under the rubric, "From Hall and Campus." A group of students, including Eric Heurlin, Karl J. "Kacie" Swenson, Elmer Ahlstedt, Oscar Ostrum, and E. O. Deere were dissatisfied with the old "Rah, Rah" yells. While studying Swedish mythology in the class of Professor J. E. Floren, these students were impressed with the power of Thor, the old Norse god, as he rushed forward through all obstacles in a chariot pulled by charging goats. This symbolized drive and strength. The students also read about a certain jarl in Sweden of old who had placed all his possessions on a log raft which was then pushed into the Baltic Sea with the intent that wherever the raft stopped, there a great city would be built. This myth symbolized the spirit of adventure and success. The students worked hard to put the ideas into the form of a yell. Several members of the class of 1904 memorized the words and immediately before a critical game they rushed on the field and gave the first public version of *Rockar, Stockar.*[7]

The meaning of the yell, as interpreted by Dean E. O. Deere, who helped to initiate what apparently Eric Heurlin had drafted in the first instance, is as follows:

ROCKAR! STOCKAR!

(The jarl wore a jacket or coat—*rockar.* He was on a
log raft—*stockar,* braving the perils of the Baltic, floating
to the peninsula where he founded Stockholm.)

THOR OCH HANS BOCKAR!

(Thor going forward with lightning speed, driving his goats
from pinnacle to pinnacle, rushes irresistibly through all
opposition.)

KÖR IGENOM! KÖR IGENOM!

(Drive on through! Drive on through!)

TJU! TJU! TJU!

(A Swedish interjection.)

BETHANIA

(Bethany)

Thus came into being Bethany's famous yell which is heard at all Bethany athletic contests and whenever Bethany groups assemble.

The resignation of "Bennie" Owen and growing criticism of football soon brought an end to intercollegiate competition which lasted for a decade. At the meeting of the Augustana Synod in June, 1905, the members passed the following resolution: "That the Synod exhorts the board of directors at our colleges to pursue such action that the so-called intercollegiate contests in 'baseball, football, and basketball' shall stop and to see to it that instruction be given in systematic gymnastics . . ." Resolutions prohibiting football were passed at several successive synods. On November 15, 1905, a motion was passed "that the [Bethany] faculty looks with disfavor upon the organization of a football team composed of some outsiders for the purpose of playing a game or games with Oklahoma University and that the faculty prohibits the use of the name of the "Terrible Swedes" or the name of Bethany College in any form whatsoever." Moreover, the following day the board of directors took the following action: "In regard to Football, resolved, that the board sustains the action of the president in prohibiting intercollegiate football at the institution."[8]

Much criticism of the ban on football appeared in the *Messenger.* In October, 1905, the editor, Elmer T. Peterson, argued: "The game itself needs no defense save its own success as a peerless source of college spirit and an all around development of muscle, will-power, courage, and the inherent quality of exhuberant animal spirit which is the basis of all desire for exercise." The editor stated: "The class of people who still think the game too rough has dwindled down to a few obese preachers and a handful of consumptives." In December, 1907, a sharp editorial criticizing the prohibition of football appeared under the rubric, "Are the Sons of Thor Extinct?"[9]

The response to the ban on football took several forms. In September, 1908, the schedule of football games was printed on the front page of the *Messenger* enclosed in a block of black lines with two black crosses. The games had been cancelled by the board of directors. When a correspondent in the *Lindsborg News* applauded the action, the *Messenger* printed the following: "A free ticket to the coming marble game to the writer of the above article if he or she has the nerve to call for same." In October the *Messenger* reported: "The greatest demonstration in the history of the college was made last Tuesday evening when the entire student body paraded the streets giving college and football yells." Homes of the professors and businessmen were visited where great encouragement was given. The article concluded: "Since the opening of school, there has been a geyser-like boiling of resentment to the thwarting of their wishes [the students]." Later that month the *Messenger* reported: "A miniature football with crossbones attached is quite generally worn by students."[10]

One Bethany student recorded in 1908 his response. He went out to the athletic field and saw only empty bleachers. As he stood leaning against the goal posts, "out of the still night air rang the cry, 'Third down, eight to gain.' From the bleachers there came from a thousand lusty throats the yell, 'Stone wall, Stone wall, Bethany.' Distinctly above all the rest could be heard one well-known voice saying—'Play fast, tackle low.' It was "Bennie" Owen urging his men to victory . . . . The Swedes crossed the opponent's goal line in a few minutes of play. A deafening roar ensued . . . . But it was a dream. And back through the sombre shadows of the night came the echo. 'How long.' "[11]

Although there were no intercollegiate football games from 1905 until 1915, an occasional intramural game was played on the campus. An unusual game was staged in November, 1909. It was between the Greek and the science departments. Professor Lund played fullback for the Greeks and Professor Deere was a tackle for the scientists. The *Lindsborg Record* reported: "The Greeks called their signals in Greek and the scientists in chemical formulas. Both teams played much stronger defense than offense and kicking was a feature of the game. The score was a tie, 0-0."[12]

When football was revived in 1915-16, E. O. Brown served as coach for one year. The record was one win and six losses. Quince Banbury, the

Coach Ad Lindsay led the 1925 gridiron Swedes to a seven-game undefeated season, scoring 143 points to opponents' 3.

great quarterback of the "Terrible Swedes," was coach 1916-17. Activity was curtailed considerably during World War I. Guy C. Omer was coach 1920-21. The squad in 1920 included George Carlson, one of the greatest athletes in Bethany's history, John Sward, Bill Ash, "Dell" Lundgren, Reuben Spong, Milton "Runt" Rehnquist, C. B. Nelson, "Ole" Olson, "Butch" Larson, Phil Pearson, and A. C. McBrian.

When Adrian "Ad" Lindsay, a former great athlete at the University of Kansas, served as Bethany's football coach 1922-26, great interest was revived in the sport. The 1925 season was all victorious. The Swedes scored 143 points to 3 for the opponents. Among the outstanding players were Lester Flohr, Stanley Skilling, Willis Carmichael, Emery Barclay, Ralph Barclay, Glenn Tarrant, Carl Sundgren, Arthur Olson, Howard Nelson, Herbert Heidel, Paris Stillion, Hugo Olson, Cecil Ferm, and Paul Swensson. Lindsay, a popular Bethany coach, later served as head football coach at the University of Kansas.

George Carlson succeeded Ad Lindsay as football coach. The Swedes placed second in the Conference in 1928, with the loss of only one game, and also in 1929. When Elmer Schaake was coach the Bethany team tied for second in 1936 and 1937. Ray Hahn started his great career in 1938, serving until the war interrupted football after the 1942 season. He returned in 1946 to continue his coaching duties until 1956. Bethany won the Conference championship in 1946 and placed second in 1938 (tie), 1939, 1948, and 1949. Succeeding coaches until 1965 were Harold Collins and Phil Miller.

Keith Rasmussen began a successful tenure as coach in 1965. Bethany placed second in the Conference in 1965 and 1971. The Swedes defeated the Missouri Valley College Vikings 17-14 in a thrilling game in the 23rd annual Mineral Water Bowl classic at Excelsior Springs, Missouri, in December, 1971, by a 24-yard field goal by Ken Pabst with six seconds remaining in the game. In 1973, Bethany as KCAC co-champion went to the Boot Hill Bowl, Dodge City, Kansas. The Swedes were decisively defeated by Millikin University, Decatur, Illinois.

More than 100 names are found on the list of all-conference teams since 1922. Limitations of space makes it impossible to include all these fine players. A representative list would include, in addition to persons previously mentioned, Marsh Hartshorne, Ernest Ireland, Bill Engstrom, Marshal Kephart, Harry Peterson, the Lindsborg Carlson

The 1971 football team, co-champions of the Kansas Conference and Mineral Water Bowl victors.

brothers—Lawrence, Roy, Bill—Bill Chandler, Dave Anderson, Bruce Nelson, Robert Ahlstedt, Jan Oleen, George Casey, and Larry Hartup.

The following football coaches have directed Bethany teams: Bennie Owen, 1902-04; E. O. Brown, 1915-16; Quince Banbury, 1917-19; Guy Omer, 1920-21; Adrian Lindsay, 1922-26; George Carlson, 1927-33; Elmer Schaake, 1934-37; Ray D. Hahn, 1938-42 and 1946-56; Hal Collins, 1957-60; Phil Miller, 1961-64; Keith Rasmussen, 1965-73.

The first athletic field was the square block of land north of Old Main. It served multiple purposes as the football field, the baseball diamond, and the area for track and field events. In 1901 the field, which was enclosed by a wooden fence, provided 450 seats in a grandstand at the southeast corner. In 1926 substantial improvements were made by the construction of a large wooden grandstand along the west side of the field. The design was primarily for a football field and a quarter-mile track. This grandstand was enlarged and renovated from time to time. Large cottonwood trees on the west and north sides provided a beautiful splash of color when frost turned the leaves into resplendent yellow. In September, 1935, the first football game under lights was played at Bethany with Bethel College following the installation of four poles and thirty-two lamps on the east and west sides.

Philip Anderson, Lindsborg, gave 12.7 acres of land in 1958, located along the northeast part of the campus, for an athletic field. Adequate space was now available for expansion. In October, 1959, the Philip Anderson Athletic Field and Stadium was dedicated. Separate football and baseball fields were provided. A concrete stadium with steel bleachers seating 2000, a new scoreboard, and improved lighting made available fine facilities for football. The old athletic field is now used for practice purposes.

Although there are references to basketball at Bethany in 1897, the earliest definite information is found in the *Messenger,* March, 1901, when the first game between two teams of the athletic association was played. In making the announcement, the editor observed: "We are glad it will be introduced here, for it is a clean manly game and full of excitement."[13]

The intercollegiate season started out well in 1903 with victories over St. John's Military Academy, Salina, 30 to 15, and Kansas State Agriculture College, Manhattan, 25 to 10. In reporting the victory over the Manhattan institution the *Messenger* observed: "On February 6 a

The 1914-15 basketball team.   *The 1929-30 Kansas Conference champions.*

large crowd saw the farmers go down to defeat before Bethany's superior skill. Manhattan failing to score during the first half, the game did not grow interesting until near the close, when Bethany commenced to relax a little." However, St. John's defeated the Swedes 36 to 18 a week later. An important factor in the loss was the following according to the *Messenger:* "Unfortunately the game at Salina was played on a waxed dance floor—something on which the Bethany boys are not yet proficient as performers. The result was that they sometimes found it difficult to preserve their equilibrium, and accordingly lost out to those who knew these grounds."[14]

In the 1907-08 season the Bethany team won ten and lost six games with Yngve Nyvall as coach. In 1914 Bethany was awarded the championship of the Kansas College Athletic Conference because Kansas Wesleyan University, a contender, had not played enough games to qualify and Bethany was in second place. The 1915-16 season was a great one in the annals of Bethany basketball. The Swedes readily won the Conference championship. Reuben Hven, Garfield, one of the all time "greats" in Bethany basketball, and Vernie Olson were selected as members of the all-conference and all-state first teams. E. O. Brown was the coach. Clarence Peterson had been placed on the all-Kansas team in 1913.

The decade beginning in 1925 was a period of great success in basketball. In 1925-26 the record was 16 wins and 3 defeats. Bethany placed third in the KCAC. Ad Lindsay was the coach. Art Olson, Glenn Tarrant, and Guy Barnes were selected as all-conference stars.

George Carlson was a successful basketball coach. The Swedes won the KCAC title three times, 1930, 1931, 1932, and placed second in 1929. Carl Larson, Kansas City, Missouri, the greatest performer on a Bethany basketball team, scored 344 points in 1929-30. In 1930 the Swedes lost to the "Olympics" of Los Angeles in the semi-finals of the National Amateur Athletic Union tournament in Kansas City, Missouri. Larson, "Buck" Vanek, and Glenn Tarrant were placed on the first all-star team of the KCAC. Larson received much recognition throughout his Bethany career. Larson also was placed on the national all-star first team. In 1961 he was elected to the NAIA Hillyards Hall of Fame for his outstanding performances.

The 1970-71 KCAC Northern Division co-champions.

When Ray Hahn became coach of all sports in 1938, the basketball team improved following the lull after the great era of the late 1920s and early 1930s. In 1939 the Swedes tied for second place in the Conference. In 1941 Bethany was Conference co-champion. Outstanding players were Harry Peterson, Alden Tilberg, Donald Olson, Lawrence Carlson, and John Grieve. Harry Peterson was repeatedly chosen on the all-conference team during his career at Bethany.

During World War II Conference competition was discontinued, but some basketball games were played with Professor Donald F. DeCou as coach. Ray Hahn returned as coach in 1946. Players and coach were greatly handicapped when Ling Gymnasium was destroyed by fire in March, 1946. Through the fine cooperation of school officials and the board of education at McPherson, the Swedes practiced and played games on the high school court. Later a surplus army gymnasium served as the facility for practice and games. When the new Lindsborg High School was completed in 1955, a cooperative arrangement was developed whereby college games were played in the high school gymnasium in this period. Dave Anderson, Smolan, established a great record and was recognized by membership on the KCAC first all-star teams. Dick Hahn, son of Coach Hahn, was chosen for the first team in 1951-52. Other Bethanyites who received Conference recognition in this period were Bill Carlson and Glen Sanderson.

In 1954 Dale R. Bloss was hired as basketball coach, thereby providing a head coach in football and a head coach in basketball. The 1959-60 team won the championship of the KCAC. Ralph Fry was selected for the first KCAC all-star team in 1954-55, Bill Thomas in 1957-58, Merlin Larson in 1959-60 and 1960-61, and Doug Ade in 1962-63.

During the first three years of John A. Hickman's tenure as coach, Bethany won two Conference championships and placed second one year. The Swedes were champions in 1963-64 and in 1964-65. The team also participated in the District 10 tournament of the NAIA all three years. Robert Ahlstedt and Paul Johnson made the KCAC all-star first team in 1963-64. Harvey Daniels and John Darrow were selected for the same honor in 1964-65. Against St. Benedict's College in the District 10 playoffs, Daniels scored 40 points for a new Bethany individual scoring record. Daniels and Gary Harder were chosen for the KCAC all-star team in 1965-66. Harvey Daniels, an outstanding player, scored 512 points during that season which broke the previous school record of 493 points which he had established the previous year. Dale Gorsky was selected on the all-conference team in 1966-67.

In 1970-71 Bethany tied for first place in the northern division of the KCAC. Sheldon Morton was an outstanding player during the season. The teams of George Stephens in recent years have had good records. Brice Leon, Bruce Nelson and Art Sommer have been good performers on the court.

Basketball coaches have included the following: Yngve Nyvall, 1907-08; Carl O. Lincoln, 1908-09, 1912-15; N. G. Wann, 1909-10; W. C. Dunham, 1910-12; E. O. Brown, 1915-17; Reginald Runbeck, 1917-20; Guy Omer, 1920-22; Adrian Lindsay, 1922-27; George Carlson, 1927-34; Elmer Schaake, 1934-38; Ray D. Hahn, 1938-43 and 1946-54; D. F. DeCou, 1943-46; Dale Bloss, 1954-63; John Hickman, 1963-67; David Anderson, 1967-70; George Stephens, 1970-.

Girls also played basketball in the early history of Bethany. The first game of the 1903 season was between the "Grasshoppers" and the "Butterflies." Although the former team had more experienced players, the "Butterflies" were reported to have played "a very plucky game making several nice plays." The "Grasshopper" players were Betty Davidson, Edna Ramsey, Edith Carlson, Eleanor Milton, and Gertrude Harlowe. The "Butterflies" were Alma Luise Olson, Annie Theo. Swensson, Bertha Roth, Eunice Clarke, and Beatrice Wayland. Basketball continued to increase in popularity and more intercollegiate games were scheduled. In 1908 the Bethany women defeated Kansas Wesleyan University and won two games with Ottawa. The members of the victorious team were Edith Edinburg, Enola Bengston, Murielle Lewin, Julia Blair, and Jessie Blomberg.

After a varied pattern of activity in basketball for some time, the Bethany women played several games in 1951. Modest interest was continued during the next several years. In 1970-71 the Swedettes were formed under sponsorship of Miss Joyce Pigge, a member of the faculty, and the college's Women's Intramural Council; twelve basketball-playing coeds competed in three games, losing once to Kansas Wesleyan and twice to Tabor College. A twelve-game schedule was played in 1971-72,

The 1973-74 basketball Swedettes helped renew the campus interest in women's athletics.

The 1974 baseball Swedes were conference champions, for the second consecutive year.

and Bethany became a member-institution of the Association for Kansas Women's Intercollegiate Sports, which sponsored the women's state tournaments. The Swedettes began their first season for women's competitive volleyball on November 1, 1972. The Kansas Association for Intercollegiate Athletics for Women held its 1974 women's state collegiate basketball tournament on the Bethany campus March 1 and 2, 1974, and the Swedettes were one of four competing teams from the fourteen member-institutions.

When Ling Auditorium was constructed in 1895, basketball games were played there. Court size was minimal and facilities limited. When the auditorium unit of Presser Hall was completed in 1928, the old "Messiah" auditorium was used exclusively for basketball and physical education. In the spring and summer of 1929 the building was renovated to provide a regulation size basketball court. The new and improved facility was designated Ling Gymnasium in commemoration of Henrik Ling, well-known nineteenth century Swedish leader in gymnastics. As noted previously, when this building was destroyed by fire in 1946, a surplus army physical education building was moved to the campus.

In December, 1961, the Ray D. Hahn Physical Education Building was dedicated. Included among the excellent facilities was a fine basketball court with two playing areas for practice and seating space for 1500 spectators in opera-type seats in the balcony and roll-out bleachers on the main floor.

Baseball was played at Bethany as early as 1882. The first game resulted in a victory for the academy students over the Lindsborg public school boys by the unusual score of 53-38. Games were played without formal organization until the college athletic association became active in the early 1900s. In 1903 the College played a schedule of eleven games with a record of six wins and five losses. The *Messenger* wrote that the crowd at the first game with K.U. was large because many "Messiah" visitors were there. Victor Holm, who later played professional baseball, was the principal pitcher. In 1905 the Swedes won five games and lost 3. The 1907 season started out brilliantly with twelve straight victories. The last four games resulted in losses. Art Runbeck was an outstanding player with a batting average of .412. Bert Shaner was the coach. Bethany had good teams in the next several years.[15]

All sports were curtailed during World War I. When a formal schedule was played again, Bethany fielded successful teams. The

Swedes were undefeated and champions of the Central Kansas Intercollegiate League in the 1922 season. Reginald Runbeck, an outstanding
former pitcher for the Swedes, was the coach of this successful team.

An important factor in the success of Bethany in baseball at this
time was the stellar pitching of Delmar "Dell" Lundgren, Lindsborg.
"Dell" Lundgren has the most distinguished record among former
Bethany students and graduates in professional baseball. He started out
as a pitcher with the Salina Millers, was sent to the Flint, Michigan
professional team, and then joined the Pittsburg Pirates of the National
League. He later played with the Boston Red Sox in the era when "Babe"
Ruth was the famous Yankee home run hitter.

After a long period of inactivity, baseball again became a part of the
athletic program in the late 1940s. In 1951 Bethany placed second in the
Conference tournament. After another period of no baseball, the sport
was resumed in the late 1950s and has continued since that time. Greater
activity in baseball developed within the Kansas Collegiate Athletic
Conference. An outstanding record was established in 1973 when
Bethany won the Conference championship, the first in the college's
history, with a record of twelve wins and four losses, and again in 1974,
with thirteen wins and three losses. These championships have been won
with Carroll Johnson as the coach.

Baseball practice and games were held for many years on the athletic
field which was also used for football. Spectators were accommodated in
a grandstand behind home plate. When Philip Anderson made available
acreage east and north of the campus, a section was set aside for baseball.
In 1961 a new baseball field was built surrounded by a chain link fence. In
1966 lights and bleachers were provided.

In November, 1907, the first track meet in the history of the College
occurred. Karl F. Miller, a student, was responsible for this development.
The college newspaper reported the participants "will strain every nerve
and muscle to win honors for their department and class." Six professors
served as judges. When the event was over, the tally of the score showed
the following: College, 43, Academy, 29, Conservatory, 23, and Commercial, 9. The performance of the winners included: Pole vault, 7'6", high
jump, 4'10", and broad jump, 16'1". The first cross country race, known
as the turkey race, found eight students in competition in November,
1907. The race started at Sundstrom's corner, Main and Lincoln Streets,
and the course brought the runners to the East River bridge and return.
The prizes were as follows: 1. a turkey, 2. a duck, 3. a rooster, 4. a goose
egg.[16]

The first intercollegiate track and field meet resulted in a 67 to 33
point victory over Kansas Wesleyan in May, 1908. Karl Miller of Bethany
was the high point man with the high total of 22¼ points. The Swedes
won first and second places in every race and also in the running broad

Track competition is improved now with an all-weather track at Anderson Field.

jump. In 1909 Bethany entered the state meet but scored no points. The Bethany athletes won the Pentangular Meet with McPherson, Kansas Wesleyan, Bethel and Sterling in 1922, 1923, and 1925. In 1923 Bethany won third place in the 880-yard relay race at the Kansas Relays. Stanley Skilling was a stellar performer in the short distance races and in the broad jump. In 1933 Archie San Romani was an outstanding competitor in the long distance races. Later he enrolled at KSTC, Emporia, and was a member of the United States Olympic track team. Bethany has never won the Conference title in track. Records indicate that fourth place finishes in 1948 and 1965 may be the highest standing of the College in Conference competition.

Track facilities were incorporated in the old athletic field north of Old Main. A dirt quarter-mile track provided limited facilities until in 1960 when the new athletic field was built on the eastern edge of the campus on land given by Philip Anderson. A quarter-mile cinder track and a 220-yard straightaway were provided at that time. In May, 1972, dedication of the eight-lane all-weather D. L. Anderson Memorial Track and related facilities made available excellent facilities for the track program.

Tennis was played at Bethany as early as the autumn of 1889, when Dr. G. A. Andreen introduced the game. The first court was described as "a sandbur patch on the northwest corner of the art hall block." The Bethany Tennis Association composed of faculty and students, men and women, developed interest in this sport. In 1909 Bethany was host to Midland College, Fremont, Nebraska, in the first intercollegiate match. The Bethany players were Donald Dilley, M. A. Anderson, and John Ekblad. Midland won in a close contest. The College participated in intercollegiate contests intermittently. In the early 1920s "Bill" Anderson, Eric Jernberg, Carl Eberhardt, and Ronald Wagner were the outstanding players.[17]

Interest in tennis continued to develop. A number of KCAC championships were won by Bethany representatives. On the basis of available information the record provides the following: Singles, Emory Lindquist, 1928, 1930; Ermal Lindquist, 1933; Birger Olson, 1942; Herb Benson, 1956; Ron Dahlsten, 1958, 1960. In doubles: Leo Liljestrom and Emory Lindquist, 1928; Melvin Allen and Emory Lindquist, 1930; Paul

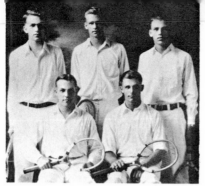

The 1929 tennis team was especially successful, with several championships.

J. Billing, R. Tideman, R. Strange, B. Anderson, S. Everhart, B. Young, and Coach Ray Hahn were 1968 KCAC Tennis Champions.

Willman and Bill Hellberg, 1933; Maurice Lysell and Carl Monson, 1938; Birger Olson and William Chandler, 1942; Bill Carlson and Art Newcomer, 1952; Gilbert Dyck and Herb Benson, 1956; Gilbert Dyck and Ron Dahlsten, 1957; Gary Robinson and Ron Dahlsten, 1959, 1960.

The greatest era in Bethany tennis began in the early 1960s and it has continued for more than a decade. A spectacular record occurred in 1973 when Bethany won the KCAC championship for the tenth consecutive year. Moreover, Bethany players won all seven tournament divisions, exceeding the record of the previous year when six of seven were victories. This superior record in 1973 was established by the following winners with the number of the division indicated before the name of the player: 1. Mike Young, 2. Shannon Everhart, 3. Bill Gusenius, 4. Ben Pigorsch, 5. Dave "Denver" Wassberg. Young and Everhart were the champions of the top division in doubles and Gusenius and Pigorsch won the second division. In 1973 Bethany won the championship of District 10 of the NAIA tournament and sent all five players to the national tournament.

In this decade of splendor for Bethany tennis two sets of brothers have been great players: Bryce and Mike Young and Scott and Shannon Everhart. The Young brothers have distinguished themselves in the number of Conference singles championships they have won for Bethany as well as being members of championship doubles teams. Ray D. Hahn has been the coach of tennis teams during this decade of unrivaled victories.

Tennis has been popular at Bethany for many years!

Bethany has superb facilities for tennis in the E. T. Anderson Memorial Courts which were constructed in 1969. These four excellent courts with chain link fences and lighting were made possible by a gift from the family as a memorial to E. T. Anderson, Commercial '04, Emporia, Kansas, cattleman, banker, businessman, and Bethany friend. The courts are also used for other outdoor recreation.

The records indicate that Bethany competition in golf began in 1929. Carl Larson, an outstanding basketball player, was also a fine golfer. In the period 1929-32 he was a low-medalist and runner-up in the Conference tournament. In 1933 George "Bud" Johnson and Harold Olson placed second. Harry Peterson was runner-up in 1939 and 1940. In the next few years Eugene Christensen was a successful representative in golf. In 1958-61 Ken Carmichael and Walt Wendel and in 1966-69 Richard Gundick and Richard Finger performed well in the golf competition. In 1974 Art Sommer finished second to the low medalist in Conference competition.

Bethany has held membership in the Kansas College Athletic Conference or the Kansas Intercollegiate Athletic Conference since the 1900s. The original Conference was a comprehensive organization of fifteen colleges and universities. In 1928 six institutions—Baker, Bethany, Kansas Wesleyan, McPherson, Ottawa, and St. Mary's (St. Mary's, Kansas)—formed the Kansas College Athletic Conference. In 1974 the membership included the following: Bethany, Bethel, Friends, Kansas Wesleyan, McPherson, Southwestern, Sterling, St. Mary's of the Plains, and Tabor.

KCAC basketball in R. D. Hahn gymnasium continues to be popular.

The stained glass windows in the chapel of the new Burnett Center for Religion and the Performing Arts have been made from windows formerly in the chapel of Old Main.

The campus is host to many visitors, speakers, performers, and dignitaries. In 1974 the Central States Synod of the Lutheran Church in America held its annual convention on campus, and President and Mrs. Hahn (left) greeted the Synod president, the L.C.A. president, and their wives—Dr. and Mrs. Harvey Prinz (center) and Dr. and Mrs. Robert Marshall (right).

13.

Campus Life

College life includes more than formal studies and academic activities. The relationships of students with one another and in groups provide important additional resources and experiences. Variety characterizes these aspects of Bethany life. Moreover, the developments reflect the changing nature of the students and differences in the general culture from decade to decade.

The youthfulness of the students in the first year of Bethany's history is reflected in an article in the *Lindsburg Localist* in October, 1882, which reported: "The Academicians play leap frog o'nights." The same account stated: "The Academy students have organized a reading room in town which is open 4-9 p.m." Community concern for the welfare of the young students appeared in the resolution signed by Carl Swensson, P. J. Berg, pastor of the Swedish Methodist Church, and K. Erixon, pastor of the Mission Convenant Church, in the *Lindsburg Localist* in December, 1881: "A father can no longer with assurance send his sons to our public schools, or to the select school at the Lutheran Church. Why? Someone may induce the innocent boy to go into the Billiard Hall and entice him to commence a gambler's life. In the name of morality and Christianity, we would therefore ask the Honorable Mayor and Council, as well as citizens of Lindsborg: Shall that Billiard Hall be tolerated?"[1]

Student life in the early years centered around societies which served academic and social functions. The Linnean Association and the Lyceum Society were organized in 1884. The former promoted interest in scientific knowledge among members and collected specimens for the museum. The Lyceum Society "met statedly for literary and oratorical exercises." The Adelphic Society was formed in 1889; three years later it was given equal rights with the Lyceum Society. It is likely that this society was first organized as the Concordia Society in 1887, which became the Eclectic Society in 1888. A healthy rivalry continued between the Lyceum and Adelphic societies for several decades. The weekly meetings included declamations, orations, debates, lectures, poetry readings, and musical numbers. A social hour with refreshments was a regular feature. Membership in one or the other of the two societies was open to all students, and generally attendance was good.[2]

Skating on the Smoky Hill River in winter months was a popular sport as students glided over the frozen surface and later warmed themselves by a roaring bonfire. The Smoky was a great attraction in the spring. In May, 1891, the junior class enjoyed an excursion to the Smoky Hill River where the members spent the day translating Latin, and in fishing and boating. There were many outings to the hills west of Lindsborg when happy throngs of students explored Björndyke and areas along the Spanish Steppes west and north of Lindsborg where Coronado and his Conquistadors had visited in 1541.[3]

Class parties were a vital feature of social life. In February, 1891, the *Lindsborg News* described the joint party of juniors and seniors at the home of Professor A. W. Kjellstrand when "after having supper, they engaged in throwing beanbags, in which the professor proved to be most efficient." Later that month students had a pleasant time at the country home of Francis Johnson where the entertainment consisted of telling ghost stories and playing "Old Maid," a popular and approved card game. The *Messenger,* December, 1903, described the seniors' "tacky" party where there were "clowns, dunces, dudes, 'gentlemen av Dublin,' hoboes, hayseeds, greybeards, and hunchbacks. To offset these there were Red Cross nurses, gypsies, Red Riding Hoods, cooks, queens, and 'peaches.' Carlbert [Dr. C. F. Carlbert] was one of the boys that night. He hadn't forgotten how to skip them a loo either . . . . The affair was a 'dinger' in every way." The freshmen class party in October, 1905, according to the *Messenger,* was an excursion to Björndyke, west of Lindsborg. The members left the campus at 4 a.m. in a variety of horsedrawn vehicles that were gaily decorated with the class colors. The day was spent in eating, exploring, taking photographs, painting, and carving names on rocks. The class flag was planted on the highest peak of the bluffs.[4]

There was considerable variety in the class parties. On October 25, 1906, the sophomore class had a clambake at Christian's Grove along the Smoky Hill River. The *Messenger* reported: "The moon, shining upon the placid waters of the Smoky, and the firelight casting fantastic shadows, seemed to inspire us like the olden time gypsies and the stories told were weird and romantic, amusing and interesting."[5]

When spring came, romance was in the air and on the campus. In March, 1894, the *Messenger* reported: "All the signs of spring are here:

FRANK NELSON, *Bethany professor, State Superintendent of Public Instruction, and fund-raiser.*

green grass, outdoor sports, and romantic walks." Two years later, in April, the college newspaper reported a recurring annual scene: "The park benches have again been placed in their position, and on moonlight evenings it can readily be seen that they are being used. You see in the uncertain light a dim figure or two in dreamy monologue or conversation beguiling away the romantic hours."[6]

In the late 1890s bicycles became popular. The *Lindsborg News* reported in 1899 that the ladies were especially enjoying their bicycles and that "there never have been so many wheels at Lindsborg at one time as is now the case." Trick bike riding and races provided thrilling entertainment. In April, 1899, the *Lindsborg News* observed: "The ladies at the college are jubilant. Why? Their sporting time has been extended from 6:30 to 7:15." Variety was also a part of the pattern as suggested in May, 1899: "Several professors serenaded the ladies at the dormitory last Tuesday." There were tricksters around too, when the college bell was silenced by students who had stuffed the bell mechanism with rags. Other students joined Professor Welin at 4 a.m. one morning in March, 1899, on the roof of Old Main to look at the stars through the new telescope purchased recently. The moons of Jupiter and the rings of Saturn were brought into clear focus for the viewers on the Plains of Kansas.[7]

The Spanish-American War, 1898, made only a modest impact upon the Bethany campus. Several Bethany students joined up with Lindsborg's Twentieth Kansas Company of the National Guard and others enlisted in the regular army. When the Lyceum Society met in May, the vacant chairs of three members were draped in red, white and blue. A reception was being held at the home of Reverend and Mrs. Swensson one evening in May when the troop train carrying Lindsborg and Bethany men was scheduled to go through Salina enroute to the West Coast. The *Lindsborg News* reported that at Swensson's request, the guests arose and sang *America*. The editor observed: "We do not recall when we heard our beautiful *America* sung with so much feeling and fervor as at the parsonage on Monday night." When members of the Twentieth Kansas returned to Lindsborg in November, an enthusiastic crowd greeted them in a program at the college chapel followed by a reception in their honor.[8]

Students shared with Lindsborg residents a number of gala occasions. A large crowd greeted Professor Frank Nelson at the Union Pacific depot in November, 1898, when he returned after campaigning successfully on the Republican ticket for state superintendent of public instruction of Kansas. He was placed in a chair decorated with American flags and carried on the shoulders of four men, preceded by the college band and followed by hundreds of people as the procession went down Main Street to his home. In November, 1900, the *Lindsborg News* reported: "A hearty welcome was accorded Dr. Swensson last Saturday evening at the Union Pacific depot. The whole college family was there. The band played and all cheered when the doctor stepped from the car." Swensson had been campaigning for the Republican ticket in eastern Swedish American communities.[9]

There were times of special excitement. The quiet of the campus was suddenly disrupted when a severe windstorm hit Lindsborg late one Monday afternoon in May, 1899. College buildings were damaged as roofs were blown off, chimneys collapsed, windows smashed, and large trees uprooted. Fortunately, no one was killed or injured. A heavy downpour of rain slashed in through broken windows to soak the contents of buildings and loosen plaster which fell in large sheets. Great damage was done to the women's dormitory.[10]

Students created their own social life at the turn of the century. Although women students were permitted to dance together in the Ladies Hall, dancing with men was forbidden. This prohibition could not prevent students from secretly dancing in Teichgraeber's mill in the south part of town which provided good facilities especially when flour was spilled on the floor to aid the dancing feet. Not all dancing was done at the mill according to the reminiscences of a student who was at Bethany in the early years of the new century. There was an upstairs room over one of the stores half-way down Main Street that was used frequently. The students reached the room from the alley side by using the let-down stairs of the fire escape.

Groups of students brought together by various causes also had their social life. In March, 1908, the *Messenger* printed this interesting account: "At 8 p.m. Tuesday evening, March 10, the members of the Bethany Fuzz Growers Association entertained their ladies at Gibson's cafe. They took possession of the booth which had been reserved for them when the most delicious eatables were served, for instance, fried chicken. Five men and five women. Next day, 'the scrubbing-brush-like appendages' had been removed from their faces." In that year fifty students had a festive Halloween party in Berggren's Hall. The students gathered at the College and paraded downtown with a Jack-O'-Lantern for a headlight. This was a tacky party and the evening was spent "playing games, cracking jokes, and enjoying refreshments." When winter came there was a variation of activity as recorded in the *Messenger:* "Last Saturday evening a jolly crowd of students engaged in a sleigh ride . . . . After some preliminary phoning, the warmth of Gibson's cafe was appreciated." But there were also expeditions out of town, as reported by the *Messenger:* "Several of the college students took the Missouri Pacific to Marquette last Sunday evening. The roller skating rink is the attraction."[11]

The calendar of events in this period indicates clearly the great interest in the Swedish background of the College. In May, 1907, there were two well-attended programs in the auditorium in observance of the bicentennial of the birth of Carl von Linnaeus, world-famous Swedish botanist. In January of the following year a public program was presented, with Birger Sandzén as principal speaker, in memory of King Oscar II who had died the previous month. On April 30, 1912, the *Svea Vitterhetssällskap* sponsored the traditional Swedish *Valborgsmessoafton*. The students assembled at 9 p.m. in front of Old Main and walked in a single file to the large square downtown singing Swedish songs. The *Messenger* wrote: "Merriment, song, and a good bonfire are the three requisites." The purpose was "to send into inglorious exile all the evil spirits that may have accumulated during the year." The *Svea* chorus, accompanied by violins, sang the Swedish patriotic numbers, *Vårt Land* and *Du Gamla, Du Fria,* and student songs. In the spring of 1913 the senior men wore the imported Swedish *studentmössor* (white student caps). The number of students with Swedish antecedents was between 360-400 in the total of about 600 in this period.[12]

Although secret organizations were forbidden on the campus, a club with the same intent as a fraternity was organized early in the 1900s. The club was first known as Pi Delta. It was reorganized in 1905 under the name of Eta Alpha Pi. The clubhouse was located directly across the street from the southwest corner of the campus known originally as the "park," and more recently as the Presser Hall block. The unpretentious shack served as a place for the sale of cold drinks and candy. The boys rented it from the owner. It served mostly as a "smokehouse" and domino and card parlor. One of the gala social affairs of Eta Alpha Pi was the annual costume Halloween party for the members and their girlfriends at Berggren's Hall.

The early attempts at founding a club or fraternity led to further developments. In 1908 two clubs were established: the Cloven Hoof, a rather strange name for an organization in a church college, for men, and Sigma Kappa Gamma for women, founded by the seniors. The former was still active in 1922. In 1909 the sorority engaged a room in Frank Lindberg's house and held their regular Saturday evening meetings there. The *Messenger* reported: "The girls have decided to make literature the main feature of these meetings, but fudge and cocoa are still as prominent as they have been in the past."[13]

Three men's clubs were founded in the World War I era: Omega Zeta Phi in 1916, Freogan in 1917, and Swastika in 1918. Freogan was still active in 1922. The women were especially interested in social organizations in this era. Between 1914-20 the following were founded: Sigma Pi Phi,

1914; Kappa Gamma Phi, 1915; Beta Chi Theta, 1915; Phi Delta Delta, 1917, and Sigma Phi Omega, 1920.

The growth and increased activity of fraternities and sororities in the post-World War I era aroused opposition especially in certain church circles. At the Conference meeting in 1920 the matter was discussed. The faculty agreed to study the complaints. In September, 1920, the faculty minutes stated that "it was decided that the faculty recommend to the board of directors that sororities and fraternities be eliminated." The next day the directors passed a resolution declaring that the "members hereby sustain the faculty in eliminating sororities and fraternities among students and faculty at Bethany College."[14]

The action of the faculty and board appears to have been largely symbolic. The organizations were soon active again. For instance, in 1925, five sororities, Alpha Mu Phi, Beta Chi Theta, Sigma Pi Phi, Sigma Phi Omega, and Kappa Gamma Phi, provided their members with a normal program of activities.

Criticism of the organizations appeared again in 1929. One objection was related to the expense of membership. In October, 1929, it was decided that the expenditure per member should not exceed $20.00 per year in the form of initiation fee, dues, and assessments, exclusive of the pin. When the board was asked at the Conference meeting in 1930 about Bethany's social organizations, a committee of the board made a study. In its report to the Conference in 1931, the following statement was made: "The faculty has on its own initiative effected measures to keep such groups within proper leash. While according them no official recognition, it has required of all members that they maintain satisfactory scholarship." In 1932 the Conference was told: "Activities of social fraternities and sororities have not been very prominent. Strict rules have been adopted for these organizations. No freshmen may become a member. These organizations are not permitted to own or lease or conduct rooming houses. All social functions must be passed on by the proper authorities."[15]

Student opinion, as reflected in the *Messenger,* ranged from high praise to severe criticism of fraternities and sororities. The proponents enthusiastically pointed to the opportunities for fellowship and personal development, the stimulation to better scholarship, more effective college citizenship, and the strong bonds of loyalty to the College that were forged by the organizations. Critics lamented the exclusive nature of membership, the divisiveness caused among students, and the possibility of negative influences. Non-campus criticism arose primarily because the fraternities and sororities promoted dances and dancing was not authorized by college policy. Church and outside criticism generally was not extensive after the 1930s.

Six Greek social organizations have been active in later years.

This Panhellenic Council of 1957 has been one of the governing bodies of fraternities and sororities.

Women students affiliate with Sigma Phi Omega, Kappa Gamma Phi, and Alpha Theta Chi. The fraternities are Gamma Kappa Alpha, Pi Sigma Chi, and Alpha Sigma Nu. Kappa Gamma Phi is the oldest Greek social organization, tracing its origin to 1915. The groups have leased houses or rooms as meeting places but not as residential quarters in recent years. Picturesque names have identified fraternity houses beginning in the 1960s. The Gamma Kappa Alpha house is known as the "Hole," the Pi Sigma Chi as the "Pit," and Alpha Sigma Nu as the "Pad." The sorority counterparts are: Kappa Gamma Phi, the "Kottage," Sigma Phi Omega, the "Pendulum," and Alpha Theta Chi, the "Flat." The Pan-Hellenic Council has governed Greek social organizations since the 1920s.

The rivalry between classes, a striking aspect of campus life in certain periods, resulted in a variety of activities, including pranks and sometimes physical conflict. When the sophomores in 1903 were staging their class program in the college chapel, the freshmen presented "a vigorous, bouncing toy elephant which cavorted around the circle upon the stage in the midst of the introductory speech of the class guardian." In 1905 the *Messenger* reported in language difficult for a later generation to understand: "The seniors had a perfectly 'tuky' [crazy] time at their watermelon hoedown September 14. No trumpets nor chards were present—only sinners tolerated. In spite of the sophomores, the seniors had a jowce of it." Occasional physical combats occurred in defense of class flags, colors, and caps. The issue became so intense that for a brief period class day activities were banned, but in October, 1905, such events were restored by action of the faculty.[16]

There were times of tension when class prestige was challenged. In their senior year the class of 1906 sought to paint their class numerals on the 175-foot high chimney of the power plant. Paul N. Carlson, Elmer T. Peterson, and Anton Peterson succeeded in making the hazardous climb on the iron rungs inside the sooty chimney and achieved their mission. But this was just the beginning. Forces were marshalled for destroying this mark of triumph on the chimney, but after an uneasy period involving some fighting, the seniors were victorious. Later in the year the seniors fought in defense of the class colors that waved triumphantly on the top of the high flag pole in front of the Swedish Pavilion.[17]

The editorial, "Class Scraps," in the *Messenger,* February, 1906, by David Haglund, expressed the editor's appraisal: "No doubt class scraps are now and then carried beyond the pale of propriety . . . but we cannot on that account indiscriminately condemn them any more than we would condemn the eating of veal because a certain voracious fellow once died from eating a whole calf. We have little sympathy with those who everlastingly cant of orderliness and harmony, who can find no justification for the spontaneous outpourings of student enthusiasm."[18]

The interest in class days tapered off gradually and became limited largely to determining whether or not the freshmen should wear their distinctive caps. In 1920 there was an exception as the *Messenger* reported: "There was a fierce battle between freshmen and sophomores. Completely surrounded, the sophs were pitched back and forth until they were a pile of helpless debris." The freshman banquet in the Tea Cup Inn was a triumphal event. The sophomore president, decked out in freshman colors, presented a trophy to the freshman winners.[19]

The Freshman-Sophomore conflicts were attacked by the *Messenger* as " . . . barbaric, but in all fairness we wish to state that this term is entirely too weak to describe the custom adequately. Why it should be considered as beneficial to the so-called spirit of a Christian institution to sanction such a survival of the primitive we are unable to understand." In September, 1921, the Student Council announced plans for abandoning the annual class fight between the freshmen and sophomores to determine the issue of wearing the blue caps with a yellow button or the more traditional green caps. Athletic contests between the classes were then instituted.[20]

The relationship of boys and girls, language used at that time to designate college men and women of a later era, was the topic for an address to the student body at chapel by Mrs. J. E. Welin, dean of women, in February, 1921. Speaking to the boys she said: "Choose a girl who can be a pal to you, one to whom you can tell your troubles and who will be a guardian angel to you." In addressing the girls directly, she observed: "In order to attract the boys, a girl need not 'doll up' and paint her face. Such things do not add to her beauty . . . . The main thing for a girl to consider in choosing her gentlemen friends is simply to be sure he's a gentleman. And a gentleman will not tempt a girl to leave her room after hours and go car riding." The popularity of automobiles created new problems.[21]

A variety of attractions were available to Bethany students in this period. In addition to many recitals and concerts, the May Day Fete with folk dances and the winding of the May Pole was a gala occasion. The

Wonderland Theatre in Lindsborg was a continuing source of entertainment for those who found the movie attractions acceptable. In the winter months of 1922 students were entertained by Katherine MacDonald and Wesley Barry in *Stranger Than Fiction,* Alice Brady in *Little Lady,* and Charlie Chan and Jackie Coogan in *The Kid,* a return engagement. Line parties at the Wonderland often helped to brighten up an otherwise dull weekend when a hope for a date did not develop. Early in January, 1922, the *Messenger* reported that a large number of students, accompanied by Prof. and Mrs. Birger Sandzén and Margaret, went to Hutchinson to see a performance by Anna Pavlova and the *Ballet Russe.* A large crowd at the "Messiah" auditorium saw a beautiful pantomime from Longfellow's *Hiawatha.* Events like those described above were one phase of student life during the decade.[22]

A perennial student complaint at Bethany had been the limited social life for students. In October, 1929, one of many editorials on this subject appeared in the *Messenger:* "The sore spot in life on the Bethany campus is the social side or rather the lack of it. Something ought to be done about it." The editor lamented the fact that school parties were too few and the social activities of sororities and fraternities offered no general solution. In that same month the faculty set up a joint committee on social affairs consisting of three faculty members and three student council representatives.[23]

The 1930s represented a subdued era among collegians as the economic depression produced serious consequences in all aspects of social life. The fraternities and sororities restricted their expenses on social functions to a bare minimum. A phonograph replaced live music at dances off campus. Olson's cafe on Main Street served as a social center where, in the back room, students danced the new dances to new tunes. When sufficient cash was available, the more fortunate, at the Wonderland Theatre saw Delores Del Rio in *The Girl from Rio* and Laurel and Hardy in *My Old Port* in 1932, and in January of the next year, Joan Bennett and Spencer Tracy in *Me and My Gal* and Norma Shearer and Clark Gable in *Strange Interlude.*

In 1935 a recreation room was provided for students across from the cafeteria in Old Main. The *Messenger* described the situation in February of that year: "The recreation room across from the cafeteria is a favorite rendezvous for some of the Nips and Tucks. The tête-à-tête hour after supper will find several of these romancing pairs enjoying a quiet chat in the twilight stillness, only to be rudely interrupted by the entrance of some yelling mob who plan a meeting of some kind in that particular sanctum. Too bad. Too bad." The students strolled leisurely out of Old Main, stopped for a drink at the old stone fountain, and meandered slowly under the friendly cottonwoods, planted in 1894, on their way to Lane Hart Hall.[24]

Lane Hart Hall was not only the focal point for picking up or returning a date but it occasionally received more corporate attention. A writer in the *Messenger* in October, 1935, observed with regret: "Your scribe is extremely annoyed because he was unable to attend the event of events—the supreme escapade of the year—the Dorm raid. What a gossip-gleaner's paradise that must have been."[25]

Thirty years later the Bethany campus saw an extensive dorm raid. In December, 1965, the *Messenger* reported a "panty raid," following two during the previous academic year. This time action was taken by the college authorities when fifty students were punished. A fine of $2.00 was imposed on each male involved, there was immediate suspension from all extracurricular activities, confinement to the dormitory during the probation period, November 22-December 13, and a letter to parents informing them of the event.[26]

Campus life was often made brighter by special events. The Fal-Da-Ral of the art department provided such an occasion in January, 1936, at the Swedish Pavilion. The *Messenger* described the setting: "Confetti, streamers, balloons, bally-hoos, torch singers, food, side-shows, and an orchestra." There was Ray Stapp, hiding behind a huge mustache and under a ten-gallon hat; Ted Butterfield dressed in loud vest and tie, selling tickets; Allan Downs in a brilliant red tam, sketching someone; Phil Fauerso jumping from chair to chair as he bellowed "Let's Play Bingo"; Irene Isaacson and Greta Kaufman distributing cards, corn, and prizes; Jean Moeller displaying the "Lindsborg Quintuplets"; Leonard Stout promoting the freak show; Junior Martin as an imported African pygmy; Lois Kilpatrick as the "Bearded Lady"; Milton Olson as the "Human Art Gallery"; Miriam Ulrickson and Sarah Jean Sterling as the "two pathetic Siamese Twins"; Margaret Hunt as "the strong man"; and Violet Fellows guarding the entrance. The climax was a gala floor show in which the orchestral music was furnished by Vernon Dentonofsky (Vernon Denton) and his Russian Reds, with such stars as Adabelle Bonner, Wayne Robinson, Archie Anderson, and "Babe" Holthoefer. And lest we forget—there was the fish pond with Dorothy Pearson in charge.[27]

Large audiences always attended the annual "Stunt Nite" sponsored by Pi Kappa Delta, national forensics society. Tracing its origin to 1926, this festive occasion provided an opportunity for fraternities, sororities, and independent groups to vie for the honor of prizes and cash awards for creative skits of various types. The *Messenger* in February, 1937, portrayed the events for its readers: First prize went to Gamma Kappa Alpha for its presentation, *Down on the Levee.* The setting was a Basin Street bar in the slums of New Orleans with a strong emphasis on the despair and helplessness of humanity, finding relief only in drink. Second prize went to the skit, *The Gods' Decree,* an impressive portrayal through pantomime of an ancient Egyptian religious rite in the temple of *Re* by

Sigma Phi Omega. *Juggernaut,* by Alpha Sigma Nu, was a protest against the cruelty and futility of war; *Pilgrim Follies* by Kappa Gamma Phi was a take-off on the rigid morals and customs of the Pilgrims; and *Moments Musical* presented interesting songs and dances in a modern setting. These skits were rather typical of Stunt Nite entertainment. The name of this annual event was changed to *Valhalla* in 1966, and in recent years has been sponsored by the Pan Hellenic Council and the *Bethanian.*[28]

In 1936 two well-known Bethany "characters" had their demise. In September the *Messenger* described the sad fate of "Sadee," a mannequin "who suffered dissemination Sunday after maltreatment at the hands of ruffians as yet unknown." Sadee arrived at Bethany in October, 1934, after spending many years in retirement in the storeroom of the Farmer's Union building in Marquette. Her first appearance at the College was in the death chambers of an all-school Halloween party. In April, 1936, the full-length obituary of "Billiken" was printed in the *Messenger.* "Billiken," an alligator, was fourteen years old when he arrived at Bethany from the Everglades of Florida in 1920 as a gift to Myrtle Ericson, a Bethany student, from her brother, Elmer Ericson. The college newspaper reported shortly thereafter that the two-foot long alligator "created not a little excitement when he escaped one day at the Ladies Hall, but Miss E. came and grabbed the ill-looking animal by the nape of the neck and all was well again." "Billiken" received a permanent home on fifth floor of Old Main in the biology laboratory. But "Billiken" met a tragic death when he crawled out of a fifth story window, fell, and broke his neck. The lamented "Billiken" was stuffed and mounted for the Bethany museum, thus gaining a kind of alligator immortality.[29]

Live theatre provided entertainment during the decade of the 1930s. The dramatics department presented the Bethany Players, who performed under the direction of Miss Annie Theo. Swensson. In the same fine manner in which Miss Swensson previously presented personal dramatic recitals to large and enthusiastic audiences, her Bethany Players continued this tradition. In December, 1931, the Christmas favorite, *Why the Chimes Rang,* was enjoyed by a large audience in Presser Hall. Other memorable performances were *Smiling Through* in February, 1932, *Little Women* in May, 1934, *The Copperhead* in May, 1936, *Pillars of Society* in March, 1936, and *The Music Master* in May, 1939. Several other full-length and one-act plays enriched the life of the campus. The Pollard Players, a traveling group, appeared frequently in this period. Annual May Day Fetes and minstrel shows, together with Stunt Nite and various carnivals, furnished interesting variety.

Social activities in the early 1940s reflected the austere impact of World War II. As increasingly large numbers of men were called to the colors, the student population was dominated by women. Sororities continued their activities on a limited scale. Fraternities were largely inoperative. The college annual listed only the names of two or three members who proudly dedicated their fraternity page to brothers in the armed services. Social functions were attuned to the war situation. Students and organizations participated in Victory bond drives and in Victory book collections. In February, 1944, a large and successful Victory carnival was held on the campus when Lilybelle Brandt, Salina, was elected Victory queen. Stunt Nite was discontinued during the war years.

The war years provided some interesting campus activities. In December, 1943, the Lucia tradition from Sweden was revived in Lane Hart Hall when the elected co-ed, adorned with a white robe and a crown of white candles, served coffee to students at an early hour. The drama department presented a variety of plays as the Bethany Players performed in *A Servant in the House,* 1940, *Our Town,* 1941, *Peg O' My Heart,* 1942, and *Letters to Lucerne,* 1944. Sigma Alpha Iota was responsible for a performance of the operetta, *Naughty Marietta,* in November, 1942, which was repeated for a capacity audience of soldiers from Camp Phillips near Smolan. In the 1950s presentations included Emlyn Williams' *Night Must Fall,* Moliere's *The Imaginary Invalid* and Noel Coward's *Blithe Spirit.*

When the war was over a new situation prevailed on the campus. The returning veterans included many married students and soon young families with children graced the campus. A married students organization was established. Twenty veterans families lived in housing units constructed on the southeast part of the campus and others found apartments in the town. Social organizations became active and included record membership. Dances were held regularly in Salina, in McPherson, and also in Lindsborg, but never on the campus where such events were banned. In November, 1945, the school dance sponsored by two sororities received editorial praise from the *Messenger.* Strong student sentiment was often expressed for campus dances but the administration and board, committed to the historic pietistic attitude, did not grant the request.[30]

The ban on campus dancing was lifted in 1955. Swede Inn, located in the lower level of Alma Swensson Hall, provided the setting for a variety of dances sponsored generally by the student social committee. In May, 1959, the *Messenger* reported "one of the most stimulating musical experiences in a long time was the jazz concert presented by Gamma Nu Chapter of Phi Mu Alpha Sinfonia in conjunction with the American Federation of Musicians . . . . It was mentioned at the program that this was the first time such an event of this nature had been presented at Bethany." When the Pihlblad Memorial Union was completed in 1964, dances were held there. Various dance bands have played on the campus. In November, 1967, the "devastating" Dinks appeared in a return

"The Clouds," produced by drama students and others in 1974, has been one of many theatre productions on the campus.

engagement. In the 1970s a variety of bands performed including The Chancellors, Denny Brooks and the Mason Profit, 1971, Deep Creek, and James Dutton and his Rose Rebellion, 1973. The Homecoming dance in the autumn is a big feature for alumni and students. In 1973 a new source of entertainment was provided through the Coffee House. In announcing this event in October of that year the *Messenger* reported: "A new late night spot is opening up at Bethany soon. A coffee house with a night club atmosphere will be a new untried experience for the student body."[31]

The 1950s witnessed great interest in opera, a pattern that was sustained into the later years. In October, 1952, Sigma Alpha Iota presented to a large audience in Presser Hall the first college performance in the United States of Gian Carlo Menotti's *Amahl and the Night Visitors.* The development of opera workshops resulted in the presentation of several operas including the *Magic Flute,* 1960, *LaBohème,* 1960, *The Marriage of Figaro,* 1961, *Hansel and Gretel* and *Madame Butterfly,* 1964, and *The Mikado,* 1965. Opera presentations have continued into the 1970s.

Drama experienced a brief lull in the 1960s which caused the editor of the *Messenger* in November, 1964, to lament the absence of a speech and drama director, declaring that this was a "disgraceful" situation in a four-year liberal arts college. He also expressed regret over the absence of debate activity. Drama became again a part of campus life. In November, 1969, theatregoers viewed the sombre message on stage of Orwell's *1984. The Glass Menagerie* was featured in March, 1972. In 1974 the excellent facilities of the Burnett Center for Religion and the Performing Arts stimulated a splendid response. The fine situation of the arts on the campus drew plaudits from the *Messenger* at the end of April, 1974, when the editor pointed out that the calendar for the following week included *Bus Stop,* an appearance by the *Preservation Hall Jazz Band,* the college choir's home concert, and the concert by the Kansas City Philharmonic at the conclusion of a productive two-day residency.[32]

A campus is a collection of young people who understandably respond in a variety of ways. Problems of discipline and discontent were not confined to any one era. In 1899 the *Lindsborg News* reported in the column, "Bethany Briefs": "Some of the students have 'caught it' this week for being naughty. Let all good students be warned by this example." In April, 1906, the faculty minutes record that fifty-three students appeared before the faculty and were "scolded" for a variety of offenses, ranging from failure to attend chapel to unsatisfactory performance of their academic work, and for matters of conduct. In the same year the faculty provided for grades in diligence and deportment with penalties ranging from 10 percent to 25 percent on their grades for reprimands from the faculty. In October, 1911, the faculty resolved that "the setting of a grade for diligence be hereafter abolished." In January of the following year a "special grade for deportment" was established.[33]

There were occasions when student restlessness took formal action. In September, 1934, the *Messenger* published an "Open Letter" to the board of directors: "Last year the student body held a mass meeting at which the majority of them signed a petition asking for certain improvements and privileges. Because they took this action they were criticized . . . . There is great necessity for being frank with young Americans. Gentlemen, why not give the students a chance to help you solve your problems?"[34]

An interesting situation developed in May, 1960, when the Student Council authorized the sending of a letter to President Lund stating their support of the personnel welfare committee concerning what were described as "flagrant violations" of school policy. By a vote of eight to three, the official student organization decided to stand behind the recommendations of the committee "concerning the expulsion of students who repeatedly violated established school policies . . . . There is no cause for continued disobedience and disregard for such things as chapel attendance, good citizenship and general good deportment." President Lund replied later that "Justice properly understood is never arbitrary nor impersonal . . . . Bethany College is pleased that its policies have corrected far more offenders than they have condemned."[35]

An "Open Letter" was published in the *Messenger* in May, 1963, setting forth student desire for "revaluing the process whereby information is filtered into the student body," for improving the situation in which "little if any prerogative has been left to the students in planning details of their own curriculum," for remedying the "undiplomatic and arbitrary rulings that have been forwarded to resident heads at both women's dormitories," and for consideration of "the perennial issue of compulsory chapel attendance." The response of J. R. Hamlin, a member of the faculty, to the "Open Letter" provided an interesting point of view: "If the sergeant was correct that a griping army is a happy army, then

Bethany could not be better and students could not be happier." A reasonable response was forthcoming to the students' concern. Sometimes the expression of discontent and criticism is a better indicator of a healthy campus than the grand silence of no response to a situation.[36]

Changes in personal appearance and dress have been characteristic of American college and university students. Bobbed hair was an innovation in hair style during the 1920s. This development was lamented as radical by many people, but it was applauded by the *Messenger* in April, 1921: "We hail with pleasure the apparent tendency of the fairer sex to uncover their ears. Not only will this give the long hidden auricles the opportunity to enjoy the pleasure of fresh air and sunshine, but it will also conserve the vocal energies of man." The vogue of using rouge and lipstick, which was regarded as a radical departure prior to 1920, spread rapidly in the succeeding years. Beauty shops made their appearance also in Lindsborg at this time. Conflicts among "pale faces" and "rouge users" were greater than a later generation understands.[37]

The muse of history on the Bethany campus has witnessed a variety of women's hair styles—high pompadours, sedate braids, bold bobbed hair, meticulous marcels, neat flip cuts—which yielded in the 1970s to straight long hair flowing over the shoulders. Moreover, heavy rouge, powder, and lipstick gave way to cosmetics which achieved a subtle naturalness. Eye shadow was applied more or less generously to provide an accent in the new mode.

Photographs of Bethany girls with modified "Gibson Girl" style of the 1890s and the preponderance of jean-clad women on the campus in the 1970s bear witness to the fact of change. Between those years women students had gone through various stages of hem lengths from "hobble skirts" to freer, longer skirts, to tighter, longer skirts, and then, through evolutionary stages of length, which in the 1970s gave the American vocabulary two new phrases, "mini skirts" and "hot pants." The vogue for both men and women in the 1970s became blue jeans (not new) for comfort, for economy, and for what some viewed as a new sense of equality and freedom.

The achievement of greater freedom for women in dress was a controversial issue. In October, 1969, a letter to the *Messenger* identified the problem. The woman writer contended: "A girl sitting in pants next to a boy in an English class won't throw him into a frenzy of sexual desire" and she doubted that in the cafeteria "a pair of bell bottoms could give anyone indigestion." Moreover, she continued: "Another important thing to keep in mind is that pants cover a lot more than a skirt, especially a mini-skirt, and especially when you sit down." A campus survey of fifty-five students produced forty-nine votes for slacks. The dean of students, in defending the dress code which forbade slacks for women in class and at the cafeteria, argued that Bethany students were more neat-ly dressed than at many colleges and universities and that this situation produced good public relations and advantages in the recruitment of students.[38]

Male campus styles had not been subject to great change, although by the 1970s the austere crew cut of the 1940s was almost extinct. Quantities of hair oil seemed no longer essential. Many college men went less frequently to barbershops than formerly, and when they sought help in trimming long hair and thick beards, a place competent in hair styling was patronized. If some of the older generation lamented long hair and beards, they should have consulted photographs of church patriarchs in the era of Bethany's founding, where they would find worthy and pious examples of the tonsorial style adopted by college men in the 1970s.

Bethany has shared in the passing fads of college and university students. "Streaking" was one of those fads in the spring of 1974. The *Messenger* reported: "On Wednesday, April 17, a group of unidentified males, apparently originating from Deere Hall, streaked across the 'million dollar circle.' The group was described by observers as 'naked as jaybirds' and 'eight or ten bare bottoms.' A group of female streakers apparently got cold feet, or something." Two days later a memo from President Hahn distributed via the college mail dealt with the subject of streaking. The memo stated that further incidents of streaking would not be tolerated and that participants would be subject to "immediate serious disciplinary action." Streaking disappeared from the campus with the same rapidity that it had appeared.[39]

The life of students is more inclusive than it is possible to portray in a chronicle of selected aspects. The composite pattern is best known by successive generations of students across the years.

Students and faculty members visit in the Wallerstedt Learning Center discussion court.

A couple strolling across today's campus.

The Thorsen Room in the Birger Sandzén Memorial Gallery, a retreat for contemplation for students, faculty and staff, and many campus visitors. It is also used for some recitals and special receptions.

Although a vanishing tradition, the Class of 1974 members wore beanies as freshmen.

Intramural sports are popular with participants.

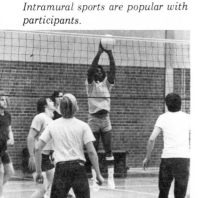

In recent years the Black Student Union has been active on campus, and its activities have included such events as talent shows.

Above: A recent group of the Youth Ministry Team. Below: Three Bethany "Swedes" of today.

Thy Kingdom Come

This "head of Christ," and others like it, have been produced by Bethany alumna artist Signe Larson. Thy Kingdom Come is world-famous, and it has been reproduced in an untold number of publications and in numerous ways. (Copyright 1933 by Signe E. Larson; used with permission.)

14.

Campus Thought

A college is a community engaged in teaching and learning. Evidence of this high calling is found partially in course descriptions, in syllabi, and in library, laboratory, and studio activities. However, there is a broader and less tangible manifestation of campus thought and concern on a variety of public and personal issues. This section is designed to recount certain of these aspects.

Although colleges and universities are often accused of having an "ivory tower" mentality, evidence identifies substantial interest in public issues. One criterion of citizenship is political concern and activity. The attitude of Bethany students toward politics has ranged from intense enthusiasm to complete indifference. In the early years the active involvement of President Carl Swensson in the Republican party was reflected in extensive student participation. A strong McKinley-for-President club was active on the campus. The Bethany band and a large number of students attended a McKinley rally in Hutchinson in November, 1894. The *Messenger* reported: "The band played and the boys yelled. In both these accomplishments Bethany was strictly on top."[1]

Theodore Roosevelt received enthusiastic support from Swensson and the students and faculty. A large crowd heard him when he spoke in the "Messiah" auditorium in October, 1900. When "T. R." held a big rally in Salina in the spring of 1903, 200 Bethanyites and the band came equipped with attractive Roosevelt banners. A beautiful embossed tribute was presented to President Roosevelt by the president of the Bethany Republican Club. President Roosevelt made the following references to Bethany as reported in the *Messenger:* "O yes, I know all about Bethany. I have been following your work right along," and

"Bethany had fine banners, didn't she?"[2]

The campus always has had a small group of Democrats who also showed their interest in developments. William Jennings Bryan was a great favorite. In 1907 the "Bryan Boosters" were organized, and in 1908 a Bryan Club was formed. It is interesting to observe that the "boosters" presented a platform which emphasized a program for extensive campus improvements. A Taft-Sherman Club was also organized in 1908.

The election of 1912 stimulated great interest on the campus. "T. R." elicited great enthusiasm when an active Progressive Club was organized. He spoke in April to a large crowd from his private car at the Union Pacific station. The *Messenger* reported: "His remarks tho somewhat rambling showed the earnestness and enthusiasm of the speaker . . . . As the train departed the students bid the colonel adieu by giving the *Rockar, Stockar* yell." The Democrats were especially active that year. Members of the Bethany Wilson Club were pleased when William Jennings Bryan spoke in behalf of their candidate to a packed "Messiah" auditorium early in October, 1912. There was a rather bitter altercation between members of the Progressive and Democratic clubs over the hoisting of a Wilson banner on the college flag pole.[3]

While traditional political parties were vying for positions of influence, Bethany women were involved in the suffragette movement. In April, 1912, the first suffragette banquet, a successful and well-attended occasion, was held on the campus. Dr. Helen Brewster Owens, Cornell University professor and a national leader in the women's voting rights action, was the guest speaker. The cause was supported by Mrs. Ernst F. Pihlblad, Mrs. Carl Swensson, and Miss Anna Carlson, and by student leaders. The *Messenger* recorded considerable interest in the suffragette movement in the following years.

Interest in politics was revived in the election of 1916. The Hughes supporters outnumbered the Wilson admirers by a ratio of two to one. In the interim between 1912 and 1916, there was great interest in socialism on the campus. The Civic League, a club sponsored by the faculty, discussed various pros and cons of socialism, Henry George's single tax proposals, and the regulation and dissolution of monopolies. Professor G. A. "Swede Pete" Peterson often presented speeches and participated in discussion of socialism.

There was apparently some decline of active interest in national politics for a considerable period of time. However, 1932 was a year of great activity. Republicans, Democrats, and Socialists presented effective campaign organizations. When the votes were taken, the results showed a Republican victory in the presidential campaign: Herbert Hoover, 122, Franklin D. Roosevelt, 85, and Norman Thomas, 25.

The campaign of 1936 produced even greater political activity as the full impact of the depression years was realized. The Young Socialist

Club was especially active. An interesting requirement was that each member must read a stipulated number of magazine articles each week. The motto of the club was: "The most good for the most people." The Democrats' motto was: "Roosevelt—Recovery—Reform." The campus Republican club used the following slogan: "Up with Alf [Landon]—Down with the Alphabet [REA, NYA, etc.]."[4]

An editorial in the *Messenger*, "Politics," reflected on the campaign as follows:

> Shall we sit by basking in a novel display of alphabet and digit juggling in that eloquent showman's private little circus [F. D. Roosevelt], a circus which no longer truthfully bears the democratic banner . . . . And those who back the Republican machine, the millionaires, the bankers, the Wall Street brokers, 'the big fellows' . . . . The Democrats, on the one hand, are sewing madly to preserve the torn cloak of democracy while the Republicans, on the other hand, are ready, if necessary, to throw aside the old cloak and substitute the iron mailed cloak of dictatorship, fascism.[5]

The campus balloting returned a decisive majority for the Republican candidate, Governor Alf. M. Landon of Kansas. The vote was as follows: Landon, 129, Roosevelt, 85, and Thomas, 10. The Bethany campus thus joined Maine and Vermont in the rejection of FDR and his program.

Political activity was sustained in the 1940s with all three parties actively involved in meetings and discussion. In 1948 Thomas Dewey won the campus election overwhelmingly by a vote of 188 to 55 for Harry Truman. Frank Carlson, Republican, Concordia, always a Bethany favorite, defeated the Democratic candidate, Randolph Carpenter, Marion, by a vote of 205 to 40 for the office of governor. In the 1950s General Dwight D. Eisenhower won an easy victory in the campus presidential election. In 1956 he routed Adlai Stevenson by a vote of 232 to 32.

Political interest increased substantially in the 1960s. The first election of that decade showed well-organized party activity and dissemination of political propaganda. An all-night election party was held at Swede Inn. Although the national results showed a victory for John F. Kennedy over Richard Nixon, the Bethany students gave Nixon a decisive victory by a vote of 194 to 68. In 1963 the Bethany Young Peoples' Socialist League was organized. The purpose of the league was to provide a forum for liberal and conservatives and to stimulate discussion of current issues. When Professor Alex Garber of the University of Colorado came to the campus to organize the local league in February, 1963, campus signs declared "YPSL's are out to lunch" and "YPS Leaguers are Finks." Twelve students were present at the meeting on Sunday afternoon and twenty were in attendance the next day. The socialist league members established a bookstore on the campus.[6]

In 1964 a poll showed that 60.7 percent favored Democrat Lyndon B. Johnson for president of the United States while only 30.3 percent favored Republican Barry Goldwater. In May, 1968, a pre-election poll produced the following results for presidential aspirants: Richard Nixon and Robert Kennedy, 102 votes each, Eugene McCarthy, 58, and Nelson Rockefeller, 34. In 1972 Richard Nixon polled 62 percent of the votes to 22 percent for George McGovern.

The pages of the *Messenger* show varied responses to critical national and international issues. At times there was silence and then again, great concern. In the post-World War I era, the editor in March, 1919, lamented the great indifference to public events at Bethany. The writer cited the indictment of students by a Bethany faculty member for their "disinterestedness in thought-stimulating, world-significant problems of the day such as the League of Nations, Bolshevism, and other great issues of national and international character." The editor lamented, moreover, the absence of groups like the Civic League which formerly had been a catalyst in the discussion of public issues on the campus. The prevailing mood currently could be best summarized, the editor concluded, by the word, "Indifference." In November, 1925, the *Messenger* grappled with the issues of isolation and internationalism, and came out with a hearty endorsement for participation by the United States in the World Court for the adjudication of disputes within its jurisdiction.[7]

In the middle 1930s when Eugene K. Nelson was editor of the *Messenger*, Bethany students were confronted with important editorials that were characterized by sensitive and perceptive insight. In November, 1936, the editor expressed grave concern about the role of the Christian church in society:

> When man's inhumanity to man forces thousands of persons to sleep in tenements where natural light has never penetrated, the church press is silent . . . . At a time when war threatens to destroy millions of lives and place a blight upon civilization, the church as a whole is raising no voice against organized murder. Because of this inaction and indifference to human misery and social problems, the church has lost much prestige . . . . Has the church in America lost its social conscience?"[8]

The columns of the *Messenger* contained much discussion of the issue of war and peace during this period. In December, 1936, the editor invited students and others to send statements on why they would go to war. Among the responses was the following: "The group of youth that would dare, as the editor has said, to say, 'I will not fight,' is composed of rank cowards, and religious fanatics . . . . This group are parasites on the resources, protection, and economic welfare of the nation." The April 6, 1937, issue of the *Messenger*, two decades after the entry of the United States in World War I, was dedicated "to the cause of Peace and International understanding." In commenting on that war the editor wrote:

"Our official reason for going to war was 'To make the world safe for democracy!' A truer explanation would be 'To make the world safe for J. Pierpoint Morgan.'" In November, 1937, a *Messenger* editorial raised the question: "How long will it be before the governments of nations decide to give Mars a permanent holiday instead of a holy day?" The role of pacificism as an alternative to military participation was a lively issue on the campus in the late 1930s.[9]

The post-World War II era produced great interest in the United Nations. A large U.N. rally was held in November, 1946, and in February, 1947. Study groups met regularly under the leadership of Alma Luise Olson, Bethany teacher and former *New York Times* Scandinavian correspondent. In 1948 and 1949 an active chapter of UNESCO, Charles Satterfield, president, presented interesting programs on and off campus. Campus interest in the United Nations was sustained. In March, 1961, a U.N. Assembly was held in which Bethany students played the roles of President Kennedy, Fidel Castro, Nasser, Kruschev, and Dag Hammerskjöld.

The relationship of Bethany to the emerging nations of the Third World was interestingly portrayed when Tanganyika gained its independence in 1961. This part of Africa is especially close to the College through alumni missionaries and through a succession of students from that area. The corridors on the third floor of Old Main rang with the shouts of *"Uhuru,"* "Freedom" in Swahili, during the night of Sunday-Monday, April 30-May 1. The celebration of Tanganyika independence led by Lalashowi Swai, senior, and his American friends began at 1 a.m., which was 9 a.m. in the home country. At the appropriate time residents of Old Main rushed out to the victory bell, which soon rang loud and clear in the Smoky Valley as a mark of identification with the new independent state in far away Tanganyika.[10]

Some Bethany students in the 1960s identified themselves in a special way with the peoples of the new world that was coming to birth. Three graduates of the class of 1966 joined the Peace Corps—Wanda Helmer, Guatemala, David B. Larson, Katmandu, Nepal, and Rosalie Peterson, Ilorin, Nigeria.

The tension in colleges and universities in the mid-1960s is reflected somewhat in the *Messenger*. The editor in November, 1965, while commenting on the situation at Berkeley and elsewhere wrote: "The burning of draftcards is an attempt to attract attention to the Extremist cause . . . . The so-called 'draftniks' are capable of mischief far out of proportion to their numbers." Referring to some of the literature of protest, the editor continued: "This type of communist-backed literature shows how the demonstration has grown way out of proportion." In contrast with the above situation, the lack of concern about contemporary affairs was reflected in an editorial, "The *Messenger* Speaks," in March, 1966:

"Current affairs . . . who cares inside Bethany, the home of chicken wire society. Yes, like many small liberal arts schools, Bethany prides itself in small town isolationism . . . . Perhaps discussion of current affairs could replace the pure unadulterated gossip which seems to obsess dormitory living. Conversations with an informative purpose would be a welcome change."[11]

As the American involvement in Vietnam increased in tempo so did the response in colleges and universities. In November, 1968, a meeting was held in the Blue Room of the Union to discuss American involvement in Southeast Asia. Seven students and one faculty member organized a group identified as the Universal Peace People. When the national moratorium on the Vietnam War was to be observed in October, 1969, the *Messenger* announced plans for campus participation: "The flag will be flown at half-mast to honor those who have already given their lives in Vietnam. Also bells will be rung periodically to honor those who will die in combat that day." A convocation was also scheduled. The college newspaper provided extensive material on the event, including the reprint of an editorial, "Into the Breach," from the *New Republic,* which set forth the liberal point of view on the responsibility of colleges and universities towards the Vietnam War. However, the *Messenger* in the next issue lamented "the lack of response and interest" as well as "the apathy" of the campus toward this great crisis.[12]

The intervention of the United States in Cambodia in the spring of 1970 intensified the feelings about the war in Southeast Asia and the death of four students on the Kent State University (Ohio) campus in an altercation with the Ohio National Guard brought a crisis situation on many campuses. Bethany students held a teach-in on May 8, 1970, which provided opportunity for discussing various aspects of the crisis. In this period a Kent State graduate student (not named), who was an eyewitness of the tragic events at the Ohio university, spoke on the campus. The editor of the *Bethany Magazine* described the situation: "In a completely non-biased, non-radical manner this former marine described and interpreted the climate and the events that led to the incident. The resulting experience on the Bethany campus was a memorable and significant effort to participate meaningfully in a crisis of these times." The *Messenger* raised two vital questions in an editorial on May 8: "Do students need to be afraid for their lives when they raise protests against government policies? Or have the students of this country fallen to such a level that they will endanger those whose responsibility it is to keep their protests within a reasonable limit?"[13]

Freedom of thought and speech has appropriately been a concern of the *Messenger.* An especially interesting development took place in January, 1926, during a period when Dr. Gerald Winrod, Wichita, evangelist and self-proclaimed "Defender of the Faith," and a controversial fundamentalist, conducted meetings in a Lindsborg church. Winrod's attacks on scientific theories violated facts and invaded the quest for truth in the academic community according to Milfred Riddle, the able editor of the *Messenger*. In a critical editorial she referred in strong language to Winrod's arguments against the Darwinian hypothesis before "the massed Christians of Lindsborg." In referring to his addresses on this and other topics she lamented the favorable assent that he was apparently receiving. In response to criticism for her article, the editor emphasized appropriately: "Bethany stands for the highest type of Christianity and teaches true science which in no way conflicts with true theology . . . . We expressed our opinions as we did because we believed that true scientific facts were being seriously misrepresented and ridiculed. It was contrary to our sense of justice for such statements to be imposed upon an intelligent community." Moreover, the editor made it clear that the *Messenger's* position represented her views and were in no way the responsibility of the College.[14]

The uproar over the *Messenger* editorial and its response to Winrod's attacks caused President Pihlblad to write a letter "To the good people of Lindsborg" in which he stated: "The management disavows responsibility for the article in question and emphatically states that it in no sense represents the attitude of the administration." The *Messenger* gave space to Dr. Winrod so that he had further opportunity to expostulate on his position. In an amicable conference between President Pihlblad and the editor, it was decided that the editor should resign. The Winrod matter came to the attention of the board of directors, who took no disciplinary action relative to alleged participation of a faculty member in the criticism of Winrod. The board asked President Pihlblad to present chapel addresses on "the Fundamental Doctrines of the Church." It should be noted carefully that he was not requested to speak on "fundamentalist doctrines."[15]

An interesting sequel to the "Winrod matter" appeared about a decade later in an editorial in the *Messenger*. The editor, in reading about the events in 1926, wrote:

> It is interesting to observe the great change of attitude that has taken place on that particular subject [evolution]. Among present day Christians the question of the truth or falsehood of Darwinism is not much of a problem. Energy is rather concentrated on the task of living up to the ideals of Jesus Christ than dissipated on the details of the development of the human body. Christians in 1937 are more concerned with the question of where they are going than they are with the question of where they came from.[16]

The editor of the *Messenger* in May, 1938, published a thought-provoking editorial on the topic of freedom of speech when Norman Thomas and other socialists were impeded from presenting their ideas in certain cities: "Freedom of speech in any institution and in any place is necessary and to be fought for . . . . Protection of those who exercise their democratic right of assembly and speech is necessary if open and honest principles are to be maintained." When the question of loyalty oaths for teachers as a class set apart in American society was under intense discussion in 1950, the *Messenger* wrote editorially: "The dangerous thing is that such a policy is an attempt to limit the right to think and speak . . . . The existence of vigorous, active minorities have produced almost everything that we value in our modern civilization . . . . I believe that the group who fired the 32 professors [University of California], Senator Joe McCarthy, and all who are in favor of such limitations should read Milton's *Aeropagitica.*"[17]

The issue of freedom of speech in the classroom was of concern to the *Messenger* in February, 1974. A letter from a student had criticized a professor for including what was alleged to be "pornographic" reference material in a course. The editor responded: "The material available to Bethany students should not be limited if Bethany is to achieve its purpose. John Milton once wrote: 'Let truth and falsehood grapple; who ever knew truth put to the worse in a free and open encounter.' What Milton said seems to be full of wisdom . . . . None will be better if we are afraid to look at controversial ideas. Hopefully, Bethany will never be afraid to look for the truth no matter how bad it may first seem."[18]

In the 1960s as America faced up more honestly than ever before to the responsibility of racial justice, the editorial columns kept Bethany students alert to their responsibility. In January, 1960, the editor declared: "Prejudice is an ugly word. Its very sound resembles the name of a horrible disease. And such it is—a horrible disease common to small minds and twisted perceptions." In March of that year, in reference to Henry Golden's well-known book, *Only in America,* the editor declared: "It is time for us as a College to join our fellow NSA member schools in applauding the courageous actions of the Southern Negro. It is time we as Americans begin to see that segregation in any form is undesirable and unwanted in our Christian nation."[19]

In 1961, in the column *Vox Pop,* a student referred to the inspiring address on the campus by an experienced civil rights worker in Mississippi in these words: "The civil rights workers today present a challenge to the youth of the United States and to the personnel of Bethany College. They challenge us to give the Negro the opportunity to better himself and our world." This statement was in contrast with that of another student who wrote: "I am getting fed up with civil rights being drummed into my head repeatedly . . . . The negroes must realize that the prejudice against which they fight is over 300 years old in this country. What to do then? I personally think that the Negroes should make better use of our courts."[20]

Other great issues were discussed in the *Messenger.* When the power of the Supreme Court of the United States was exercised to declare certain New Deal legislation unconstitutional, the editor wrote in February, 1937: "In recent years the Supreme Court has gone beyond the realm of the judicial into the realm of the legislative. The president's proposal [to pack the Supreme Court with new favorable members] is in the direction of destroying dictatorship rather than establishing it." Support was given for the trade union movement in an editorial in April, 1937: "If the goal of a reasonably complete unionization of workers is accomplished, we may look for a decrease in industrial strife." A strong endorsement of the child labor amendment appeared in March, 1937.[21]

"Earth Day" was observed in April, 1970, when President Hahn addressed students in a convocation. The *Messenger* devoted much space to drug use and abuse. Reports of limited student surveys in 1972 showed wide disagreement about the use of marijuana, but a substantial majority felt that it should be legalized. Similarly, the columns of the *Messenger* indicated differences of opinion on legalized abortion. In the column, "The *Messenger* Speaks," the writer stated that although the Supreme Court of the United States had never ranked in his "personal 'Ten Most Admired' column, this past month they certainly increased their rankings . . . . The reason? Legalization of abortion without restrictions imposed by any form of government."[22]

A real but intangible factor on a campus is best described by the mood which seems to prevail. Often the culture of the broader social community, of which a college is a sort of microcosm, is reflected in that mood. Aspirations and hopes for the future are often articulated through the vehicle of criticism and protest. The college newspaper is generally the vehicle for expressing this criticism and these hopes on a college campus. In two eras editors of the *Messenger* were especially effective in identifying their concern about the campus situation.

In the middle of the 1920s, Milfred Riddle, editor of the *Messenger,* portrayed the mood among sensitive students in an editorial at the beginning of the academic year, 1925-26: "The earmark of the able college student fifteen years ago was receptivity in the classroom and loyalty to 'great ideals.' The earmark of the able student today is, more and more, cynicism, irony. He is not fooled by anybody. The illusions of his father have less and less meaning for him." Factors cited as the cause of this cynicism were the extreme materialism and self-aggrandizement of contemporary America on the one hand, and in contrast, the new sense of values coming to college students from the emphasis in the Student Volunteer Movement, the Y.M.C.A. and the Y.W.C.A. The implications of the situation were stated in this sobering question: "Does a nation which is saturated with national provincialism, commercial greed, and race prejudice have any right to preach anything to the world?"[23]

Editorials in the *Messenger* in 1959 by Larry Danielson had a prophetic quality in warning students of the consequences of apathy and conformity on college campuses and in American life. In September, 1959, the *Messenger* warned editorially: "A great problem on today's United States campuses is apathy—a dark shapeless blob that crawls about, smothering individual student participation and interest. This monster called 'Apathy' also creeps among the U.S. public as a whole." In October of the same year the youthful editor provided another sensitive analysis of the times: "There is a disease among us. It spreads rapidly and its effect is blighting. Like a slow cancer it grows almost unknown. Too often the harm is done before the malignancy can be removed. The disease is conformity. It has been creeping about the country since Ford and mass-production . . . . Individuality is your right. Enjoy it!"[24]

In 1961 an interesting series of articles appeared in the *Messenger* under the rubric, "Through the Looking Glass. World Views of James Darnell." The importance of the articles is indicated by some of the topics discussed: "On the United Nations," "Laos, Congo, Algeria," "Issues in Communism," "The Bay of Pigs, Cuba and JFK," "The United States and Man in Space," and "The John Birch Society." The article on the latter topic expressed the writer's views: "I think that we are going to hear quite a lot about this group. They bear watching."[25]

Convocations have been a feature in later decades. Visiting lecturers—scholars, religious leaders, politicians, authors—as well as faculty members have participated. In 1947 the series included presentations on such vital subjects as the following: "Knowing Other Races and Peoples," "Is Inflation Inevitable?" "China's Struggle for Democracy," and "Implications of the Atomic Bomb." Issues of current importance have generally formed the basis for these lectures across the years. When attendance became compulsory, some students objected. In October, 1973, the *Messenger* printed a cartoon which identified this protest. A student stood in front of a Bethany bulletin board, reading the following: "Today 12:30, Prof. Zadius speaks on the financial future of *Radish* farming. You will attend. You will be interested. You will applaud." Other students have responded enthusiastically. Extensive showing of documentary and other films has enriched campus life and thought in recent years. The famous series on the cultural life of western man, Professor Kenneth Clark, writer and narrator, presented in 1973 is an indication of this emphasis.[26]

The life and thought of the campus has been enriched by hundreds of visiting lecturers on a great variety of subjects. A selective but not exhaustive list includes the following: Preston Bradley, religion (1922), Anton J. Carlson, science (1947), Upton Close, author (1928), James Francis Cooke, music (1931), Charles A. Ellwood, sociology (1922), Hamilton Holt, journalist (1909), Henry Goodard Leach, Scandinavian culture and literature (1915, 1950), Kirby Page, religion (1938), Judge Ben Lindsay

(1922), Richard Llewellyn, author (1951), Private Peat, war and peace (1930), Bishop William Quayle (1919), Carl Sandburg, poet and author (1922, 1923), Charles M. Sheldon, author and religious leader (1912, 1926, 1937), Jerry Simpson, populist leader (1896), Dr. E. A. Steiner, sociologist (1905, 1911, 1933), Loredo Taft, sculptor (1926), Count Ilya Tolstoy, son of Leo Tolstoy (1924), Vilhjalmur Stefansson, explorer (1929), Elton Trueblood, religion (1949, 1950), Philip Van Dyke, author (1933), and Albert E. Wiggam, author (1919). Kansas governors and United States Senators have often appeared at a variety of campus and community functions.

Visitors from Sweden have been numerous across the years. Prince Wilhelm presided at ground breaking ceremonies for Presser Hall in March, 1927, and later lectured on his trip to Africa. Two Swedish Ambassadors to the United States have been guests of Bethany during "Messiah" week: Ambassador and Mrs. Herman Ericksson in 1946 and Ambassador and Mrs. Erik Boheman in 1950. Ambassador Gunnar Jarring spoke at the opening of the Swedish exhibition in the Birger Sandzén Memorial Gallery in 1961. Bishop K. H. G. Von Schéele was a Lindsborg visitor in 1893, 1901, and 1910. Bishop Hjalmar Danell was a guest of Bethany Church on the occasion of the sixtieth anniversary in 1929. The internationally famous Swedish sculptor, Carl Milles, a close friend of Dr. and Mrs. Birger Sandzén and Oscar Thorsen, visited Bethany and Lindsborg in 1929, 1931, and in 1935. Carl Sundbeck, journalist, spent several days in the community in 1902 as did also Helge Nelson, geographer, in 1921. P. O. Waldenstrom, theologian, was a speaker in 1889 and in 1901.

Many Swedish Americans, in addition to Carl Sandburg and Dr. Anton J. Carlson mentioned above, lectured or addressed public meetings on the campus. Almost all presidents of the Augustana Lutheran Church were presented at college or community functions. Other Swedish Americans who spoke on the campus include Dr. Theodore W. Anderson, president, the Evangelical Covenant Church of America, Dr. Amandus Johnson, the historian of the Swedes in America, and journalists and authors, Jakob Bonggren, John Enander, Ludwig Holmes, F. A. Lindstrand (Onkel Ola), E. W. Olson, Anders Schön, and Ernst Skarstedt. Conrad Bergendoff, president of Augustana College and Theological Seminary, was a frequent visitor and lecturer in the later decades. "Ole i Skrathult," Swedish humorist, appeared in the "Messiah" auditorium in 1929 in a return visit to Lindsborg.

Bethany Song.

CRUSELL.

J. B & P H. P.

Maestoso. f

1. Hail Thee, our Beth-a-ny! For peace and har-mo-ny
2. The seeds of no-ble truth Sown in the spring of youth,
3. In har-vest thousand fold, The sto-ry shall be told,

Pave the way! Strike dis-may To foes of
To the skies Shall a-rise And bless the
Hail to Thee. Beth-a-ny, May thou be

prog-ress ev - er! Pave the way!
boun-teous giv - er. To the skies
loy - al ev - er! Hail to Thee,

Strike dis-may To foes of prog-ress ev-er'
Shall a-rise And bless the boun-teous giv-er.
Beth-a-ny, May thou be loy-al ev-er!

CODA. f

I. II.

Hail Thee, Hail Thee, Hail Thee our Beth-a-ny! -ny!

The first of the most important Bethany College songs is reproduced here (the original Swedish words are below).

BETHANY SÅNG
(Melodi: Hell dig du höga nord.)

Hell dig, vårt Bethany!
Till frid och harmoni
Fostra du!
Hygg itu
De bojor mörkret smider!

Lyft högt ur jordens grus
Mot himlens klara ljus
Ädel sådd,
Som i brodd
Slår ut i vårens tider!

Må odlarns bön bli hörd
Och tusenfaldig skörd,
Vittne bli,
Bethany,
Hur DU vå odling sprider.
Lefve, lefve, lefve, vårt Bethany.

15.

Campus Interests

A college campus provides a wide variety of opportunities for developing talent and interests. Certain aspects involve campus-wide commitment to the purposes of the college while others are more personal. This section is designed for consideration of those interests including religion, student organizations, forensics, publications, and other areas at Bethany College.

The role of religion was identified clearly in the founding of Bethany. The name of the College traces its origin to that Bethany of old where Jesus loved to be with His friends. A statement in the catalogue of the second year of the school's history identifies the spirit and intent: "Bethany Academy is a Christian institution and all the learning and influences of the College are concentrated as much as possible upon this one point." Nine decades later this commitment is expressed in the catalogue in these words: "The ultimate aims of Bethany College are to educate students who will contribute significantly toward the development of constructive Christian thought and expression in human life and society, and to provide for the Church of Christ on earth dedicated and informed leadership to assist in the determination and implementation of its future goals."[1]

The basic commitment of the College to the Christian view of life and learning has been supported historically by required courses in religion, by a major in religion and philosophy for a part of the college's history, by compulsory chapel services until recent years, by college chaplains, pastors, and faculty members with Christian commitment, and by the activities of religious organizations.

The requirement that religious studies form a part of the student's academic program has a continuous history from earliest times to the present. In the first decade courses in Bible, sacred history, and ethics were required every term or semester for all students enrolled on a full-time basis. In the 1890s the required studies for liberal arts and normal students were described as Bible, sacred history, dogmatics, church history, apologetics, and ethics. In the business department the requirement was described as "lectures on religious topics and character building two hours a week." Students in applied music were not generally required to enroll in religious courses every term although many students enrolled in these classes.

The common pattern in liberal arts and sciences during the first two decades of the twentieth century was a requirement of nine to twelve semester hours of religion for graduation. In the next three decades there was a minimum of four two-hour semester courses. In the middle 1950s the requirement in religion for fine arts graduates was equalized with that of liberal arts. When the new alignment of courses was introduced in 1968, two units or approximately eight semester hours were required of all graduates. In 1971 the requirement was reduced to one unit of four semester hours.

The academic program provided a major in religion and philosophy beginning in 1944 for more than two decades. In the reorganization of the curriculum and the elimination of several emphases as recommended by consultants in September, 1968, this major was discontinued. The courses have traditionally emphasized Biblical studies, church history, and ethics. In the mid-1950s the catalogue listed "Bible Orientation," "New Testament," "Life of Paul," "Christian Education," "Christian Doctrine," "Church History," and the "Prophets." Fifteen years later, in 1970, reflective of modern trends, the four courses in religion in the curriculum were "Biblical Concepts and Today's World," "Contemporary Christian Thought," "Religious Perspectives On Man, History, and Nature," and "Denominations and Sects."

Compulsory chapel services were a vital part of the life of the College at the time of the founding and until recent years. The earliest official statement (1882-83) read: "The school session is opened daily with devotional services. All students are required to attend these services. They are also to attend services on the Lord's day at the church preferred by them." Later, religious services were held on Sunday afternoon and evenings. Students were expected to attend these services.[2]

In the early years, daily devotional services were presented by Carl Swensson whenever he was in Lindsborg. Chapel services were held in the former Lindsborg public school building until Old Main was occupied in 1887, when the beautiful and commodious chapel on second floor became the focal point of the campus every day. Former Bethany students and graduates were singularly blessed by the inspiring and eloquent chapel talks of Carl Swensson and Ernst F. Pihlblad. Accounts by former

December 1902
Volume 6 Number 3

Motto: "Qui legit regit"

When the December 1902 issue of the
BETHANY MESSENGER was produced,
it had become a student publication.

The small chapel in Anna Marm Hall is
one of the informal worship centers on
campus.

The Luther League on campus had several names over the years while it was a formal
organization. Here it is in the early year of 1913.

Today's chapel services are not always held indoors.

students provide impressive testimony of the abiding values that came from their addresses. In the absence of Swensson or Pihlblad, faculty members and guest speakers conducted the services. In the later period the college chaplain was generally responsible for the chapel services.

Although compulsory chapel attendance was not seriously questioned in the early years of the College, there were some problems nevertheless. In 1894 the *Messenger* reported a new policy, namely, "All unexcused absences will be known to all after morning services on Thursday." In the early 1900s there was growing criticism about compulsory chapel attendance. However, the editor of the *Messenger* expressed generally the student attitude when he strongly endorsed the policy, and in doing so, he quoted Emerson while a member of the board of overseers of Harvard: "I would not deny the young men the opportunity of assuming once a day, the highest attitude man is capable of, that of prayer." In 1905 the faculty decided that "students with three unexcused absences from chapel would be called before the president for warning and with three additional absences the student would be called before the faculty for severe reprimand." In 1906 the faculty set up a pattern whereby excessive absences from chapel could lead to expulsion from school.[3]

In October, 1908, in the midst of campus unrest over the banning of football, the *Messenger* reported the following:

> Many complaints have been heard about those students who insist upon sitting down during the entire morning chapel exercises. Anyone should be able to stand up the five or six minutes that are required to sing a hymn, read the text of the responsive readings, and repeat the Lord's Prayer . . . . There has been a great deal of laughing and talking at times during the chapel exercises.

There were also periodic complaints by the students for the poor faculty attendance.[4]

Various attempts were made to enforce compulsory chapel attendance. In 1926-27 the college catalogue provided the following statement: "Unexcused absences from chapel will affect the scholastic standing of the student and cause a reduction of honor points." This regulation appeared for the last time in 1948-49. Serious efforts were also made to counsel with the offenders who usually constituted a small minority. The regulations were not strictly enforced for considerable periods of time.[5]

In the 1950s efforts were made to face up to the problem. In November, 1954, the *Messenger* reported that "the attempt to enforce attendance has been flouted disgracefully." In that year the daily chapel was replaced by chapel services three times a week on Monday, Wednesday, and Friday. In 1956 students voted down a proposal for voluntary chapel attendance. In the count of 276, which was 90 percent of the students, 154 or 56 percent favored compulsory chapel to 122 or 44 percent who favored voluntary participation.[6]

In 1962-63 a change in terminology from the statement, "Every student is expected to attend chapel services," to the more positive, "Every student is required to attend chapel services," brought a response in the "Open Letter" of student leaders when they cited ". . . the perennial issue of compulsory chapel attendance as one of the factors of low campus morale." In March the following item had appeared in the *Messenger:* "Since there may be some confusion about chapel absences, it was announced by Dean Shannon this week that, commencing with Chapel, Monday, March 18, 1963, all those who have three unexcused absences as of that date and who subsequently have an additional unexcused absence will be campused the weekend following the infraction." This decision was arrived at through a subcommittee of the Personnel Committee.[7]

The issue of compulsory chapel attendance continued to be unresolved. An irate student wrote in the *Messenger* in November, 1966, that he had received a letter informing him that he was "a five-time chapel cutter" with the attendant penalties. He observed: "The point of mandatory chapel attendance has about as much value to a Bethany student as a can of Prestone does to a Volkswagen owner." Since the criticism of the chapel policy mounted, a decision was made in the academic year 1967-68 that chapel attendance was no longer mandatory. However, attendance at one weekly convocation was required.[8]

Voluntary chapel attendance has prevailed since that time. Devotional services are held twice a week. The new and attractive Burnett Center for Religion and the Performing Arts provides a chapel for about 100 worshippers and is well-adapted to religious services.

A variety of religious organizations have served the campus. Saturday evening prayer services were held early in the history of the College and they have been sustained in some form almost continuously. Between 1927-47 the group was known as the Prayer Circle. In 1947 it was called Saturday Evening Devotions consisting of "a group of young people who meet regularly on Saturday evenings for a quiet hour of meditation and prayer under the sponsorship of the Bethany Home and Foreign Missionary Society."[9]

The campus shared in the programs of the YMCA as early as in 1890 and the YWCA was organized a few years later. These groups were generally active until the late 1920s when they merged with new organizations known as the Bethany Christian Womanhood (BCW) and the Bethany Christian Brotherhood (BCB). In 1900 there is a reference to a college Luther League for Young Ladies and a continuous history of a Luther League from 1908 until 1940 when the BCB and the BCW merged with the Luther League to form the Bethany League. In the late 1920s, the BCB, the BCW, the Mission Society, the Luther League, the

Lutheran Brotherhood, a men's Christian group, and ten Bible classes with a total membership of 150, presented a strong Christian emphasis. The 1920s also brought great interest in the Student Volunteer Movement. The state convention was held on the campus in 1921. In February, 1929, the Third Christian Conference of the Augustana Luther League brought 300 delegates from many states for a series of sessions on the campus.

In 1908 the Bethany Mission Society was organized with the objective "to be a factor in promoting the evangelization of the world." In 1927 the mission activity was reorganized with the formation of the Bethany Home and Foreign Missionary Society. Its motto was: "The love of Christ constraineth us." In the several decades of its history, the missionary society stimulated commitment to full-time Christian service for a considerable number of Bethany students. In February, 1950, two hundred delegates from all over the nation attended the World Missions Institute of the Augustana Lutheran Church on the campus.

The interest in preparation for the ministry furnished the basis for the Pre-Sem Club which has had a long history. The group met weekly for worship and discussion of the church and church vocations. This organization promoted fellowship and developed interest in the high calling of becoming a pastor. Many members of the Pre-Sem Club have served as supply pastors for shorter or longer periods. All but a few members have entered Augustana Theological Seminary, Rock Island, Illinois, and the Lutheran School of Theology, Chicago. Bethany has always been well-represented at the seminary of the church. The impressive number of thirty-three Bethanyites were enrolled in the Rock Island institution in 1952. The Pre-Sem group took the name *Ichthos* in the 1960s. The Prohibition League formed in 1906 and active for several years recruited many members from the Pre-Sem group and from other religious organizations.

In the 1970s the student religious organizations on the campus centered around the activities of the Religious Life Committee, *Ichthos*, the pre-seminary organization, the Campus Crusade for Christ, which was organized in 1968, and the Youth Team Ministry. The latter group witness consists of students whose Christian life is shared in a variety of programs on and off campus. In 1969 eighteen students presented twenty-five programs. The college chaplain has responsibility for coordinating and developing the religious programs and activities.

In the spring of 1970 the "Pastor on Campus" program was inaugurated with the Reverend Jearald J. Shaft, St. James Lutheran Church, Kansas City, Missouri, as the first designee. Other pastors have been on the campus in a continuation of this program, which makes available additional pastoral and residential counseling for students while at the same time enabling the visiting pastor to become familiar with student life and thought.

A symbol of the Christian emphasis is meaningfully portrayed in the official college seal which was adopted in April, 1906. A committee was appointed to present a design for the seal which was to be affixed to all diplomas and official documents. The committee recommended a circular pattern which was dominated by a sunflower as the central symbol. This proposal was rejected by the board, and after additional reflection, the present seal was adopted. The central symbol is the Lamb and the Cross, which are identified with the most intimate aspects of Christian faith and doctrine. Beneath this symbol are the Latin words: *Domini, Domino,* "Of the Lord, for the Lord." The college seal furnishes its own eloquent testimony to the purposes and aims of Bethany College.[10]

Students are involved in a variety of organizations related to departments, extra-curricular activities, and service projects. More than a hundred organizations have been active for longer or shorter periods in the college's history from the founding of the Linnean Association and the Bethany Lyceum in 1884. In the early history of the College many of them were described as literary societies. These organizations included the following with the date of founding: Lyceum, 1884; Concordia, 1886; Eclectic, 1888; Adelphic, 1889; Sapho, 1889; Young Ladies Reading Circle, 1890; Friends of Belles Letters, 1893; and Vim, 1899. The English Club was organized in 1939. It continues to be active.

Several organizations were related to foreign language and literature. *The Geiger Society,* 1895; *Svea,* 1899, which was succeeded by *Svea Vitterhets Sällsskapet,* 1910, and *Tegnérförbundet,* 1908, represented the language and culture of Sweden. The decreasing pattern of immigration and developing Americanization diminished these activities in the late 1920s. Early informal German clubs were succeeded by *Die Rundtafel,* 1925. The current organization is the German Club. The French language is represented presently by Pi Delta Phi, 1973, honorary scholastic fraternity.

Svea Vitterhetssällskap has been one of the Swedish-interest organizations on the campus, as shown here in 1909.

The Linnean Society of Science, shown here in 1919, was an early organization for those interested in natural sciences.

Social Sciences represent a later development in American higher education. The Social Science Club, 1926, furnished the background for Pi Gamma Mu, 1931, honorary scholastic fraternity, which no longer has a chapter on the campus. The current group is a chapter of the Midwest Sociological Society. Phi Alpha Theta, honorary scholastic history fraternity, represents student interests in that area. The International Relations Club, 1939, affiliated with the Carnegie Endowment for World Peace, carried on an active program for about two decades. The Business Club, founded in 1958, is still active.

The Linnean Association, 1884, which emphasized the natural sciences, was the first society and had a long history. In 1900 it was reorganized to form the Linnean Society of Science. The Society observed the hundredth birthday anniversary of Charles Darwin in 1909 with a festive program. The Alpha Delta chapter of Theta Chi Delta, honorary scholastic chemistry fraternity, founded in 1925, is active presently. A chapter of Lambda Sigma, honorary scholastic biology fraternity, was formed in 1936 but it is no longer active. Interest in chemistry and biology are stimulated currently by chapters of the American Chemical Society, 1954, and the American Institute of Biological Science, 1971. The Mathematics Club, 1921, has a long history which is represented at the present time by the Mathematics and Physics Club.

Speech and drama have provided many opportunities for participation and performance. The historic emphasis upon debate until recently is discussed later in this chapter. The Kansas Mu Chapter of Pi Kappa Delta, honorary scholastic fraternity in forensics, was established at Bethany in 1923. The Bethany Players, founded by Professor Annie Theo. Swensson, is very active, and Alpha Psi Omega, 1935, is also active currently. In addition the Drama League stimulates interest in performance.

Interest in art has been stimulated through the *Pro Artibus Society,* 1897, the Smoky Hill Art Club, 1913, and Delta Phi Delta, 1920, the honorary scholastic art fraternity. The important role of the Smoky Hill

Art Club under the leadership of Birger Sandzén has been discussed elsewhere.

The traditional emphasis upon music produced several student music clubs and organizations in addition to ensemble groups. Included among them are the Lyric Club, 1908, the Bethany Operatic Society, 1909, the Musical Art Society, 1912, the Bethany Music Club, 1913, the Alpha Alpha Chapter of Sigma Alpha Iota, 1927, honorary music fraternity for women, and the Gamma Mu Chapter of Phi Mu Alpha, 1940, honorary scholastic music fraternity for men. The later organization was preceded by Zeta Phi Omega, 1915, the first Greek scholastic fraternity on the campus. The chapters of Sigma Alpha Iota and Phi Mu Alpha Sinfonia are active presently.

A vital aspect of campus musical interests across the years and presently is related to senior recitals. Hundreds of students recall the extra rehearsals and coaching that eventuated in the graduation recital, usually in the spring of the year. This was and is a gala time of music, flowers, applause, and receptions. Faculty recitals have been and are presently important events. Moreover, recitals by visiting artists on occasions other than the Messiah Festival have enriched campus life. Historic examples are the three concerts by E. Power Biggs, famous organist, and recitals by Jussi Björling and Jan Peerce.

The emphasis upon teacher education is reflected in clubs and societies. An early organization was the Bethany Normal Society, 1905. The Dr. W. L. Brooks chapter of the Future Teachers of America was formed in 1947. Two educational groups are active in 1974: the Bethany College Student Education Association, 1960, and the Bethany Chapter of the Music Educators National Conference, which was preceded by the Music Education Club, 1944.

Enrollment in recent times reflects the changing pattern of American colleges and universities in the increased attendance of students from minority groups. The Black Student Union was organized in 1970. This organization represents the interests of minority students and conducts a series of programs identifying the contributions of Blacks to American life and the problems confronting all minorities. Convocations, visiting lecturers, worship experiences, and articles in the *Messenger* are included among the activities of the BSU.

Blue Key and Gold Key, student service clubs, were founded in 1961 and continue their activities.

Student instrumental ensembles of various types developed from time to time. The Blue Dozen, the most famous of them, has had a continuous history since its organization in 1925. In the autumn of that year a group of students met on the steps of Carnegie Library to organize a pep band. There was need for a small band that could readily travel out of town for athletic contests. Carl Eberhardt suggested the name, "The

When the Blue Dozen pep band was organized, it added much musical color to the campus. The group is shown here in 1926.

Blue Dozen." This suggestion was adopted and it still designates the current pep band a half century later. Twelve players formed the personnel. August San Romani and Andrew H. Baker served jointly as leaders during the first year; Baker was the director during the second year. The first uniforms were white duck trousers, football jerseys, and an overseas type blue cap. The founding members include Bethanyites who have had distinguished records in music and in other fields: Fred Kienzie and Russell Anderson, clarinet; Lloyd Malm and Orville Anderson, saxophone; Marion Madison and Carl Leaf, trombone; James Hawkins, bass; Clarence Sawhill, baritone; Carl Eberhardt, snare drum; Lee Smith, bass drum; August San Romani and Andrew H. Baker, cornet. Spirited renditions of *Tiger Rag* by the Blue Dozen will be remembered by many generations of alumni and former students. The Blue Dozen has also presented many concerts in Lindsborg and on tour.[11]

American colleges and universities have developed varied patterns for student government. The first public discussion of the need for a student government association appeared in a *Messenger* editorial in October, 1908, "Why not a Student Council at Bethany?" In April of the following year the issue was again discussed: "Bethany needs a student council, and needs it bad. Several instances have occurred during the past year which we believe would have been more quickly and satisfactorily settled if students had an authorized representative body to speak for them." In April, 1911, the faculty authorized a student council of eleven members. Hugo Haterius was the temporary chairman.[12]

The student council has operated across the years through standing and special committees. In the developing pattern of responsibilities, a student court for adjudication in specified areas was established in 1957 with Danny Nelson as the first chief justice. In that year President Mortvedt and his associates arranged for a leadership conference for students at sessions which were held at Camp Webster. A new constitution was adopted in April, 1966. The new organization was called "Associated Students of Bethany College." The key element was identified as the Interclub Council. Representation was provided from clubs, organizations, classes, dormitories, and officials of campus student publications.

In 1968 an editorial in the *Messenger* complimented the College on the success of the Student Congress. The editor pointed out that the student organization had initiated action in regard to women's dormitory hours and teacher evaluation and that the students had gained representation on the curriculum, interterm, and student standing committees.[13]

In later years the Student Congress has had direct relations with the board of directors. In April, 1974, the board approved fifteen of nineteen revisions in the *Student Handbook* proposed by the Congress. One was turned down and three were referred for further consideration. The rejected student proposal was the one "which would have allowed the possession and consumption of alcoholic beverages on campus."[14]

The constructive role of debate in stimulating interest in public issues and in providing important educational values has long been recognized among American colleges and universities. The early history of Bethany provides ample evidence of the recognition of the importance of student participation in debate activities. In 1889 there were five debating clubs—Vega, Webster, Platonian, Ciceronian, and Alpha Beta. In 1905 debating activities were organized through the Debating Club, and provision was made "for the special benefit of new and young students who are timid and just learning the secrets of the art of debating." Its successor was called the College Debating Club, which was organized in 1907 "with the aim to create mental activity in the cerebral hemisphere and to train its members in public speaking, to discuss questions in history, art, science, politics, etc., and also to become familiar with parliamentary rules and practices." This club was active until 1922.[15]

Debating was also an important part of the program of the Adelphic and Lyceum literary societies in the early years of the twentieth century. In December, 1903, the first annual debate between the two societies was held on the subject, incredible as it may seem in our era, "Resolved, that the negro should be deported from the United States." In commenting on the debate, the *Messenger* observed: "We hope that this debate may serve as an eye-opener to the students and friends of Bethany. A college to be first class must not only excel in athletics—which after all is only of secondary importance—but also in literary lines."[16]

In 1903 there was active interest in arranging an intercollegiate debate. Negotiations had been made with Augustana College, but as the *Messenger* reported: "The debate did not come off as they would debate with us only on condition that we allowed their seminary students to participate." Arrangements were finally made with Augustana so the first Bethany intercollegiate debate was held on May 8, 1908, on the Bethany campus. The topic was, "Resolved, that disputes arising between capital

Lorin Sibley, coach Martin Holcomb, and Emory Lindquist in 1930 brought forensics at Bethany to a new level, including a second-place in the National Pi Kappa Delta Tournament.

The Kansas Mu chapter of Pi Kappa Delta forensics fraternity at Bethany in 1940 included debaters who placed high in the national tournament at Knoxville, Tennessee.

and labor should be settled by compulsory arbitration." The Bethany debaters, Andrew Ostrum, Oscar Peterson, and Roscoe Peterson, were the victors. Debates were a part of the program in later years with Augustana, Gustavus Adolphus, and Midland colleges.[17]

When Martin J. Holcomb joined the faculty in September, 1920, a new and great era of intercollegiate debate was inaugurated. The record reveals the great success of Bethany debaters. In 1924 Bethany won the championship of the Kansas State Men's Debating League through the fine achievement of Carol Holmberg, Walter Ostenberg, Lavern Soderstrom, and Clifford Swenson. In 1926-27 the debate squad won thirty-one and lost sixteen debates. The Bethany women tied for first place in the Kansas State Women's Debating League. In the regional Pi Kappa Delta tournament two Bethany men's teams tied for first honors among twenty-six teams. The Bethany debaters were Marie French, Margaret Shelley, Eleanor Yowell, Opal Miller, Agnes Hyrup, Lucille Condit, Merle Yowell, Alvin Yordy, Arthur Rydell, Cecil Lamb, Lloyd Malm, Carl Lindahl, and Carl W. Segerhammar. In 1928 the Bethany men debaters ranked ninth out of 122 teams in the national Pi Kappa Delta tournament at Tiffin, Ohio. Bethany's success was sustained under the leadership of Professor Holcomb. In 1929 Lorraine Stromquist and Irma Lann tied for first place in the women's division of the regional Pi Kappa Delta tournament. Bethany also won the championship of the Kansas State Men's Debating League. The men debaters were Cecil Lamb, Carl W. Segerhammar, Emory Lindquist, Lorin Sibley, and Keith Morrison. In the 1929 season Bethany debaters won thirty out of forty-two debates for a record of 72.5 percent.[18]

The fine record of the Bethany debaters was sustained in 1930 when there were thirty-two victories in forty-three debates for a win percentage of 74.4 percent. Harvey E. Anderson, Kenneth L. Peterson, Maynard Peck, and Lorin Sibley placed third out of forty-two teams in the Tri-State tournament at Winfield, Kansas. The Bethany women won the championship of the Kansas-Missouri Women's Debating League. The debaters were Marie French, Irma Lann, Mary Lawrence, Mildred Holmstrom, Marie James, Katherine Bolin, and Ellen Esther Ericson. The men's team, Lorin Sibley and Emory Lindquist, went to the finals of the national Pi Kappa Delta tournament where they were defeated by a 3-2 decision. They placed second among the ninety-two colleges and universities in the tournament.[19]

Following a leave of absence 1930-31, Professor Holcomb returned for his last year as coach before assuming a speech and debate professorship at Augustana College. In 1932 at the biennial national convention of Pi Kappa Delta at Tulsa, Oklahoma, "Bethany made one of the best records ever set up by college representatives in the great national event." Bethany entries reached the semi-finals in three events. Malena Jane Berglund, Esther Ritter, and Melba Olson lost to UCLA in the semi-finals of the women's debate section. Lettie Pierson and Carl Lund-Quist reached the semi-finals in women's and men's oratory. Moreover, in men's debate, Lorin Sibley and Carl Lund-Quist ranked twelfth out of 122 teams.[20]

The outstanding success of Martin Holcomb's years as coach is apparent in the fact that Bethany debate teams won approximately 70 percent of all debates in the period 1925-32. In the four national tournaments of Pi Kappa Delta victories resulted in 66 percent of all contests. Moreover, this outstanding record was achieved by using a large number of debaters. The maximum number was reached in 1929 when thirty-five students entered the debate squad try-outs and twenty-five participated in intercollegiate debates during the season. There are ninety names on the list of debaters for the years 1925 to 1932. The *Messenger,* in commenting on Holcomb's achievement observed: "Columns could be written on the merits of the debate coach, Professor Martin J. Holcomb, but we only repeat an expression often applied to the aforementioned coach—'The best debate coach in the USA.' And we mean it!"[21]

Although the Holcomb era is the greatest in Bethany's debate history, the fine tradition that he had established was quite well sustained. In 1933 and 1934 Carl E. Olson and Kenneth L. Johnson were outstanding debaters. In the autumn of 1934 Estred Johnson and Linda Ulrickson won the invitational women's debate tournament at Southwestern College in competition with forty-three colleges and universities. In 1936 Bethany debaters won first place in the Hutchinson Junior College tournament. They were victorious in fifteen of eighteen decisions. Melvin Ostlin and Harold Sandberg were undefeated in six debates. Bethany won the Kansas State Women's League championship. LaVerne Hoch Billings and Roberta Dearing won first place in the women's division of the regional Pi Kappa Delta tournament. The women debaters again won the league championship in 1937. In the Mid-South tournament at Conway, Arkansas, two teams, Helen Johnson and

Barbara Lacquement and Frances Rosander and LaVerne Billings, reached the semi-finals, the former team losing in the finals. Earlier, in the invitational tournament at Southwestern College, Frances Rosander and LaVerne Billings were undefeated.[22]

The 1938 season produced fine results for Bethany women debaters. Anne Bengtson and Barbara Lacquement placed second in the Mid-South tournament at Arkadelphia, Arkansas. Miss Lacquement won the outstanding debater's award. Bethany won first place in the women's section of the Kansas Province of Pi Kappa Delta. The Bethany men's and women's teams won first place in the Kansas State Debating League. Frances Rosander and LaVerne Billings were undefeated and Harry Benson and Harold Sandberg won four out of five debates. In the national Pi Kappa Delta tournament Frances Rosander and LaVerne Billings won seven out of eight debates. Only one team ranked higher. The Rosander-Billings combination had an outstanding record of twenty-two victories in twenty-five debates during 1938. Emory Lindquist was the debate coach 1933-38.[23]

Kenneth L. Johnson, '34, who became debate coach in the academic year 1938-39, had established a great record as coach in his tenure at Canton, Kansas, High School. He produced an outstanding record at Bethany. In the invitational tournament at Southwestern College in December, 1938, one women's team, Frances Rosander and Barbara Lacquement, won a superior rating, undefeated in six rounds, and one other women's team and two men's teams won excellent ratings. The squad won eighteen of twenty-four debates. In the Abilene, Texas, tournament, Rosander and Lacquement placed second; in the McPherson College tournament, they won first place. In the provincial Pi Kappa Delta tournament, the men's team of Harold Sandberg and Harry Benson, and two women's teams. Rosander and Lacquement, and Gertrude Byrn, Marion Lorimer, and Elizabeth Swanson, won superior ratings. The Rosander-Lacquement team lost only three debates during the entire season.[24]

The following years brought additional victories to Professor Johnson's debate teams. In the McPherson College tournament in January, 1940, Bethany's men's team was one of three undefeated among forty-eight entries. In the Kansas Debate League tournament in March, Paul Engstrand, Jr., and John Carroll tied with two other teams for first place and Barbara Lacquement and Gertrude Byrn were undefeated, winning team honors. In the national Pi Kappa Delta tournament at Knoxville, Tennessee, Lacquement and Byrn won the rank of superior, one of six teams to be thus honored among 156 colleges and universities. Paul Engstrand, Jr., and John Carroll were ranked excellent. In 1940-41 a men's team and a women's team ranked excellent in the Southwestern College tournament; similar rankings were gained in the Mid-West tournament at the University of Oklahoma. Ethel Parsons and Parthena Grigsby won first place in competition with twenty-three women's teams in the Pi Kappa Delta Province of the Plains tournament.[25]

The 1941-42 debate season was also successful. Signore Fornberg and Ethel Parsons won a superior rating at the Mid-West tournament, Norman, Oklahoma; they won first place in the tournament at East Central State College, Ada, Oklahoma; and they were undefeated in the women's division of the Kansas Debate League. The next academic year brought many victories. In the McPherson College tournament four Bethany teams won fourteen out of twenty debates. In the women's division of the Kansas Debate League, Signore Fornberg and Lois Lindeman were members of the only undefeated team. The men's team placed second. The men debaters included John Adams, Einar Jaderborg, and Virgil Lundquist.[26]

Forensic activities were discontinued during the late war years. Debate was resumed shortly after the end of the war. There has been no intercollegiate debate participation in recent years.

The cultivation of the fine art of public speaking through oratorical contests was developed early in the history of Bethany. Opportunities were available for the use of both the Swedish and English languages. In May, 1891, the *Lindsborg News* recorded the following: "Friday evening the first oratorical contest in Swedish was held in the chapel. This was not only the first in America but the first of its kind in the history of the Swedish nation. Each class was represented. J. D. Danielson, a junior, won first place." Local Swedish oratorical contests were held regularly for many years and prizes were awarded from the W. W. Thomas, Jr., fund for excellence in oratory. A Swedish contest was held as late as 1937.[27]

The local contest served as the occasion for selecting the Bethany representatives in Swedish intercollegiate oratorical contests. Such contests were held for several years with Augustana College and Gustavus Adolphus College beginning in 1903. Bethany was the winner that year when the oration of Adolph Anderson was given first prize.[28]

Intercollegiate oratorical contests in English were held earlier than the Swedish events. The Bethany activity was sponsored by the Oratorical Association which was organized in 1890. Bethany held membership in the Central Kansas Oratorical Association. The *Messenger* described the interest in 1894 when A. W. Fredrickson was the Bethany representative in the association contest held at McPherson: "An excursion train was run to accommodate the Bethany delegation. The train was crowded by students from the college and quite a number of citizens of Lindsborg. The Bethany delegation was more numerous than all the rest put together."[29]

Oratorical contests in English were also held with Gustavus Adolphus College for several years. The Minnesota institution won some early victories but in 1907 the Bethany representatives won first and second places in the contest held in Lindsborg. The *Messenger* described the response of the audience in the college chapel when the judges' decision was made known: "When it was announced that the first prize had been awarded to Mr. Nelson and the second prize to Mr. Ostrum, the Bethany students who had been quiet up to this time could restrain their feelings no longer, but gave vent to their pent-up emotions by means of *Rockar, Stockar,* Bethany's time-honored barbarian yell." In 1911 Wilbur Tilberg, who had won the local W. W. Thomas contest, was the winner in competition with Gustavus Adolphus College.[30]

There was a lessening of interest in oratory for a considerable period of time until in the 1930s. In 1932 Lettie Pierson, who was the Kansas champion, was a semi-finalist in the National Pi Kappa Delta contest. Alice James won the women's division of the state oratorical contest in 1934. In 1937 Ruth Chamberlain won the title in women's oratory in the provincial contest of Pi Kappa Delta. Miss Annie Theo. Swensson was the coach in oratory. The Mr. and Mrs. F. O. Johnson oratorical contest has presented speakers on a variety of issues in recent years.[31]

The life and thought of the College have been reflected in a variety of publications. At the outset several short-lived journals appeared including *Kansas Posten,* 1882-83, *Academica,* 1884, *Pedagogen. Kristlig Skoltidning,* 1885-86. Carl Swensson and Edward Nelander were the leaders in founding and editing these journals in the Swedish language.

More success occurred when Swensson, who was president of the Bethany Publication Company, announced the establishment in 1887 of the *Lindsborg News,* a weekly, successor to the *Smoky Valley News* which was founded in 1881. J. A. Udden, the first full-time Bethany teacher, was the first editor of the *News.* The office was on the campus until 1889 when it was moved to a back room in the Farmer's State Bank. The *News* merged with the *Lindsborg Record* in 1912.

Two more attempts were made by Swensson to establish Swedish newspapers in Lindsborg before success was achieved. *Framåt,* a weekly Swedish newspaper which was founded in 1887 in Lindsborg and edited by Swensson, was merged with *Fosterlandet,* Chicago, in 1889. *Bethania,* a journal designed to gain support for the College, had a brief history in 1891. However, the founding of *Lindsborgs-Posten* in 1897 was successful. This Swedish monthly had a continuous history until 1930 when it was succeeded by the *Kansas Conference Lutheran.* Swensson was the editor and publisher in the early years. Professor Hans J. Hoff was the last editor. *Lindsborgs-Posten* was a semi-official publication of the Kansas Conference. It rendered heroic service again and again in generating support for the College. In 1892 Swensson launched the first *Bethany Messenger* (1892-97). It appeared four times a year at the outset and the editors were members of the faculty. The purpose was to promote

Bethany.

P. H. P.

AULD LANG SYNE.

SOLO or QUARTET.

1. To Beth - an - y, O friends, we'll sing, A mer - ry strain we'll sing!
2. We love thy clas - sic shades and halls, Thy park and camp-us too;
3. Oh, there the brightest dai - sies grow, And there they long-est bloom;
4. Tho' seas may roll and moun-tains rise Between us and thy halls,

With sport and cheer and sounds of joy Let hills and val - leys ring!
And hap - py were the days we spent Be - neath thy skies of blue.
And there the mer - riest voi - ces ring In dusk of moonlight gloom.
We'll fond - ly cher - ish all our days What mem - o - ry re - calls.

CHORUS.

O Beth - a - ny, hur - rah! hur - rah! We'll live to dare and do,

And to our Col - lege on the plains We'll be for - ev - er true.

A second Bethany song, which preceded the current Alma Mater Song (see pages 232 and 266), is reproduced above.

Bethany College and to describe the college program. Occasional issues of a Swedish edition, *Budbäraren (The Messenger),* appeared during this period of the publication's history. The first issue was January, 1896.

The publications of the College include collections of songs in Swedish and English. In the Swensson era *Bethany's Sånger,* consisting of thirty selections, was published. Included were such well-known compositions identified with life in Sweden as *Hell dig, du höga Nord,* and Runeberg's famous *Vårt Land,* patriotic numbers, and *Värmlandsvisa,* a famous melody related to the area from which the founders of Lindsborg had emigrated.

The official Bethany song in that era was *Hell dig, vårt Bethany.* The lyrics of Jakob Bonggren, Swedish American poet, were set to the tune of *Hell dig, du höga Nord,* a Swedish patriotic song. When Bethany students in the twentieth century were better served by the English language, Bonggren's lyrics were translated by Professor P. H. Pearson. *Hail Thee, Our Bethany* then became the official college song until the 1930s.

Two collections of Bethany songs were published in English. The first consisted of seven Bethany and Kansas songs. The five distinctive Bethany lyrics, written or translated by Pearson, included *The Bethany Song* (translation), *Bethany,* to the tune of *Auld Lang Syne, Echoes from Bethany, Kansas and Bethany,* and *Twilight at Bethany.* This collection was reprinted in 1915. A collection of twenty-eight American patriotic and folk songs was also published.

The *Bethany College Alma Mater Song,* with the familiar opening words, "Sing for dear Bethany, Let your voices ring," was introduced in the late 1930s. LuRuth Anderson, '40, provided the lyrics and Lloyd Spear, '39, and Ralph Harrel, '39, composed the music.

The College in the Swensson era sold pianos and organs carrying the "Bethany" mark. Arrangements were made with instrument makers to provide Bethany pianos and Bethany organs.

Several student publications have appeared from time to time. *Cornucopia,* the earliest on record, was described by Professor P. H. Pearson in his reminiscences of 1886. It was apparently sponsored by the Lyceum Society. Pearson wrote: "One of its most marked traits was the power it had of getting the editors into all kinds of scrapes and difficulties." The *Cornucopia* was short-lived. Another student publication with a brief history was *The Organizer* which appeared in 1891. In March of that year the *Lindsborg News* observed: "We would say that shall this paper be the organ through which school reform is to be brought about, we surely hope that the reformed school will aim higher in its literary attempts than *The Organizer* is doing presently." *The Gleaner,* a publication of the Adelphic Society had a brief history in 1895. *The Optimist* was a Lyceum Society journal in that year.[32]

The current *Bethany Messenger* traces its origin to 1902 when the first issue appeared in October of that year. It was normally a twenty-two page magazine type of journal published by students at the beginning on a monthly and later on a bi-monthly basis. The first editors were Alma Luise Olson, Oscar Freeburg, and Carl O. Olson. The first two persons became highly successful professional journalists. The Lyceum and Adelphic Societies were responsible for the *Messenger* in its early history. Some issues were edited and published by a class or by the Conservatory of Music.

In September, 1908, the *Messenger* became a weekly with newspaper format. The first editor was Alden Anderson. It has had a continuous history since that time. Various patterns have prevailed in supporting the *Messenger*. A board of publications has been the normal situation. Editors have been elected by the students or appointed by a board or committee. The *Messenger* has played an important role in reporting campus events, in providing a forum for expressing student concern, and in identifying goals of the College.

The year 1908 introduced *The Daisy,* Bethany's college annual. The "Jolly Juniors" were responsible for launching this important publication. George Anderson was the first editor and A. R. King was business manager. The annual received its name from the beautiful daisies which in springtime covered the "park," or the Presser Hall block as it was called later. Literal descendants of these daisies are found in the flower gardens of several Lindsborg residences and around the homes of Bethanyites elsewhere. The name of the annual was changed to *The Bethanian* in 1959. *The Daisy* and *The Bethanian* recorded important activities as well as information about individuals and groups in the ongoing history of the College. The Bethany annual reflected generally the trend in such publications with features like the most popular girl and boy and the most beautiful girl. In 1927 the expert help of Flo Ziegfeld of Ziegfeld Follies fame was used to select the most beautiful girl.

The Bethany campus has had several independent student publications in more recent times. In the 1950s, *The Fledge,* and in 1961, *Tidning,* made their appearances. Both journals presented student authors in various literary forms. *Tidning* (journal or newspaper in Swedish) was published by the English Club. One issue featured the "Cantata of the Black People" by Larry Danielson. In the spring of 1969 *The Black Moon* confronted campus readers. This was a literary journal but its contents included comments on campus life. One issue showed a revised version of the Bethany motto, "Bethany College—A Retreat for Learning," with changes on a signboard which substituted "Bethany College—A Retreat from Reality." The *Messenger* showed hostility in commenting: *"The Black Moon* represents a very small segment of the student body (perhaps minute is a better word) and one of the many at-

tributes of this group is the ability to be destructive in their endeavor
. . . . It is obvious that the contributors and editors are dedicated to no
one cause. *The Black Moon* does not appear to be authentic or sincere
about anything." It is somewhat ironic that the same issue of the
Messenger which attacked *The Black Moon* printed without comment
the "Joint Statement on Rights and Freedoms of Students" developed by
the National Committee on Students.[33]

In 1972 the Sociology Club published *The Yellow Brick Road.* Attention was given to serious subjects dealing with sociology and religion,
earth day, and problems of modern society. In 1974 *Agape,* a publication
designed to promote Christian life, and as the Greek title suggests, to
emphasize love, appeared on the campus. This journal presented book
reviews, exposition of passages of Scripture, personal testimony, and
special articles. One issue emphasized Christian unity. Another issue
featured an article, "Carl Hansen Says a Bunch of Stuff," setting forth
some ideas of this teacher of religion and philosophy.[34]

These independent student journals were generally short-lived. They
represented, nevertheless, an opportunity for students to present their
ideas in various literary forms and they showed an intellectual and
literary vitality that transcended their usually very modest format and
short life.

Included in the activities of the Associated Colleges of Central Kansas is the publication of the *Creative Arts Magazine.* Bethany students
have been regular contributors. In 1973 Donna Molander was the first
Bethany student to serve as editor-in-chief.

In 1961 the Bethany Teachers' Wives (B.T.W.'s), known later as the
Bethany Dames, published *Measure for Pleasure,* an excellent cookbook
featuring *Hyllningsfest smörgasbord* recipes. The success of this volume
resulted in the publication of a second edition, *The New Measure for
Pleasure* (1970). The latest edition contains 219 pages and 429 recipes.
The income over expense is used for scholarships at Bethany. In the
period 1961-74, 20,000 copies have been sold and $24,400.00 has been
made available for scholarships.

When radio became popular in the 1920s Bethany students showed
great interest as receivers were placed in public areas and later in
students' rooms. In February, 1927, radio station B-E-T-Y made its
appearance in Old Main. Paul Allen and Walter Heline were the
promoters. This was a five watt station, 270 meters on the dial, with a
reception of twenty-five miles. Live programs and recordings a few hours
a week constituted the program of B-E-T-Y which had a brief history.[35]

In October, 1970, KLBC, a more substantial undertaking, was heard
for the first time at 630 kilocycles for campus listeners. The program
scheduling provided for a fifteen-hour day. Chris Abercrombie was the
general manager. Rebroadcasts from KEYN, Wichita, provided the ma-

jor programming. Engineering problems shut down the station in the next academic year. KLBC resumed broadcasting during the following year with full programs in 1974. The station is located on the top floor of Presser Hall. The *Messenger* described KLBC in February, 1974, as "having albums galore, loads of 45s, a good tape system, mod jocks, and D.J.s who have freedom to play whatever they like."[36]

Commercial radio has transmitted a variety of programs from the campus, including renditions of the *Messiah* and *The Passion of Our Lord According to St. Matthew.* In 1939, and in the 1940s, a half hour music program was broadcast on Sunday afternoons by remote control from Presser Hall by KSAL, Salina.

Ludvig Nelson has been a generous benefactor, and the trust established by his will continues to provide funds for the College.

Mrs. Gene (Barbara) Burnett, and Mrs. E. C. (Mary) Mingenback are among the major non-alumni donors who support Bethany

1881 - 1975

Bethany College — Alumni Directory

Published April, 1975

An Alumni Directory, now being released by the College's alumni office, provides the names of all graduates and former students, as well as current addresses.

Dr. and Mrs. Alvar G. Wallerstedt were guests of honor at the 1970 "Day of Dedication." They are shown here at the dedication of Wallerstedt Learning Center. In the background are Governor Robert Docking and Dr. Harvey Prinz.

16.

Alumni Achievement

In addition to students and faculty in residence, Bethany College embraces a far larger number of graduates and former students who have an enduring relationship with their alma mater. Various designations have been given historically at Bethany to identify the completion of different courses of study including certificate, diploma as distinct from degree, and a variety of baccalaureate degrees. Since 1972 the bachelor of arts degree has been the sole designation of a graduate.

In slightly more than nine decades, the total number of graduates of all types has been 5,795. The distribution has been as follows: liberal arts and sciences, 2,667; fine arts: certificates, diplomas, and degrees, 1,757; commercial, 954; academy, 277; and normal, 140. These graduates have entered a wide variety of professions and vocations. This section is designed to identify representative alumni among the thousands who have shared and are sharing in the world's life and work.[1]

A survey of alumni reported in 1970 indicates the general trend of professions and vocations. The data used in projecting the distribution provided the following: clergy, 230; college and university teachers, 240; elementary school teachers, 500; secondary school teachers, 600; management and business officials, 100; social workers, 40; physicians, 35; and a varied number in other professions and vocations.[2]

Available studies at various periods confirm the above findings. In 1921 after forty years, the total number of graduates with certificates or diplomas was 1,996. Detailed data for the 397 college graduates, 297 men and 100 women, verified the 1970 study. Among graduates, 120 or 30 percent were teachers, and 80 or 27 percent of the male graduates were clergymen. On the fiftieth anniversary, 1942, the number of graduates of all types was 3,593, and again, the 435 teachers and 159 clergymen formed the two largest professional groups.[3]

The initial desire to chronicle in detail alumni achievement proved to be an exciting goal, but soon it became an impossibility. The number of names soon reached more than 200 and the list grew with amazing rapidity in numbers and in achievement. Since it is not possible to record adequately all alumni achievement, representative selections from various fields are cited. No one can possibly regret this limitation more than the author.

Evidence already presented indicates the meaning for Bethany of the general prayer of the Augustana Lutheran Church across the decades that the colleges of the church "might send forth men and women to serve Thee in the ministry of the Word, the ministry of mercy, and all the walks of life." Not only have hundreds of parishes of various denominations been served by Bethany graduates, but the general work of the church has been blessed by the dedication of Bethany alumni.

In world missions there are familiar names within the Lutheran Church—Charlotte Swenson, Normal '94, the first commissioned woman missionary in the Augustana Lutheran Church whose service has been described as "one of the greatest gifts which the Lutheran Church has given India"; Agnes Christenson, '15, with a lifetime of service in the Rajahmundry district of India; Dr. George N. Anderson, '09, for thirty years a missionary and church leader with the Iramba tribe of Tanganyika (merged with Zanzibar to form Tanzania in 1964), later president of the Augustana Lutheran Mission and the first chairman of the Lutheran Mission Council in that area; Lillian Larson (Mrs. Elmer R. Danielson), '27, who served the Lutheran Mission in Tanganyika for forty years; and at least twenty other Bethanyites who served in Africa. Esther Anderson, '20, '23, was a missionary in China for many years prior to the Communist invasion, and later in Hong Kong and North Borneo. Other Bethanyites of various denominations have served world missions in other areas.

A close relationship between Bethany and Tanganyika and Tanzania developed through students who have enrolled at Bethany beginning in 1953. They have made significant contributions to their country following graduation. The highest office in public life of any Bethany graduate was held by Solomon Nkya Eliufoo, '55. He served as a member of the legislative council of Tanganyika and was president of the Chagga people, which approximates the governor of a small state in the United States. When Tanganyika became independent in 1961, he was appointed minister of education and information of the Republic of Tanganyika. He was mourned in his native country and at Bethany when a serious illness brought his untimely death in 1971. The Bethany scholarship program, established in 1952 under the leadership of Dr. Emmet Eklund, professor of Christianity, and supported also by the Lutheran Church of Northern Tanganyika and the National Lutheran

Council, introduced a rewarding pattern that has been continued subsequently.

Bethany has been closely identified with the administrative aspect of world missions through Dr. Rudolph Burke, '30, who served as associate director and director of the board of world missions of the Augustana Lutheran Church and executive secretary of Africa in the world mission program of the Lutheran Church in America. Pastor Donald E. Trued served as a missionary in Tanganyika and as assistant executive secretary for world missions, Lutheran Council in the USA.

Dr. Carl Lund-Quist, '32, was executive secretary of the Lutheran World Federation 1952-62 with headquarters in Geneva, Switzerland. This is one of the most important positions in world Lutheranism. His responsibilities were especially great in post-World War II Europe. After many years of exacting and constructive leadership, he passed away in 1965 following a long illness, mourned in many parts of the world. He was buried in the cemetery of the rural Freemount Lutheran Church near Lindsborg, his home congregation. Carl Lund-Quist's achievement was recognized by the award of honorary degrees from European and American colleges and universities and by the Order of Merit, conferred upon him by the German Federated Republic in 1957. His distinguished career with the Lutheran World Federation and in other important church offices identifies him as an outstanding Bethany alumnus.

The Reverend James Claypool, '34, was a leader in the Lutheran World Relief Agency in Korea, 1955-58, and was director of Korean Church Relief. He was recognized on two occasions by the Korean government for distinguished service to the people of Korea.

Nine Bethany alumni have served as presidents of conferences or synods within the Augustana Lutheran Church or the Lutheran Church in America. They include Philip Andreen, '92, California Conference; A. W. Lindquist, '95, G. A. Dorf, '93, and Victor Spong, '10, Kansas Conference; Hugo Haterius, '12, and Merton Lundquist, former student '36-37, Texas Conference; Emil Swenson, '09, Minnesota Conference; Carl W. Segerhammar, '29, California Conference and Pacific-Southwest Synod; Raynold J. Lingwall, '36, Iowa Conference and Iowa Synod. Dr. Segerhammar is a nationally known churchman, having been vice-president of the Augustana Lutheran Church, a member and leader of important ecumenical groups and committees, the preacher on nationwide radio pulpit series, and an author of several religious volumes.

Dr. G. Elmer E. Lindquist, '08, was known nationwide for his work with the American Indians as secretary for thirty-five years of the Society for the Propagation of the Gospel (an inter-faith group), as a member of the federal government's American Indian Commission, and as an author of several books on the American Indian.

Teacher education has been a vital aspect of the Bethany program from the earliest years. Bethany graduates have taught in various fields and at all levels. Several have held important administrative positions and have been recognized in leadership positions with professional organizations. Four graduates have been presidents of the Kansas State Teachers Association or its successor, Kansas-NEA: Amos Glad, '16; W. M. "Osty" Ostenberg, '24; Joe Ostenberg, '24; and Don Anderson, '61. John Manley Eklund, '31, is a former president of the American Federation of Teachers, AF of L.

Administrative posts in collegiate institutions have had the services of Bethany graduates. Several alumni have been presidents of colleges, universities, and conservatories: Ernst F. Pihlblad, '91, Bethany College; A. W. Fredrickson, '96, North Park College, Chicago, Illinois; Axel Vestling, '00, Olivet College, Olivet, Michigan; Harrison Keller, '07, New England Conservatory of Music, Boston, Massachusetts; and Emory Lindquist, '30, Bethany College and Wichita State University. Joseph E. Maddy, '08, '09, was founder and president of the National Music Camp, Interlochen, Michigan, and William W. Perry, '15, served as president of the Tulsa College of Music, Tulsa, Oklahoma. Eighteen Bethanyites have served as deans, directors of conservatories, or in equivalent positions. Included among these administrators are Dr. Wilbur Tilberg, '11, dean of Gettysburg College, and Dr. Roy Underwood, chairman of the department of music, Michigan State University, until their retirement. Dr. Gilbert Dyck, '57, is dean of admissions and registrar at the University of Kansas, Lawrence. Several county superintendents of instruction are numbered among graduates as well as employees of state departments of education.

Approximately 300 Bethany graduates have taught in colleges and universities. The number and achievement is impressive. Limitations of space necessitates the identification of only a few as representative of others. Dr. Vivian A. C. Henmon, '95, is quite likely the best-known alumnus in academic circles. He was a professor of psychology and education at Columbia, Colorado, and Wisconsin universities, and a visiting professor at Harvard and Yale. He was co-author of the famous Henmon-Nelson Test. Henmon was a prolific author of books and articles in learned journals. He conducted research in perception as a measure of differences in sensation, in achievement testing, in intelligence testing, and in the study of modern languages. Dr. Terence Pihlblad, '17, '18, is a well-known sociologist who was chairman of the department of sociology and anthropology at the University of Missouri for many years. He was a Fulbright research scholar at the University of Oslo in 1953-54 and the recipient of other awards for research. He is the author of several books and professional articles. Dr. Kenneth L. Johnson, '34, professor of natural sciences, Long Beach State University, has a fine record as a teacher and scholar. He also served as chairman of the division of science, mathematics, and engineering at Long Beach State University, California. Henmon, Pihlblad, and Johnson are former Bethany professors.

Dr. Martin J. Holcomb, '16, former Bethany and Augustana professor, is nationally known in collegiate speech circles. His great record as a Bethany debate coach is discussed elsewhere. His Augustana College debate teams established an unrivaled record of being invited in all but three years during more than two decades of the history of the national West Point debate tournament. Augustana won first, second, and third place trophies. He was national president of Pi Kappa Delta, forensics fraternity, 1942-47. He received awards for distinguished service to forensics from George Washington University, Redlands University, Dartmouth College, the University of Kansas, and the United States Air Force Academy. Holcomb was chairman of the department of speech at Augustana, 1933-66, and he organized the Speech and Hearing Center at Augustana and was the director, 1942-66.

Milfred Riddle McKeown (Mrs. Russell J. McKeown), '26, has had an important career in clinical speech pathology and related fields. She has participated in national and international conferences as a specialist in aphasia therapy. An authoritative volume, *Aphasia Handbook for Adults and Children,* first published in 1959, with a 1975 revised edition, and several articles are included among her professional publications.

Music graduates have been teachers and performers in large numbers. In music education they range in time from J. Leon Ruddick, '15, '17, former supervisor of instrumental music in the Cleveland, Ohio, schools and W. Arthur Sewell, '18, former supervisor of music at Tucson, Arizona, to Thaine Tolle, '50, '54, presently chairman of the department of music at Southern Methodist University, and recently national coordinator in the Comprehensive Musicianship project sponsored by the Music Educators National Conference. Another range of interests is from G. Lewis Doll, '22, with a long and successful career in music education with special emphasis upon orchestras, resulting in a special award from the National School Orchestra Association "for his fifty years of distinguished service to music education through his significant contribution to the development of orchestras in America," to Bruce Montgomery, '50, first director of musical activities at the University of Pennsylvania, conductor of that university's glee club, director of the Gilbert and Sullivan Players, Philadelphia, composer of *Herodotus Fragments,* a choral composition, which received notable attention in 1970 when the Philadelphia Orchestra gave the world premiere at the Philadelphia Academy of Music.

A substantial number of music alumni have been well-known performers including Ernest Davis, former student 1910-12, leading tenor of the Boston Opera Company for several years and a frequent soloist with the New York Symphony Orchestra and the London Symphony Orchestra; Stewart Wille, '13, concert pianist and accompanist for Lawrence Tibbett; Alma Rosengren Witek (Mrs. Anton Witek), '13, violinist; George Griffin, former student 1926-28, a Victor recording artist, who has had a professional career as singer and coach in New York and Hollywood; Max Walmer, '38, pianist and accompanist, New York, are among this group of artists.

Several Bethanyites have won recognition as band directors. Clarence Sawhill, '29, is known nationally as the former conductor of the bands at the University of Southern California and the University of California at Los Angeles and as director of band clinics throughout the nation. Two brothers, Archie San Romani, '29, Arkansas City, and August San Romani, '32, McPherson, were outstanding Kansas band leaders.

Many Bethany music graduates have served as directors of church choirs and as church organists. Several alumni have brought the tradition of singing Handel's *Messiah* to their communities. A still larger group have promoted music performance and appreciation as private music teachers.

Art graduates have an impressive record of achievement. Oscar Brousse Jacobson, '10, was a fine painter, director of the school of art at the University of Oklahoma, author and illustrator of several books on the American Indian, and an elected member of the Oklahoma Hall of Fame. Samuel Holmberg, '05, '10, a young painter, the first art teacher at the University of Oklahoma, had a promising career interrupted by his untimely death. Myra Biggerstaff Holliday (Mrs. William Holliday), '26, '30, has won several awards and prizes for her paintings and was included in "The Watercolor Series" in the *American Artist* in 1953. Sue Jean Hill Cavacevich, '27, is well-known as a teacher and painter. Her murals have won special distinction. Signe Larson, '31, has received international recognition for her famous print, *Thy Kingdom Come,* a head of Christ, which has been reproduced a million times in single copies and religious books and periodicals. Zona L. Wheeler, '32, who has won national recognition in fine arts and graphic design, is presently Senior Art Director at McCormick-Armstrong Company in Wichita. Charles B. Rogers, '42, is a painter whose works are found in the Metropolitan Museum in New York, the National Museum in Washington, and the Library of Congress. Two volumes illustrating his paintings have been published. Anton Pearson, '18, was a popular Lindsborg woodcarver, stonecutter, and painter. Dale Oliver, former student 1939-42, has been with the Walt Disney Studios for twenty-five years, principally as an animator.

The list of Bethany art graduates with achievements in various art media is far greater than can be included within the limitations of space. Representative of that list are Anna Keener Wilton, '16, '18; Alba Malm

Almquist, '19; Dolores Gaston Runbeck, '27; Margaret Sandzén Greenough, '31, '32; Louis Hafermehl, '40; Lloyd Angell, '39; Fern Aspelin Cole, '40; and Pat Wolf, '58. In the field of art education, representative persons are Annie Lee Ross, '35; Ray Stapp, '37; Gladys Hendricks, '38; Carl W. Peterson, '42; Donald Weddle, '47; Clyde Watson, '52; Harry Hart, '57; and David Ritter, '64.

A sizeable number of alumni became authors and journalists. Alma Luise Olson, '03, was the *New York Times* Scandinavian correspondent for many years and the author of the authoritative volume, *Scandinavia. The Background for Neutrality* (1940); Elmer T. Peterson, '06, had a distinguished record as an editorial writer for the *Wichita Eagle and Beacon,* the *Oklahoma City Daily Oklahoman,* editor of *Better Homes and Gardens,* contributor to *Harper's, McClure's,* the *Saturday Evening Post, The Independent,* and author of several volumes, including *Trumpets West* (1934) which describes the tradition of Swedes in America; Muriel Lewin Guberlet (Mrs. John E. Guberlet), '09, and Mary Marsh Buff (Mrs. Conrad Buff), '13, were authors of many children's books; Allison Chandler, '34, is an authority on trolleys as a form of transportation and has published books and articles on his specialty. Several other alumni have served as editors and journalists or have written volumes of poetry, science fiction, biography, and history. Among alumni with publications in poetry is Jessie Lofgren Kraft (Mrs. Charles Kraft), '34, who has published two volumes. Ruth Bergin (Mrs. John Billdt), '18, is a well-known translator of volumes from Swedish to English.

Many Bethany graduates have devoted their lives to pure or applied science. Dr. Bror L. Grondal, '10, was professor of forestry and director of the forest products laboratory at the University of Washington, Seattle, for many years. He was recognized as an authority on the theoretical and practical side of forestry. Dr. Harold Barham, '21, had a successful academic career as a chemistry professor and then continued as a research chemist with special contributions in cereal chemistry. Dr. Vernon Holm, '28, was a research chemist with the metalurgical division of the Bureau of National Standards, Washington, D.C., and was involved in fundamental studies of the physical properties of uranium during World War II.

Dr. Arthur W. Lindquist, '26, is an internationally known entomologist. In 1961 he received the U.S. Department of Agriculture distinguished service award with the citation: "For original research and forceful leadership in improving the health and welfare of man and livestock through the development of new methods for controlling insects of medical and veterinary importance." He has served on important committees of the U.S. Atomic Energy Agency, the Food and Agriculture Organization of the United Nations, and in seminars sponsored by the

North Atlantic Treaty Organization related to agriculture. Dr. Lloyd E. Malm, '28, former professor of chemistry at the University of Utah, was nationally known in the field of chemistry education. He lectured at many colleges and universities under the auspices of the National Science Foundation. He was an author of books and periodicals in his field of specialization.

Business careers of various types have engaged the interest of Bethany graduates from earliest times to the present. Representative of this range in time and area are Paul N. Carlson, '06, who until his death was head of the construction firm which added many impressive buildings to the Seattle skyline, and C. A. Rolander, former student 1938-41, a past president of General Atomic Company and General Atomic International and now senior vice-president of Gulf Oil Corporation with responsibility for all corporate public affairs activities. Bernard Malm, '33, formerly an executive with Sears, Roebuck, and Company, is president and chief executive officer of the DeSoto Chemical Coatings, Inc., Des Plaines, Illinois, and a member of the board of the Sears Bank and Trust Company. Several alumni with majors in chemistry hold important administrative and production posts in a variety of companies and corporations.

A representative number of alumni have entered the field of medicine and the healing arts. Dr. Gayfree Ellison, M.D., '90, served for many years as bacteriologist for the State of Oklahoma and was an authority on preventive medicine, sanitation, and public hygiene. Dr. Rudolph Oden, M.D., '03, Chicago surgeon, received the first citation in the history of the board of regents of the American College of Surgeons for twenty-five years of service on their thesis committee. Dr. Herbert J. Rinkel, M.D., former student '16-19, a specialist on food allergy, was the author of books and of articles in American and foreign medical journals. Dr. Paul Lindquist, M.D., '29, has had an active career in public health with city, county, and state governmental units and under the auspices of the federal government in Italy, Austria, and Greece. Dr. Edward L. Johnson, M.D., '53, was chief of the section of urology and director of medical education of the Kansas City General Hospital and Medical Center before establishing his medical practice at Albuquerque, New Mexico, in 1964. He is chief of the section of urology and surgery at the Presbyterian and St. Joseph hospitals. He has published several papers in medical journals. He has also been the recipient of the J. William Hinton, M.D., Surgery Award, 1963, and of the Yearbook of Urology Award in 1964 for hypertension research. Other alumni have fine records in private practice, in public health, and in teaching medicine.

Several alumni have been closely identified with institutions of healing and mercy. Dr. A. W. Lindquist, '95, was the key person in founding Trinity Lutheran Hospital, Kansas City, Missouri. He served as chairman of the board for many years. Elmer E. Ahlstedt, '04, administrator of Trinity Lutheran Hospital, was one of the founders of the Blue Cross hospital insurance program in the Missouri-Kansas area. Dr. Karl J. Swenson, M.D., '04, was a leader in founding Lutheran Hospital, Portland, Oregon.

The legal profession has attracted several alumni. Three members of the class of 1904 became attorneys. Karl Miller was judge of the Kansas 31st judicial district for many years with his residence at Dodge City. Oscar Ostrum was a successful practicing attorney and served for many years as Russell County, Kansas, county attorney. Luther D. Swanstrom was a member of a well-known Chicago law firm, an assistant United States district attorney, and author of legal books and articles. Other Bethanyites have been active in private practice, and have served as county attorneys, officials of legal aid societies, and as legal counselors.

Public service has provided the career for several Bethanyites although only a few entered politics, and then principally as members of state legislatures or assemblies in Kansas, New York, Oregon, and Wyoming. The range in government service has been from the career of Dr. Alfred Pearson, '93, who served as American Minister to Poland and later in the same diplomatic position in Finland, to Dr. Jack W. Juergens, '42, whose varied career with the U.S. Information Agency included assignments as cultural affairs or public affairs officer in Ethiopia, Nigeria, Sierra Leone, educational assignments in Thailand, and currently as deputy executive director on the Joint Department of State-U.S. Information Agency Board of Examiners, Washington, D.C. As noted earlier in this section, Solomon Nkya Eliufoo, '55, was minister of education and information in the Republic of Tanganyika.

Hundreds of alumni have been members of the armed services during times of national crisis. They rendered loyal and effective service in various branches of the armed services at home and abroad. A considerable number have had careers in the military. Several have received important awards for outstanding service. Dr. Karl J. (Kacie) Swensson, M.D., '04, was decorated by General John G. Pershing with the Distinguished Service Cross for outstanding contributions to the hospital corps in World War I. He also received the French *Croix de Guerre*. Dr. Swensson had a distinguished career in medicine including the assignment as head of surgery in the University of Oregon school of medicine. The highest known military rank of any alumnus was held by Brigadier General Conrad Staffrin, Commercial '99, Dallas, Oregon, in World War I.

Alumni throughout the nation and in various parts of the world continue direct affiliation with the College through the Bethany College Alumni Association. The Alumni Association of Liberal Arts and Sciences was organized at Augustana Theological Seminary, Rock

Island, Illinois, in November, 1891, by the four graduates of that year. Eric Glad was the first president of the four-member group. The Alumni Association of the School of Fine Arts was formed in April, 1917. Oscar Lofgren, '02, served as the first president. The two associations had their own constitutions, officers, and programs. In April, 1941, the two groups merged into the Bethany College Alumni Association. Dolores Gaston Runbeck, '27, was the first president of the merged association. Seven elected representatives and the past president as an ex officio member constitute the board. L. Stanley Talbott, '46, has been the director of alumni affairs since 1967.

The alumni association has presented annual awards of merit to selected graduates since 1951. The basis for the award is continuing interest in Bethany and one of the following: noteworthy achievement and service to humanity in public or church life; a contribution of creativity in the arts or sciences; or heading a recognized organization or outstanding leadership or participation in such an organization.

The following persons have received alumni awards of merit: Esther Anderson, '20, '23; Ruth Bergin (Mrs. Ruth Billdt), '18; Myra Biggerstaff (Mrs. William Holliday), '31; Dr. Arthur Byler, '21, '23; Maurice Callahan, '37; Paul N. Carlson, '06; Agnes E. Christenson, '24; Rev. James H. Claypool, '37; Dr. John O. Cole, '39; Dale P. Creitz, '32; Dr. Emil O. Deere, '04; Agnes Engstrand, '16; Rev. David Haglund, '06; Rev. Norman Hammer, '37; Doris Hedeen (Mrs. Bernard Spong), '31; Dr. Martin Holcomb, '16; Dr. Vernon C. F. Holm, '28; Kenneth E. Holt, '36; Carl Jacobs, '31; Ethel M. Johnson, '35; Dr. Edward L. Johnson, M.D., '53; Kenneth C. Johnson, '37; Elvira Larson, '31; Lillian Larson (Mrs. Elmer Danielson), '27; Signe Larson, '31; Muriel Lewin (Mrs. John Guberlet), '09; Howard Lincoln, '39; George E. Lindell, '17; Dr. Arthur W. Lindquist, '26; Dr. Emory Lindquist, '30; Dr. Paul Lindquist, M.D., '29; Alba Malm (Mrs. Edward Almquist), '19; Bernard Malm, '33; Dr. Lloyd E. Malm, '28; Anna Marm, '09; Robert E. Martin, '40; Luther Monell, '33; Dr. Rudolph J. Oden, M.D., '03; Joe Ostenberg, '24; Walter Ostenberg, '24; Oscar Ostrum, '04; Arthur Palmquist, '21; Elmer T. Peterson, '06; Gladys Peterson, '31; Roscoe Peterson, '08; Dr. C. Terence Pihlblad, '16; Howard Sandberg, '38; August San Romani, '32; Margaret Sandzén (Mrs. C. P. Greenough 3rd), '31; Clarence Sawhill, '29; Lorin E. Sibley, '32; Kenneth L. Sjogren, '57; LaVern W. Soderstrom, '24; Rev. Bernard Spong, '35; Jens Stensaas, '01; Dr. Verne S. Sweedlun, '23; Norman V. Swenson, '43; Annie Theo. Swensson, '03; Dr. Wilbur Tilberg, '11; Oscar Thorsen, '02; Zona Lorraine Wheeler, '32; Anna Keener Wilton, '18.

Bethany College has conferred honorary degrees on forty-nine alumni ranging from graduates in the first class of 1891 to the class of 1959. The following have been honored by their alma mater: George N. Anderson, '09, D.D.; Dr. Harold N. Barham, '21, Sc.D.; Lloyd L. Burke, '33, D.D.; Rudolph Burke, '30, D.D.; A. A. Christenson, '15, D.D.; Solomon Eliufoo, '55, L.H.D.; Paul M. Esping, '10, D.D.; Bror Grondal, '10, Sc.D.; Hugo Haterius, '12, D.D.; Doris Hedeen (Mrs. Bernard Spong), '31, LL.D.; Martin Holcomb, '16, '17, '18, LL.D.; Oscar Jacobson, '03, '10, D.F.A.; C. O. Johns, '99, Sc.D.; Harrison Keller, '07, Mus. D.; Anza Amen Lema, '59, LL.D.; Julius Lincoln, '91, L.H.D.; A. W. Lindquist, '95, D.D.; Arthur W. Lindquist, '26, Sc.D.; Emory Lindquist, '30, L.H.D.; G. Elmer E. Lindquist, '08, D.D.; Carl E. Lund-Quist, '32, D.D.; Lloyd E. Malm, '28, Sc.D.; Luther Malmberg, '98, D.D.; Nellie P. Johnson (Mrs. Daniel Martin), '20, LL.D.; W. Karl Miller, '04, LL.D.; Gottfred Nelson, '98, D.D.; Wendell C. Nystrom, '17, Litt. D.; Joshua Oden, '02, D.D.; Dr. Rudolph Oden, M.D., '03, Sc.D.; Julius Olsen, '98, Sc.D.; Walter M. Ostenberg, '24, Ed.D.; Elmer T. Peterson, '06, Litt.D.; Gladys Peterson, '31, L.H.D.; C. Terence Pihlblad, '16, '17, L.H.D.; Ernst F. Pihlblad, '91, L.H.D.; Clarence E. Sawhill, '29, Mus. D.; Carl W. Segerhammar, '29, D.D.; Emil Swenson, '09, D.D.; Oscar Thorsen, '02, D.M.A.; Roy Underwood, '16, Mus.D.; Alvar G. Wallerstedt, former student 1909-13, LL.D.

BETHANY COLLEGE ALMA MATER SONG

Words: LaRuth Anderson '40

Music: Lloyd Spear '39
Ralph Harrel '39

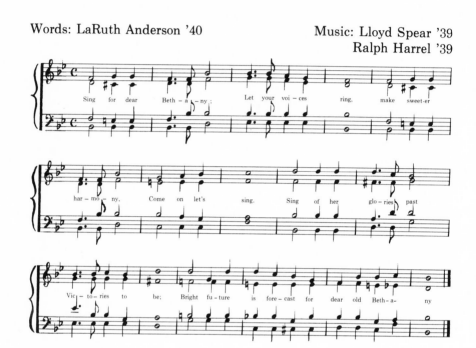

Sing for dear Beth-a-ny; Let your voi-ces ring, make sweet-er har-mo-ny, Come on let's sing. Sing of her glo-ries past Vic-to-ries to be; Bright fu-ture is fore-cast for dear old Beth-a-ny

Cheer for dear Bethany,
  Cheer with all your heart,
Support her loyally
  Come, do your part.
Fight on ye "Terrible Swedes"
  Strive courageously,
Show the world by noble deeds
  That you're from Bethany.

Here's to dear Bethany
  How we love that name.
She has her dignity,
  Glory and fame.
Long may the gold and blue
  Bring to memory
Those happy days we knew
  At dear old Bethany.

This is the current Alma Mater Song for Bethany College.

17.

Alumni Remember

Among the abiding resources of a college are the remembrances of alumni and former students about life and learning in youthful years. When the mind turns the clock backward, the portraits in the temple of memory may not always be as clear as formerly but what comes into focus is often a source of great meaning and it builds a bridge of affection from the past to the present. There is both continuity and renewal through memory among generations of Bethanyites soon spanning a century. The remembrances are as varied as the many students who have experienced them.

Dr. Julius Lincoln, a native of Lindsborg, recalled that summer day in 1882 when he watched the old Lindsborg public school house placed on rollers. He walked expectantly with many spectators to the future campus of Bethany Academy where the old frame structure became the first building. Ten years later he was a member of the first baccalaureate graduating class of four members. His temple of memory always included the living and distinct portrait of Bethany's founder, Carl Swensson, and his dynamic words for that day and later: *"Kunskap är makt"*—"Knowledge is power." Julius Lincoln subsequently described Dr. Swensson in a memorable address with the title, "Being Dead Yet Speaketh."[1]

Julius Lincoln also provides fascinating reminiscences about faculty members from the founding period of the College. J. A. Udden, "a man of quiet habits, masterly scholarship, kaleidoscopic changes of the beard, the 'Agassiz' [Louis Agassiz, great natural scientist and teacher] of the Augustana Synod"; Edward Nelander, "whose devotional and practical talks as *rektor* were so much enjoyed by the entire student body"; Gustav Andreen, "the electric dynamo in the chair of Greek and German, a linguistic genius"; P. T. Lindholm, "the strict moralist and disciplinarian"; J. E. Gustus, "the farm boy from Illinois, whose suave manner and easy speech made him so popular and who taught us to write by the latest whole-arm, oblique-pen Spencerian movement"; William A. Granville, "whose powers to clarify the air of a recitation room might be likened unto the fresh northerly winds of Minnesota, whence he hailed."[2]

The great company of former teachers whose memory Julius Lincoln cherished included also: A. W. Kjellstrand, "the blackeyed tyrant of *grammatica Latina* à la Harkness, who in the classroom held the thunders of Jupiter in his right hand, and hesitated not to hurl them, and in his left, the trident Neptune, a perfectly designed instrument to quicken the sluggish energies of the climbers upon the heights of classical lore, but who on the campus would hob-nob with the boys"; Philip Thelander, "the terror of my boyhood days, whose stentorian voice I could hear even in my righteous sleep, who since then, however, has become a dear friend, a co-laborer in the vineyard"; C. F. Carlbert, "gentlemanly, dignified, and true gold all the way through"; N. A. Krantz, "the inimitable 'Gubben Noah' and his colleague, Victor Lund, formed a pair, the like of which, I dare say, will not soon appear on the scene again; for originality of expression, good humor, and fellowship they were absolutely unapproachable."[3]

Variety truly characterized early Bethany faculty members as Julius Lincoln recalled the past. There was Charles Purdy, "the most versatile man who has ever been connected with Bethany, the Barbarossa of the conservatory of music, educated in this country and Europe, his excellent native endowments had aided him in appropriating everything which he came by on the road of learning." Lincoln was also favorably impressed with the ladies on the faculty: "We remember Miss Ellen Lawson's dramatic recitation of *The Bells* by Edgar Allen Poe; before she had concluded, every stick of wood in the old 'Academy' had a metallic ring and vibrated to the professor's voice." He remembered Miss Harper, "the dear little lady, whom we all honored but seldom obeyed, who was so good and kind that she looked forward to ultimate rather than immediate results and passed some of us unworthy young reprobates into the next class without any other qualification than probably long life ahead of us." Finally, there was Fröken (Miss) Peterson, recently arrived from Sweden, "who had difficulty to find her bearings amid the conditions of a country which was entirely strange to her . . . but her memory is blessed."[4]

P. H. Pearson recalled Bethany when he was a student prior to the construction of the building known tenderly as Old Main: "Greek was taught in a room formerly used as a dry goods store. We drilled on Greek verbs and wrote paradigms on the rough boards, from which the paper had been stripped or scraped . . . . The commercial branches were taught in what had formerly been a blacksmith shop. We used to stroll up there [Old Main under construction] between four and six of afternoons and watch the bricklayers and carpenters at work. By April 15, 1887, the work had progressed so far that four or five recitation rooms could be used . . . . More than once Caesar's campaigns in Gaul and Cicero's oratory in the Capitol were interrupted by the clangor of iron striking against iron in some remote part of the building." Pearson later became an esteemed Bethany teacher.[5]

On the last day of August, 1899, Hannah Granville (Mrs. F. O. Johnson) arrived in Lindsborg from Vasa, Minnesota, to enroll at Bethany. As the Union Pacific train from Salina approached Lindsborg, she was thrilled by the sight of five-story Old Main which loomed large on the prairie landscape and by the high-spired Bethany Lutheran Church. Soon she met President and Mrs. Carl Swensson, who inspired her unforgettably by their kindness and enthusiasm for Bethany. Like so many Bethanyites she had pleasant remembrances of the people of Lindsborg. At the service in the Bethany church she saw J. O. Sundstrom, his vest adorned with a heavy gold watch chain and wearing spats, taking his regular pew on the south side, and Francis Johnson in his white vest always sitting in a pew on the north side, and many other interesting Lindsborg characters closely identified with Bethany College. She remembered *"Kol"* Pearson, the custodian, who at sundown on Saturday evening climbed the stairs of the tower to ring the church bell loud and long as his successors have done, sending a kind of benediction upon college and community, then and subsequently, on the eve of Sabbath. In the autumn of 1899 Hannah Granville was full of anticipation as she assembled with many singers in the college chapel for her first rehearsal of the "Messiah" chorus. Victor Lund was the conductor. She began membership that day in the oratorio society which lasted for five decades.[6]

In 1896 Hannah Blomgren (Mrs. Martin Holt) left Fort Dodge, Iowa, to enroll in Bethany with three new dresses in her trunk. On the train between Kansas City and Salina President Carl Swensson noticed a resemblance of the young lady to Hilma Blomgren (Mrs. J. E. Welin), her sister, who was teaching at Bethany, and he inquired as to her name. Young Hannah was thrilled to meet Bethany's great founder and president, who spoke enthusiastically about life at the College. Enroute Carl Swensson pointed out landmarks and showed her fields where a new Kansas crop, alfalfa, was growing. Hannah studied botany with J. E. Welin, she went buggy riding with a handsome "beau" (Oscar Berglund, well-known Lindsborg druggist), and she spoke the piece, "When McKinley goes into the White House," when she was initiated into one of the literary societies.[7]

Beatrice Wayland (Mrs. English Smith), Washington, Kansas, enrolled at Bethany in 1902 to study violin. After seven decades she has happy memories of her Bethany years. She reflects with gratitude about her fine teachers—Fredrik Holmberg and Vendla Wetterstrom, violin, Samuel Thorstenberg, piano, and Theodore Lindberg, conductor of the orchestra. Joining her in the front row of the second violins in the symphony orchestra was Harrison Keller, who later was president of the New England Conservatory of Music. When the chorus sang the "Hallelujah Chorus" of the *Messiah,* singers and orchestra arose to perform their scores, but since the heavy folios on the music stands sometimes crashed to the floor, the pattern was changed and the orchestra was seated during the performance.

There were many remembrances by Beatrice of talented fellow students, among them Arvid Wallin and Oscar Thorsen, later Bethany professors. Unforgettable were the "Messiah" festivals with the long lines of special trains from all over Kansas and the great crowds of people everywhere. College life also had other aspects. As a member of Bethany's first girls' basketball team she had as teammates Annie Theo. Swensson and Alma Luise Olson. She recalls the excitement created by the string of football victories of "Bennie" Owen and the "Terrible Swedes" and the problems for "American" students when they first tried the Swedish yell, *Rockar, Stockar.* Beatrice lived in the well-known "Bethany Flats" located on the top floor of the Bethany Book Concern on the corner of Main and State streets in the business district. The Bethany restaurant on the same floor served tasty meals in a pleasant atmosphere. Beatrice was an "American" among many "Swedes," but she loved them and wishes that she had learned Swedish when she was a young student at Bethany.

Beatrice Wayland Smith also remembers that sad February day in 1904 when the memorial service for Bethany's dearly beloved president, Dr. Carl Swensson, was held in the "Messiah" auditorium. When the long service was concluded, she walked with faculty, students, and several hundred mourners as the funeral cortege moved slowly toward Elmwood cemetery to the music of a muted band.

The remembrances of Dean Wilbur Tilberg, the distinguished dean emeritus of Gettysburg College, who was a student at Bethany 1907-11, are clear and fascinating. He turns memory backward to the nickelodeon on the east side of the north block of Main Street where students for a nickel saw the Keystone Cops and robbers chase each other uphill and downhill. There was that autumn day in Lindsborg in 1907 when he saw his first automobile. After hesitatingly asking the owner if he could borrow it to take his girl for a ride, he received the answer, "Sure," with instructions on how to crank the engine, then hurry to the gas throttle to keep the engine running, and the fundamentals of driving. Dean Tilberg reports that Vitalia Nelson was impressed. Four years later they were married.

Dean Tilberg has many clear memories of life and learning on the campus. The faculty was composed of interesting and capable persons—P. H. Pearson, "scholarly and conscientious"; J. E. Welin, "well-informed and kind, offering students the hospitality of the Welin home"; Birger Sandzén, "one of the most lovable characters I have ever met"; G. A. Peterson, "who truly loved the Swedish language, but who loved people more as indicated by his philosophy and by his later years of service to humanitarian causes"; Walter Petersen, "scholarly, stating propositions in psychology and philosophy clearly and concisely as he sat parallel to the class, looking out of the window, seeing nothing"; Alma Luise Olson, "keen mind and good personality"; Gus Lund, "a good teacher, who taught Latin as if it were an exact science."

Amusing experiences are found in the memories of Dean Tilberg. There was Dr. Carlbert, professor of history, a small, five-foot, six-inch, fastidious man who sought the advantage of standing on an upper step in the stairway of Old Main to overcome a height disadvantage, and hurrying especially to do so in conversations with Dr. Alf. Bergin, large and distinguished-looking pastor of Bethany Church. Tilberg also recalls the slide-lecture in Old Main when Professor Deere was presiding, quite unmindful of the passing of time. When three girls left in the semi-darkness to hurry to the dormitory before the 10:00 p.m. mandatory closing time, the shadow of one girl's head fell on the screen. Deere, unmindful of the situation on the screen, continued in a booming voice: "And this, my friends, is the magnified leg of a grasshopper," wondering at the howls of laughter which greeted his statement. Dean Tilberg is correct in pointing out that this young professor became a legend in later years. Tilberg also remembers with delight both the musical experience and the personal relations when as a member of the oratorio society his place in the tenor section was between G. N. Malm and Andrew Monson, distinguished Lindsborg citizens.

Wilbur Tilberg worked toward the payment of college expenses as organ pumper between 5:00 a.m. and 7:00 a.m. six days a week at the rate of fifteen cents an hour. He stood in the hall outside the chapel, pumping by hand the bellows for the chapel organ. His body swayed up and down in rhythm with the button in a slot indicating whether or not the organ was getting the proper amount of air. There he stood, pumping with one hand and holding a textbook in the other, absorbing culture and paying for his meals. The regular pumper was known as "Professor Wind." It is reported that when "Professor Wind" was at odds with an organ student, he would silently but successfully cut down the supply of air for the organ, to the chagrin of the student. Although electricity had been installed earlier, it was not until 1909 that an electric motor replaced the future dean of Gettysburg College and "Professor Wind" in furnishing the motive power for the chapel organ. Progress was also made when Old

Main's "outhouses" were replaced by a building with modern plumbing. The girls called their old structure "Sammy," but research has not divulged the origin of this nomenclature. The boys' old facility apparently went unnamed.

After eight decades of a busy life, Iva Winters Schmoker reflected on her years at Bethany when in 1912 at the age of seventeen she received a diploma in piano. She has gratitude for Christian resources that were greatly enriched. High on her list of remembrances was a fine young teacher in piano, Arvid Wallin, whose name is written large in Bethany history. The Reverend Carl Bengtson became a Bethanyite in September, 1913. People stand out in his remembrances. There was Birger Sandzén with his care and concern for students in foreign languages; the brilliant mind of President Pihlblad who taught a class in "Christian Evidence"; the sincere Christian life of Anna Carlson, the inspiration from her teaching of a large Bible class in Bethany Church, and her leadership in developing an interest in foreign missions. Dr. Carlbert's passion for building a warless world in his class, "World Governments"; the skill of "Greek Pete" (Walter Petersen) and "Swede Pete" (G. A. Peterson) in languages; and E. O. Deere with his enthusiasm for science and his leadership on Arbor Day in 1914 when hundreds of trees were planted on the campus. Like so many other alumni and former students he remembers well Bethany boosters among Lindsborg people, like G. N. Malm, Andrew Monson, and J. O. Sundstrom.

When F. S. (Fritz) Gustafson arrived on the campus in the autumn of 1915, he was impressed with the beauty of Lindsborg and by the statue of Carl Swensson, a symbol of greatness. He, too, has kind remembrances of fine and dedicated teachers—"Bethany professors have had a lasting influence on my life." "Messiah" week was a memorable time with concerts by Schuman-Heink, Galli-Curci, Pablo Casals, Eugene Ysaye and others and then the supreme thrill of singing the *Messiah* under the baton of Hagbard Brase. But Fritz Gustafson is also appreciative of his fellow students—Esther Anderson, Carl Glad, Arthur Bengtson, Daniel Martin, Armour Edberg, Arthur Christenson and others like them, who at that time, and subsequently, made fine contributions to others through their ideals and dedication.

G. Lewis Doll, '22, remembers clearly his first meeting with Arthur E. Uhe and the impression made on him when his future violin teacher played the Pagannini *Caprice* and a Max Reger composition for solo violin. He recalls Birger Sandzén's chapel appearances when students heard him tell Hans Christian Andersen's stories "which are treasured memories for he told them so delightfully." There were capable fellow students—Arthur Byler, Leslie Scoville, and others who shared their interest in music. Also enshrined in his memory is the delightful experience of living in a Swedish home north of the College.

Hulda Mattson, '23, Windom, Kansas, remembers after fifty years the beautiful profusion of blooming daisies on the Presser Hall block devoid then of buildings, the leisurely Saturday walks on unpaved country roads to Coronado Heights, and the sessions of Dr. Welin's astronomy class on the roof of Old Main as students viewed the universe anew through a telescope. Students' costs were indeed modest. Three meals a day for a week at the dining hall cost $2.50 a week and $200.00 took care of all expenses. Swedish declamation contests formed a link with the pioneer world of the Swedish immigrants. Astrid Glidden Runge received a bachelor of expression degree in 1924. Most meaningful in her Bethany experience was a teacher, Annie Theo. Swensson, to whom she feels everlastingly grateful for constructive influence and abiding inspiration. She writes sensitively: "When I stood by Miss Swensson's grave a few years ago, I felt I was on holy ground."

Dr. Evert A. Larsson, M.D., a native of Lidköping, Sweden, came to Bethany in 1925, less than a year after his arrival in the United States. He had no money, little knowledge of English, but great and impelling desire to get an education and become a physician. On an off day from his job on the railroad section crew at Lindsborg, he went to the campus and when wandering around Old Main he "fortuitously met a tall, lean man with a little black mustache, friendly inquisitive eyes, and a faint smile, who spoke Swedish exceedingly well." The man was Dean E. O. Deere, who from that moment became a friend of the struggling Swedish immigrant. Dr. Evert Larsson, whose dreams about becoming a physician were realized by great sacrifice and determination, has many interesting and perceptive remembrances about faculty, courses, students, and the spirit of the campus. He has summarized a vital, total impression in these words: "The prevailing Swedishness of Lindsborg imparted a sense of security free of any discordant feelings of alienation or strangeness. But there was also something else contained in the very atmosphere of the place which I interpreted as regard for the individual, lack of social distance between man and man, a desire to be of assistance, and a high respect for academic and cultural pursuits." Then Dr. Larsson concludes: "The value placed on the individual, the encouragement and support so fully given, I considered typically American. I actually thought I had come to a most distinctive American place and never thereafter did I find any reason to think otherwise."[8]

Milfred Riddle (Mrs. Russell McKeown), '26, was editor of the *Messenger*. She was supported by James C. Hawkins, '26, associate editor and by Merle Yowell, '27, business manager. Milfred was a dynamic person who shared college life enthusiastically. Her remembrances are as full as her life at the College. In the forefront are wonderful people—President Pihlblad, in a tight situation with a segment of the community as a result of Milfred's rather harsh direct attack upon "scientific" views of Dr. Gerald Winrod, a visiting evangelist, in the *Messenger,* reluctantly relieving her as editor but in a spirit that brought understanding and admiration; Otto Hawkinson, Marquette banker and long-time board member, who made a personal delivery of a loan so that she could meet an urgent payment of college expenses; Professor Sandzén, assisting Milfred when rather brashly she went to the studio with brushes and paints, stating she wanted to paint a picture, and leaving with a highly cherished watercolor (a proud possession now) that Sandzén had assisted her in completing; Professor Bonander meeting with her for several hours four or five times a week during a summer term so she could complete an urgent graduation requirement in German; Professor Deere's kindness when Milfred's obligation at Mrs. Mead's famous boarding house on Second Street made her regularly late to classes, and his humor when he cooperated with Jim Hawkins and her in permitting them to use stuffed birds from the biology laboratory to play a trick on Bill Stensaas when he returned one night to his room in Old Main.

Milfred Riddle McKeown conveys something meaningful about Bethany in the following words: "I certainly was not the typical Bethany student. I was not a Lutheran, I was not Swedish, I did not go to Sunday School, I had grown up as a railroader's daughter whose life was not as sheltered as that of many Bethany students. It was difficult for me not to be able to go to dances and to be in the house at a stipulated hour and not to ride a bicycle whenever I could get the loan of one (the dean of women called me in and told me not to ride a bicycle on the campus because it was not lady-like). In spite of this and other things like it, not a single person at Bethany was ever rude or cross or showed any prejudice." In the background of these observations, her response to the College seems especially interesting: "So many of the things that now are abhorred were not at all objectionable to me: being marked in attendance at Chapel, for example. I didn't care much about what the speaker said, I just wanted to be there in case I might miss something important. Required courses in religion: I wasn't interested in the courses (but would be tremendously interested today) but I was entirely in accord with the proposition that a college had a right to impose its own regulations." Milfred acquired a porcelain doorknob during the sale of Old Main items by the Bethany Dames, but she would have preferred above everything else a square foot of the bright red wallpaper from the turn of the last century that hung on her practice-room walls in Old Main.

Almost forty years had passed between the matriculation of Helen Holt, Des Moines, Iowa, in 1934, and her mother, Hannah Blomgren in 1896, but the remembrances of the mother, referred to above, and daughter have the same framework of reference. Esteem for faculty was a common denominator. Helen Holt shared as did her mother in the patient and effective teaching of science by Dr. J. E. Welin; she recalls the great gentleness and capability of Vendla Wahlin in teaching creative writing ("I will always write poetry"); and she reflects on the classes of E. B. Doering, who unfolded the whole glorious world of English literature with wit and erudition. Helen also thinks with gratitude about her fellow students, whom she describes as "genuinely nice people." Moreover, she recalls aspects of student life in the lull before the great storm caused by World War II: "We found pleasure in simple things: walking out to Coronado Heights, going to the bakery for toasted cheese sandwiches and tomato soup, or to the drugstore for 'chocolate smooths'; getting dressed up for social events; taking off for shopping trips in Salina in an old rented car (or perish the thought—by hitch hiking); holding forbidden parties on third floor of Lane Hart Hall; and always, everywhere, the glorious sound of music. We were the college generation that wanted international peace. After our graduation came World War II."

Alumni reflections are fashioned in a variety of circumstances. Natalie Miller, '41, came to Bethany from Texas in 1937. She expresses her remembrance of the Bethany spirit: "The friendly, positive attitude of both students and faculty did much to encourage me when I took my first steps into a completely sighted world. They did not set me apart as different." She recalls clearly the long discussions on controversial social issues with well-informed Dr. George Kleihege, professor of sociology, on a variety of topics during her first year while living in the friendly home of the Kleiheges. She also enjoyed other fine teachers—Oscar Thorsen, Birger Beausang, Ellen Strom, sharing their great musical knowledge, and Dr. Brase, and the unforgettable experiences during "Messiah" week. The Bethany years brought many good friends, including Margaret Kyner, '39, Wilson, Kansas, with whom Natalie has shared most of the subsequent years as each has continued her professional career in the Chicago area. Margaret Kyner also recalls dedicated teachers and delightful experiences. In reflecting on the campus she observed: "Although the buildings were not new—Old Main, the Library, Lane Hart Hall, the Old Gym ["Messiah" auditorium], and Art Pavilion, the whole complex of the campus was a homey, vital place."

When Paul Moore, '37, Caldwell, Kansas, came to Bethany as a transfer student, he soon found good friends, rewarding studies, and a stimulating environment. He writes: "One of the highlights was the daily chapel service which provided not only an opportunity to pause and reflect and be thankful, but also a vehicle which brought the administration, including President Pihlblad, and the faculty and the students in close contact. Chapel was a meaningful experience." There were great people too—the privilege of private piano lessons with Dean Lofgren, singing in the choir and oratorio society under the baton of Dr. Brase, participating in the wonderful theater productions under the direction of

Miss Swensson, having classes with Professors Doering and Kraft, who were "tough but impressive," and learning about teaching public school music from a skilled instructor, Geneva Smith. Living in the community of Lindsborg with its enriching cultural resources was also a great experience.

When World War II cast its shadows upon the family of man, the mobility of population took many people from the campus, but it brought some who otherwise would not have been there. Marian McBroom (Mrs. J. H. McBroom, Jr.), whose husband was a young artillery officer stationed at Camp Phillips, near Smolan, enrolled in 1943. The McBrooms lived in Lindsborg. Three decades later Mrs. McBroom shares her remembrances as her thoughts turned to the College and the community. People are clearly remembered with great appreciation: "piano lessons with Arvid Wallin, so gentle, so brilliant, and so patient"; organ lessons with "charming Hagbard Brase in the chapel of Old Main, and the thrill that it gave me"; Donald DeCou, economics, "helpful and kind"; the great friendliness of Margaret and Pelham Greenough. Marian McBroom came from magnolia country, but she cherishes Bethany and Lindsborg: "My brief interlude there enabled me to absorb a touch of Swedish culture, to appreciate more fully music and art, to know beautiful people on campus and in town, and to share in an overall atmosphere that I have somehow managed to keep with me throughout the years." In the almost century-old farm house in Tennessee, near the university where her husband is a professor, are spindles and lintels from Old Main which form the basic structure of the stairrail down to the formal dining room, a pleasant reminder of former days in the Smoky Valley of Central Kansas.

Bethany during World War II provided the setting for the remembrances of Rosalie Carlson Nelson (Mrs. Merle Nelson), who was awarded a degree in 1945, following matriculation in 1941. She recalls the steady decline, then the dramatic drop in enrollment until there were only about 130 students in 1945, including only twenty males. Classes were underway for only a few months when the traumatic news of the bombing of Pearl Harbor spread over the campus that December Sunday in 1941. Letters were sent regularly from the campus to previously unheard-of military addresses in this country and to A.P.O.'s in distant places. Classes were small and activities limited although organizations strove valiantly to sustain their programs. Teachers continued to stimulate learning and develop talent. As a voice major Rosalie reflects with deep appreciation about private lessons with Thure Jaderborg, a dedicated and able musician, who not only taught scales, breath control, diction, and an interesting repertoire, but who also inspired the student with his accounts of great composers and performers. Moreover, he was generous in giving time to the individual student and to the women's quartet composed of Martha Christenson, Helen Olson, Doris Nelson, and Rosalie Carlson, who presented many concerts throughout Kansas.

There are other Bethany personnel in Rosalie's remembrances—Oscar Thorsen, with his fine musicianship and great culture; Ellen Strom, "eyes sparkling behind glasses and hair marcelled, always generous with her time at the college and in entertaining students at her home"; Ruth J. Martin, "an outstanding sight-singing and ear-training teacher"; Elinor Gahnstrom, "the finest resident head anyone could have in that 'hall of fame,' Lane Hart Hall"; David Anderson, giving long hours of tutorial effort to enable her to meet a chemistry requirement for graduation. She reflects with happy memories about other college personnel—Irene Thorstenberg, manager of the cafeteria, and administrative office personnel, Aileen Henmon, Delia Berglund, and Leona Holmberg.

A memorable occasion in the experience of Rosalie Carlson was the special rendition of the *Messiah* in packed Presser Hall for the 94th division stationed at Camp Phillips near Smolan prior to their departure for distant battlefields and a concert for the troops who again filled Presser Hall for a performance of *Naughty Marietta*. Camp Phillips and Schilling Air Force Base nearby were the settings for concerts and programs and provided dates and romances. Chapel services were rewarding, with "thoughtful chapel messages which were like pebbles thrown into a pond making ever wider circles by which to guide ourselves." Rosalie vividly recalls dormitory life: "The living quarters in Lane Hart Hall where I lived for three years were cramped, the steps tiring, the mice scary, but the camaraderie was unequaled, my roommate unparalleled, and there I had the most fun I have ever had. We've since had a daughter live there and another who wishes to live there." She concluded her recollections with these words: "In retrospect, those four years at Bethany were priceless in terms of friendships made, vision enlarged, spiritual life and faith deepened, along with the learning that was hopefully acquired."

When the tragic years of World War II ended, a new generation of students brought their talents and then left the campus for a bigger world with deep affection for Bethany. One of those students was Bruce Montgomery, '50, from an Ivy League Philadelphia family, whose father, James Montgomery, was a frequent tenor soloist with the oratorio society and one of the all-time favorites. Bruce describes his remembrances as "fragmentary thoughts about some of the personal experiences and impressions that flood back to me." They are cited because they have a timeless as well as a specific content in the Bethany tradition. Selections follow:

The thrill of performing the *Messiah* and the *Saint Matthew Passion* during Holy Week . . . the additional thrill of having my father as the tenor soloist during my first two years . . . the stunning shock of the performance of the *Messiah* when Arvid Wallin's beat became unintelligible and the chorus and orchestra simply petered out in shocked silence as Mrs. Wallin stepped from the soprano section and, with great calm and nobility helped her seriously ill husband from the stage . . . and the quiet authority of old and retired Hagbard Brase, leaving his seat in the audience, mounting the stage, picking up the idled baton, and with dignity and resolve completing an inspired performance.

Lindsborg's ghastly water rusting the three-faceted drinking fountain outside "Old Main" . . . the worn metal treads on every step of the building . . . chapel services that always ended with announcements . . . the president catching Pattie Taylor and me dancing (*ach! verboten!*) in the Art Pavilion late one night . . . ice skating on the football field one cold winter . . . listening at all the practice room doors on the top floor of Presser Hall to find an idle piano . . . excellent and inspiring sermons by Emmet Eklund . . . Emil O. Deere never having learned that his car had a second and third gear.

Singing and travelling in various parts of the nation with the Pitch Pipers—Carol Anderson, LaRue Olson, Wayne Holmstrom, and myself . . . designing mammoth and impossible floats for Homecoming parades . . . Painting the windows of almost every store in town for the Swedish Festival . . . the beautiful *Julotta* services at the college and in the churches, hating *lutfisk* and loving *sill* and *ostkaka* . . . never tasting coffee that could stand beside King Oscar . . . the old bandstand that stood near where the Sandzén Gallery is now . . . learning so much useful technique from Lester Raymer and Charles Rogers . . . sitting for hours at a time with Margaret and Pelham Greenough and Frida and Birger Sandzén and learning history and the arts and simplicity in their presence . . . going into raptures over one of Irene Thorstenberg's rhubarb pies one day in the cafeteria and having her reach under the counter for the next three years when she had saved a piece for me . . . Living at Kalmar Hall with the Ray Hahns as marvelous house parents and realizing with astonishment that a husky football coach could like poetry, music, and art.

And then Bruce Montgomery concludes: "Oh, how easy it is to ramble on and on with a steady stream of memories and influences of four years that helped so much to shape my life forever."

Betty Nelson Swenson (Mrs. William G. Swenson), '54, reflects on dorm life, "an experience that never can be duplicated; companionship day and night; sharing of problems and being able to talk them out with friends; being late or forgetting to sign out and then being campused; sunning on the roof top of Alma Swensson Hall; finishing our days with devotions in each other's rooms." Monette Burnison Johnson (Mrs. Charles K. Johnson), '65, among other things recalls "building and stuffing homecoming floats, the annual Artscaval, bow day, and the special feelings and memories of being a member of a sorority."

Larry Danielson, '62, a native of Lindsborg, was early identified with Bethany. The college years deepened his insight and understanding. Classroom experiences broadened his knowledge of the world of books and ideas. He writes: "The bright, intellectual lights on the faculty in the late 1950s were John Adams, who frightened most students and even his

English majors with his persistently intellectual queries; Warren Kliewer, always stylish, a little cynical, delighting in the double-entendre, an actual writer who published his poems, and interested in interesting things; and Bill Unrau, who delighted those few campus liberals with his outspoken political allegations and made distant history lively and exciting to the most reluctant student." He concluded his observations: "The music department, too, had its colorful and talented faculty members. I played in the college band for several years with Lowell Boroughs . . . who demanded excellence in performance, and freely applied the epithet 'buckethead' to careless musical behavior. His band became one of the best musical groups in the state under his talented direction. Elmer Copley was an important music faculty member, in my opinion. His work with the college choir was impressive, and his direction of the "Messiah" Chorus was an inspiration."

David Goldberg, '74, transferred to Bethany as a junior and soon felt at home. He lived in Carlton Hall and later at Deere Hall, often referred to as the "zoo." He has pleasant remembrances of teachers and classes, friends and activities. He writes: "I remember the Saturday night dances, the soft snow falling against the dorm window at night, and the smell of fresh coffee every morning in the dining room . . . . I remember the friends also, the best part!—Vicki, Parsha, Wanda, Tom, Tony, and others. I remember Rev. Jerry Shaft and what he meant to me . . . . I remember most of all one afternoon when we were to find out if Dr. Hahn would leave or stay. I remember him saying, 'I have decided to stay.' I remember the ovation, laughter, tears, and happiness."

The remembrances of individuals, named and unnamed, form only a part of a greater whole. Although there are many variations, a common theme prevails. Esteem for faculty, appreciation for fellow students, respect for learning, and gratitude for great spiritual and cultural resources seem to be the basic elements in a glorious heritage. Activities and events loom large as Bethany offered many opportunities for participation in organizations and groups. All of them fashion a kind of unwritten saga about Alma Mater and happy student years.

President Arvin W. Hahn also has his lively and vivid feeling about Bethany College and in expressing these sentiments, he articulates the feelings of alumni in the context of their remembrances:

Bethany College is *Someplace Special;* this college in Lindsborg, Kansas . . . .

Maybe it's the setting in a community unlike most small communities, since Lindsborg has undertaken deliberate efforts to retain its European heritage and its dedication to the fine arts . . . .

Maybe it's the relatively quiet though stimulating surroundings which provide an unhurried atmosphere in which students may wrestle with the creation of ideas . . . .

Maybe it's the deliberate intent to emphasize Christianity and the value systems that it implies, expressed in acts of person-to-person concern . . . .

Maybe it's such events as the Messiah Festival and other cultural events for which the College and community are well noted . . . .

More than likely it's all of these factors and more that make Bethany College—*Someplace Special* . . . .

18.

Retrospect and Prospect

When the annals of history have been read and the resources of memory recalled, it becomes apparent that a college operates in a dimension of space and within the changing forces of time. The former is a specific factor and for Bethany College it is that area of good earth at Lindsborg in the Smoky Valley of Central Kansas known as the campus. But that is not an adequate description. Bethany is really wherever graduates and former students participate in the world's life and work. This dimension reaches beyond the boundaries of Kansas and the United States. In faraway India there is another Bethany, a girls' school, named to honor an alumna whose path of Christian service brought her to that country. Elsewhere it is less tangible in the legacy of the Bethany spirit, fashioned in youthful years and enriched with the passing of time. This broad concept of Bethany is valid in retrospect and increasingly so in prospect.

The time element in the life of a college has about it a continuous reality from the "then" to the "now" and beyond. In retrospect the point of departure is that October day in 1881 when the Reverend Carl Swensson and J. A. Udden met in the sacristy of the Bethany Lutheran Church with a few students. The future was heavy with the promise of greater things. Ninety and more years have passed and the cumulative numbers have reached several thousands. The prospect is for greater growth in service.

A glance backward to the time of origin brings the observer to a Swedish community in the early process of Americanization. The Swedish settlers had lived there for only slightly more than a decade. The common language in the homes, churches, business firms, and newspapers was Swedish. In the early years a large majority of the college students was Swedish-born.

Although the college catalogue was always printed in the English language, the early promotional literature was in English and Swedish.

In 1883 the board of directors passed a resolution declaring that English and Swedish were to have equal status. The report of the president of Bethany College to the church Conference was in Swedish until 1923. Students with Swedish antecedents were expected to study the Swedish language until the middle 1920s.

When yellow and blue became the college colors, the Swedish flag was the source. When *Rockar, Stockar* was adopted as the college yell, the background and words were Swedish. When the official college song, *Hell Dig, Vårt Bethany*, was designated in the early years, the lyrics were written by Jakob Bonggren, well-known Swedish American poet, and the music was from *Hell Dig, Du Höga Nord*, a Swedish patriotic song of the homeland. An English translation, *Hail Thee, Our Bethany*, was still sung in 1930. Swedish festivals and Swedish clubs further identified the cultural origin of the College.

The Swedish antecedents brought important cultural resources to Bethany. Coming directly to the campus from the old country were greatly esteemed professors—Hugo Bedinger, Sigfrid Laurin, Birger Sandzén, Hagbard Brase, Oscar Thorsen, and many others. Moreover, the Swedish culture of the community and of the church constituency in the Smoky Valley added elements that were unusual in the Plains area and in America generally. Professor M. C. Hansen has written appropriately: "The immigrant brought with him European culture . . . . If they did not come in loaded with culture, at least they were plentifully supplied with the seeds of culture, that, scattered in a fertile soil, could flourish mightily."[1]

Although the Swedish character of the College and community was dominant, the result was not a closed, exclusive society. Carl Swensson was American born and thoroughly conversant with the American idea. In July, 1887, in an article in *Lutersk Kvartalskrift,* he declared: "We do not wish even if it were possible, which it is not, to build a little new Sweden in this country. That would be as childish as it would be wrong, but on the other hand we do not wish to become Americanized at the turn of the hand." Two years later in a "Swedes Day" address at Chautauqua, New York, he emphasized: "America is now our fatherland . . . . May we cherish that sense of gratitude that so well becomes us as the beneficiaries of this new and unexcelled civilization."[2]

Attempts were made early to overcome the language barriers for non-Swedish students and faculty. English religious services were held in the Bethany Lutheran Church and in the college chapel. In 1902 the Bethany congregation at the annual meeting passed a resolution affirming that non-Swedish speaking persons were welcome as members. In 1908 the Messiah Lutheran Church was organized for the purpose of providing worship services in the English language for Bethany students, faculty, and Lindsborg residents.

The process of Americanization continued steadily. In the 1920s it was completed. World War I had been an important factor in moving forward the process. The new generation of students was increasingly less bilingual than previously. But a large residue of Swedish and Swedish American culture remained and has been cherished subsequently. An interesting manifestation was the first *Svensk Hyllningsfest* in October, 1941. This gala festival is a tribute to the Swedish immigrants by a new generation. Swedish crafts, folk dances, music, food, and historical exhibits recall the early days. It is interesting to observe that Dr. William Holwerda, M.D., who traced his ancestry to Holland, conceived the idea and purpose of the festival. The College participates actively in the events of the *Svensk Hyllningsfest* which is held in October of odd-numbered years.

In retrospect, Bethany College figuratively speaking has sunk roots deep in Kansas and American soil. The rich Swedish heritage, which also has been cherished among the general American public, has witnessed the forces of change across the years. The Swedish origins have become more of a reminiscence than the pervasive reality of earlier decades. Bethany students in this era represent a cross section of American youth and are not basically different from collegians elsewhere. The national origin of faculty members is scarcely different from other colleges in the area. The curriculum contains no special marks of identification with the culture of the immigrant founders. The pietistic background, which prohibited social dancing on the campus until the 1950s, is no longer an important factor. There is nevertheless continuity with the past that provides distinctive resources for the present and future. The College recognizes fully that the twin forces of tradition and innovation enrich student life and thought.

Since history deals principally with the resources of retrospect, it is understandable that the greatest emphasis in this volume has been upon that element. But there is abiding truth in the familiar saying, "The past is but prologue." This emphasizes the future as the decisive legacy from history. That prospect, reinforced by the magnificent progress of the last decade, which has produced the largest full-time enrollment, the greatest financial support, and the finest campus buildings and facilities in Bethany's history, is indeed splendid. Moreover, the foundations for this hope-filled prospect have been wisely and firmly established. The dual forces of a rich legacy and current vitality produce an encouraging prospect for the shape of things to come.

Legend has it that when Indians long ago viewed the Smoky Valley from the range of hills northwest of Lindsborg and saw the mystic haze on spring and autumn days, they believed that the valley was endowed with some unusual quality. Later, the Swedish residents described not the legendary but the real when they wrote to relatives and friends in the homeland that America and this area was indeed *"framtidslandet,"* "the land of the future." Legend and history, although so different, may join to describe and inspire. There is much inspiration in Bethany's history and there is great reason for confidence in the college's future.

The founders often used the familiar Swedish word, *"Framåt!"* "Forward!" to express their belief about the College in the world of tomorrow. This imperative, "Forward!" is still valid. Faith in God and in the Bethany idea will enable succeeding generations to write additional glorious chapters in Bethany's history.

Another commencement is over, as the academic procession leaves Presser Hall.

Echoes From Bethany.

P. H. P

1. Where the clas - sic Smo - ky Riv - er, Beth - a - ny, Beth - a - ny,
2. Thou hast writ a wond-rous sto - ry, Beth - a - ny, Beth - a - ny,
3. All, thy vig - or and thy beau - ty, Beth - a - ny, Beth - a - ny,

Rolls its stream a - long for - ev - er, Beth - a - ny, Beth - a - ny,
And thy strug-gles and thy glo - ry, Beth - a - ny, Beth - a - ny,
When thy coun - try calls to du - ty, Beth - a - ny, Beth - a - ny,

Comes an ech - o loud and clear; List-en, and the name you hear.
Shall re - ech - o in the song Of the com - ing gal - lant throng,
Shall in ser - vice brave and true To the red and white and blue,

O'er the prai - ries far and near, Beth - a - ny, Beth - a - ny,
That shall pass thy name a - long, Beth - a - ny, Beth - a - ny,
Crown the deeds that thou shalt do, Beth - a - ny, Beth - a - ny,

O'er the prai - ries far and near, Beth - a - ny.
That shall pass thy name a - long, Beth - a - ny.
Crown the deeds that thou shalt do, Beth - a - ny.

—Reprinted from an early Bethany
College songbook, Bethany Songs.

PILGRIMS OF THE PRAIRIE.

I.

God smiled upon the new-created earth,
And, lo, the Eden of the East stood forth.
His face to sunward turned, God smiled again,
And into being sprang the Western Plain.

Upon the bright and limitless expanse
The cloudy hosts of heaven in sunlight dance.
The verdant prairies into blue hills rise
To match the sapphire glory of the skies.

God saw that it was good. "Who will arise
And plant me here another Paradise?
They who shall till for me this idle sod
Shall be my chosen people." — Thus spake God.

The call rang out o'er all the lands and seas.
A thousand ships, urged by the westward breeze,
Sped gladly to the New World's beckoning shore —
Each argosy its share of pilgrims bore.

II.

The fields beneath the polar star
Took up the call and sent it far,
Till from the dales a dauntless band
Embarked for this new Promised Land.
They left their altars and their fires,
They left the green graves of their sires —

All that they loved on native sod,
All — save unflinching trust in God.

This cantata by Ernst William Olson, with music by Carl Busch, was a dedicatory cantata for Presser Hall auditorium; it was presented by the Bethany Oratorio Society on March 29, 1929.

What men were these — true-hearted, stout!
What women — faithful and devout!
And there, the stalwart heart of youth,
Afire for freedom, right, and truth!

Into the pathless wilderness
The prairie pilgrims onward press.
These guardsmen on the wide frontier
Fight back the desert without fear;
These volunteers at God's behest
Plant Him a garden in the West,
And every plow that turned the sod
Made straight the highway for our God.

They wrought — and worshiped as they wrought —
With but one consecrated thought:
To lay foundations firm and strong
For State and Church, enduring long.
The soil they watered with their tears
Full oft, these praying pioneers,
Through years on toilsome years.
— — — Then broke their song!
With echoes of their cheers on cheers
The vault of heaven rang loud and long.

III.

Then stood forth from out the numbers
Master builders among men,
Men endowed with clearer vision,
Gifted with diviner ken,
Seers who saw the great ideal,
The Creator's nobler plan
For the multiplying masses,
For the destinies of man.

From the sacramental altars
Rose the incense of their prayer
To the Lord of Hosts who granted

For our use this garden fair.
Lauds and hallelujahs hovered
Godward on the wings of song,
While the Spirit wafted blessings
O'er the pioneering throng.

Spade and trowel here they wielded
While the Spirit's sword they swung,
Frontier forts for culture builded;
From the turf their temples sprung;
And the works they wrought so wisely
Through devotion, might, and skill
Stand as monuments eternal
Praising their dead builders still.

IV.

Nay, are they dead whose radiant mind
Light into countless souls has shed?
To live in those they left behind
Is to live on. — They are not dead.

That Shepherd of the Smoky Hills
Who gathered here a scattered flock,
He comes in spirit when he wills
And smites again the gushing Rock.

That grand Apostle of the West
And sainted Prophet of the Plain,
That man of God supremely blest
This day is in our midst again.

O Learning's shrine, bone of his bone,
Thy halls ring with his voice for aye —
A mighty sermon, preached in stone,
God's witness to eternity!

O temple of the Seraphims,
Earthly abode of heaven-born song —
The fathers' praises, prayers, and hymns
Their children's children shall prolong!

NOTES

Abbreviations:

BCC—Bethany College Catalogue.
BM—Bethany Messenger.
CSSM—Central States Synod Minutes (1963-74).
KCM—Kansas Conference Minutes (1924-58).
KKP—Kansas-Konferensens Protokoll (1870-85).
KKR—Kansas-Konferensens Referat (1886-1923).
WCCM—West Central Conference Minutes (1959-62).

PART I

1. Founding and Early Years, 1881-1891

1. Carl Swensson, *"Huru Bethany College blev till," Prärieblomman Kalender för 1903,* pp. 78-86; *Kansas-Konferensens Protokoll, 1884,* p. 35; *1876,* p. 39. *Kansas-Konferensens Protokoll* hereinafter cited as *KKP.*
2. *KKP, 1884,* pp. 35-36.
3. Swensson, *"Huru Bethany College blev till,"* p. 82.
4. "Bethany Academy Journal and Account Book, 1881-82."
5. Swensson, *"Huru Bethany College blev till,"* p. 82; Monica Heiman, *A Pioneer Geologist. A Biography of John August Udden* (1936), p. 5.
6. "Bethany Academy Journal and Account Book, 1881-82"; *KKP, 1884,* p. 36.
7. *Lindsburg Localist,* June 1, 15, 1882; *Smoky Valley News,* Nov. 8, 1882.
8. *KKP, 1884,* pp. 36-37; J. A. Udden, *"Minnen från min tid i Lindsborg"* in Alf. Bergin, *Lindsborg Efter Femtio År* (Lindsborg, 1919), p. 178. Translated by Ruth Billdt and edited by Elizabeth Jaderborg with additional items and published with title, *The Smoky Valley in After Years* (Lindsborg, 1969).
9. *Smoky Valley News,* Oct. 6, 1882.
10. *Bethany Academy Catalogue, 1882-83,* pp. 3-4.
11. *Ibid.,* p. 2.
12. Emory Lindquist, "Enrollment Statistics, Bethany College, 1882-1973," pp. 9-11. Hereafter cited as "Enrollment Statistics."
13. *Bethany Academy Catalogue, 1882-83,* pp. 3-4; *KKP, 1886,* pp. 38-39.
14. Udden, *"Minnen från min tid i Lindsborg,"* p. 178.
15. J. A. Udden to C. A. Swensson, Aug. 15, 1882.
16. *Förgät-Mig-Ej. Årskalender, 1902* (Lindsborg), pp. 38-39.
17. *Bethany Academy Catalogue, 1883-84,* pp. 8-9; "Protokoll av Board of Directors, Bethany College," Aug. 28, 1883.
18. *Smoky Valley News,* Nov. 28, 1885.
19. *Bethany Academy Catalogue, 1883-84,* pp. 10-11.
20. *KKP, 1884,* pp. 42-43.
21. *Ibid., 1886,* p. 40.
22. "Protokoll av Board of Directors," Dec. 2, 1885; *KKP, 1887,* pp. 32-35; Emory Lindquist, *Smoky Valley People. A History of Lindsborg, Kansas* (Lindsborg, 1953), pp. 89-90. .
23. *Smoky Valley News,* Nov. 27, 1885.
24. "Protokoll av Board of Directors," Sept. 13, 1886; *KKP, 1877,* p. 32.
25. *Bethany College and Normal Institute Catalogue, 1886-87,* p. 7.
26. *Kansas-Konferensens Referat, 1887,* pp. 34-35. Hereinafter referred to as *KKR.* Successor to *Kansas-Konferensens Protokoll (KKP).*
27. T. N. Hasselquist to C. A. Swensson, Oct. 20, 1885; C. A. Swensson to T. N. Hasselquist, Oct. 27, 1885.

28. *Ungdoms-Vännen* (Rock Island), Sept. 1, 1882.
29. *KKR, 1889,* p. 41; *Förgät-Mig-Ej. Årskalender, 1902,* p. 47; M. A. Nordstrom, "Edward Nelander," *Korsbaneret, 1916,* pp. 145-48, surveys Nelander's career.
30. *Förgät-Mig-Ej. Årskalender, 1902,* p. 47; E. W. Olson, *Olof Olsson. The Man, His Work, and His Thought* (Rock Island, 1941), p. 220; *Lindsborg News,* Apr. 3, 1891.
31. *Lindsborg News,* Sept. 20, 1889. An excellent study of Carl Swensson's objectives in founding Bethany College is presented in the master's thesis at the University of Chicago of Dr. Emmet Eklund, '41, with the title, "A Study of Bethany College and Its Educational Objectives As Interpreted By Its Founder, Dr. Carl Aaron Swensson From 1881 to 1904 (1958)."
32. *Bethany College and Normal Institute Catalogue, 1891-92,* pp. 6-11.
33. *Ibid.,* p. 30.
34. *KKR, 1891,* pp. 40-41.
35. *Bethany Messenger,* Dec., 1893, p. 4. Hereinafter cited as *BM.*
36. *KKR, 1892,* pp. 32-33.
37. *Bethany College and Normal Institute Catalogue, 1890-91,* p. 47; *Minnen från Commencement-Veckan och den förste Student-Examen vid Bethany College, Lindsborg, Kansas, 1891,* p. 5.
38. *Minnen från Commencement-Veckan,* pp. 6-8.

2. Struggle and Victory, 1891-1904

1. *Bethany College Catalogue, 1900-01,* pp. 9-17. Hereinafter cited as *BCC.*
2. *BM,* Nov.-Dec., 1896, p. 5.
3. *BCC, 1900-01,* pp. 61-62.
4. *Ibid.,* p. 73.
5. *Ibid.,* pp. 74, 81.
6. *Ibid.,* p. 94.
7. *Ibid.,* p. 101.
8. *Förgät-Mig-Ej. Årskalender, 1902,* pp. 88-92.
9. *BCC, 1900-01,* pp. 105-11, 97.
10. *KKR, 1902,* pp. 39-41.
11. *BCC, 1900-01,* p. 139.
12. *Förgät-Mig-Ej. Årskalender, 1902,* p. 98.
13. *KKR, 1893,* p. 34; *1894,* p. 42; *BCC, 1900-01,* p. 93.
14. *The Yale Alumni Weekly,* quoted in *BM,* Nov., 1902, p. 9.
15. *Lindsborg News,* Jan. 4, 1889.
16. Lindquist, *Smoky Valley People,* pp. 99-100.
17. *KKR, 1889,* p. 34: "Minutes of Board Meeting," Jan. 12, 1891; *KKR, 1895,* p. 31.
18. J. Seleen, *This Valley of Tears. Memoirs* (1971), Ruth Billdt, translator, Elizabeth Jaderborg, editor, pp. 51, 53, 63.
19. *KKR, 1895,* p. 39; *"Protokoll av Board of Directors,"* Sept. 11, Nov. 14, Dec. 5, 1895.
20. *KKR, 1897,* pp. 41,45.
21. *Lindsborg News,* Oct. 15, 1897.
22. *KKR, 1897,* p. 41; "Minutes of Board of Directors of Bethany College," May 19, 1898. Hereafter cited as "Minutes of Board of Directors."
23. J. E. Telleen to C. A. Swensson, Jan. 31, 1891.
24. "Minutes of Board of Directors," July 12, Nov. 15, 1898; Jan. 12, 1899.
25. C. A. Swensson to Board of Directors, May 3, 1895.
26. *"Protokoll av Board of Directors,"* July 3, 1895.
27. *Topeka Capital,* Oct. 6, 1895.
28. *KKR, 1892,* p. 20; *1901,* p. 42; *Lindsborg News,* Jan. 4, 1895.

29. *KKR, 1903,* p. 23; *BCC, 1902-03,* pp. 13-18.
30. *BCC, 1902-03,* p. 18; *1904-05,* pp. 20, 47; *BM,* May-June, 1904, p. 15.
31. *Kansas City Star,* Jan. 23, 1903; *BM,* Feb., 1903, p. 6.
32. *Topeka Daily Capital,* Jan. 28, 1903; *Kansas City Times,* Apr. 16, 1903.
33. Elmer T. Peterson, "Senior Reminiscences," *BM,* May, 1906, pp. 14-15; Mrs. John Holmquist, "Diary," Feb. 16, 1904.
34. *In Memoriam. Dr. Carl Swensson* (Lindsborg, 1904), 79 pp., provides detailed information about the memorial service.
35. Ernst Skarstedt, *"Läroverkspresidenten Carl Swensson," Prärieblomman Kalender för 1905* (Rock Island), p. 85. Various aspects of Carl Swensson's career in politics, colony promotion, etc., are presented in a comprehensive and scholarly study by Dr. Daniel Pearson, '63, in his Ph.D. thesis at the University of Minnesota entitled "The Social and Political Thought of Dr. Carl Swensson 1879-1904: A Study of Acculturation Using the Gordon Model (1973)."
36. *Fosterlandet,* Feb. 17, 1904; Julius Lincoln, "Being Dead Yet Speaketh," *Conference Echo. The Radiant Life Conference* (Lindsborg, 1929), p. 196.
37. Skarstedt, *"Läroverkspresidenten Carl Swensson,"* p. 80; *Kansas City Star,* quoted in *Lindsborg Record,* Feb. 19, 1904.
38. *Lindsborg Record,* Feb. 19, 1904.

3. Consolidation and Growth, 1904-1921

1. *Dr. Ernst F. Pihlblad. In Memoriam* (Lindsborg, 1945), a 51-page booklet provides much information about Bethany's president, 1904-41.
2. *BM,* May-June, 1904, p. 186; Oct., 1904, p. 5.
3. Ernst Pihlblad, "Inaugural Address," May 31, 1905.
4. *KKR, 1905,* p. 50; "Minutes of Bethany College Faculty Meeting," Mar. 8, 1906. Hereafter cited as "Minutes of Faculty Meeting."
5. *Lindsborgs-Posten,* Jan. 2, 1907; *BM,* Jan., 1907, p. 15.
6. *Lindsborgs-Posten,* Feb. 12, 1899; Mar. 31, 1909.
7. *"Minutes of Board of Directors,"* Dec. 16, 1889; Anton Peterson, *"The College Bazaar," BM,* Nov., 1905, p. 13.
8. *KKR, 1913,* pp. 35, 56; *1915,* pp. 49, 34-35; *1917,* p. 50.
9. *Ibid., 1917,* pp. 41-42; *1918,* pp. 36-37.
10. *Ibid., 1918,* p. 39.
11. *Lindsborg News-Record,* Oct. 4, 1918; *BM,* Oct. 5, 1918.
12. *BM,* Oct. 26, 1918.
13. *Lindsborg News-Record,* Nov. 15, 1918.
14. *Ibid.*
15. *Ibid.,* Apr. 13, 1917.
16. *BCC, 1918-19,* p. 7; *1927-28,* p. 12.
17. *BM,* Oct. 25, 1919.
18. *BCC, 1918-19,* p. 8.
19. *Ibid.*
20. *KKR, 1919,* p. 42.
21. *Ibid.,* p. 49.
22. "Minutes of Faculty Meeting," Sept. 8, 1919.
23. *BCC, 1918-19,* pp. 27-28; "Minutes of Faculty Meeting," Apr. 19, 1922.
24. *KKR, 1919,* p. 63; *1920,* pp. 46, 56-57.
25. *Ibid., 1921,* pp. 45-53, *passim;* financial data, p. 41, in report of chairman of the board.
26. *Ibid.,* p. 46.
27. *Ibid.*

28. *Ibid.*, p. 53.
29. *Ibid.*, pp. 61-63.
30. *Ibid.*, pp.42-43.

4. Academic Enrichment, 1921-1941

1. "Minutes of Faculty Meeting," Sept. 4, 1921.
2. *KKR, 1923*, p. 48. The "President's Report" was presented in English for the first time in 1923. The report of the chairman of the board of directors appeared for the first time in English in 1924.
3. *Kansas Conference Minutes, 1924*, pp. 52-56. The proceedings of the Kansas Conference, *Kansas-Konferensens Referat*, became an all-English document in 1924, known as the *Kansas Conference Minutes.* Hereinafter cited as *KCM.*
4. *Ibid.*, p. 61.
5. *KKR, 1923*, p. 63; *KCM, 1924*, pp. 42-43.
6. *BM*, Sept. 27, Oct. 4, 1924.
7. *KCM, 1925*, p. 45.
8. *KKR, 1923*, p. 42; *KCM, 1927*, p. 45.
9. *Golden Jubilee Festival. Bethany Oratorio Society, 1881-1931*, pp. 4-5.
10. *KCM, 1926*, p. 41.
11. *Ibid., 1925*, pp. 41-55; "Enrollment Statistics," p. 3; *BCC, 1961-62*, p. 123.
12. *KKR, 1905*, pp. 59-60; *KCM, 1929*, pp. 59,64.
13. *BM*, Apr. 2, 16, 1932.
14. *KCM, 1932*, pp. 35-36, 42; *1933*, pp. 32-33.
15. "Enrollment Statistics," pp. 5-6.
16. *KCM, 1931*, p. 41; *1935*, p. 38.
17. *Ibid., 1931*, pp. 39-43; *1936*, pp. 37-39.
18. *Ibid., 1932*, pp. 34-35; *1934*, p. 28; *1935*, p. 28; *1937*, p. 28.
19. *Ibid., 1935*, p. 28.
20. *Ibid., 1934*, p. 35; *1937*, p. 36; *1935*, p. 30.
21. *BCC, 1933-34*, pp. 12-13; *KCM, 1938*, pp. 34,36.
22. *KCM, 1938*, pp. 34,36.
23. E. O. Deere, "Brief History of Senior Comprehensive Examinations at Bethany College" (1946), pp. 1-2.
24. *A Challenge to Greater Opportunities. Bethany College* (ca. 1940), 30 pp.; *KCM, 1942*, pp. 37-38.
25. *KCM, 1941*, p. 38.
26. *Ibid.*, p. 40.
27. *BM*, Mar., 1907, p. 36; *KKR, 1923*, p. 42; *KCM, 1928*, p. 62.
28. *Topeka Daily Capital*, Dec. 11, 1943.

5. World War II Years and Later, 1941-1958

1. *KCM, 1941*, p. 42.
2. Emory Lindquist, Inaugural Address, "Things Truly Believed," Sept. 21, 1943.
3. *BM*, Nov. 21, 1939.
4. *KCM, 1941*, p. 31; "Enrollment Statistics," p. 7; *KCM, 1943*, p. 36; *BCC, 1944-45*, p. 92.
5. *KCM, 1942*, pp. 33-34.
6. *Lindsborg News-Record*, May 10, 1945.
7. *Ibid.*, Aug. 16, 1945.
8. "Enrollment Statistics," p. 6; *BCC, 1944-45*, pp. 24-25.

9. "Enrollment Statistics," p. 6; *BCC, 1947-48*, p. 95.
10. *KCM, 1951*, p. 54.
11. "Enrollment Statistics," pp. 6-7.
12. *KCM, 1950*, p. 45; *BCC, 1948-49*, pp. 33-34.
13. *KCM, 1942*, pp. 38-39; *1945*, p. 60.
14. *Ibid., 1953*, p. 68; William H. Taylor, "Bethany College Fiscal Data, 1950-74", p. 1. Hereinafter cited as Taylor, "Bethany College Fiscal Data."
15. *KCM, 1946*, p. 40; *1947*, p. 34; *1949*, p. 41.
16. *Ibid., 1952*, pp. 50, 53-54; *1957*, p. 64.
17. *Ibid., 1944*, p. 38; *1954*, pp. 57-60.
18. *Ibid., 1953*, pp. 62, 54-55.
19. Robert A. L. Mortvedt, Inaugural Address, "Education Within the Shadow of the Church," Nov. 12, 1953.
20. *The Lutheran Companion* (Rock Island), Dec. 9, 1953.
21. "Enrollment Statistics," p. 7; *KCM, 1955*, p. 54; *1956*, p. 62.
22. *KCM, 1954*, p. 50.
23. *Ibid., 1955*, pp. 54-55.
24. *Ibid., 1958*, p. 77; Taylor, "Bethany College Fiscal Data," p. 2.
25. *BM*, Dec. 16, 1955; Taylor, "Bethany College Fiscal Data," pp. 10-11, 14-15.
26. *KCM, 1956*, p. 65; *1957*, p. 66; *BCC, 1955-56*, pp. 77-78, 68-69, pp. 46-47.
27. *KCM, 1958*, p. 78; Taylor, "Bethany College Fiscal Data," p. 23.
28. *KCM, 1955*, p. 70; *1957*, pp. 60-71.
29. *Bethany College Alumni News*, May, 1958, p. 4.

6. A Decade of Change, 1958-1967

1. *BM*, Oct. 10, 1958.
2. "Enrollment Statistics," p. 7.
3. *BM*, Sept. 25, 1964.
4. *KCM, 1958*, p. 79.
5. "Minutes of Board Meeting," Feb. 3, 1959; *KCM, 1959*, pp. 66-67.
6. *KCM, 1960*, pp. 70-71; *1959*, p. 70.
7. *Ibid., 1961*, p. 78.
8. *Minutes of the West Central Conference of the Augustana Lutheran Church, 1962*, appendix; *Central States Synod Minutes, 1963*, annex. The *Kansas Conference Minutes (KCM)*, 1924-58, became the *West Central Conference Minutes (WCCM)*, 1959-62. The latter became the *Central States Synod Minutes (CSSM)* beginning in 1963.
9. *BCC, 1960-61*, pp. 28-29.
10. *Ibid.*
11. *KCM, 1960*, p. 72; *CSSM, 1965*, p. 66.
12. *KCM, 1959*, pp. 68-70; Taylor, "Bethany College Fiscal Data," pp. 2-3, 5.
13. Taylor, "Bethany College Fiscal Data," pp. 11,24.
14. *CSSM, 1965*, p. 68; *BM*, Oct. 2, 1964.
15. *Bethany College Alumni News*, Oct., 1965, pp. 2-3.
16. *Bethany College Progress Fund* (1965), 14 pp.; *BM*, Apr. 22, 1966.
17. Francis C. Gamelin, "Toward Significant Survival. A Status Study of Bethany College, 1966," 38 pp.
18. *Ibid.*, pp. 24-26, 34.
19. *Ibid.*, p. 2.
20. *CSSM, 1967*, p. 66.
21. *BM*, Mar. 25, Apr. 29, 1966.

22. *CSSM, 1967*, p. 66.
23. *BM,* Feb. 11, 1967.
24. *Ibid.*
25. *CSSM, 1967*, p. 66.
26. *The President's Report for 1966-67*, pp. 4-5.

7. A Miracle in the Making, 1967-1974

1. *Bethany Magazine,* July, 1967, p. 1.
2. *Ibid.,* Oct., 1968, p. 8.
3. *BCC, 1967-68*, pp. 9-10.
4. "North Central Association. Bethany College Basic Institutional Data, 1969," pp. 61-62.
5. *Bethany Magazine,* Jan., 1968, p. 7; "Minutes of Faculty Meeting," Jan. 12, 1968; "Minutes of Board Meeting," Dec. 18, 1967.
6. Emory Lindquist, "Study of Bethany College Graduates, 1884-1974," pp. 2,5.
7. *Bethany College Bulletin,* Apr., 1968, 4 pp.
8. *CSSM, 1968*, p. 57.
9. *BM,* Oct. 10, 1968.
10. *Bethany Magazine,* Mar., 1970, p. 6.
11. *Ibid.,* Oct., 1970, p. 6.
12. "To Make a Miracle," *President's Report, 1966-67*, p. 1.
13. *Bethany Magazine,* Oct., 1970, p. 1.
14. *Someplace Special. Bethany College Centennial Decade Development Program, 1972-81*, p. 21.
15. *Ibid.,* p. 19.
16. *Bethany Magazine,* "News Special," Fall, 1972, 4 pp.

8. New Horizons, 1967-1974

1. "Enrollment Statistics," pp. 7-8.
2. "Educational Statistics," Lutheran Council in the USA, 1973.
3. *CSSM, 1973*, p. 32.
4. Taylor, "Bethany College Fiscal Data," pp. 25-26.
5. *BCC, 1968-69*, pp. 44-45; *1971-72*, pp. 44-45.
6. *Bethany Magazine,* July, 1973, p. 1.
7. Taylor, "Bethany College Fiscal Data," p. 9.
8. *Ibid.*
9. *Ibid.,* pp. 3,12; *The President's Report, 1973-74*, p. 14.
10. *BCC, 1973-74*, p. 32.
11. *CSSM, 1974*, p. 37.
12. *Ibid.*
13. *CSSM, 1972*, pp. 40-41.
14. *BM,* Feb. 9, 1968; *Bethany Magazine,* June, 1970, p. 2.
15. *BM,* Sept. 7, 1967; *Bethany Magazine,* Oct., 1968, p. 8.
16. *The Wichita Eagle,* Mar. 2, 1974.

PART II

9. Colleagues and Co-workers

1. The data on faculty is based on Jacquelyn Black, "Study of Bethany College Faculty, 1881-1974," 21 pp., and on College catalogues.

2. A more detailed discussion on art and artists is found *infra,* pp. 178-83.

3. *KCM, 1936,* p. 32.

4. *Ibid.*

5. *Infra,* pp. 244-45.

6. *BM,* Sept. 23, 1961.

7. *Ibid.,* Sept. 30, 1960.

8. *Bethany Magazine,* May, 1973, p. 3.

9. The data on members of the board of directors is based on Emory Lindquist, "A Study of the Bethany College Board of Directors, 1881-1974," on the minutes of the board of directors, Conference and Synod minutes, and College catalogues.

10. *KCM, 1956,* p. 78; *CSSM, 1968,* p. 57; "The Constitution of Bethany College, 1968," 8 pp.

11. *BM,* Oct. 4, 1904.

10. The Lindsborg "Messiah" Tradition

1. Olof Olsson, *Helsningar från fjerran. Minnen från en resa genom England och Tyskland år 1879* (Moline, Ill., 1880), pp. 25-28.

2. *Ungdoms-Vännen* (Rock Island), May 15, 1881; Conrad Bergendoff, *Augustana. A Profession of Faith. A History of Augustana College* (Rock Island, 1969), pp. 59-60.

3. *"The Messiah." Quarter Centennial Anniversary, 1882-1907,* pp. 3-5.

4. *Smoky Valley News,* Dec. 8, 1881.

5. *Ibid.,* Dec. 15, 1881.

6. Program of the first rendition by the Handel Oratorio Society, Lindsborg, Kansas.

7. *Lindsburg Localist,* Mar. 30, 1882.

8. *Ibid.; McPherson Republican,* Mar. 30, 1882.

9. *Lindsburg Localist,* Mar. 23, 30, 1882; *Saline County Journal,* Mar. 30, 1882.

10. *Smoky Valley News,* Apr. 20, 1882.

11. *Ibid.,* Nov. 2, 9, 16, 1883.

12. *"The Messiah." Quarter Centennial Anniversary, 1882-1907,* p. 9.

13. *Ibid.,* p. 7.

14. *Lindsborg News-Record,* Mar. 16, 1923; Emory Lindquist and Jacquelyn Black, "Study of Bethany College Oratorio Society Membership" (1974), pp. 2-4. Hereinafter cited as "Study of Oratorio Society Membership."

15. "Study of Oratorio Society Membership," pp. 2-4; *Lindsborg News-Record,* Jan. 9, 1964; Mar. 13, 1974.

16. *Lindsborg News-Record,* May 31, 1918.

17. *Kansas City Star,* Mar. 18, 1960.

18. *BM,* Apr., 1907, p. 4.

19. *Ibid.,* Apr. 10, 1922; *KCM, 1930,* p. 45.

20. *Ladies Home Journal,* Apr. 10, 1900, p. 15.

21. *Independent* (New York), May 8, 1913, p. 1051; *Literary Digest,* Apr. 15, 1922, pp. 37-38; *Kansas City Star,* Mar. 22, 1970.

22. *New York Times,* Mar. 26, 1939; *Reader's Digest,* Apr., 1944, p. 86.

23. *Washington Star,* Apr. 5, 1953.

24. *Kansas City Star,* Apr. 11, 1960.

25. *Topeka Capital-Journal,* Apr. 2, 1972.

26. *New York Post,* May 24, 1973; *New York Times,* May 27, 1973.

11. Art and Artists

1. *BCC, 1890-91,* p. 31.

2. *Hemlandet* (Chicago), quoted in *Lindsborg News-Record,* Nov. 25, 1926.
3. Birger Sandzén, *"Något om svensk konst i Amerika. Målarekonsten,"* *Prärieblomman Kalender för 1902* (Rock Island), p. 109.
4. *BCC, 1894-95,* pp. 36-37.
5. Sandzén, *"Något om svensk konst i Amerika,"* p. 115.
6. *Ibid.*
7. *Kansas City Star,* July 8, 1934.
8. *Ibid.,* Apr. 25, 1915.
9. *Ibid.,* Feb. 16, 1922.
10. Birger Sandzén, *"Våra svensk-Amerikanska konstskolor,"* *Prärieblomman Kalender for 1903* (Rock Island), pp. 49-50.
11. *Ibid.,* p. 52.
12. *BCC, 1913-14,* p. 25.
13. For a description of the achievement of art graduates *vide,* pp. 260-61. The bibliography on Birger Sandzén is extensive. A brief list includes the following: *Kansas City Star,* Feb. 16, 1922, "New York Lauds Sandzén," contains reviews by Peyton Boswell of the *New York American* and other critics; Margaret Greenough, "From Sweden to Kansas," *American Artist,* Jan. 1961, pp. 26-32, 72-73; Emory Lindquist, "Birger Sandzén. Six Decades of Artistic Achievement," *The American-Scandinavian Review,* Dec. 1954, pp. 329-35; *Catalogue. Centenary Retrospective Exhibition of Birger Sandzén, 1971* (Sandzén Memorial Gallery, Lindsborg, Kans.); *Utställning, 1-18 Maj 1937, Gummesons konsthall . . . .* Foreword by Carl Milles (Stockholm); *Kansas City Times,* June 26, 1954; *Wichita Eagle,* June 8, 1958; Sept. 15, 1974.
14. For a description of the Mingenback Art Center, *vide* pp. 116,118.
15. The Birger Sandzén Memorial Art Gallery is described *vide,* pp. 90-91.

12. Intercollegiate Athletics

1. *Lindsborg News,* Jan. 1, 1892; *BM,* Oct., 1893, p. 3; Dec., 1893, p. 4.
2. *BM,* Nov. 10, 1894, p. 3.
3. "Minutes of Board Meeting," Feb. 4, 1894; *Topeka Capital,* Mar. 10, 1895.
4. "Minutes of Board Meeting," May 29, 1901.
5. Harold Keith, *Oklahoma Kick-Off* (Norman, Okla., 1948), pp. 84-86, 189-91, 132-33; E. Keith Rasmussen, "A History of Intercollegiate Athletics at Bethany College, 1881-1966," Master's degree thesis (1966), Kansas State University, provides much valuable information on athletics at Bethany College.
6. Lindquist, *Smoky Valley People,* p. 224.
7. *BM,* Dec., 1902, p. 7.
8. *Augustana Synodens Referat, 1905,* p. 125; "Minutes of Faculty Meeting," Nov. 15, 1905; "Minutes of Board Meeting," Nov. 16, 1905.
9. *BM,* Oct., 1905, p. 7; Nov., 1905, p. 17; Dec. 5, 1907, pp. 14-15.
10. *Ibid.,* Sept. 11, Oct. 9, Oct. 25, 1908.
11. *Bethany Daisy, 1908,* pp. 92-93.
12. *Lindsborg Record,* Nov. 10, 1909.
13. *BM,* Mar. 1, 15, 1901.
14. *BM,* Feb., 1903, p. 11.
15. *Smoky Valley News,* Dec. 1, 1882; *BM,* Apr., 1903, p. 13; May, 1903, p. 16.
16. *Lindsborg Record,* Nov. 15, 22, 1907.
17. *Bethany Daisy, 1908,* p. 105.

13. Campus Life

1. *Lindsburg Localist,* Oct. 26, 1882; Dec. 8, 1881.

2. Elmer T. Peterson, "Historical Sketch of Bethany Lyceum and Adelphic Literary Societies," *BM,* May-June, 1904, pp. 194-200.

3. *Lindsborg News,* May 8, 1891.

4. *Ibid.,* Feb. 13, 27, 1891; *BM,* Dec., 1903, p. 73; Oct., 1905, p. 26.

5. *BM,* Nov., 1906, p. 26.

6. *Ibid.,* Mar., 1894, p. 4; Apr., 1896, p. 5.

7. *Lindsborg News,* Mar. 17, Mar. 24, Apr. 14, May 26, 1899.

8. *Ibid.,* May 26, 1898.

9. *Ibid.,* Nov. 11, 1898; Nov. 9, 1900.

10. *Ibid.,* May 26, 1899.

11. *BM,* Mar. 16, Oct. 30, 1908; Jan. 22, 1909.

12. *Ibid.,* May-June, 1907, p. 22; Jan. 30, 1908, p. 25; May 4, 1912; *KKR, 1913,* pp. 38-39. An interesting and thorough study of the festival idea with special reference to the Lindsborg *Svensk Hyllnings Fest* is found in the Ph.D. dissertation of Dr. Larry Danielson, '62, at the University of Indiana in 1972. The title is "The Ethnic Festival and Cultural Revivalism in a Small Midwestern Town." This scholarly study presents an analysis and evaluation in a wide context.

13. *Bethany Daisy, 1908,* p. 150; *BM,* Jan. 29, 1909.

14. "Minutes of Faculty Meeting," Sept. 6, 1920; "Minutes of Board Meeting," Sept. 7, 1920.

15. *BM,* Oct. 19, 1929; *KCM, 1931,* p. 37; *1932,* p. 33.

16. Elmer T. Peterson, "Senior Reminiscences," *BM,* May, 1906, pp. 13-14; *BM,* Oct., 1905, p. 19; Nov., 1906, p. 21.

17. *BM,* May, 1906, p. 15; Anton Peterson to Emory Lindquist, May 17, 1952.

18. *BM,* Feb., 1906, p. 17.

19. *Ibid.,* Dec. 4, 1920.

20. *Ibid.,* Mar. 5, Sept. 17, 1921.

21. *Ibid.,* Feb. 26, 1921.

22. *Ibid.,* Apr. 14, 1921; Jan. 14, 1922.

23. *Ibid.,* Oct. 19, 1929.

24. *Ibid.,* Feb. 5, 1935.

25. *Ibid.,* Oct. 1, 1935.

26. *Ibid.,* Dec. 3, 1965.

27. *Ibid.,* Jan. 28, 1936.

28. *Ibid.,* Feb. 9, 1937.

29. *Ibid.,* Sept. 17, 1936; Dec. 11, 1920; Apr. 7, 1936.

30. *Ibid.,* Nov. 20, 1945.

31. *Ibid.,* May 8, 1959; Oct. 19, 1973.

32. *Ibid.,* Apr. 26, 1974.

33. *Lindsborg News,* Feb. 22, 1899; "Minutes of Faculty Meeting," Jan. 22, Apr. 5, 1906; Oct. 11, 30, 1911; Jan. 22, 1912.

34. BM, Sept. 25, 1934.

35. *Ibid.,* May 6, 1960; Jan. 27, 1961.

36. *Ibid.,* May 3, May 10, 1963.

37. *Ibid.,* Apr. 2, 1921.

38. *Ibid.,* Oct. 10, 24, Nov. 7, 1969.

39. *Ibid.,* Apr. 26, 1974.

14. Campus Thought

1. *BM,* Nov. 2, 1937, quoted from *BM,* Nov., 1894.

2. *Lindsborg News,* Oct. 5, 1900; *BM,* May, 1903, p. 11.

3. *BM,* Apr. 27, Oct. 5, 19, 1912.
4. *Ibid.,* Oct. 20, 1936.
5. *Ibid.,* Oct. 29, 1936.
6. *Ibid.,* Feb. 1, Dec. 6, 1963.
7. *Ibid.,* Mar. 29, 1919; Nov. 14, 1925.
8. *Ibid.,* Nov. 17, 1936.
9. *Ibid.,* Dec. 1, 1936; Apr. 6, 1937; Nov. 2, 1937.
10. *Ibid.,* May 5, 1961.
11. *Ibid.,* Nov. 5, 1965; Mar. 4, 1966.
12. *Ibid.,* Nov. 1, 1968; Oct. 10, 24, 1969.
13. *Bethany Magazine,* July, 1970, p. 11; *BM,* May 8, 1970.
14. *BM,* Jan. 16, 23, 1926.
15. *Ibid.,* Jan. 30, 1926; "Minutes of Board Meeting," Jan. 26, 1926.
16. *BM,* Apr. 6, 1937.
17. *Ibid.,* May 3, 1938; Oct. 28, 1950.
18. *Ibid.,* Feb. 22, 1974.
19. *Ibid.,* Jan. 15, Mar. 25, 1960.
20. *Ibid.,* Mar. 19, 1965.
21. *Ibid.,* Feb. 9, Mar. 9, Apr. 20, 1937.
22. *Ibid.,* Apr. 24, 1970; Apr. 28, Dec. 2, 1972; Feb. 2, 1973.
23. *Ibid.,* Sept. 25, 1925.
24. *Ibid.,* Sept. 25, Oct. 16, 1959.
25. *Ibid.,* Jan. 27, 1961.
26. *KCM, 1947,* p. 37; *BM,* Oct. 19, 1973.

15. Campus Interests

1. *BCC, 1883-84,* p. 6; *1973-74,* p. 9.
2. *Ibid., 1882-83,* p. 4; *1895-96,* p. 41.
3. *BM,* Nov., 1894, p. 3; Nov., 1905, p. 17; "Minutes of Faculty Meeting," Sept. 6, 1905; May 24, 1906.
4. *BM,* Oct. 16, 1908; Feb. 12, 1909.
5. *BCC, 1926-27,* p. 12; *1948-49,* p. 29.
6. *BM,* Nov. 5, Oct. 8, 1954; Nov. 2, 1956.
7. *Ibid.,* May 3, 1963; Mar. 15, 1963.
8. *Ibid.,* Nov. 4, 1966; *BCC, 1967-68,* p. 15.
9. *BCC, 1947-48,* p. 20.
10. "Minutes of Board Meeting," Apr. 2, 1906.
11. *BM,* Oct. 3, 1925; Nov. 6, 1960.
12. *Ibid.,* Oct. 23, 1908; Apr. 16, 1909; "Minutes of Faculty Meeting," Apr. 29, 1911.
13. *BM,* Sept. 20, 1968.
14. *Ibid.,* May 3, 1974.
15. *BCC, 1905-06,* p. 26; *BM,* Sept. 30, 1907, p. 27.
16. *BM,* Jan., 1904, p. 96.
17. *Ibid.,* Nov., 1904, pp. 10-11; May 15, 1908.
18. *Bethany Daisy, 1927,* p. 117; *1929,* p. 91; *BM,* Mar. 23, Apr. 13, 1929.
19. *Bethany Daisy, 1930,* pp. 84-85; *BM,* Dec. 16, 1929; Mar. 22, 1930.
20. *BM,* Apr. 2, 1932.
21. Martin J. Holcomb, "Preliminary Report: History of Debate Activities at Bethany College" (1974), pp. 4, 5, 8-9; *BM,* Mar. 23, 1929.
22. *BM,* Dec. 18, 1934; Feb. 23, Nov. 30, 1937; *Bethany Daisy, 1937,* p. 65; Eugene K. Nelson, "A Sketch of the Kansas Mu Chapter of Pi Kappa Delta" (1937), 9 pp.

23. *BM,* Feb. 22, Mar. 8, May 3, 1938; Apr. 4, 1939; *KCM, 1939,* p. 35.
24. *BM,* Nov. 29, 1938; Feb. 21, Mar. 7, 21, 1939.
25. *BM,* Jan. 16, Mar. 12, Apr. 9, Dec. 3, 1940; Feb. 25, Mar. 17, 1941.
26. *Ibid.,* Dec. 16, 1941; Mar. 10, 1942; Mar. 9, 1943.
27. *Lindsborg News,* May 8, 1891; *BM,* May 18, 1937.
28. *BM,* May, 1903, p. 12.
29. *Ibid.,* Feb., 1894, p. 3.
30. *Ibid.,* May-June, 1907, pp. 140-41; May 27, 1911.
31. *Ibid.,* Apr. 2, 1932; *Bethany Daisy, 1937,* p. 65.
32. *BM,* Feb., 1903, p. 4; *Lindsborg News,* Mar. 6, 1891.
33. *BM,* Mar. 14, 1969.
34. *Agape,* Apr. 15, 1974.
35. *Lindsborg News-Record,* Feb. 17, 1927.
36. *BM,* Feb. 8, 1974.

16. Alumni Achievement

1. *BCC, 1961-62,* p. 115; Emory Lindquist, "Study of Bethany College Graduates, 1884-1974," pp. 1-3.
2. *CSSM, 1970,* p. 41.
3. *KKR, 1921,* p. 46; *KCM, 1942,* p. 34.

17. Alumni Remember

1. Julius Lincoln, "Being Dead Yet Speaketh," *Conference Echo. The Radiant Life Conference* (Lindsborg, 1929), pp. 193-201.
2. Julius Lincoln, *"Sic Vos, non Vobis," Bethany College Bulletin,* Oct. 20, 1911, p. 14.
3. *Ibid.,* pp. 14-15.
4. *Ibid.,* pp. 15-16.
5. *BM,* Feb., 1903, p. 3.
6. Mrs. F. O. Johnson, "Echoes from a Vanished Past. Lindsborg and Bethany Reminiscences, 1889-92," 7 pp.
7. The sources for the following personal accounts are letters to the author from the persons involved or from their relatives unless otherwise noted.
8. Dr. Evert A. Larsson, M.D., "America Fever," 36 pp., an unpublished manuscript, pp. 22-25, 33.

18. Retrospect and Prospect

1. M. L. Hansen, *The Problem of the Third Generation Immigrant.* Augustana Historical Society (Rock Island, 1938), Publication 8, part 1, pp. 7-8.
2. Carl Swensson, *Lutersk Kvartalskrift,* July, 1887, pp. 139-40; Carl Swensson, "A Lecture. The Swedes in America" (Topeka, 1889), p. 14.

INDEX

Bethany in Kansas

In 1881, slightly over a decade after Swedish immigrants arrived in the Smoky Valley of Central Kansas, the institution which was to become Bethany College was created.

On October 15, 1881, in the sacristy of Bethany Lutheran Church, Lindsborg, Kansas, founder Carl A. Swensson and first-teacher J. A. Udden met with ten students who became the first Bethany students. From those humble beginnings, the life of Bethany College has included many exhilarating high points in its history — as well as many traumatic and trying events. Through it all, this church-related institution of higher education has enjoyed a proud and often enviable record of service, in many fields, for generations of students.

Bethany College is an institution of Lindsborg, of surrounding communities, and far beyond! Over the years the state of Kansas and the Great Plains area have pointed with pride to Bethany College — especially in relation to the Messiah Festival, the fine arts traditions, and the educational record. The supporting Lutheran churches, reaching into much broader areas, have continued and strengthened their infusion of developmental and spiritual sustenance. Since the early years, Bethany graduates, former students, and friends have helped mould and improve many of the factors that make up this institution. Supporting businesses, foun-

(CONTINUED ON BACK FLAP)

dations, and various sympathetic and creative news media have shared effectively in the historical development. The everchanging "on campus" community (which at the same time has a changeless strength from its heritage) in itself makes an interesting study and chronicle.

Emory Lindquist in this volume has skillfully woven the major historical threads which precede Bethany of today. For many readers, the book will help put into perspective that which has been. At the same time, it can help identify what might be in the near future.

The Bethany spirit is a spirit of individuals and groups. But it is more. There is something that belongs to this institution which never can be reduced to a sum of individual parts.

Bethany is dedicated to educational goals viewed with a philosophy of life and values which goes beyond that which is transitory.

Bethany is, as has been stated recently, "someplace special." *Bethany in Kansas: The History of a College* helps tell why.

BETHANY COLLEGE
LINDSBORG, KANSAS

An artist's conception of the campus, circa 1888.